RANK AND FILE

RANK AND FILE

Updated Edition

Personal Histories by Working-Class Organizers

Edited by
Alice and Staughton Lynd

Haymarket Books
Chicago, Illinois

First published by Beacon Press, Boston, MA
© 1973 Alice and Staughton Lynd
"How I Became Part of the Labor Movement" copyright © 1973
by John W. Anderson.

Accounts by Vicky Starr, Marshall Ganz, Mia Giunta, Bill DiPietro, Ed Mann,
James Trevathan, Andrea Carney, and the Chinese Staff and Workers' Association, are reprinted from *The New Rank and File*, edited by Alice and Staughton
Lynd. Copyright © 2000 by Cornell University. Used by permission of the
publisher, Cornell University Press.

This edition published by Haymarket Books in 2011
P.O. Box 180165
Chicago, IL 60618
773-583-7884
www.haymarketbooks.org
info@haymarketbooks.org

Trade distribution:
In the US, Consortium Book Sales and Distribution, www.cbsd.com
In Canada, Publishers Group Canada, www.pgcbooks.ca
In the UK, Turnaround Publisher Services, www.turnaround-uk.com
In Australia, Palgrave Macmillan, www.palgravemacmillan.com.au
All other countries, Publishers Group Worldwide, www.pgw.com

This book was published with the generous support of Lannan Foundation and
the Wallace Global Fund.

Cover design by Josh On. Cover image of thousands rallying in support of
sit-down strikers in Detroit in March 1937. Associated Press photo.

Printed in the United States by union labor.

ISBN-13: 978-1-60846-150-9

Library of Congress CIP Data is available.

10 9 8 7 6 5 4 3 2 1

MIX
Paper from
responsible sources
FSC® C012752

Contents

Jon Kelley Wright
Workers' Memorial Book Series

On September 22, 2007, the Chrysler Corporation murdered Jon Kelley Wright. After working over twenty years at their Kokomo, Indiana, die-casting plant, the machine he operated crushed him to death because faulty safety equipment had been disabled instead of replaced. Kelley was an outspoken critic of management's dangerous practices and an advocate for safety on the job. Months before his death, he helped organize meetings where management said that replacing the safety equipment "wouldn't be cost effective."

As the beneficiary on one of my uncle's modest life insurance policies, I endowed the Jon Kelley Wright Workers' Memorial Fund through the Center for Economic Research and Social Change. This fund allows Haymarket Books to publish a series of books about the labor movement and struggles of working people to change the world.

Thousands of people are killed on the job each year in the United States alone. We invite anyone who has lost someone due to an unsafe workplace to memorialize their loved one through this book series. To read the memorials and find out more, please visit: http://WorkersMemorialFund.org.

I hope that the Jon Kelley Wright Workers' Memorial Book Series will inspire others to dedicate their lives to the struggle for a world where safety on the job is more important than profits, and that it will help keep the memory of my beloved uncle alive.

In solidarity,
Derek Wright

To contribute to this project, please send tax-deductible donations to the fund payable to "CERSC" (with "Workers' Memorial Fund" in the memo) to:

CERSC
P.O. Box 258082
Chicago, IL 60625

Acknowledgments

W E WISH GRATEFULLY to acknowledge many kinds of help. Helen Michalowski spent many, many hours transcribing tapes in an effort to deepen her own understanding of history. Jim Wright and Fred Stern provided some of the first introductions. Betty Balanoff generously shared her own resources in oral history. Alfred Young, Ann Gordon, and the editors of *Radical America* and *Ramparts* took this work seriously and made it possible for us to publish fragments.

Since the first edition of *Rank and File*, Julia Reichert, Jim Klein, and Miles Mogulescu have added richly to the accounts of Christine Ellis, Stella Nowicki, and Sylvia Woods in producing the film *Union Maids*. We are indebted to these filmmakers and to New Day Films for excerpts from the film script.

Cal Winslow and Steve Early suggested that we do a sequel to *Rank and File*. Dick Flacks knew how to locate Marshall Ganz. Stan Weir put us in touch with Andrea Carney. Jeannette Gabriel introduced us to the Chinese Staff and Workers' Association. Frances Goldin, friend, sometime tenant organizer, and latter-day literary agent, led us to Cornell University Press and Fran Benson. We were surprised and gratified when Anthony Arnove and Haymarket Books approached us with the suggestion that we publish a new edition of *Rank and File*. We acknowledge with appreciation the permission of Cornell University Press to add eight accounts from *The New Rank and File*. We thank them all.

Above all, we wish to thank the individuals in the accounts, and their friends and families, who opened their lives to us.

Alice and Staughton Lynd
October 2010

Introduction to the Expanded Edition

This expanded edition of *Rank and File* contains all the stories
by working people in *Rank and File: Personal Histories by
Working-Class Organizers,** a book that we edited and published in 1973, and eight accounts from its sequel, *The New Rank and
File,*[†] published in 2000. This book, like the earlier ones, is directed especially to rank-and-file workers, and to young people who are seeking
long-term service in the labor movement.

In the early 1970s, the real wages of working people in the United States
began to decline. By the late 1980s, workers' movements were on the defensive. Concessionary contracts surrendered hard-won gains. Employers pushed "jointness," the "team concept," "quality circles," and other
forms of labor-management cooperation, to co-opt workers and to
weaken the union as an exclusive mechanism for problem solving in the
workplace. Collective bargaining agreements tended to become "living
agreements," subject to perpetual modification by small groups of company and union negotiators. Even for companies not in financial difficulty, concession bargaining became the norm. Ten- and twelve-hour
shifts became commonplace as management sought to operate expensive equipment continuously. Two- and three-tier wage schemes weakened solidarity by giving incumbent workers more than the younger
workers coming into the shop. Multinational corporations could make
more profit by "disinvesting" from traditional industries like steel, so
plants closed and destroyed whole communities. As labor's defeats multi-
plied, so too did the disappointment and disaffection of union members.

*Rank and File: Personal Histories by Working-Class Organizers, first edition
(Boston: Beacon Press, 1973); second edition (Princeton, NJ: Princeton University
Press, 1981); third edition (New York: Monthly Review Press, 1988).
†*The New Rank and File* (Ithaca, NY: Cornell University Press, 2000).

During the last thirty years of the twentieth century, a number of re-formers sought election to top union offices. They thereby brought about modest improvements in several labor organizations. But union reformers have not challenged the fundamentals of the existing eco-nomic system, such as management's supposed right to shut down fac-tories unilaterally. These leaders are committed to what labor historians call "business unionism": the goal of signing collective bargaining agree-ments complete with management prerogative and no-strike clauses; the dues check-off as the means of funding union bureaucracies; the pro-tection of jobs in one's own nation at whatever cost to workers in other countries; and the capitalist system that puts profits before people.

At century's end, the trade union movement had not yet reversed the decline of "union density" in the United States. Organizing successes, when they have occurred, have been largely in service occupations where the workplace cannot easily be closed and moved, such as the public sector, clerical work, food services, hospitals, home health care, auto repair shops, trucking, and airline transportation.

Union organizing today is typically top-down "blitz organizing." The ob-jective of blitz organizing is to increase the number of workers who belong to unions and the amount of dues they pay. Far from consulting workers, devising strategy with them, or otherwise empowering those who are to be organized, the blitz organizer induces workers whom he or she hardly knows to vote for a union the worker has barely met. Typically the blitz or-ganizer is recruited from a college campus and trained at some central think tank. He or she is likely to be "parachuted" into an unknown setting and to check out of the motel the day after the NLRB election, win or lose.

The contributors to this book offer a different, more bottom-up model, in which the worker is an on-the-job organizer. Or, if the organ-izer is not on site, the organizer and the worker relate as equals. The worker is the expert on his or her own experience, on the way the con-tract is actually applied, on the culture of his or her fellow workers and the values and objectives the worker and the organizer seek to achieve.

The *labor movement* must find ways to be more visionary, more in-clusive, more democratic, and more willing to take risks than the *union movement* can be expected to be.

The labor movement is in crisis. No one has all the answers as to how we can address the effects of globalization and new technology. Workers will need qualitatively different kinds of organization and qualitatively new forms of struggle. This book is by and for people struggling with these problems.

SOLIDARITY UNIONISM

The outlook of the rank-and-file organizers in this book might be described as "solidarity unionism." Solidarity unionism is the idea that in the absence of effective national organizations from which they can seek help, rank and filers turn to each other and reach outside the workplace, into other workplaces and into the community, to create horizontal networks for mutual support.*

For John Sargent and Nick Migas at Inland Steel in the late 1930s, unionism was solidarity unionism. Settlement of the Little Steel Strike of 1937 permitted Local 1010 of the Steelworkers to represent only those workers who wished to belong to it, and no others. Members paid dues voluntarily, not by means of a dues check-off. There was no contract between the company and the union. These circumstances would be viewed as signs of weakness and immaturity from the standpoint of conventional unionism. But according to Sargent and Migas, greater gains were made under these conditions than after achievement of a union shop, the dues check-off, and a contract.

In meatpacking, Stella Nowicki says, when people were fired, the whole department just closed down. People refused to work until this person was put back.

In steel, Nick Migas says, when the company increased production

---

*See Staughton Lynd, *Solidarity Unionism: Rebuilding the Labor Movement from Below* (Chicago: Charles H. Kerr, 1992). See also the examples of solidarity unionism collected in *"We Are All Leaders": The Alternative Unionism of the Early 1930s,* ed. Staughton Lynd (Urbana: University of Illinois Press, 1996); and Staughton Lynd and Daniel Gross, *Labor Law for the Rank & Filer: Building Solidarity While Staying Clear of the Law* (Oakland, CA: PM Press, 2008).

goals without increasing pay, the department began to slow down. Nobody told anybody to strike. They knew what was necessary.

Stan Weir describes the Oakland general strike after World War II. No
one called it, he says. The strikers simply formed committees on the
street corners.

Christine Ellis and Stella Nowicki describe the reluctance of women to
become involved in unions, and the resistance of men in allowing women
equal status within unions. Women often did harder work for less pay. As a
young woman in the 1930s, Stella Nowicki joined the YWCA, played basketball, went bowling, and learned to play pool in order to contact other
young people. She organized young women's groups. They loved to
dance and she loved to dance, so they went dancing together and she
talked to them about the union. She asked her coworkers, what happens
if you get sick, or what happens if the foreman says he doesn't like you and
he wants somebody else to have your job? After a while they saw that the
union could win bread and butter things for them.

Christine Ellis and Mia Giunta proposed rotating layoffs or reduction
in hours for everyone in the shop rather than deprive anyone of work.
Jordan Sims said it was not right to work overtime if a union brother or
sister was laid off.

Solidarity unionism makes demands that pull people together. Stella
Nowicki called on others to "Sit, stop" when a woman's fingers were
caught in the meat chopper. Ed Mann tells about a walkout in response to
the death of a worker after the company had turned a deaf ear to their
safety grievance. Ken Tucker's union brought up pollution at the bargaining table as a health and safety issue affecting the community. Mia Giunta
describes a tragedy that led to the dedication of Workers' Memorial Day.

While solidarity unionism is often expressed in spontaneous group action, the rank and filers in this book also saw the necessity for organization. John Anderson saw hundreds of workers walk out and mill around
in the street, but they did not know what to do. They had no organization and no one to speak for them. So he got up on the fender of a car and
found words for the ideas passing through the minds of the protesting
workers. As Ed Mann says, somebody has to be there when the workers
say, "This is enough."

When Marshall Ganz went to work for the Farm Workers, his first assignment was to provide personal service in immigrant communities with all kinds of problems, not only on the job, but also with drivers' licenses, or with the Immigration and Naturalization Service. "You made the organizing credible by beginning to do something about those problems."

After winning a strike and preserving the union shop, Bill DiPietro defended a former strikebreaker. Why? Because that's what unions are about, "not whether I like you or don't like you." He wound up with a better group of men coming to the union meetings than before the strike. You're not going to organize by zooming into town and talking to people, he says. People want to see what you do.

Andrea Carney belonged to a local union in which newly organized janitors, many of whom were recent immigrants from Central America, and Anglo health care workers like herself formed a Multiracial Alliance. When the Multiracial Alliance candidates were elected to the union's executive board, a trusteeship was imposed and the elected leadership was removed. She turned down offers of full-time union staff jobs believing that she could learn and do so much more "by being rank and file."

We see workers reaching out to help others and asking for help from a wider community. James Trevathan was a member of a union but never wanted to be involved in it. He was able to move from the Mason Department to the Machine Shop as the result of a Consent Decree in the steel industry. But in his experience, the union did just what it had to do for blacks—the least possible, no more. As an elderly man, he became a volunteer for the NAACP and the Urban League, investigating complaints of racial discrimination. "I may help two little young Black people keep their jobs. I can't do anything for these forty or fifty other ones. But I may help these two. And maybe, some of that will rub off on one out of the two, and maybe he'll go and help two more."

Virginia Yu and Wing Lam of the Chinese Staff and Workers' Association, like many other rank and filers, believe the labor movement should not narrow itself to the purely economic concerns of a particular trade. They ask for help from a wider community than their own workplace, and conclude that the only way to make change is by organizing workers of all trades in the community.

Rank-and-file organizers are on the spot, in touch with abusive situations and the people affected. They have a sense of what others can be called on to do and they lead by example.

SELECTION OF ACCOUNTS AND QUESTIONS OF METHOD

The contributors to this book are not unique. We feel sure they would wish us to say that many others like themselves can be found in shops and offices across the United States, and throughout the world.

We interviewed people whom we knew and were able to observe in action over a period of time, or who were recommended to us by persons we trust. Because we wanted to be sure that the individuals we interviewed actually did "walk their talk," a disproportionate number of the accounts come from the area near where we lived in Chicago before 1976 and Youngstown, Ohio, since 1976. It was less important to us that every occupation, nationality, or part of the United States involved in the labor force should be represented in the book. We acknowledge gaps in this regard, especially in the South, and hope that others will step forward to fill them.

No attempt has been made to update all of the headnotes. What appears in the present tense reflects what these men and women were doing at the time the accounts were compiled. Since then, many of the individuals have died or gone on to further activities. Stan Weir and Wayne Kennedy lost their cases in the United States Supreme Court.

In this expanded edition of *Rank and File,* with the permission of Cornell University Press, eight accounts from *The New Rank and File** include new material by two people who spoke in *Rank and File,* Vicky Starr (who appeared as Stella Nowicki in *Rank and File)* and Ed Mann, who was part of the Rank and File Team with John Barbero. The later accounts reflect organization in new sectors, such as clerical and health care workers, and restaurant and sweatshop workers. Marshall Ganz describes the organization of the Farm Workers under the leadership of César Chavez.[†]

---

*Staughton Lynd and Alice Lynd, *The New Rank and File* (Ithaca, NY: Cornell University Press, 2000).

[†]We have tried not to duplicate stories already well told elsewhere. For this reason we do not offer accounts of dramatic strikes in the 1980s at southwestern copper mines, or

There were only three women in *Rank and File,* "Christine Ellis," "Stella Nowicki," and Sylvia Woods. Inspired by their stories, three film-makers interviewed these women, added archival material and songs, and in 1976 produced the documentary film, *Union Maids.** In *Union Maids,* Christine Ellis is identified by her real name, Katherine Hynd-man, and Stella Nowicki was no longer hesitant to use her real name, Vicky Starr. When, at a preliminary screening of the film with the three women and ourselves, Sylvia Woods saw the footage of Black laundry workers shaking out sheets, she cried, "That's just how it was!"

In memory of Katherine Hyndman, we quote a couple of passages from the transcript of *Union Maids* to supplement her account in *Rank and File:*

> My father's mother was a very unusual woman. The rule was, when a young man got married and brought his bride home, she had to get up early the next morning and make breakfast for the entire household to show that she was worthy of being a part of that family. So she deliberately stayed in bed! She waited until she figured everyone else was up and in the kitchen waiting for breakfast. And she said, "I want to make it clear, here and now, I am not going to be a servant here. I am not going to come here and show you my worth as to what a good cook I am, what a good housekeeper I am, all those things. I am not going to do that. But I'll tell you what I will do. I'll go out and work with the men. I'll do the plowing. And I challenge any male member of this household to outdo me when it comes to work." I've often said, "I hope I've inherited some of my grandmother's fighting spirit."

And, near the end of her life:

> There have been times when members of my family, especially in recent years, in my old age when I'm not in good health anymore, said, "Humph, you had to open your big mouth! Now, with your intelligence, you could have been something. And what are you now? You're nothing!" And I said, "Well, that's your way of looking at it but it's not my way." I have no regrets. I felt there was a purpose in my life. There were very difficult times, but I am proud to say that I survived them.

against the Hormel meatpacking corporation, the International Paper Company, and Pittston Coal. Nor do we draw from the innovative organizing by clerical workers at Yale or steel industry retirees in Youngstown. All these experiences are accessible in other books.

*The film *Union Maids* by Julia Reichert, Jim Klein, and Miles Mogulescu is available from New Day Films, 190 Route 17M, P.O. Box 1084, Harriman, N.Y. 10926; or www.newday.com

I still believe in socialism, but I don't know if there is any single European country that has the kind of socialism that I would want. To me, socialism should mean that the greatest say-so should be the people themselves. Let the people decide.

ABOUT THE EDITORS

The reader may find it helpful to know something about the editors. While gathering the accounts for *Rank and File,* we met workers who needed legal assistance. Often the union was part of the problem, and the worker could not find a lawyer who knew labor law but was not already working for either management or organized labor. Later, as coordinators of a team of health professionals and local union activists who worked on occupational health and safety, we could not find lawyers who knew environmental law and industrial hygiene, or, if they did, would give the time needed to educate or represent rank-and-file workers. So we decided to go to law school ourselves, Staughton in the 1970s, Alice in the 1980s.

As a lawyer, Staughton represented individual discharged workers, many of whom were not protected by a collective bargaining contract or represented by a union. For a number of years he also devoted much time and energy to fighting plant closings and trying to develop worker/community ownership of abandoned steel mills.* When companies went bankrupt and reneged on their commitments to retirees, retirees sought legal assistance concerning their pensions and health insurance benefits.† Alice made that one of her fields of concentration, along with employment discrimination.

As lawyers, we jointly assisted a group of visiting nurses to form their own union. We represented African-American operating engineers who

---

*Staughton Lynd, *The Fight Against Shutdowns: Youngstown's Steel Mill Closings* (San Pedro: Singlejack Books, 1982); "The Genesis of the Idea of a Community Right to Industrial Property in Youngstown and Pittsburgh, 1977–1987," in *Living Inside Our Hope: A Steadfast Radical's Thoughts on Rebuilding the Movement* (Ithaca: Cornell University Press, 1997), pp. 159–188.

†Staughton Lynd and Alice Lynd, "Labor in the Era of Multinationalism: The Crisis in Bargained-For Fringe Benefits," *West Virginia Law Review,* vol. 93, no. 4 (Summer 1991).

were not being fairly referred to work by union dispatchers. We helped to create the Workers Solidarity Club, an organization of retirees known as Solidarity USA,* and Workers Against Toxic Chemical Hazards (WATCH).† We retired from employment as Legal Services attorneys in 1996.

We dedicate this expanded edition of *Rank and File* to the future of the labor movement, which needs the dauntless spirit, imagination, integrity, dignity, and vision of solidarity that has inspired generations of rank and filers.

---

*Alice Lynd and Staughton Lynd, "'We Are All We've Got': Building a Retiree Movement in Youngstown, Ohio," in Gary Bellow and Martha Minow, eds., *Law Stories* (Ann Arbor, MI: University of Michigan Press, 1996).

†Alice Lynd and Staughton Lynd, *Stepping Stones: Memoir of a Life Together* (Lanham, MD: Lexington Books, 2009), pp. 100–125.

Introduction

I

T HE INDUSTRIAL UNION organizing drive of the 1930s was a movement for democracy. Talk to the mass production workers who took part in it, and they will tell you that what they wanted more than anything else was dignity. They wanted freedom from the petty harassment of a foreman who could send a man home at will and reward those who curried his favor with steady work, preferred jobs, and promotion. They wanted "unions of their own choosing" which could stand up to the power of corporate employers and bargain on equal terms. Like democratic movements in America before and since, they believed that the human right to a job should take precedence over the property right to manage an enterprise as the employer sees fit.

After World War II the labor movement fell silent, and the democratic impulse made itself felt in movements of blacks, students and women. These movements insisted that American society claims to be democratic but the reality is often the reverse. They asked, how can a society which calls itself democratic prevent blacks from voting? How can it treat students as IBM cards, and women as sex objects? How can it make war without consulting Congress, let alone the people? All these movements agreed that people should participate in the decisions which affect their lives.

Now American working people are stirring again. They are beginning to question foremen and corporation executives whom they did not elect, and union officials who have lost touch with their membership. The groups which took part in the cultural revolution of the 1960s are moving into the workplace. Blacks have become a majority in many automobile plants and steel mills, students have graduated and taken jobs in white-collar bureaucracies, veterans are returning from Vietnam, women have gone out to work in larger

numbers than at any time since World War II. A new restlessness
is evident in wildcat (unauthorized) strikes, in rank-and-file rejection
of contracts, in demands for humanizing work and for a pollution-
and hazard-free work situation.

Two events in 1972 symbolized the ferment. At the General
Motors assembly plant in Lordstown, Ohio, workers struck against
speed-up and arbitrary discipline. Their average age was under
twenty-five. Many were veterans. Long hair and New Left life styles
were common. In the Appalachian coal fields, the Miners For
Democracy ousted the incumbent leadership of the United Mine
Workers. Their movement grew in part from a campaign against
unnecessary mine disasters and the slow death of Black Lung from
breathing excessive coal dust.

It is by no means clear whether the lasting impact of the new
working-class consciousness will be progressive or reactionary.
Miners For Democracy is widely supported by working people but
so is George Wallace. Even supposing (as we do) that the thrust of
working-class revolt is essentially democratic, what will protect it
from betrayal by those whom it elects to office? Among rank-and-file
working people there is universal resentment about union reformers
who, once in office, kick the ladder away and forget to look back.
It is hard to know how to prevent this.

Thus difficult problems present themselves as workers sense their
power and make their feelings known. This book is by and for
people struggling with these problems.

II

In the following pages, a number of men and women tell of their
experience as organizers. About half were active mainly in the 1930s
and about half since World War II. About one third are currently
involved in rank-and-file movements. Most grew up and worked in
the Midwest and many in the steel industry, since this is the principal
industry in the Chicago area where we lived while making the book.

They were not selected at random. What unites these remarkable
individuals is that, in our judgment, they belong to a tradition of
working-class democracy. "Go see so-and-so," we would be told,
"if you want to meet someone who expressed the spirit of the rank

and file.'' Led in this way from one person to the next we put together *Rank and File.*

What do working people mean when they say "rank and file"
and what do we mean by using it for the title of this book? Rank
and file, in a general way, refers to workers on the job, not paid
union leadership. Rank-and-file activity usually means people on the
job taking whatever action they think is necessary, doing something
for themselves rather than waiting for someone else to do it for them.
It means people acting on their own, based on their own common
experience. In the words of Percy Llewellyn, who helped to unionize
Ford in Detroit,

> It wasn't the international [union]* doing it. We were doing it. This
> was on our own. We knew what the problems were in the plant,
> and we didn't have to go to some political officer to tell him we
> needed some help on this problem. We just went out and did it. And
> that was the big reason that Ford was organized. Ford was organized
> mainly because the workers in there did the job themselves.

Rank-and-file activity may be directed against an intolerable
employer or an unresponsive union bureaucracy. Neither the
individuals in this book, nor we ourselves, are anti-union. "Don't
get me wrong," says Clarence Stoecker, a retired farm equipment
worker from the McCormick Works in Chicago (site of the strike
which led to the Haymarket "Riot" of 1886). "I'll never say that
you're better off without a union, that you'd do better to save that
five bucks a month or whatever the dues is. You just can't do that."
The fact remains that too many industrial unions have become
bureaucratic closed corporations, like the craft unions of the old
AFL. At best they are concerned with material benefits for their own
members, not with the welfare of working people everywhere. At
worst they have become a new kind of company union, financially
independent of the rank and file because the company deducts union
dues from the worker's paycheck (dues check-off) and politically
all-powerful because the contract takes away from rank and filers the

*National unions (as opposed to local unions) in the United States refer to them-
selves as "internationals" when they include Canadian members.

right to strike (no-strike clause). This is the situation that makes some union men and women say that they have two enemies, the company and their union leadership.

How did this degeneration of the trade unions come about? The collective action of working people springs from the need for self-protection. Those who are in a position to decide what others will do, when, where, and how they will do it and how much they'll get paid, have tremendous power over the lives of the people who work under them. It is extremely difficult for any single individual or any single local union to deal with that power. When the industrial unions were being organized, they were up against the power of national corporations which could transfer operations from one plant to another, or could take a loss for a while in one place and make it up in another. So workers turned to the CIO and to national unions which could match the corporations in money, full-time staff, lawyers, and access to media, and which could shut down all the plants of a corporation at the same time.

But this power came at a price. Once unions gained recognition and union dues were automatically taken out of the workers' paychecks, unions took on a new character. The militancy, democracy, and local union autonomy which flourished in the organizing period faded away or were crushed. Taking leadership in the union, which once meant working for nothing and living with the risk of being beaten or killed, became a way of moving ahead personally. It was a way of getting out of the workplace and getting a higher income. A successful local union officer could then go on to a career on the staff of the international union or, having come to the attention of management as a person with supervisory ability, a better-paying job with the company.

The typical rank-and-file leader seeks to be neither a union staff man nor a foreman. Characteristically, he or she does not want to become separated from the people in the shop. Like Eugene Debs, the rank-and-file leader feels, ''When I rise it will be with the ranks, not from the ranks.''

The rank and filers in this book felt, in addition, that there had to be basic social changes. They were both militant, in demanding changes within their unions and workplaces, and radical, in the sense that they tried to democratize the larger society. They imagined both a union and a society which were more just, more humane, more of a community.

They came to feel that the union alone could not bring all this about and they turned to political parties or community organizations as well. Most were some kind of socialist. Many belonged at some point in their lives to an organized radical group. Some still do. Regardless of their political beliefs or associations, those who took a forthright stand in confronting either management or the union were commonly attacked as Communists, and in this way forced to deal with the question of radicalism.

Of those who joined or worked closely with an organized radical group, most of the organizers who were active in the 1930s were connected with the Communist Party, while those active after World War II worked with other groups. We did not set out to select those we interviewed with this pattern in mind. We think it reflects the extent to which working people felt the relevance or shortcomings of these organizations.

Among the organizers who tell their stories here, therefore, there are people who vigorously disagreed with one another's politics. We do not believe that any of the organized radical groups had a monopoly of wisdom in the 1930s, nor do we think any of them do today. As we see it, there is a rank-and-file experience shared by all the participants in this book (and of course by countless others) which is deeper than the words used by different individuals to talk about it. Even when two people use words which are contradictory, they may have in common the goal of building a movement of ordinary people for the general good.

III

When we came to interview people we would offer the following explanation. We believe that most of labor history is created neither by famous leaders nor by faceless masses in crisis situations. We believe that the labor movement draws its life from many thousands of committed persons who work, day in and day out for years, to bring unions into being, to resist their bureaucratization, and to better the lives of others, not just themselves.

We asked the people we interviewed about their childhood, how they became involved with the labor movement, what they did, how their ideas were shaped, and what they might like to say to young people today. Many famous events in labor history are recounted or alluded to in this book—the Pullman strike of 1894, the McKees Rocks strike of 1909, the steel and packinghouse strikes of 1919, the San Francisco general strike of 1934, the Memorial Day Massacre, the Taft-Hartley Act, for instance—but these events figure largely as background to the personal development of those who lived through them.

Although most of our material was edited from tape recordings, Christine Ellis and John Anderson both wrote personal histories of book length. We regret that we could only publish portions. Some accounts (Patterson, Reese, Sargent, Sims, and the three miners) were edited from speeches; others (Tucker, and in part Ellis and Nowicki) from presentations to a small group, the Labor History Workshop in Gary, Indiana. Mario Manzardo permitted us to incorporate in his account a moving memoir which he wrote about his father, and Nick Migas' account includes a leaflet which was passed out at the 1948 Steelworkers convention. John Barbero's account combines the transcript of a discussion with John and other members of the Rank And File Team (RAFT) with the transcript of an interview with John alone.

All accounts were trimmed to reduce repetition of the same material or themes. A few names and places have been changed, lest unsympathetic members of the family or employers become distressed. Every account was read and corrected by the person or persons concerned.

It may be said, ''The individuals in this book were not typical.'' True, the individuals in our collection were organizers. They were leaders. They had radical ideas. But precisely because they did not start out as organizers or leaders or radicals, their accounts throw light on what has been experienced or may be experienced with variations by a much larger number of people.

Again, it is often said, ''American workers do not develop radical ideas on the basis of their own experience, but only if influenced by middle-class intellectuals or foreigners.'' This book challenges that belief. A few of these organizers inherited their outlook on the world from their parents. Most did not. Moving through a variety of frustrating and demeaning jobs, finding themselves involved in struggles often not of their own making, rethinking what they had taken for granted, the contributors to this book developed their ideas on the basis of what they saw and did, felt and tried.

Even the details were sometimes similar. Christine Ellis and John Anderson rejected the church when it failed to respond to human need or to deal rationally with the world. The flag of the United States was a significant symbol to resist or uphold for Sylvia Woods, Stan Weir, and George Sullivan as children. Mario Manzardo and (after the period dealt with in their accounts) John Anderson and George Patterson were drafted almost immediately after they did things which stirred up the wrath of the international union. As members of the Armed Forces, George Sullivan and John Barbero were disgusted by the way Americans disregarded other cultures and gained respect for people on a worldwide scale. This experience had a profound effect on Sullivan and Barbero, foreshadowing the impact of Vietnam on other young working men in the 1960s and 1970s.

For all the organizers in this book, experience was the heart of the matter. But often a friend—Marko for Christine Ellis, Frank Cedervall for John Anderson, Herb and Jane March for Stella Nowicki, Mamie Harris for Sylvia Woods, a fellow seaman for Stan Weir, the United Labor Party for John Barbero—put into words a context for what they were feeling and offered a sense of direction for dealing with unresolved life situations.

We would be pleased if our book could play the part of such a friend in the experience of those who read it. Rank-and-file groups tend to be isolated from one another. Individuals trying to transform their work situations (among whom we include ourselves) are also isolated in a deeper sense. Family, church, school, army and workplace combine to make us distrust our own feelings and to be fearful that the dream of solidarity and human dignity is, after all, only a dream. This book stands at the side of anyone doing such dreaming. Here is a roomful of travelers who, after long journeying, still believe that all men and women *can* live as brothers and sisters, still affirm that democracy *must* be made to work in the plants and offices where Americans work. We have found them encouraging friends in seeking our own way from the movement of the 1960s into the very different kind of movement which the 1970s require. We hope readers will gain from this book encouragement to work in their own lives for the release of the human spirit.

CHRISTINE ELLIS

C HRISTINE ELLIS recalls in detail the experience of immigrants coming to America and the support the foreign born gave each other in political as well as economic and cultural ways.

She joined the Communist Party, served as an organizer of the unemployed in the early 1930s, and was active in the Party for many years. Later she became disillusioned with the Communist Party as a possible instrument for creating a more just society.

After the period described in this account, Christine Ellis lived in Gary, Indiana and married a steelworker. She opposed the Korean War for reasons similar to those of the Vietnam War protesters. This led to efforts of the Justice Department to have her deported under the McCarran Act. She was jailed without bail for ten months in 1952–53.

While in jail she began to write the story of her life on the backs of Christmas and Easter cards sent her by supporters. After we met her she added to these recollections, writing about some incidents and telling others to us personally or to the Labor History Workshop in Gary during the summer of 1971. What appears here are several highly condensed fragments from a mass of vividly-remembered material.

CHRISTINE ELLIS

People Who Cannot Be Bought

I

ALTHOUGH I WAS ONLY FIVE when we left what is now Jugoslavia, I remember the compound where we lived and the tiny village where many of the poor peasants lived in thatch-covered huts. Both my mother and father came from ancient communal families. We lived in huge compounds, two stories high, built of thick stone walls. There was a common kitchen and dining room where all the members of the family ate together.

In order for a commune to exist in the twentieth century, it had to have good management. At one time our family had owned a lot of land, with vineyards, many sheep, olive trees, etc. With the death of my great-grandfather our fortunes began to suffer.

My father was a good-hearted soul but he wasn't exactly a hard worker. He served his time in the army of Emperor Franz Joseph where he learned to be an excellent marksman. His marriage to my mother was pre-arranged. They hadn't even met.

My mother came from the village of Nadim, walking distance from our village of Tinj. Her mother was the head of the family in their compound. She was a widow most of her life. But she was a good manager and was the undisputed head of the household.

My mother bore twelve children but only six survived. The first four, all male, either died at birth or in early infancy. Then she had three girls.

The land-holdings of the family had dwindled to a very low point and we lived in poverty. My father, perhaps in disgust that he had lost four sons and now had three daughters, decided to go to America. He left in 1911.

His first job was digging with pick and shovel the foundation for the St. Louis, Missouri, City Hall. When that was done he joined some other Croatian immigrants in building railroad tracks in Minnesota. The extreme cold weather there did not appeal to them. Some of the men said there were coal mining towns in southern Iowa where a large number of Croatians lived, and that is how Papa came to Jerome, Iowa. Between these various jobs he managed to save up enough money to send us the fare to come to the United States via steerage on a German steamship plus train fare from New York City to Jerome, Iowa.

I can never forget the misery and suffering we endured on the ship. We traveled steerage which means down in the hold where there are no portholes for air. The place was jammed tight with double and triple bunk beds, very thin mattresses so that if a child slept in the bunk bed above you there was every chance of the urine dropping down on you. Passengers who were seasick simply vomited all over the place and the stench is impossible to describe. Early every morning everyone in the hold had to go out on deck. If a passenger was too ill to walk up, stewards came and dragged the person up the steps and threw them on the deck floor. Then buckets of sulphur were burned in the hold so that the fumes of the burning sulphur would kill the stench. The passengers had to stay out on the deck all day, regardless of the weather or their physical condition. If a passenger was seasick and lay vomiting where he or she was the stewards would come along and spill a pail of water over their heads. Sometimes they added a kick in the ribs as well.

I was the least seasick of our family. Mama suffered the most. She spent almost every day just lying on the deck floor, too ill to move or do anything. There were sinks on deck where you could wash your face or your clothes. I felt quite well and decided to wash my stockings. I foolishly hung them to dry on the ship's railing. Naturally they were gone when I went to look for them. The sad part of it is that I had only that one pair of stockings and had to do without stockings the rest of the trip.

We arrived in New York in late September so it was already getting chilly. Some enterprising immigrant showed my mother how to take any kind of paper but especially newspapers, wrap my feet in one section and then wrap another section around my legs and tie it so it stayed up. I imagine Mama must have had some string or she tore something into strips so that she could tie the newspaper securely to keep my legs warm—so I arrived in America without even a pair of stockings and my feet and legs wrapped in newspaper.

The story of our wait for three days on Ellis Island and what we had to go through because I was lame is a story in itself. Since we spoke no English we all had identification tags, our names and our destination, etc.—my mother, two sisters and myself. Mama was terribly frightened of America. She had been told in the old country that in America men rape women on the streets, openly. There was another strange thing we noticed—so many men without mustaches. Where we came from all men had mustaches, only the priest was clean-shaven. Mama was puzzled—so many priests and yet so many sinful men.

We were herded like cattle—first we were stripped naked (males in one room, females in another room) and then we were forced to walk through a huge pool of water that had Lysol in it. That was our bath. Then we went to a de-lousing room where they sprayed something on our hair to kill the headlice. After that, still naked, we each had to have a complete physical examination.

I had a congenital hip dislocation and had a limp. The doctor said I could not be admitted to the United States, that only completely healthy people could be admitted and that I would be returned to my grandmother in Europe by the first boat. Mama, though a timid and very frightened woman, totally illiterate, told the doctor very firmly that unless I was admitted she and my two sisters would also return to Europe—she would not tolerate the breaking up of the family. There was a long and very heated argument but Mama stood firm. The doctors had me walk back and forth, asked many questions. I was confused and frightened. The idea of being separated from Mama was beyond comprehension even though I loved my grandmother very much. Finally the doctors gave in and said I could stay.

The authorities [at Ellis Island] kept us in huge waiting rooms on wooden benches. There was a huge dining room where we ate at long tables. The food was so dreadful that even we who had known real hunger in Jugoslavia could hardly eat any of it. The rule was that the new immigrants had to wait till their name was called to board trains for their destination. When the immigrants arrived a telegram was sent to the person sponsoring the immigrants. Then when a return telegram of verification was received the immigrants' names would be called and they would be directed to the boat that took them to shore and to the proper railroad station. Usually it was only a matter of a few hours or a day at the most.

We sat on the benches on Ellis Island for three days. Mama was sure that either something had happened to Papa or he had changed his mind and we were stranded on Ellis Island. She wept a great deal in her helplessness. Mama was hard of hearing and that made matters even worse. An employee on the Island would go through the waiting rooms calling out the names of those whose telegrams of verification had arrived. Our name was simple enough, Stanich, but how the employee pronounced it I do not know. Fortunately for us a woman who sat near us, a Slavic woman, perhaps Polish, asked us our name and when we told her she informed us that our name was being called for the last two days. She helped us locate an Island employee and that sped up our departure from Ellis Island.

I remember very little about the long train ride from New York City to Jerome, Iowa. We had huge tickets pinned on like labels on packages and were herded on and off trains since there was no direct route from New York City to Jerome. I do remember that the seats in the trains were made of braided cane and were hard. There was no such thing as a reclining seat so we had to sit up straight on the hard seats all the way.

The "home" that awaited our arrival in Jerome was a miserable three-room frame company house, built on a dirt street along the railroad tracks and across the road from the coal mine. The year was 1913.

We lived in the company shack for several months. Across the road from us and right next to the coal mine were a number of black families. My sisters and I made friends with black children and spent most of our play time with them. I remember the delicious cookies one of the black mothers gave us. It wasn't too long before my parents were told by other Croatians that they must not allow us to play with black children. It was forbidden and we would get in trouble. So that was the end of our friendship and delicious cookies.

We moved from the company shack to other houses where we stayed only a short time. Later we moved to a long-neglected farm in Rathbun.

Rathbun was and still is basically a Croatian town. (Rathbun is the oldest Croatian settlement in Iowa and very proud of its history and tradition. Now almost a ghost town, its old-time residents hang on—their children, scattered everywhere, return for celebrations and religious festivals.) The majority of its residents were Croatian, with a few Italian families, one Czech family, and a small number of native American families.

Whereas in most places it is the foreign born who have an inferiority complex because of language problems, etc., with us in Iowa it was just the opposite.

The early settlers were of English descent. They lived off the land and income from services to those moving west. In contrast to the new immigrants, the Anglo-Saxons had a past in America, a past that had been exciting and ever-changing. Now things had settled down. Railroads criss-crossed the land, people settled in towns, industries flourished.

With the digging of coal mines, immigrants from Central Europe began to arrive. These new immigrants were peasants, long experienced in getting food from the soil. They were also ready and eager to enter industry. The new arrivals felt insecure in a foreign land. The need to have a piece of land on which to raise food, a house you could call your own for shelter in your old age was a driving force which enabled them to withstand all kinds of difficulties, to live frugally, to save for the lean years. They had no past in America, only the future and the future was unsure and unpredictable.

Perhaps in their longing for the old days the old settlers blamed the new immigrants for the change that was taking place. At any rate the old native American families around Rathbun never acclimated themselves to coal mining which became the chief source of earning a living in the hilly country thereabouts. Their farm holdings became smaller and smaller as they sold sections of land to the new immigrants who combined farming and coal mining.

Foreign-born people used to make disparaging remarks about the native American women sitting in the shade in the summer heat fanning themselves while the foreign-born women sweated in their kitchens putting up hundreds of jars of beans, tomatoes, preserves, jellies, pickles, beets, fruits of all kinds. Instead of putting up vegetables, meat, etc. for the winter, native Americans bought canned goods from the store. None of the foreign-born women would be caught dead with store bread on the table. Every bit of land was carefully cultivated and cared for.

When work was slack many of the native American families had to apply for county ''charity'' which was something none of the foreign-born families would even contemplate. In the old country there was no such thing as public relief. They didn't expect it or look for it in America. The foreign born all belonged to fraternal societies which provided sick benefits and insurance. In case of accident, sickness or death the foreign-born miners made provisions for the care of their dependents.

Native Americans had no fraternal organizations nor did they make provisions for their families in case of long illness or death. When misfortune came their way they had to get help from the county. The foreign born resented this. They felt that they were paying taxes to maintain people who were too lazy and thoughtless to care what happened to their women and children.

Religious prejudices entered into the picture also. All of the foreign born were Roman Catholics and they maintained a church. The native Americans were Protestants. They didn't have a church. They held their occasional religious services in one of the school rooms.

It was a matter of record that the foreign born were the most loyal and devoted union members. Some of the native Americans had to be forced to join the miners' union [United Mine Workers].

In other words, the foreign-born people had nothing but contempt for the native Americans. In our eyes they were worthless and shiftless. No self-respecting son or daughter of a foreign-born family would think of marrying into native American families.

Disturbing events deepened the prejudices and antagonisms and finally resulted in bitter hatred and distrust in the 1920s.

During World War I a large number of southern white families migrated to the mining and industrial areas in Iowa. During the war the mines worked every day. When the war was over, work in the mines slackened. The mines worked during the winter months but only a day or two a week during the summer.

The coal operators were quick to react. Wages were cut. Union miners protested and went on strike [November 1, 1920].

I've already described how the native Americans lived. When hard times came they were totally unprepared. Native Americans were willing to work for any wages. Some of the smaller pits in predominantly native American towns remained open. Native Americans became scabs.

The two mines in the town where I lived remained closed. No one dared scab. The town where I lived was made up of perhaps 95% immigrants who were staunch union men.

Coal operators and politicians fanned the prejudices that had so far remained only near the surface into open warfare. Epithets like "hunkies," "flat-heads" were hurled at the foreign born. The foreign born retorted with "johnny-bulls." Not even the children escaped from the brewing storm. The school yard in Rathbun became divided between "flat-heads" and "johnny-bulls" and heaven help the "flat-head" that tried to be neutral.

The Ku Klux Klan took the offensive. The combination of resentment of the new by the old settlers and the influx of native stock southerners who found kindred souls in the old native settlers during World War I was what gave the KKK its mass base for a number of years.

Night riders in white robes and hoods invaded Rathbun night after night, shooting pistols and shotguns into the air. The fiery cross appeared often in front of the Catholic Church and on the tip of the slag pile of the slope mine. Dynamite was exploded night after night. Crops were destroyed, barns and haystacks were burned down. Livestock was slaughtered. The Klan had a newspaper, "The Iowa Fiery Cross," which was sold publicly on the streets of Centerville (the county seat) by small boys.

Native Americans in Rathbun never dared admit they belonged to the Klan although there were suspicions about some of them, including the Scotts, our nearest neighbors.

The reign of terror lasted for about three years, although its peak was 1920–21. During that time my father always had a loaded rifle near his bed at night. We had quite a few boarders in this period. All of them had shotguns for hunting. My father let it be known that every man in our household had guns, ready for use, and if anyone dared come on our farm at night the men would shoot first and ask questions later. Nothing was touched on our place.

In order to keep the ignorant, prejudiced and poverty-stricken native Americans loyal to the Klan their leaders promised them that as soon as the "foreigners" were driven out the Klan leaders were going to give, I mean *give*, homes and farms to the native Americans. They went so far as to designate which house, which farm was to be given to whom. It was not unusual for a Rathbun resident to be approached on the street in Centerville by a Klan member and told, "You damned foreigner, when we drive you out I'm getting your house, free."

When the Klan began its open warfare against the foreign born throughout Appanoose County a delegation went to the county sheriff demanding protection for the foreign born and restraining action against the Klan. The sheriff laughed in their faces and told them he was a leader of the Klan. Every county official except the assessor was a member of the Klan. When our people discovered that the county officials were leaders of the Klan they appealed to the governor but the governor turned a deaf ear to their pleas. We were completely on our own.

The Klan was unable to carry out its threats. The foreign born were outnumbered in the county population as well as the state. It was impossible to launch any kind of counter-offensive but the foreign born were determined to sit tight and weather the storm. In time the Klan terror began to subside, especially when it became evident to the rank and file that the promises of houses and farms were nothing but empty boasts.

The way the strike was settled also helped to break the backbone of the KKK, at least in Appanoose County. The strike went on all winter, the following spring and on into the summer of 1921. The union miners were getting desperate. We were running out of food. The company stores would not give credit and the few independent

store owners were running out of money and could not get supplies
from wholesalers. The shelves in the small stores were almost bare.
The union (Lewis, etc.) deserted the striking miners. Not one penny
came to our aid. In desperation the local union leaders decided they
had to use force to get the scabs out of the mines.

In early September 1921, the union miners met in the town where
I lived. They were armed with shotguns and rifles. I remember my
mother weeping and begging my father not to go with the caravan.
She said, "Think of me and the children." My father said, "It's
because of you and the children that I go."

So the armed caravan in broken down jalopies left our town and
headed towards a nearby town where scabs worked the mine. When
they arrived at the mine they found the entrance to the mine guarded
by southern white women and teenagers armed with shotguns and
rifles.

Instead of shooting it out right there on the spot, the union leaders
wisely put their guns on the ground and approached the women and
youth with outstretched hands. A spokesman said, "We mean you
no harm. We don't want to shoot you. We know your men are working for low wages but in doing so they do harm to you and to us.
Our children are hungry. All we want is for your men to come out
with us. If we all stick together all of us will gain. Our children
won't go hungry and neither will yours. We want you in our union
so that together we can improve our wages."

The women and youths listened, put down their guns and allowed
a delegation of union miners to go into the mine and talk to the
men who were scabbing. The delegation succeeded in getting the
men to come out. Then the southerners who had been scabbing
joined the caravan and they went from one scab-operated mine to
another, only now it was white southerners who acted as spokesmen
and convinced the others to come out. In one day the companies
were defeated—no one scabbed and the strike was settled and the
enmity between southern whites and the immigrants gradually wore
itself out.

This was an important episode in my early years. These events
left a deep impression.

A number of people have influenced my life profoundly but

perhaps none so much as Marko. I was fifteen years of age. My oldest sister and her husband had been living in Cleveland. My brother-in-law was a steelworker. There were big layoffs [1922] and work was scarce. They wrote and asked Papa if they could come back and live with us. They also asked if they could bring a friend with them. This friend was a man whose health was bad and he needed a place to rest and recuperate. Marko had been in jail, one of the victims of the Palmer Raids.

I was fanatically religious. It was mainly the fault of radicals in the Iowa mining fields who made religion instead of capitalism the main issue. The more religion was attacked the more I defended it.

There was a reason why I clung to religion. One has to have a reason for living, a guiding philosophy, a purpose, a goal. While in school my teacher had encouraged me to study. She predicted a great future for me as a teacher or social worker. I had beautiful plans for high school and college. There were no limits to the things one could accomplish in America. But no one in my family shared my ambitions.

Instead of going to high school I went to work. My disappointment was crushing. I wanted to die, literally. I prayed for death. I had no interest in living. There was nothing to live for. I blamed my father entirely. I refused to accept the fact that it was financially impossible for my father to send me to school. All I could see was my world crashing about me. There was no future in a place like Rathbun. Nothing awaited me except housework. I was lame. No man would want to marry me. In my desperation I turned more and more to religion. There was nothing to live for except the reward I would get in heaven when I died. When my father and his friends attacked religion they attacked and tried to undermine the only thing left to me, my only purpose in living.

One hot summer day I was reading a history book in the shade of the grape arbor. I wore glasses, the same glasses I had worn since I was about nine years old. Marko came and sat across the table from me. He was interested in what I was reading and was very much surprised that it was a history book. He spoke words of encouragement about studying. This was the first bit of interest I had evoked in anyone about my dreams and hopes for an education. Here for the first time was someone who valued and respected books.

He told me he noticed that I needed new glasses. That opened the door to the resentment against my father which was hidden deep inside. I unburdened myself of all the bitterness I felt at being cheated of an education.

Then slowly, skillfully he picked up the pieces and put each in its proper light and perspective. First he took up the question of the glasses. He explained that he understood the glasses were important to me but had I talked to my father about my need for new glasses? No, I hadn't. He showed how it was that my father, a man who had never gone to school, a man harassed by economic worries, a long strike the previous year, could not be expected to know and understand what went on in my mind.

Then, most important of all, he took up the issue of higher education. Deftly, he asked one question after another. My answers to each of his questions cast a light on who was to blame for my broken dreams. Up to then my father was the culprit. It was he who stood in my way. It was he who had ruined my life.

Marko asked how many students had been in my graduating class. I told him. How many of them had gone to high school? Two. Who were they? Elizabeth Mills and Billy Robinson. Were their fathers coal miners? No. What did their families do for a living? Mr. Mills was manager of the company store. Billy was a nephew of the mine superintendent, his mother a clerk in the company store. Had any son or daughter of a coal miner in Rathbun ever gone to high school? No. Did I believe that all coal miners were cruel and deliberately prevented their children from getting an education? No. Are there any rich coal miners in Rathbun? No. How far is it to the nearest high school? Centerville, about eight miles. Is there free transportation to school? No. Does the student have to buy his own books? Yes. Is there a tuition? Yes.

I was ashamed of myself for thinking such terrible thoughts about my father. Marko talked some more. He didn't preach but in clear and simple terms explained why it was impossible for a coal miner to be rich, to give his children an education, to take care of their health properly. I saw things then as I had never seen them before.

Father Kaufman, the Catholic priest of the area, made the final contribution that swung the balance of power on Marko's side. The priest came to our house one cold winter day to ask for a donation of chickens for a banquet to be held in Centerville to raise funds for the Church. The priest was a large man, blustery, aggressive and overbearing. He was also under the influence of too much home-made wine by the time he got to our house.

Papa was home that day. There was no love between Papa and the priest. Instead of sitting on a chair the priest sat on the table. That was an insult that could not be overlooked.

When Marko walked in I left the room and hid behind the door of the bedroom where I could observe and hear everything that went on. Marko went to work on Father Kaufman—it was an opportunity he couldn't miss. Politely and calmly he began asking questions which challenged religious dogma, dogma that had been refuted by science. Blow by blow every pillar on which I had leaned toppled over. The priest could not prove anything. All he could say was that it was a matter of faith, that it was written in the Scriptures, that it was proclaimed by Pope so-and-so. On his side Marko had science, logic and man's own experience learned through centuries of investigation, trial and error. The priest couldn't take it any more. He became very angry. He bellowed, "Go to hell with your questions and science." He pointed an angry finger at Papa, "Mr. Stanich, Sunday from the altar I'm going to expose you and have you run out of town." With that he stalked out of the house.

Marko announced that he would attend Mass Sunday morning to hear what the priest had to say. He dared me to attend. I couldn't refuse.

The priest gave his sermon on the sinfulness of women. I could hardly believe [that he did not live up to his threat]. It was a great relief but at the same time a great disappointment. Why didn't Father Kaufman show the same courage as Marko and fight for his beliefs? Was it possible there was really nothing to defend and fight for? I would have admired and respected the priest if he had carried out his threat. Perhaps I would even have been won back to the fold. . . .

I began to earn my own living at the age of thirteen, and at the age of fifteen I left home to earn my living in industry, first in Cleveland and then Chicago.

I went to work for the American Can Company. I had to walk up five flights of stairs to go to work. They put me painting milk cans by hand.

Most of the fifth floor was the lithographing department. The piece of tin is painted and then it is dried through the kilns, through gas ovens. Men with leather gloves would take these pieces of hot tin and stack them up as they came out of the kiln. It was impossibly hot working up there.

The men who took the tin off the kilns had some grievance. Apparently they all agreed. They wanted higher wages. They went to the boss and the boss refused. So these men stopped working. Then what did the boss do? He called on the girls and other young men who were painting, like myself, and put us to work because there was a certain amount of tin already in the ovens that had to come through. They didn't even give us any gloves or anything. I worked only a few minutes handling this hot tin. I almost cut off three fingers. The tin cut to the bone through three fingers. So I went home, this hand all bandaged up.

And my brother-in-law said, "What happened?" So I told him. He said, "You dirty scab." He said, "Serves you right. You should have known." I knew about unions. My father was a union member. And I knew it was wrong. But you're frightened. You don't know what to do. The boss tells you, "Do this." And this is what you do.

There were many places in the old days where you had to sign what they called a yellow-dog contract. In order to get a job you had to sign a statement that you would not join a union as long as you were employed by that company.

In factories where I worked, with the American Can Company and with the Continental Can Company, if a man did something that wasn't right, that was deducted from his wages. Not only was that deducted from his wages but he would get bawled out. I have seen grown men stand there and take such horrible abuse that the tears ran down their faces and they just stood there. They had nothing to say because there was no seniority, nothing. You took all the abuse, whether you liked it or not, because any time the boss could fire you from your job, and he could bring somebody else there. This whole question of what unionism meant and why these people sacrificed so much was so that they could have some dignity, so they wouldn't have to stand the abuse.

I came from Cleveland to Chicago when I was about sixteen. In those days nobody worked a whole year at a time. You worked a few weeks and then you had layoffs for a month or two and then you got another job and you worked a few weeks. In my early youth, there was nobody that I knew who ever worked steady. There were layoffs constantly.

I finally got a job at Bauer and Black, makers of medical supplies and athletic supports. Bauer and Black was one of the nicest places I have ever worked for. I was quite happy there. The work had to be perfect. The stitches had to be small. Their machines were in good shape. It was clean. I made many friends there. The wages were only thirty cents an hour, but they had an extra Christmas bonus. You got $50.00, I think, for the first year. My last bonus was $200.00.

When the Depression came, when the big crash came in '29, they went bankrupt. They were bought up by the Kendall Corporation which still owns Bauer and Black. The Kendall Corporation decided to modernize the place. So they started bringing in different kinds of machinery. My sister worked for the American Can Company and she told about all the modern machinery that they were bringing, all the people they were laying off and the modern machinery that was taking the place of people. So I became very much concerned.

When I first started at Bauer and Black I worked in the corn plaster department. You put certain things on the corn plasters by hand. Well, shortly, they got machinery and the whole thing just went one-two-three. The machine put out by the thousands. I could see machinery taking the place of human beings and the people who didn't have an education would be without work.

Meanwhile, I had become [a member of the Communist Party]. When I came to Chicago, all kinds of cultural organizations were led by progressives. They had choruses; they had the various amateur acting groups in which we took part and which I liked very much. And I had become acquainted with a whole number of people who were Communists. The leading Communists among the Croatian people were cultured, educated, kind, devoted people. Among them were editors of a Croatian language newspaper. Most of the leaders were skilled workers, but in the group were factory workers and just plain laborers. The thing that impressed me the most was the stress on education, culture, respect for others, devotion to a movement that would by its example win the masses to the cause of communism.

So when I became very much concerned as to what was going to happen to the working class with the introduction of machinery, I went to a meeting. They were organizing a conference of working women. Well, I worked in a place with working women. So I talked to some of the girls in the department where I worked and told them that this would be a good thing and some of them promised to come. They thought the program was excellent, the idea of organizing women, but I was the only one who came to the conference.

When I came to the conference I saw a woman in disguise. She was the personnel director of Bauer and Black. So I thought, oh boy, there it goes, I'm going to be fired. When I got to work on Monday, instead of being fired I got promoted. I got promoted to assistant forelady (at the age of twenty) and they raised my wages to $20.00 a week salary, which was something! And so I decided that I would use my position to talk to the girls since I had to teach new people as they came to work.

When they changed the managers of the factory they called a meeting of all the foreladies, assistant foreladies and so on. The whole bonus system was done away with. All the paternalism was gone. The company picnics, everything was gone. They announced that they were going to make big layoffs, that they were going to keep only the most efficient employees. We had to increase the production so that the production would be the same with about fifty per cent of the employees. They had to be heartless. Regardless of how long these people had worked there, only the fastest workers were to be kept, and it was up to us, the foreladies and the assistant foreladies, to decide who was going to be laid off.

So they said, "Does anybody have anything to say?" Well, how can I sit there? I am so naive. So I raised my hand. I said, "I protest!" Everybody's flabbergasted. So I said, "What do you want these girls to do?" There were a number of elderly women who worked as inspectors and there were others who were slow workers. I said, "What do you expect some of these old women to do, go down to Indiana and 22nd to be prostitutes?" They were quite shocked. And [a man] said, "What do you recommend?" "Well," I said, "a beginner, at least, at least split the shift. Split it in half, that each of the girls work three days so they won't starve, they won't have to walk the streets." And he says, "I'll have you know that you are working for the *company* now. You are *company* representatives. We have to think of the company first," and so on.

Then I wrote an article for the *Daily Worker* in which I said that the company was going to lay people off regardless of how many years they had worked in the factory. They were going to keep only the most efficient and they would have to produce to make up for all those that were going to be laid off. Of course, I didn't sign my name to it. I ordered about six copies to be sent to me personally. I clipped this article out, I brought some thumbtacks, and as I was sent on errands through the different departments I stuck up this article that I had written in different parts of the factory.

I put it on the bulletin board in my own department. In the meantime, I had some messages to deliver to the main office. When I came back to my own department the whole place was a bedlam. The forelady was ready to tear her hair out. Nobody was working. Somebody was standing up on the work table, everybody was gathered around, and she was reading this article that somebody found on the bulletin board. It dealt with the workers at Bauer and Black, and they thought it was wonderful. Hooray! Somebody cares about us. Listen, it's in print. It's in a newspaper. Look at what they said, about us, about layoffs and all this. And the forelady and everybody else came running in and put everybody back to work. Nobody said a word to me.

It was my job at the end of the day, after all of the girls left, to make sure all the windows were closed, that the aisles were clear, the machinery was shut off. The forelady would leave right away at quitting time. But this particular day the forelady was still sitting at her desk. I finished, cleared the aisles, shut off the machinery, checked the fire escapes. Then she said, "Christine, you're wanted in the office."

I came down to the office and there was the woman in charge of personnel. She says, "Christine," in her highest Bryn Mawr or eastern college fashion, she says, "We don't think you're happy here. And we think it's best that we sever all connections. Here's your pay."

II

Our first test in organizing the unemployed was about May 1931. Another man and myself were assigned to organize the unemployed on the near west side [of Chicago] in an all-black neighborhood. We found a small storefront and we paid the rent on it. We cleaned it up, got some chairs, mimeographed a leaflet. We didn't know a soul—went from door to door to distribute the leaflets. In the evening a lot of people came. The little hall was full.

We spoke simply, explained the platform, the demands and activities of the unemployed council. And then we said, "Are there any questions?" There was a rather awkward silence. Everybody looked at each other to see who was going to speak up.

Finally, an elderly black man stood up and said, "What you folks figure on doing about that colored family that was thrown out of their house today? They got no place to go. They're still out there with their furniture on the sidewalk."

So the man who was with me said, "Very simple. We'll adjourn this meeting, go over there, and put the furniture back in the house. After that, anyone wishing to join the unemployed council and build an organization to fight evictions, return to this hall and we'll talk about it some more." That's what we did. We adjourned the meeting.

They didn't walk with us. They discreetly walked just a little behind us because they didn't trust us. They wanted to see what we were going to do.

The evicted family was just around the corner a block away, at 13th and Loomis. It was a little frame house. (All the houses were small, frame, one-family shacks.) We walked up to the front door. There was a big padlock on it. So the man who was with me said, "Does anybody have any tools? We've got to break this lock." In a matter of minutes men came with all kinds of tools. We broke the lock on the door. Once he and I started taking in the chairs, everybody else pitched in, began to haul in every last bit of furniture, fix up the beds, set up the gas stove and break the seal that had shut off the gas, and so on; and when that was all done, went back to the hall. The hall was jammed! And we organized the best and most effective unemployed council in the city of Chicago.

Later some of the landlords got together and they decided that, come hell or high water, they and the police were going to put an end to this business of people breaking the locks and putting the furniture back in, turning on the gas and everything else.

Some family had been evicted early in the morning. People had been coming there all day long trying to put the furniture back in. Hundreds of people had been arrested.

We had a little meeting in the hall and I said, "Well, let's go. We've got to get that furniture back. It's getting night. We have to help this family." So we did.

Over on 13th Street, there was the woman and her children and her furniture at this house. But there was not another soul on the street anywhere, not even a dog. So we think, all right, we'll go.

A handful of us marched up to the house where this woman and her children were. As soon as we got there—the police had been hiding around different buildings—the police came and surrounded us. They were ready to arrest us.

I tried to go up to the house. So one of the detectives jumped up on the steps of the house with a sawed-off machine gun and he says, "The first son-of-a-bitch that sets foot on these stairs is going to have his head shot off."

Well, you can't let that go unchallenged! So I stepped forward, and behind me comes a young white man, and behind him comes a black man and his wife. And the four of us marched up, right in the face of the sawed-off gun.

When we four went on the stairs the people came out of their houses. They came swarming out and they surrounded the police.

And the detective didn't dare kill us. He just held his gun uselessly in his hand. The four of us stood triumphantly up at the top of the stairs and were kicking on the door.

And then the chief, or whoever was in charge, said, "Now look. We've arrested hundreds of people here today. The hell with it." He took off his hat. He said, "Take up a collection. Whatever we collect, that's going to be the rent." They took up a collection among all the policemen and everybody who was there.

The landlord was there and the policeman told him, "That's your rent." The landlord wasn't satisfied. And the policeman told him, "Now you take this money or you get nothing. We've had enough trouble with this one house. I don't want to hear another word out of you." He said, "These people are going to break down the door. Now you take this money and you go open that door." So the landlord had to take the padlock off the door.

In July 1932, I [became an organizer for District 10]. District 10 comprised Texas, Oklahoma, Arkansas, Missouri, Nebraska, Kansas and Iowa. At first the district headquarters was in Kansas City, Missouri. We had isolated organizations in all of these states plus some devoted contacts in all kinds of small towns and rural communities.

In Kirksville, Missouri we had one lonely contact. He wrote to the office in Kansas City and said that he'd like to have me come out and speak. He had come to see us in Kansas City and he wanted me to come to Kirksville. He would organize a meeting in front of the court house on a certain Saturday morning.

I had been up in northern Iowa, so I hitch-hiked from northern Iowa down into Kirksville. They had been forbidden a permit to meet. They decided, to hell with this, permit or no permit we would meet. So somebody brought an empty barrel and first a man by the name of Mr. Martin, a local man, spoke on this barrel. The police came along and arrested him.

As soon as they arrested him I asked the fellows to hoist me up there on the barrel. Somebody had pointed out the mayor of Kirksville and the mayor of Kirksville was a real dandy! He must have had a Brooks Brothers suit on. Kirksville used to be a shoe manufacturing town and here the people were barefooted. So, being a very practical person, I pointed to the mayor. I said, "There's your mayor." I said, "I bet his suit and his shoes and his beautiful shirt and tie cost more than you spend for a month's groceries." And that won the people over.

Meantime, they had taken this man to jail. And I said, "What do you say we all march down to that jail and get Mr. Martin out? He has committed no crime." They said, "OK, let's go!" They took me off the barrel and all of us, hundreds and hundreds, marched down to the jail.

The mayor and the keeper of the jail said they wanted to talk with me. I said, "No sir! You're not talking to me. You talk to *all* of us." No, they wouldn't, they'd talk to me. I said, "I'll tell you what, we'll compromise. Let the people here elect a committee so that nobody can say I made a deal with you."

The people there elected a committee and we went inside. We made it plain to the jailer and to the mayor that these people were not leaving until Mr. Martin was released. Since all these angry people were out there, they had better let Mr. Martin go. But first the mayor told me, he said, "You don't know this guy Martin. He's a no good slob! He wouldn't work if he had a job. He's lazy, he's good-for-nothing, he's no good," he's this, he's that! And he just slammed the man down as if he was absolutely dirt and wasn't worth fighting for. But then finally he agreed to release Mr. Martin.

So one of the turnkeys brings Mr. Martin out. The mayor comes out on the porch, puts his arm around Mr. Martin and he says, "Fellow citizens! We are releasing Mr. Martin. And just to show you that my heart's in the right place," (Mrs. Martin was pregnant, they had a baby in a few days) "just to show all of you," he says, "that my heart's in the right place, I'm going to treat Mr. and Mrs. Martin to the best meal they've had in a long time."

Mr. and Mrs. Martin walked with the mayor to a little restaurant at the west side of the square, and all these hundreds of people following. They went into the restaurant and the mayor told Mr. and Mrs. Martin to order whatever they wanted.

Mr. and Mrs. Martin ordered a glass of water! And that's *all* they ordered. The mayor pleaded with them. He *pleaded* with them to order something else. They said, "No. This is all we want—a glass of water."

By the time we got to Martin's house there was a layette, there were blankets, there was coal, there was food, there were all kinds of things. And then we organized an unemployed council in Kirksville. I think I stayed there about three days to get the thing organized. We had sowbelly bacon—it's just nothing but fat, soft fat, and that's what these people got from the relief—sowbelly bacon and homemade biscuits and gravy and black coffee three times a day. But these people organized. And there are people like Mr. Martin everywhere who cannot be bought by the mayor or by anybody else.

And the women were more militant than the men. For instance, in Joplin, Missouri, a young housewife had a whole bunch of kids. She made a slab. She took a pole and she took a piece of board and she tacked it on. And then she took the sowbelly bacon that she got from the relief and tacked it onto this board. And she led the demonstration through town.

The women were usually the most outspoken because they had the children to feed and they had to provide the food for the family. You found women pounding their fists on the desks as well as the men.

I remember a big gathering once in Grand Island, Nebraska. Have you ever heard of Mother Bloor? She was an old-time radical and a marvelous speaker. She and her husband owned a farm in North Dakota and they brought a whole truckload of farmers from North Dakota.

There were thousands of farmers gathered and they had inexperienced leadership. People had gotten together but nobody knew what to do. Mother Bloor decided somebody ought to do something. She got up on top of the truck and she said (she had a voice that really carried, she should have been on the stage), "Would you like to hear greetings from the farmers in North Dakota?" "Yeah!"

So she told them about farming and the miseries of farming and then she said, "I hear that some of you men complain about modern equipment for the women. You think women are having life too easy. Well," she said, "let me tell you the women's side of the story."

She said, "Did you ever go to a cemetery and take a look at the gravestones? Here lies Joe Smith. Here lies Jane Smith, his first wife. Here lies Mary Smith, his second wife. Here lies so-and-so, his fourth wife." She said, "A man outlived four or five wives because the women had to work so hard. . . ."

I have to tell you about the Sears, Roebuck sales. Let's say, Farmer Smith's farm is up for sale and he has 200 or 300 acres of land. He has a tractor, he has a couple of horses, he has cows, he has a wagon, he has a buggy, maybe he has a car, he has furniture, all the different implements. Everything is brought out.

All the neighbors from miles around gather. The auctioneer gets up and he says, "What am I offered for this first-rate Jersey cow?" "Ten cents!" "Does anybody raise the price? Ten cents offered, ten cents, ten cents, ten cents." Nobody offers more than ten cents. "This first-class Jersey cow is sold for ten cents."

"What am I offered for this tractor?" "Fifteen cents."

"What am I offered for this stove?" "Five cents."

"What am I offered for this. . .?"

And then they would get the bills of sale from the auctioneer and everybody would turn back these bills of sale to the farmer and help him put back all his stuff.

The farmers, without anybody telling them how to organize, knew how to organize. And do you know where they met? They didn't meet in any small hall. They met in the school house! They were American citizens, they were native Americans, that school belonged to them. They paid the taxes.

Every meeting started with a song. In the middle of the meeting there was singing. At the end of the meeting there was singing. And then they served coffee and cake if they had it.

In the '30s an organizer did not have a car and there was no money for bus fare. Organizers had either to ride the rails or to hitch-hike. [But one time] our people in Sioux City thought it might be dangerous for me to hitch-hike back to Kansas City so they managed to get enough money together to buy me a bus ticket to Kansas City.

The bus wasn't a large one, not a Greyhound, but some smaller independent company that probably ran buses in the rural areas of the region. All the seats were filled. A young woman, she didn't look to be more than twenty to twenty-five years of age, had four small children with her. They looked as though they were scarcely more than a year apart. She was thin and poorly dressed, her hair straggly and poverty was clearly written all over her and the four children. They were all squeezed into one seat, the mother holding the youngest on her lap.

Not long after the bus got started we ran into a heavy summer storm. There was thunder and lightning and at times the rain was so heavy the bus driver could hardly see the road. The pace was agonizingly slow, the storm so violent it was impossible to sleep. The four children became fretful and restless, some of them were crying—probably a mixture of hunger, fear, and being so tightly squeezed in such a small space.

Now in ordinary times the other passengers would have cursed the woman and her crying children, disturbing all the passengers in the bus and making the trip even more miserable than it already was. But these were not ordinary times. The Depression was a thing known to all. Hard times, hunger, worry, fear of tomorrow, was like a dark cloud hanging over the country.

Instead of being angry with the poor young helpless woman and her restless and fretful children, one passenger after another, male and female, came to her and each passenger took one of her children to cuddle and soothe, holding the children in their arms and trying to get them to sleep. I had seen kindness and consideration for others before but nothing to match the wonder of human sympathy and help that I saw that night. The passengers took all four children so the mother could get some rest. Soon all the children went to sleep in the arms of total strangers, and in my heart I felt that this is the true America, this is the America where I belong and feel at home.

I am very happy that I was sent out of Chicago because then I really got to know American working people. I have such undying confidence in the American people, that once they understand what they are fighting for, nothing in hell can beat them. I saw it in Joplin. I saw it in Kirksville. I saw it in Des Moines. I saw it in all kinds of small towns in Nebraska. I saw it in small towns in Kansas. I saw it in Chicago.

Some day, I hope soon, the youth of America will build a new movement. I hope that they will take that which was pure and noble from the old and add new ideas and methods of leadership that will one day convince the American people that socialism is the answer, a socialism based on the history, best traditions and the courage and fighting ability of the American people.

JOHN W. ANDERSON

J OHN W. ANDERSON was a rank-and-file activist in the United
Automobile Workers from its beginnings until his retirement in
1966. These pages, which tell of his early life, are part of a
book-length manuscript he has written on his career in the UAW.*

After the Briggs strike in 1933 with which this selection closes,
John Anderson joined the Industrial Workers of the World. This was
the union at that time which most emphasized the need for industrial
rather than craft unions. For workers to build a strong enough force
to deal with massive corporations, it appeared to Anderson, it was
necessary to organize on an industry-wide basis. So for three years
preceding the launching of the CIO, Anderson was a volunteer
organizer for the IWW.

In November 1936, he was hired at the Fleetwood Fisher Body
plant in Detroit where he worked for the next thirty years. During
the General Motors sit-down strike of January–February 1937,
Anderson was chairman of the Fleetwood strike committee. As a
delegate to the conference which ratified the GM strike settlement
and the first GM contract, he argued that the union should insist on
a shop steward system. This was one of the first occasions on which
Anderson as a spokesman for the rank and file clashed with Walter

*This material is copyrighted by John W. Anderson. It may not be reproduced
in whole or in part without his written permission.

Reuther. In 1938, he left the Socialist Party and became a founding member of the Socialist Workers Party.

John Anderson served the UAW in many positions. In 1947, he was elected president of Local 15 and initiated a massive demonstration in Cadillac Square against the impending Taft-Hartley Act. As local union president, from 1947 to 1949, Anderson agitated for a cost-of-living clause in the GM contract. He was defeated for reelection in 1949 during a period of widespread and intense red-baiting throughout the American labor movement. When he left office, a sign reading "An Injury to One is an Injury to All" was taken down from the wall of the local union headquarters.

Many themes run through John Anderson's account of his early years and his gradual radicalization which also occur in the narratives of Christine Ellis, Stella Nowicki, and George Patterson: the desire for education; the irrelevance of religion as a solution to social and economic problems; the hunger and hardship of the Depression and their effect in destroying love and family life; the outgrowing of a narrow national loyalty and the ripening in its place of a sense of solidarity with working people everywhere.

JOHN W. ANDERSON

How I Became
Part of the Labor Movement

I WAS BORN on a farm in Lincoln County, Wisconsin, May 12, 1906. Merrill, the county seat, is located two hundred miles northwest of Milwaukee. At the turn of the century and until the early twenties Merrill was a sawmill and lumbering town.

Many of the farmers worked the land in summer and were employed in the logging industry during the winter. The climate in this part of Wisconsin is not good for some crops. I have known it to freeze every month except July. There is much swamp land, many lakes, steep hills. In some areas there are so many stones that it is too expensive to clear the land of them. The farms have no ready market for their product.

My Norwegian grandfather homesteaded a hundred and sixty acres [nine miles north of Merrill]. To this wooded area he brought his wife and five children from Norway about 1890. After a few years he divorced his wife and returned to Norway. My father, Alex A. Anderson, at the age of fifteen became the principal breadwinner of the family. He had to quit school to work on the farm and in the woods. As he grew older, in the spring of the year he followed the log drives. These drives took place when the rivers were swollen from melting snow. Men like my father were skilled at riding the logs down to the sawmills. When a log was held up on some obstruction a log jam piled up. It was then the task of the drivers to find the key log that was causing the jam. Finding this log was difficult and dangerous work. When the jam was broken hundreds and some-

times thousands of logs shot forward down the river. Breaking a
log jam resulted in injury and death to many drivers.

Father knew all the skills of the lumberjack. In winter he helped
cut the trees down, cut them into logs and pile them up by the river
or at a landing where they were taken to the mills by sleighs or
by train. In summer he sometimes peeled the bark from hemlock
logs. The bark was used in the tanneries.

My mother was one of six children of Swiss immigrants who settled in Nakoosa, Wisconsin. Her mother died of childbirth when
my mother was only nine years old. She had to quit school after
the third grade and go to work as a domestic in the home of a well-
to-do family. Her wages were low and the hours long. She often
told us how hard she had to work and the indignities she suffered.
She married my father in 1902. From March 1903 to February 1913,
my mother gave birth to six children. My brother Carl was the oldest, my sister Julia came next, and then me.

My most vivid childhood experience is of a terrible forest fire
that swept over our farm and the surrounding area in early August
1910. There had been no rain for a period of forty days. Our nearest
neighbors were a mile away. The one to the west had been clearing
land. He let a brush fire get out of control.

My father, like the rest of these part-time farmers, had no knowledge of how to fight a forest fire. Hardly more than an hour before
this holocaust swept across the landscape burning our house, barn
and most of the livestock, my father put us on a wagon and took
us down to the lake located on the southern part of the farm. A
neighbor from the south of us joined my father in protecting us from
the fire. We children were made to lie on a bog on the edge of
the lake. We were covered with a blanket. My father and the
neighbor kept throwing buckets of water on us, on each other, and
on the wagon and horses standing at the edge of the lake.

My mother narrowly escaped death in the flames when she tried
to save some of the cattle by driving them into the lake. We found
several cows burned to death within a hundred yards of where we
lay. I remember seeing the flames shooting hundreds of feet in the
air over the lake. All that we saved was a team of horses with the

wagon, a few belongings and a cow. For hours after the fire there were burning embers everywhere. As far as the eye could see the landscape was black, not a green tree or bush in sight.

This fire was a harsh turning point in the life of our family. We went to stay with my grandparents who lived about seven miles from the farm. My grandmother had married again. After a week or so the rest of the family went back to the farm to build a log house and barn before winter set in. I lived with my grandparents for almost four years.

My grandmother was a domineering woman. Although her profane and derogatory remarks were in Norwegian, I soon learned what she meant. She sometimes pulled my ears if I didn't immediately do as I was told.

I started school at the French Ridge school. It was a one room school where the teacher had to teach more than thirty children in all eight grades. I got little attention and sat idle most of the time. I had no trouble in school but going to and from school I was harassed by some older boys.

I was very young when I began doing some chores. I brought in the wood for the night. I fed the goat, got the cows from the pasture and helped in other ways. A small creek ran through the farm. I enjoyed it because it gave me a place to go fishing and swimming.

Only once in my youth do I remember getting a gift for Christmas. The daughter of one of the neighbors was a school teacher. One Christmas she bought me a pail and a shovel. This kindness I never forgot.

In the summer of 1914 I returned home. I had seen little of my father or other members of the family during the years I lived with my grandparents.

My dad was a brutal man with a violent temper. We children and mother as well as the animals suffered from it. He said he wanted to make us boys tough to meet the hardships of life. To be kind and loving for him was to show a weakness. There was little love shown by either parent toward each other or toward us.

From eight years of age I cleaned the barn, drove the cattle to

water, hauled water from the lake, and milked the cows. I picked
rocks from the fields, planted, helped with the haying and the harvesting. In the fall I trapped muskrat and skunk for their skins. In
winter I snared rabbits thus supplying most of the meat for the table.
I often had to ride a horse when it pulled the cultivator or other
farm machinery. As I grew older I broke the colts we raised so that
anyone could ride them.

In the summer when it rained we went fishing. We were permitted
to swim in the lake on hot summer days when there was little work
to do. While we were rarely allowed to visit the neighbor children
we did make friends at school.

My six years in the Heineman school were not happy ones. The
teacher relied on the rod to punish those who failed to learn as well
as those who broke the rules. I believe I got more whippings than
any two children in the school. Yet even this school was better than
staying home to work on the farm. We had a mile and a half to
walk each way. Temperatures of thirty degrees below zero were not
uncommon. Sometimes we had four feet of snow and there were
no snowplows. Our school lunch, which was sometimes frozen solid,
was most often bread and syrup or peanutbutter. We seldom had
any meat, eggs or butter. These had to be sold to the store to buy
clothing and the other necessities of life we couldn't raise on the
farm.

I was baptized a Lutheran and sometimes attended church with
my grandparents but from 1914 until 1925 I had no religious training. This didn't prevent me from developing strong personal ideas
on conduct and life. My parents instilled in me an intense feeling
against any alcoholic drink. My dad smoked but always spoke
against it. We knew about sex only what we learned from the animals or from some older boys. With this strict discipline, together
with a philosophy of work, I avoided most of the pitfalls of youth.
We were forced to suppress our emotions. My dad would scold us
if we laughed or if we cried.

Religious bigotry and nationalistic pride on the part of the adults
were the principal cause of friction among the children at school.
The farmers who sent their children to the Heineman school were
of many nationalities. Father made derogatory remarks about people

of other nationalities except American and Norwegian. From my parents we acquired a strong bias against Catholics and other religious minorities. The fights and arguments I had in school originated from this bias. It prevented close friendships and the happiness that might have been derived from them.

In 1916 our log house burned down. (I was to learn from my mother that Dad had set the house on fire to collect the insurance. He needed it to pay the taxes and the interest on the mortgage.) Following the fire we were forced to live in a small frame building that had been used as a chicken coop and granary. My brothers and I all had to sleep in the attic, not more than four feet from the floor to the ridge of the roof.

During World War I we were getting high prices for butter and eggs and other farm products. My dad was getting high wages in the lumber camps; my older brother, my sister and I were bringing home our wages. We, like most farmers, were prospering. My folks saw the need for a new home. They mortgaged the farm for twenty-five hundred dollars to build the house and buy necessary equipment for the farm.

After paying off the old mortgage and buying needed farm equipment there was not enough money to complete the house. The interior remained unfinished and there were no bricks on the outside. It was impossible to keep it warm during the cold winter months. A couple of years after the mortgage debt was incurred the price of farm products began to fall. It was not long before the income from the farm would not meet the expenses.

My older brother and sister and I were the only children graduating from the Heineman school who went to high school. Because of our poor preparation and home environment all of us had difficulties with our studies. Our parents wanted all of us to get an education. Their important contribution was in encouraging us, in permitting us to leave the farm and giving us what little financial help they could. I rode a bicycle to school during the spring and fall when weather permitted. I worked on the farm on weekends and during most of the summer vacations.

After school was out in May 1923 when I was only seventeen, I got a job in a logging camp. I drove a team of horses skidding logs from the woods to a sawmill. It took all the strength I had to throw the harness over their backs in the morning and take it off at night. I slept in the bunkhouse with the other lumberjacks, ate my meals with them and thus observed first hand the life of these men. In later years when I heard iww members refer to these men as "timber beasts" I knew what they meant. There were no facilities for taking a bath. Laundry facilities were non-existent or poor. This lack of sanitation facilities resulted in a strong odor in the bunkhouse. The food was good and we ate all we wanted. It was high adventure for me to work and live with these lumberjacks for six weeks. In this way I learned how my dad spent most of his life.

The logs we brought to the mill were cut into lumber and timbers for the construction of a dam at the Grandmother Falls a couple of hundred yards down the river. When the logging job was completed I went to work for a construction company building Grandmother dam.

We were paid four dollars for an eight hour day. They deducted a dollar a day for room and board. One day two men were hired who began suggesting that we ask for more money. They were going to ask for five dollars per day. They spoke about strikes that had taken place in Lawrence, Massachusetts and Paterson, New Jersey. Because of their references to those strikes in the textile industry I concluded many years later these men had been members of the iww. They got little response from the workers for a strike demanding higher wages. I was prepared to support any demand for more money.

When I returned to school in September 1923 I had almost a hundred dollars, hardly enough to carry me through a year of school. Some of my earnings I had to loan to my parents. I was always trying to find work on Saturdays or after school. I joined the Wisconsin National Guard. For each drill period I would get one dollar. Even this amount seemed a lot of money in those days.

During the fall I had another experience that was to have a long term effect on my life. I fell in love. Not wanting to embarrass the girl I decided not to date her or do more than speak to her when we met. Being in love with her made me more determined than ever not only to finish high school but to go to college. I felt that only by this means could I escape poverty and the hard life of a worker. My love for her inspired me to work harder. From then on I seemed to be working for a cause thus making the bitterest toil more acceptable.

As soon as I graduated from high school I bought a train ticket for Milwaukee. With no previous experience and no one to advise me, I went from factory to factory asking for any job that was listed on bulletin boards at the employment offices. After two or three days of job hunting I was hired at A. O. Smith, a large employer making seamless tubing for the petroleum industry and car frames for General Motors cars. A. O. Smith was an anti-union company that checked the record of its new hires for union activity. My coming from a farm was assurance enough that I had no union ideas.

When I first went to work assembling frames by hand it took four or five men to assemble each frame. The parts for the frame were not only oily and dirty but they had sharp edges on which one could be seriously cut. The air was filled with smoke and dirt. At the end of a twelve hour day I would be completely exhausted.

By November of 1925, A. O. Smith had developed a machine that eliminated the difficult hand labor. It was controlled by one man on a raised platform. They could produce the same number of frames with two hundred men that they previously produced with twenty-five hundred. On this machine my wages were cut and I worked fewer hours.

When my roommate got a job metal finishing at Seaman Body I decided to follow him there in January 1926. It took me about a month to learn the metal finishing operation. We used a soldering iron, several heavy files, finishing hammers, and emery cloth. It required skill to use a soldering iron so that a minimum of finishing was needed; then one had to learn how to use a file to make the solder and metal perfectly smooth. The more skill one had the easier the work was. It was necessary to wear canvas gloves, not only to protect the hands but also to feel the smoothness of the metal. We wore out a pair of these gloves every day or so and we had to buy our own gloves.

It was a piecework job. When I began working on the job the company was paying seventy cents for finishing one door. It was estimated that the best finishers could earn up to a dollar and ten cents per hour. If too many of them began turning in more than that a cut in the piecework rate could be expected.

After I had been on the job about three months the piecework rate was cut. Now they were going to pay us only forty cents per door. When the men were notified of this most of them refused to work. They didn't walk out but just sat around talking about what ought to be done. There was no union or talk about a union. There was some hostility toward those men who turned in too many pieces and thus brought about the cut in piece rates. Some of us got tired of standing around. We went home at noon and returned the next morning. Most of the men had returned to work at the reduced piecework rate.

From June 1925 until September 1926 I held eight different jobs and saved over twelve hundred dollars. That was a lot of money for that time. My love for my high school sweetheart hadn't dimmed. All the hard work had been made easier just thinking of her. To gain her hand was one of the strongest motives for my going to college.

I wanted an education in order to escape from the drudgery of work that I had known ever since I was a child. I didn't know how to study. I am sure I read at a very low level. If fatigue is an enemy of the mind, as no doubt it is, then my entire educational experience had been handicapped by it. I had often been told that "knowledge is power." I decided to study economics because I thought it would give me a better understanding of the political and economic system under which I lived.

I registered at the University of Wisconsin in Madison, fearful that I wouldn't be able to do the work. By mid-term I was on probation and I continued on probation for the rest of the year. It took several months before I recovered from what turned out to be an unsuccessful love affair and a year and a half before my scholastic problems were cleared up. My studies took most of my time when I didn't have a job earning extra money for my expenses. My financial condition didn't permit me to devote much time to social activities.

When I went to the University I joined the Christian Science Society there. Later I joined the Mother Church in Boston. I looked to religion for answers to all my problems—economic, health and scholastic. Although a faithful adherent for eight years I found neither health nor freedom from poverty.

In the spring of 1928 I signed an agreement to sell a book about scientific agriculture in Marquette County, Wisconsin. I saw the book as a valuable help to the farmers. I was soon to learn that just as my folks were forced to abandon our farm in Lincoln County in 1925, many of these farmers were no better off than we had been. The depression had hit these farmers in 1921, soon after World War I. They were not too receptive to a book that would enable them to grow more crops on fewer acres. They wanted to know how to get higher prices for the crops they had to sell. When I began making deliveries I found that at least twenty per cent of the farmers who said they would buy the book either had changed their minds about its value or didn't have the money to pay for it.

I ate most of my meals with the farmers and often stayed with them overnight. I soon learned not to judge people by either their nationality or their religion. During that summer I went to a number of different churches with the farmers. There was ignorance and bigotry as well as intelligence and tolerance among these people regardless of nationality or religion. Some regarded institutions of higher learning as an evil forced onto the taxpayer. The majority believed in education and admired anyone who tried hard to get an education. I knew that some of those buying the book did so to help me, not because they were interested in the book. The summer was rich in experience but poor in financial returns.

Returning to school in September I found it necessary to find odd jobs to pay for my room and board. I knew students who didn't have enough money for food and clothing. Waiting on table for banquets, the difference in living standards between the rich student and those of us who had to work was impressed on my mind. This condition caused a number of us to organize a union of working students. We held a number of meetings but as far as I can remember we made no wage demands on our employers. I do remember making some pretty militant speeches.

It was too difficult for me to work and keep up my studies so I decided to take a year off and build up my finances. At the end

of the semester I quit school and bought a bus ticket for Detroit.
I heard that the auto industry was having a good year. Detroit had
a reputation for paying high wages. I felt certain I would be able
to find a job as a metal-finisher.

In a day or two I was hired at the Chrysler Kercheval plant. Metal-
finishing had changed considerably since I began finishing at Seaman
Body. Soldering had become a separate trade and a power tool, the
disc grinder, was used to do most of the work. There were two
of us doing the same operation, one man on each side of the body.
As we worked our disc grinders threw a stream of lead particles
in the face of our partner. It was impossible to avoid it. It was a
hard dirty job.

We were paid a piecework rate. I had only worked there about
five weeks before we got a cut in our piecework rate. I got in a
sharp argument with the foreman and I was soon escorted from the
plant. This was the first time I was fired from a job.

The 13th of March 1929 was cold and the wind was blowing about
forty miles an hour. I knew on such a day very few men would
be looking for jobs; my chances of getting hired would be good.
There were no workers in line that day when I went in to the employment office of the Briggs Mack Avenue plant. I was hired for the
second shift.

We were paid on a bonus plan which none of us could figure
out. We were earning about seventy-five cents per hour so we didn't
complain too much. The men were crowded together giving us little
room to work in. The floor was covered with dust and dirt. We
worked ten hours per day. It took me almost an hour on the street
car to get there.

I didn't work long at the Mack plant because one day I went to
Fisher Body plant No. 18 and was hired. I was able to walk to work
in about ten minutes. Working conditions were much better than at
Briggs. I was working on Buick bodies. Again this was a piecework
job and again I was to have the usual experience of having the
piecework rates cut when we made over a dollar per hour. The men
walked off the job, some leaving the plant while others sat around
outside.

A Communist union, the Auto Workers Union, put out a handbill advertising a meeting to be held in the evening in downtown Detroit. I went to the meeting which was attended by about sixty men. I didn't recognize any of them as my fellow workers at Fisher Body. The speaker, a leader of the CP in Detroit, didn't make a good impression on me. He did not appeal to the workers and there was no real representation of the people involved in the strike. There was no discussion. Workers were afraid to speak up because of spies being present and their general inability to speak, express themselves or have any program. They went to these meetings just to see what was being offered, more out of curiosity than anything else. After three or four days the men went back to work. I believe some concession was made to the workers.

At this time my two younger brothers came to Detroit looking for work. Chester and I got work together as metal-finishers at the Briggs Mack plant. He was put to work on a body line with me so that I could teach him the trade and help him out until he was able to take his turn on the line. In a week or ten days he was doing the work of a metal-finisher. We were receiving a dollar per hour and we were working ten hours a day six days per week. In the heat of the summer metal-finishing is an especially exhausting job but Chester knew he was quitting to go to the University in September 1929, and I would only be working until the end of January 1930. We were highly motivated because we thought by working hard for a few months we would eventually escape this bitter toil.

I was working at the Briggs Highland Park plant when the stock market crash came in October 1929. In a matter of days they started to lay off men. After the first layoff of ten per cent, the rest worked so much faster that it was necessary to lay off another twenty per cent to reduce production by ten per cent. The slowest man was always in danger of being laid off. The greater the number of unemployed the greater the effort on the part of those working. As the Depression deepened, the men tended to work close to the limit of their capacities. It was this speed-up which became unbearable and finally caused the workers to organize.

Most of the workers had no savings. There was no unemployment compensation or other relief available from local, state or the federal government. Workers sold everything they had, including their clothes, at bargain prices in order to buy food. Millions of unemployed workers went back to the farms they had come from. The future for many Americans looked gloomy. I was little affected by this gloom for I continued to work until I returned to the University.

I had been back in Madison about a month when one day a resentful thought about my father crossed my mind. I had a feeling of guilt at entertaining the idea. When I went back to my room there was a telgram there from Mother saying Dad had been critically injured. At fifty-three years of age he was doing a very dangerous job loading logs on flat cars. The job should have been given to a much younger man. I left for home at once but he had passed away before I got there.

The last time I had seen him was at Christmastime 1928. He made a weak apology for his treatment of the family during past years and he was not a person to readily admit his mistakes. He took great pride in the fact that he had two sons who were going to college. This was something that few workers could boast about in 1930.

My last three semesters at the University, from February 1930 to June 1931, were the most enjoyable and productive. I studied economics under Professors John R. Commons, Selig Perlman, and Don D. Lescohier. In the spring of 1931, I attended meetings in the state capitol where the legislature was debating and holding hearings on an unemployment compensation law. I heard the president of the Wisconsin Federation of Labor debate the issue with the head of the state Manufacturers Association. The AFL spokesman made a good case but it was 1936 before the law was passed and took effect.

While some of the professors and instructors did raise my interest in the labor movement they didn't influence me in a radical direction. They were satisfied with the craft unionism of the AFL. They couldn't envision anything like the CIO being formed. They didn't foresee the Depression lasting ten years or the coming of World War II. They spoke of the Depression ending in less than two years.

I dated a classmate who I would have proposed to if I had had prospects of a good job. Proposing marriage to her before I had a job was out of the question. When I kissed her goodbye in June 1931, I expected to be able to return to her in a year or so. We corresponded for a couple of years but as time passed our letters were farther and farther apart. The disruption of family life caused by unemployment and the breaking up of young people who wanted to get married was the cause of much unhappiness and suffering during the Depression.

When I received my B. A. degree in June 1931, I hoped to get a job in the personnel department of some large corporation. I had minored in personnel management in college. I wrote letters of application to General Motors and other companies but received no reply. It had long been the policy of General Motors and other large companies to use a labor spy system to deal with their hourly employees rather than employing personnel men to deal with the workers or a union. I was to learn years later that only ten per cent of the class of 1931 were able to get jobs in their field of study. The other ninety per cent had to make a living any way they could.

From June 1931 until December 1932, I tried to earn a living selling various commodities door to door. I signed an agreement with the Real Silk Hosiery Company to sell their products in Columbus, Ohio. To appeal to the anti-union elements, part of our sales pitch was that, "Real Silk is made by non-union labor." We salesmen soon learned that the Depression had eliminated hosiery and lingerie as necessities of life.

I was hired by the Chamberlin Weatherstripping Company. We told our customers the weatherstripping would pay for itself in smaller fuel bills but few people could afford it. I tried selling the Hoover Vacuum Cleaner in Lancaster, Ohio. In Cleveland, I went to work for the General Electric Company trying to sell refrigerators. Wherever I went I got the same story. Most people were having difficulty buying the necessities of life, food, clothing, and shelter. Workers were unemployed, working part-time, or were afraid of losing their jobs. What I had to sell, few could afford. I, like thousands of other salesmen, was unable to earn a living.

Near Lancaster I saw an apple orchard in December where the fruit hadn't been picked. The ground was covered with large red apples. In spite of this, workers and their children in the city of Lancaster were going hungry. I could see no reason for this hunger in the midst of plenty. It was my impression that the wealthy families in the community were doing little or nothing to help the poor.

One day I was walking near the heart of Cleveland when I felt dizzy. I was broke and hadn't eaten that day. I decided to go to the office of a Christian Science practitioner nearby. I had been seeing him for my problem. I told him I was from Wisconsin and was somewhat critical of our economic and political system which I thought was responsible for the problems of the unemployed. He saw nothing wrong with it. He said my problem was caused by my erroneous thinking. When I left he gave me fifty cents to buy food.

In the spring of 1932 I decided to return to Detroit to get work as a metal-finisher. Arriving in Detroit the latter part of April, I learned there was no hiring in the auto plants. They were laying off workers. I tried more door-to-door selling of a number of products.

During the summer and fall of 1932 I almost starved. I rented a room for two dollars a week and ate in the Penny Pantries. These were places where restaurants had been and they were remodeled to feed the unemployed. From fifty to a hundred people could stand at a counter or sit at small tables to drink coffee, milk or buttermilk, with stale rolls or donuts. Nothing cost more than a nickel. Two or three times that summer I pawned the expensive watch my father left me. The pawnshop would loan me five dollars on it. That was enough to keep me a week.

It seemed ironic that from the time I was eight years of age until I graduated from college I never had time for a vacation. During these days of Depression when I was in my most productive years I couldn't earn a living although I had the trade of a metal-finisher and a college degree. The only place I could afford to go was to the public library. I went there to read the help wanted ads and the latest reports on the state of the economy. That summer was the most depressing period of my life.

Detroit, like Cleveland and other cities, made no provision for the feeding and housing of single men. At one time thousands of them were sleeping on army cots in vacant factory buildings where in the boom days of the '20s they made bodies for cars. Promiscuity was common in the rooming houses where single men and women found shelter. Men didn't have to pay prostitutes because there were so many women looking for a meal or a place to sleep. There was little publicity given to these reports but quite often one learned of the bodies of men being found in box cars and other places where migrants hung out. They died of cold, malnutrition and lack of medical attention.

As the time approached for the auto makers to start hiring workers for the 1933 model cars, I began going to employment offices. Men and women would stand in line from four o'clock in the morning until the employment office closed in the afternoon. When there were reports of hiring, the lines in front of the employment offices would sometimes be two or three blocks long. Thousands of workers would assemble before the Ford Rouge employment offices and at times they were driven away by mounted police or with water hoses.

These employment offices were the most uncertain way of finding a job. Many workers bought their jobs through an employment agency. Others were related to a foreman or knew someone with influence at the employment office. Still others gave the foreman a gift such as whiskey or money to obtain a job.

The employers preferred young single men from out of town. These men were at the age when they have a maximum of physical stamina. This is what the employer wanted on the production line. Also they felt no responsibility to these men when they laid them off.

The unorganized worker during the Depression had no bargaining power at the employment office. He accepted the hours, wages and working conditions without question. If you didn't have a trade you bluffed your way into a job by claiming experience in any job you thought you were able to do. With hundreds of workers in line you didn't get much time to talk to the man at the window.

I was hired at the Dodge plant of the Chrysler Corporation on

December 2, 1932. I worked from twelve to fourteen hours a day seven days a week from the day I was hired until December 24, Christmas Eve. Not having done any hard physical labor for almost three years, the killing pace left me completely exhausted at the end of the day but being twenty-six years of age I was able to keep up with the other workers.

It was common knowledge that a worker in the auto plants was so tired at the end of a day that he had no energy left for his family. He came home, threw himself on a bed, lay there and rested; he got up, ate his supper and went to bed for the night. A man was just a machine that worked, brought home the paycheck and lived a bare existance. From this extreme he went to the other extreme of being unemployed. One of the grievances of the wives of the production workers was that many of their husbands could not play their sexual roles when employed in an auto plant.

The metal-finisher had other serious grievances besides that of becoming exhausted. He had to contend with the lead dust, iron filings, and the sand thrown into the air by the emery wheels and disc grinders. There was no attempt to ventilate the work areas or to take the pollutants out of the air. Lead poisoning was contracted by breathing the lead dust into the lungs, through eating with hands that had not been washed after working with lead which was used to solder the joints of the body. It was an accepted fact that thousands of metal finishers in the auto industry suffered from lead poisoning but at that time it was not recognized as an occupational disease. Those who received proper medical attention soon enough avoided permanent damage. Those who died, those who were crippled, suffered merely from neglect. (At the South Bend UAW Convention in 1936, I. Ruskin, M.D., reported 13,000 lead poisoning cases during the Depression years, 4,000 cases during 1934 and 1935.)

There were other grievances that weren't so well publicized. For example, the female not only had to do the bidding of the foreman on the job; to hold her job she was sometimes forced to go out with him and do his bidding off the job. It was common talk around the shop that some men, in order to hold their jobs, had to respond to the wishes of the foreman with their wife or daughter. The foreman would visit the home or take them out.

To call ourselves free men or free labor would have been a complete distortion of the truth. Men were forced to work under these conditions in order to feed themselves and their families. To complain of the working conditions might have meant the loss of your job.

On Christmas Eve 1932 at seven o'clock, my foreman came to me and said, "You are being laid off until further notice. We'll call you when we need you." During the twenty-three days I had worked almost three hundred hours and had earned about $150. The hourly rate of the metal-finisher was fifty-two cents. There was no premium pay for overtime, Saturdays or Sundays. Metal-finishers were among the highest paid workers in the auto industry at that time.

Knowing that the production season only lasted four or five months for most of the auto workers during those years, I didn't wait to be called back to Dodge's but went to find another job. Between Christmas and New Years I was hired at the Briggs Highland Park plant. This plant was making Ford bodies.

Because of the bad working conditions the Briggs plants were referred to as slaughter houses. In 1927 there was a fire and explosion in the paint department of the Briggs Harper plant that took the lives of over two hundred workers. Although Ford had other body and supplier plants, Briggs was by far the largest. It was said that the contracts Ford signed with his suppliers didn't allow for a large margin of profit except at the expense of the workers; the suppliers reduced the wages in order to increase their profits.

On being hired at Briggs I was given a job on the line finishing the roof rail, a strip of metal running from the front to the rear on the top of the body. There were about twenty men doing the operation. They worked as teams on opposite sides of the body. Every man was required to take every tenth body. The conveyor line could always be speeded up giving the men less and less time to do their operation. Whenever the foreman thought he could get more work out of the men he speeded up the line. To get behind in your work might mean a layoff or discharge.

Working conditions at Briggs were worse than at Dodge's. The air was full of dust particles. The floor was covered with dirt. There were no adequate facilities for washing your hands, none for taking a bath. There was no cloak room or dining area.

When we went to work in the morning we never knew how many hours we would work. The metal-finishers on repair were working as much as twenty hours per day. Workers in other departments doing work on sub-assemblies were often sent home without earning their carfare. This sometimes went on for weeks and months at a time. I was working near the limit of my capacity but it was only eight hours per day, sometimes less.

Briggs paid their employees on three different bases: some were paid at piecework rates, some on a bonus system, and others an hourly rate. When you worked on a bonus rate it was virtually impossible to figure how much money you had coming on payday.

I was hired at fifty-two cents per hour, the same rate I had been earning at Dodge's, but I was never paid that rate at Briggs. When I received my first check I discovered I had not been paid the rate on my hiring slip. I was paid forty-five cents per hour. I wanted to complain regarding the shortage but when I learned that everyone had been shortchanged I remained silent waiting for some of the older workers to speak up. None of them did. The following week everyone received a further cut in wages. Now we were getting forty cents per hour. There was a lot of grumbling among the men but there was no concerted move to raise the question of our rate of pay with the foreman.

The next week the men on the line began discussing their rate of pay among themselves. When Friday came and instead of getting forty cents per hour we only received thirty-five there was real anger and discontent among the metal-finishers. We were called in to work Saturday and Sunday. By Sunday noon the workers had become so stirred up by the shortages in our pay that most of us walked off the job and went home without notifying the foreman.

Monday morning several of the men refused to work. They wanted an explanation why they weren't being paid at the rate at which they were hired. The foreman's answer was, "If you don't like your job why don't you quit?" and "There are a lot of people waiting outside to take your jobs." For about two hours the men would work a while and then go to the foreman for some understanding as to what our wages were. Finally the foreman said, "Either go to work or quit." That statement provoked the strike. (Briggs spokesmen told the press the workers had been driven from their jobs by strangers armed with clubs.)

We decided we weren't going to walk out as individuals. We left the sixth floor in a body after changing into street clothes. The word "strike" was soon heard throughout the plant. From the sixth to the first floor the workers marched out. Soon there were hundreds of workers milling around in the street. They didn't know what to do. They had no organization, no one to speak for them. I had seen these situations before. The men stayed out a few hours or a day or two and then went back to work without having made any gains.

Now because of my experience and education, I felt an obligation to stand up and speak for these men. I got up on the fender of a car and put into words the ideas I thought were passing through the minds of these protesting workers. I spoke about our principal grievance, the shortage in our pay. I told them I thought we ought to meet with the company and demand that we be paid the fifty-two cents an hour called for on our hiring slips.

I spoke no more than five minutes and then suggested that a committee be selected to meet with Briggs management. There was general agreement. I volunteered to go if I could get two or three others to go with me. After some persuasion, two other workers volunteered to jeopardize their jobs by acting as spokesmen for the other workers. All of those on the committee were metal-finishers. Because of their large number and skill, the metal-finishers were the most militant of the workers. They had the most experience in work stoppages and strikes.

It took upwards of thirty minutes to arrange the meeting with Briggs management. After waiting this time we were taken to the sixth floor where the office of the plant manager was located. Mr. M. L. Briggs was the spokesman for the company. He asked us what the trouble was and we explained that in three weeks our hourly wage rate had been reduced from the hiring rate of fifty-two cents to thirty-five cents an hour.

Mr. Briggs agreed to restore our wage rates. I suggested that he put it in writing. This he refused to do. I told him anything that couldn't be put in writing was not worth telling the men. I thought if we didn't have something in writing we would have nothing to prove that Mr. Briggs had agreed to restore our wages.

We hadn't been in Mr. Briggs' office more than ten minutes when he looked out the window and saw someone speaking to the workers. He turned to us and said, "The Communists have now taken over the strike." We continued to argue for a written statement from the company assuring the men of the restoration of their pay scale. Mr. Briggs finally said, "We will put nothing in writing. If you cannot take our word for it you can leave." We left without making any promise of getting the workers to return to work.

On the outside we found Phil Raymond, a well-known organizer of the Communist Party and secretary of the Communist-controlled Auto Workers Union and John Weissman, alias John Mack, speaking to the strikers. They asked them to go to Yemans Hall in Hamtramck where many Communist Party activities were carried on. Most of the strikers, not wanting to take an active part in the strike, dispersed and went home or to neighboring bars. Two or three hundred went to Yemans Hall. A meeting was held to discuss the issues of the strike. A strike committee was elected.

I didn't go to Yemans Hall because I didn't want to become identified as a leader of the strike. I still had hopes of getting a job in personnel management. I didn't want to kill my chances of becoming a white collar worker. Instead of going to the meeting I went to the Michigan Department of Labor and Industry to report that the Briggs Company was violating the law by working women more than fifty-four hours a week. I had seen the women working ten hours a day six and seven days a week.

The man I spoke with was sympathetic to the strike. He belonged to the AFL. He told me his office had neither the staff required to inspect the factories nor the power to enforce the law. He said, "Unless you have a union you can't enforce the law." He further stated that the only way for the auto workers to improve their wages, hours, and working conditions was to organize.

I went back to my room in Highland Park wondering what to do and what might happen. The next morning I went to see if the strike was still in progress. A block from the plant I met a worker who recognized me as the one who had acted as their spokesman the day before. Not knowing my name he said, "Shorty, you were elected to the strike committee." I knew nothing about being elected to the strike committee. He said, "We were told what you said to management yesterday, so they elected you to the strike committee." Reluctantly I accepted the responsibilities of that committee.

I began my activities by helping organize a picket line that marched on Manchester Avenue in front of the employment office and other entrances. It was a cold winter day to plunge into the charged air of a picket line. We had difficulty in getting the strikers out of the restaurants near the plant and onto the line. Before long we had upwards of a thousand marching in the line which sometimes stretched the three block length of the plant. This picket line was referred to as Anderson's and Murphy's army. Murphy was the name of another striker who led the picketing.

John Weissman, the CP member put in charge of the strike in Highland Park, was German-born and trained as a tool and die maker. He called a meeting of the strike committee for the purpose of electing a chairman and assigning duties to each member. I, among others, was nominated for chairman. A worker with a Polish name immediately raised a storm of protest. None of us were anxious to be chairman so the protester was elected chairman by a unanimous vote. He turned out to be a spy for Briggs management. I became chairman of the publicity committee.

Within a day or two after the Highland Park plant went on strike, three other Briggs plants were struck. There were nearly fifteen thousand workers on strike from the four plants. A strike of this size required an organization and men with experience to direct it. During the first crucial weeks of the strike the CP and its Auto Workers Union helped formulate the demands of the strikers; they provided the organizers, the meeting halls, the legal defense, and the money to pay most of the expenses. The strike was directed for the first weeks by Phil Raymond at the Mack Avenue plant, John (Weissman) Mack at Highland Park and [another] John Anderson, CP candidate for governor of Michigan in 1932, representing the

International Labor Defense. The ILD provided most of the money
during the first month of the strike. If it hadn't been for these three
men and the resources they had at their disposal the strike would
have been broken in a few days with no important gains made.

The membership of the Auto Workers Union was largely unemployed. The workers on strike didn't feel that their interests were
the same as those of the unemployed. Their language was not always
that of the worker but rather that of an agitator. Two of them were
foreign born. In spite of their important contribution to the strike,
Phil Raymond and the CP were largely discredited before the end
of the strike.

The mayor of the city of Detroit in 1933, Frank Murphy, was
a liberal but the two most important city officials dealing with the
strike were conservatives. Harry S. Toy, the police commissioner,
was a Republican. I met with him to get a permit for a parade
through the city. He refused to give us permission for such a parade.
We held it without his permission. There can be little doubt that
he gave the orders which finally broke up the picket line at the Mack
Avenue plant.

Joseph Ryan occupied the most important post in the city government during the strike. As commissioner of public welfare he determined the policy of not only denying the strikers any relief but order-
ing people on welfare to apply for jobs at Briggs; if they refused
to accept a job in the struck plants they would be removed from
the welfare rolls. Two suicides were reported to the strike committee. They were workers who couldn't bear to see their families go
hungry and cold. One left a note saying, as a widow his wife would
be able to get welfare.

When the strike was called, it was reported that the editors of
the three Detroit metropolitan newspapers had met and agreed that
there would be no publicity given to the strike. And there was no
publicity for the first three or four days. Following that there were
a few headlines branding the strike as Communist-inspired and led.
These headlines were of a nature that would antagonize public opinion. I, as chairman of the publicity committee, met with the city
editor of the *Detroit Times*. With me were two other members of
the committee. We had no experience at publicity work and had pre-

pared no statement for the press. We were not successful in getting any favorable publicity for the strike.

As a Christian Scientist, I went to see a practitioner who told me to go and see the Detroit representative of the *Christian Science Monitor*. He worked for the *Free Press*. When I told him that I represented the Briggs strike committee he backed away from me as if I were a carrier of the plague. He didn't want to hear anything about the strike. That is when I decided the church was on the side of the corporations rather than the workers, and I was going to break my affiliation.

Since our efforts at publicity brought no favorable results I and other members of the publicity committee devoted our efforts to other strike activities. There was no strike fund. It was necessary to set up a strike kitchen and serve food and coffee. To get money and food, women from the strike, Communist Party sympathizers and other left-wing groups, organized what were known as chiseling committees to solicit business places and others with money who were in support of the strike.

During the first few days of the strike we were able to keep a picket line of several hundred at the gates of the Highland Park plant. As the strikers ran out of money and the strike kitchen ran out of food the picket lines were harder to keep going. Sometimes there were less than twenty pickets. Then after much effort on the part of the strike committee we might get a hundred men in the line.

To break the strike at the Mack Avenue plant the company moved thousands of army cots into the plant where several thousand men and women were kept from Monday through Friday. They were fed by the company. Because of the economic pressure on the strikers the number of scabs sleeping in the plant and walking through the picket lines continued to grow. Since Briggs was the principal supplier of bodies to Ford, Ford was forced to lay off most of their force of a hundred thousand workers. Ford supplier plants in turn were forced to close.

Briggs officials never admitted there was anything wrong with wages and working conditions in their plants. Yet on January 27, 1933, without fanfare or publicity they corrected the worst evils.

Hours of work became more regular and there were improvements in sanitation. Although the strike committee learned of these developments we held out for union recognition, a dollar an hour for metal-finishers and comparable wage increases for other classifications. We also demanded the return of all the strikers to their jobs without discrimination, and the thirty hour week so as to employ more of the unemployed. We had no hope of winning all these demands. But we knew that without a union the gains that were granted could be cancelled without notice.

Every few days there was a new attempt to break the strike. One morning when I was leading the picket line in Highland Park, I saw some twenty or thirty big burly men coming toward the picket line. They were immediately recognized as Ford service men. (The service men were plant guards who were used to intimidate and sometimes physically attack the Ford workers.) Ford had three thousand of these men at the Rouge plant. They had a reputation for brutality against protesting or striking workers. They received much publicity in March 1932 when five unemployed hunger marchers were shot to death at the Ford Rouge plant. The pickets seeing these men were afraid; they scattered. I followed several into the waiting room of the Briggs employment office. Someone recognized me as a leader of the strike and offered me a good job if I would get the men to return to work. When I refused I was escorted from the building.

The Detroit police arrested many members of the strike committee and rank-and-file members on strike. We would be held in one precinct station for twenty-four hours, which was supposed to be the maximum length of time a person could be held, and then taken to another precinct station and held for another twenty-four hours. It was a legal way of kidnapping the strike leadership in order to discourage the strike.

After about a month a number of organizations, rivals and sometimes enemies of the CP, became interested in the strike. The Proletarian Party passed out two leaflets to workers in the area of the strike giving them support. The Socialist Party began holding public meetings in Detroit and New York City for the purpose of raising money and gaining public support for the strike. As a result of meetings sponsored by the Detroit branch of the Socialist Party I decided to join that party. But sp support of the strike was limited to holding meetings and collecting funds. The afl had previously labeled the strike as a wildcat, which meant that picket lines need not be respected, but now Frank X. Martel, president of the Detroit afl, came out in support of the strike.

The iww rented an upstairs flat in Highland Park which they used as a soup kitchen and an office for the purpose of recruiting new members and giving support to the strike. John Oneka, George Lutzai and other iww members went to the farms around Detroit and collected truckloads of potatoes, carrots, onions and cabbage to make soup for the strike kitchens. They went to the bakeries and got day-old bread, buns and rolls. They went to the dairies and got surplus milk and chocolate milk that otherwise would have been dumped into the sewers for lack of customers who could afford the milk. The iww fed all who came to their hall.

A number of developments changed the leadership of the strike. The cp, wanting to exploit the strike for its own purposes, called a meeting of the strikers at a hall called Dance Land. Having had no previous experience with left-wing politics, a number of strikers and members of the strike committee attended the meeting. They got me to go on the platform to say a few words. When we realized that the purpose of the meeting was to recruit new members to the Communist Party, we knew we had been used by the cp. The reaction on the strike was immediate.

At about this time Phil Raymond was arrested by the Detroit police and held for several days. He wasn't charged with anything. They knew he was a member of the Communist Party and a leader in the strike. It took a writ of habeas corpus to get him out.

During Raymond's incarceration, Frank Cedervall of the iww was invited to speak to the strikers in their hall on Mack Avenue. Cedervall was an unemployed plasterer who had never worked in an auto plant but he was a powerful speaker of great sincerity and ability who did much to build up the morale of the strikers. The strike committee, now hostile to the cp, voted to remove Phil Raymond as the speaker at our daily mass meetings and invited Frank Cedervall to replace him. Phil Raymond and his group then announced that they would no longer support the strike and they urged the strikers to return to work.

Cedervall soon won the respect of not only the strike committee but of most of the strikers. He was looked upon more as an individual. While most of us knew the IWW was a radical organization it did not have the foreign connotation of the CP. It was more of an Americanized approach.

I spent most of my time at the Mack strike committee headquarters. We had a joint strike committee, I being the representative from Highland Park. Once when we were holding a mass meeting we received a call from the Highland Park strike committee saying that the Michigan State Police were about to break up the picket lines there. We rushed all the strikers we could get to reinforce the Highland Park picket lines. Our forces were too small to defy the State and Highland Park police. Picketing came to an end there the latter part of March.

Soon after the busting up of the picket lines, I was walking from the IWW hall and kitchen toward the plant. The Highland Park police picked me up and took me to police headquarters. I was brought before the chief of police, Dan Patch. He seemed a kindly man who was sympathetic to the workers on strike. He said he had attended some of the mass meetings and that I had a strong influence over my audience. After hearing me speak he was of the opinion that I was a potentially dangerous man. When he said the strike was instigated by Communists I asked him, "Was the Boston police strike of 1920 led by Communists?" He made no reply.

After the strike had been in progress for about six weeks Mayor Frank Murphy appointed a committee to investigate the causes of the strike. He wanted to bring Briggs and the strike committee together in a meeting. The committee had no legal power and was not able to get company representatives to testify or give them any information. Several members of the strike committee, including myself, testified before the committee and gave a detailed report on hours, wages and working conditions in all the Briggs plants. The committee, trying to remain neutral, got little notice in the press.

The mayor's Fact Finding Committee issued its report on April 24, 1933. None of the recommendations of the committee were carried out. Whatever improvements in wages and working conditions were brought about came as a result of the strike, not of the mayor's committee. The committee served the political interest of the mayor. It did nothing to improve the conditions of the workers on strike.

A week or so after the mayor's committee held their hearings, a meeting was arranged between Mr. Walter O. Briggs and four or five members of the strike committee. Mr. Briggs had been vacationing in Florida and was forced to cut short his vacation. I was selected by the Highland Park strike committee to represent them on the joint committee that was to meet with Mr. Briggs. George O. Cornell, Earl Bailey and two or three from the Mack committee were present. Cornell had been a Briggs foreman before the strike. After the strike he became a conservative Detroit politician.

We went to the main office of the company on Mack Avenue. We sat down across the table from Mr. W. O. Briggs, president, and other company officials. Mr. Briggs being the owner of the Detroit Tigers, it was natural to open the conversation with a few words about the Tigers and the coming baseball season. To my surprise this conversation continued for about fifteen minutes. When I became convinced that neither Mr. Cornell nor any other member of the committee was going to raise the issue of the strike I decided to do so. The response to my question was stunned silence. Mr. Briggs and Mr. Cornell looked at me as if to say, "You have broken the agreement." After a few moments the other members of the committee resumed the polite discussion of subjects that had nothing to do with the strike.

It didn't make sense to me going to see W. O. Briggs and not raising the issues of the strike and union recognition. Evidently other strike leaders had been told by Cornell that these issues were not to be raised. The purpose of the meeting, it seems, was to have it on record that the Briggs management had met with members of the strike committee. The failure of the committee to raise the issues of the strike gave some credence to the company's position that there

were no serious grievances. To me it was disgraceful. Since we were
no longer having mass meetings, few of the strikers learned of what
took place at the meeting.

On March 4, 1933, Franklin D. Roosevelt took office as president
of the United States. A few days later a banking crisis shook the
nation. Most of the Detroit banks were closed for several weeks.
Soon after the inauguration of Roosevelt, Hitler came to power in
Germany. Following this event, FDR established diplomatic relations with the Soviet Union. All of these important events took the
public interest away from the strike.

The number of pickets had declined to about two hundred at the
Warren entrance of the Mack plant. One afternoon while the pickets
were walking there, nuts, bolts and other metal objects were thrown
from the upper floors on to the heads of the pickets. They picked
up these objects and started throwing them back where they came
from, breaking the windows.

As if they had been assembled for that purpose, several hundred
Detroit policemen moved against the pickets and the spectators on
the sidewalk. I was standing a half block from the plant. Soon I,
like everyone in the area, was blinded and choking from tear gas.
We hurled some of the tear gas bombs back at the police but the
outnumbered pickets and their sympathizers were soon on the run.
I saw shots being fired at the strikers as they fled from the scene
although I don't believe any live ammunition was used at the time.
Some strikers were injured by the policemen's clubs.

We were in no position to challenge the Detroit police. After this
riot the picketing was discontinued. At the end of April members
of the Highland Park and Mack strike committees met and voted
to end the strike. We got no agreement of any kind from Briggs.
While most of the workers went back to work in their various jobs,
all the active leaders of the strike were blacklisted.

Little publicity was given to the gains made as a result of the
strike. The gains were many and important. The wages of metal-
finishers, which were thirty-five cents when the strike was called,
went up to sixty-two cents an hour. That was a phenomenal raise
for Depression times. Wage rates likewise went up for other classifications. Hours of work became more regular. Deductions for lost

or broken tools were ended. Other arbitrary deductions were no longer made. There were improvements in sanitation. Women were no longer worked more than the fifty-four hours permitted by law.

Not only did the Briggs workers benefit but plants throughout the Detroit area raised wages and improved their working conditions to avoid strikes. General Motors and Chrysler feared that this strike might spread to their plants. Some other supplier plants did have short work stoppages.

Equally important as the economic gains was the educational development of the workers. Willing slaves became rebellious men and women. An understanding of the economic power of the workers was impressed on the minds of most of us who took an active part in the strike. Several leaders of the strike were to become organizers of the UAW-CIO.

I had no radical ideas when the Briggs strike began. But we learned that it was only the radical parties that were on our side. The left-wing groups, the Communists, Socialists, the IWW and other groups of the left, were the inspiration and the leaders of strikes. The Republican and Democratic Parties and their official representatives in state and local government were on the side of the company. My joining the Socialist Party put me in contact with young people my own age who wanted to do something about changing society. It was in the SP that I was to meet May Wolf, Roy, Victor and Walter Reuther as well as several other socially-minded workers. My experience in the strike made me aware of the political and philosophical differences dividing worker organizations. I saw enough of the CP and its leadership in action so that I never became identified with it. The strike also brought me in contact with Frank Cedervall and the IWW which I joined some months later.

Taking up a picket sign and walking the picket line was a difficult emotional experience for workers in 1933. Few of us had ever seen a picket line much less walked in one. The fear of physical injury or even death in those days were deterrents to workers joining a picket line or engaging in other strike activity.

One day I bought a copy of the *Detroit Times* and found a few lines on the front page telling of finding the body of a worker by the railroad track in southwest Detroit near the Ford Rouge plant. He had a bullet through the head. It stated he had been selling the *Daily Worker* in the area near the Rouge plant. The tone of the article was that the Communists should be shot and nothing should be done about it. Nothing was done. There was no further publicity of the murder. The *Times* treated the murder as if he were some gangster and good riddance. This worker, who had a wife and an eight-year-old daughter, had been murdered because he wanted to educate the workers. I felt that this might have happened to me or anyone else who was a leader in the strike.

I became immune to fear of physical danger when I was active in the struggle of the workers. I think this was true of many of the radicals who led strikes and carried on political activities for the left-wing parties.

Although I didn't want to become involved in the strike when it was first called, it was to become the turning point in my life.

STELLA NOWICKI

S TELLA NOWICKI was for ten years an organizer in the meatpacking
industry on Chicago's southwest side, beginning in the early
1930s. This was the third major attempt to organize the packinghouse workers. Strikes had been crushed in 1904 and 1921, and it
was not until World War II that the United Packinghouse Workers of
America were recognized.

A major figure in the Packinghouse Workers Organizing Committee was Herb March. Through close association with him and his
family, Stella Nowicki became involved not only in meatpacking
but also in the political activities which were flowing through the
Marches' home.

The Back of the Yards Youth Council organized by Stella Nowicki and several other young people preceded the community organization for which Saul Alinsky is best known, the Back of the
Yards Council.

After World War II, Stella Nowicki married and had children.
Three times in her lifetime she felt she was part of the ferment that
was making history. Although her family responsibilities kept her
from being as involved in the civil rights movement as other members of her family were, she belongs to a women's liberation group
and again has the feeling that this movement will change events.

This account was compiled from two interviews. The first one,
in October 1969, took place in Stella Nowicki's home with a group

of young people who wanted to do community organizing in the area which had been known as Back of the Yards. The second was a presentation to the Labor History Workshop, Gary, Indiana, in the fall of 1971.

Back of the Yards

I RAN AWAY from home at age 17. I had to because there was not enough money to feed the family in 1933 during the Depression.

I was brought up on a farm. We really roughed it. We had no electricity. We had outdoor privies. We baked our own bread, churned our own butter, raised and butchered our own hogs, made our own sausage, did our own smoking of meat. All the things young people are into today we did because it was a necessity. We worked hard and long hours.

We used to fell our own oak trees, my older sister and I. We would cut eight or nine foot logs with a cross cut saw and we'd lift those logs up on the wagon and drive home, then pick them up and run a buzz saw on them. We did all kinds of other heavy work.

My father was a coal miner at one time and he instilled pro-unionism in us as youngsters. The coal miners, at least the foreign born, were of socialist background. My father bought a few books about Lenin and Gorky from socialists in the coal fields. I learned Polish through these revolutionary books but only years later did I make the connection.

I remember when Sacco and Vanzetti were executed. The foreign-born people were in mourning for a week after that, and they were not all pro-socialist. My mother was and still is a practicing Catholic.

My father used to have this slogan, "No work, no eat." That's a socialist slogan, he said. It was really carried out at home. If we didn't work we really didn't eat.

I would challenge my father many times. Before I left home I had gone to a dance with a group of girls against my father's word. For two or three nights I slept in the barn and my mother would bring me food.

Agnes, a woman from Chicago, was on our farm for her health. She was going to have an experimental operation in which a bone would be transplanted from her leg to her back to help correct a curvature. She asked me to come back to Chicago with her. We hitch-hiked to Benton Harbor and then caught the boat. I then lived with Agnes and her family who were radicals.

One of the family was Herbert March. Herb March was a member of the Young Communist League. He was a young man. When he was just out of college at seventeen or eighteen years old, he felt that here was this country, very rich, yet all these people were out of work. Maybe college didn't mean much and maybe he should go into organizing people for socialism, maybe capitalism wasn't the answer.

I was not really introduced to socialism until I came to Chicago and the Marches began telling me about it. I lived with them at 59th and Ashland. They lived on the second floor and on the third floor they had bedrooms and an attic room. Anyone who didn't have some place to live could always find room there. It was near the streetcar intersection and when there were meetings blacks could come. (This was a real problem at that time.) The Marches would have meetings of the YCL in the attic and they'd ask me to sit in. The terminology was like a foreign language. I thought that I better join this outfit so that I would know what they were talking about.

They pointed out things to me that, in my very unsophisticated and farm-like way, I saw. There was so much food being dumped —the government bought it up—and people were hungry and didn't have enough to eat. (There were days when I didn't have anything to eat. That's when I picked up smoking. Somebody said, "Here, smoke. It'll kill your appetite." And it did.) I realized that there was this tremendous disparity. The people in our YCL group told me that the government was set up to keep it this way. They thought that instead of just thinking about ourselves we should be thinking about other people and try to get them together in a union

and organize and then maybe we would have socialism where there
would not be hunger, war, etc. They initiated me into a lot of political ideas and gave me material to read. We had classes and we would
discuss industrial unionism, the craft unions and the history of the
labor movement in this country. We talked about Debs, we talked
about the eight hour day, many things.

I was doing housework for $4 a week and I hated it. I would
cry and cry. I was horribly homesick because I hated the restraint
of being in a house all the time. I was used to being out a lot on
the farm. So Herb suggested that I get a job in the stockyards.

Herb was working at Armour's at the time. He bought me a steel,
with which one sharpens a knife, and I took it with me. He took
me down to the stock yards and (he tells this story) I said, "Those
beautiful cows! They can't kill those beautiful cows!" At home we
just had cows for milking. But here were all these cows and they
were going to be killed and they were crying, mooing, as they were
going to be killed. But one had to get a job!

One of the ways to get a job was to go down to the employment
office. Every morning you got there by six or six-thirty. There were
just so many benches and they would all be filled early. They would
only need one, maybe two people. This woman, Mrs. McCann,
women's hiring director, would look around for the biggest and
brawniest person. At seventeen I weighed 157 pounds coming from
the farm, rosy-cheeked and strong. "Have you had experience?" I
said, "Well not in the stock yards but we used to butcher our own
hogs at home." I carried this big steel and that impressed her. Mrs.
McCann hired me.

I was in the cook room. At that time the government bought up
drought cattle and they were killed, canned, and given to people on
relief to eat. The meat would be cut into big hunks and steamed.
Then it would come on a rail and be dumped out on the table. The
women would be all around the table and we would cut the meat up,
remove the gristle and bad parts, and make hash out of it. The government inspector would come around to see that bad meat wasn't
being thrown into the hash. But as soon as his back would be turned,
the foreman would push this stuff right down the chute to go into the
cans—all this stuff we had put aside to be thrown away he would

push right down in, including gloves, cockroaches, anything. The company didn't give a damn.

The meat would be so hot and steamy your fingers almost blistered but you just stayed on. In 1933–34 we worked six hour shifts at 37½ cents an hour. We would have to work at a high rate of speed. It was summer. It would be so hot that women used to pass out. The ladies' room was on the floor below and I would help carry these women down almost vertical stairs into the washroom.

We started talking union. The thing that precipitated it is that on the floor below they used to make hotdogs and one of the women, in putting the meat into the chopper, got her fingers caught. There were no safety guards. Her fingers got into the hotdogs and they were chopped off. It was just horrible.

Three of us "colonizers" had a meeting during our break and decided this was the time to have a stoppage and we did. (Colonizers were people sent by the YCL or CP into points of industrial concentration that the CP had designated. These included mass basic industries: steel, mining, packing, and railroad. The colonizers were like red missionaries. They were expected to do everything possible to keep jobs and organize for many years.) All six floors went on strike. We said, "Sit, stop." And we had a sit-down. We just stopped working right inside the building, protesting the speed and the unsafe conditions. We thought that people's fingers shouldn't go into the machine, that it was an outrage. The women got interested in the union.

We got the company to put in safety devices. Soon after the work stoppage the supervisors were looking for the leaders because people were talking up the action. They found out who was involved and we were all fired. I was blacklisted.

I got a job doing housework again and it was just horrible. Here I was taking care of this family with a little spoiled brat and I had to pick up after them—only Thursday afternoon off and every other Sunday—and all for four dollars a week of which I sent two dollars home. I just couldn't stand it. I would rather go back and work in a factory, any day or night.

A friend of mine who had been laid off told me that she got called to go back to work. Meanwhile she had a job in an office and she

didn't want to go back to the stockyards, so she asked me if I wanted
to go in her place. She had used the name Helen Ellis. I went down
to the stockyards and it was the same department, exactly the same
job on the same floor where I had been fired. But it was the afternoon and Mrs. McCann wasn't there. Her assistant was there. Her
assistant said, "Can you do this work?" I said, "Oh yes, I can.
I've done it." She told me that I would start work the following
afternoon.

I came home and talked with Herb and Jane. We decided that
I would have to go to the beauty shop. I got my hair cut really
short and hennaed (similar to tinting today). I thinned my eyebrows
and penciled them, wore a lot of lipstick and painted my nails.
Because I hadn't been working, I had a suntan. I wore sandals and
I had my toenails painted, which I would never have done before.
I came in looking sharp and not like a country girl, so I passed
right through and I was hired as Helen Ellis on the same job, the
same forelady!

After several days the forelady, Mary, who was also Polish, came
around and said, "OK, Helen, I know you're Stella. I won't say
anything but just keep quiet" if I wanted to keep the job. I answered
her in Polish that I knew that the job wouldn't last long and I thanked
her. She knew I was pro-union and I guess she was too, so I kept
the job as Helen Ellis until I got laid off. (Later on I was blacklisted
under the name Ellis.)

Out of the fifteen dollars, I'd have to try to save half of it almost,
to carry me when I was out of work. I remember that at one time
I had a three-room furnished apartment on East 47th Street and I
was paying fifteen dollars a month rent. Sometimes there would be
fourteen people living there besides myself. Those who worked supported those who didn't. Anybody who worked put the money in
the one pot and we shared it.

At this time, Herb was in the AFL and was asking for an industrial
form of organization. The American Federation of Labor was
organized along a craft basis. In the stockyards there might have
been some electricians or some steam fitters or mechanics who were
organized in their own separate unions. The mass of workers who
were working on the assembly lines and on the kills—the sheep kill,

the beef kill, the hog kill—and in the canning rooms, the women, they were not organized. The wage scale was way down.

The AFL really wasn't interested in getting masses of people in because large numbers threatened their position. Being as they were in crafts they didn't want to see the expansion because they would lose control. They had nice-paying jobs. They were bought off in a sense.

There were many battles within the AFL. A group of people, including Herb March, would raise questions at union meetings whenever they could get the floor. Many times they couldn't get the floor to speak and were carried out of union meetings bodily because they insisted on speaking on questions that the workers were concerned with—conditions of employment, wages, and other things. Herb nearly lost his life a couple of times because AFL racketeers were tied up with the meat-packers. Then the left-wing group organized a Trade Union Unity League as sort of an answer to the craft organization.

The Trade Union Unity League used to meet on 47th and State. We would walk [a couple of miles] from 47th and Ashland to 47th and State for meetings—we didn't have car fare and were out of work much of the time—to get together and talk about how we were going to organize the stockyards. The meetings were with blacks and whites.

Even at that time we raised the question of more Negroes on skilled jobs. The proportion of Negroes when I started in 1933 was, I suppose, fifteen to twenty per cent at most. By the time I left in 1945 it was maybe sixty per cent.

William Z. Foster and Jack Johnstone used to come and talk with us. In the twenties William Foster and Jack Johnstone worked together in organizing not only steel but also the stockyards. So when the thirties came around and we started trying to organize the unorganized industrial workers, we had these meetings with them and they would tell us about what they did in the 1920s with steel. We took advantage of their experience in the 1919–1921 steel and packinghouse strikes as to how to try to organize this mass industry of unorganized packinghouse workers.

They talked about the kinds of tactics to use, step one, step two and step three! One of the pamphlets that William Z. Foster wrote was "What Means a Strike in Steel?" and this was our Bible. It discussed how you did all sorts of things, how you contacted workers —through the church, through their organizations, through your nationality groups, including relatives. Just like in the steel industry, the packinghouse workers were made up of different ethnic groups. They were in the main Polish and Lithuanian, some Bohemian, Croatian, some Mexican and there were the German, the Irish and the Negroes (as we called them at that time).

When we met with Jack Johnstone and William Foster, we talked with them about people that they knew. They were able to remember names of people and they gave us these names. There was a small shop called Roberts and Oake and there was this Polish guy, Stan, that they talked about. Somebody said, "Does anybody know where Stan is?" Sure enough, Stan was still working in Roberts and Oake and he was contacted.

It was very underground because if you even talked union you were fired. Jobs were at a premium. You didn't have the law which guaranteed people the right to organize. So we actually had secret meetings. Everybody had to vouch for anyone that they brought to the meeting, that they were people that we could trust, because as soon as the company found out that people were trying to organize, they would try to send in stool pigeons. They paid people to come in and try to get information.

What they didn't know was that the secretary to the vice-president of one of the companies was the wife of one of the people who was interested in organizing. We were able to take advantage of this. We made copies of material and were able to use it to expose many of the anti-union tactics of the company.

I remember one of the first big CP meetings when we had William Foster come to talk. The hall wasn't big enough. Somebody had gotten hold of a loudspeaker (they were very difficult to get in those days) and we hooked that up so that people could hear down the steps and into the street.

We had a YCL/CP unit. (There weren't enough people in either the YCL or the CP to meet separately and so we met together, younger and older people.) We would have meetings and marches and classes on Marxism and Leninism. We would write articles on the history of Marxism and Leninism which we would then discuss. These would go into *The Yards' Worker*. We asked the old time friends of Bill Foster from the different plants for news of what was going on.

We contacted young people who were at the University of Chicago and they helped in editing and getting funds. They would help us in writing up material for leaflets and by distributing material at the stockyard gates. They would get up real early and be there at 6:00 or 6:30 in the morning. (We would start work at 7:00.) They did this because we could not do so, for if we were caught giving out leaflets we would be fired. On the inside, we had to wear uniforms all the time and any packages we carried in were examined. The only way we carried in these leaflets about organizing was in our underclothes, in our bras (the men too, in their pants). I would come in real busty. Then I'd go into the washroom and leave the papers around.

When I look back now, I really think we had a lot of guts. But I didn't even stop to think about it at the time. It was something that had to be done. We had a goal. That's what we felt had to be done and we did it.

We got into sending people all over to different groups and into different shops so that when union organization picked up we would have people everywhere.

The broadest contacts of the left at that time were in the International Workers Order which was set up as an insurance organization for people to have sickness benefits and insurance, and culturally they were able to have their own social affairs. We had our songs, folk dances, and picnics where we would have ethnic foods. Every nationality had its own chapter which would meet monthly and recruit whole families. The IWO was much larger than the CP and the YCL. They were pro-labor because they had been coal miners at one time and they were organized in a Miners Union and had had experience. When we set up meetings with these groups we would cue them in as to who were stool pigeons, learn from them about stool pigeons whom they knew, and who doesn't have a big mouth who we can trust.

We had what we called fractions, made up of CP members and sympathizers, many of them from the IWO, who would get together periodically to discuss major strategy within the organizing campaign. We would decide what things to take up, who would take up what and where and how, who would support whom, who would make the motion, who would second it and so forth. It was very important that people know how to do this; otherwise they would be overwhelmed by the politicians.

The predominant organization in the community was the Catholic Church. I was the only ex-Catholic in our YCL group. When I lived around 59th and Ashland I joined the Sodality (a Catholic young women's organization) and I became a member of the basketball team to have contact with other young people and to be around people who were out of the realm of the left.

I joined all the youth organizations that I could. We didn't work steady so we had a lot of time. I'd work for two or three months and then there would be a layoff.

Then it was decided that I should start to learn about casings —guts that you make hotdogs out of. You wore rubber boots and a rubber apron. It stinks like hell because it's shit work: you clean all the shit out. I went to work under the name Kramer at the Independent Casing Company and I worked there for six or seven weeks.

I had also joined the YWCA Industrial Division and was active in their sports program. I came in contact with other women in the Y. Women were not about to come into unions but they were in the Y. The Y was offering scholarships to young workers. In 1936 they had this School for Workers in Industry at the University of Wisconsin. They would select young people through the different industries and I was selected from the Back of the Yards Y to go with all of my expenses paid to Madison, Wisconsin for six weeks. There we learned about labor history, parliamentary procedure, public speaking, how you run meetings. It was Social-Democratic in outlook. We had a mock Farmer-Labor convention there and the three political positions were presented: the left, the center, and the right.

When I came back the YCL group decided after discussions with me that I should try to get a job at Swift's. We had people at

Armour's and we had some people in Wilson's but there was no-body at Swift and Company. They employed anywhere from two to five thousand workers and we wanted to get some of them into the CIO.

Swift's was in a different class than Armour's. Everyone who worked in Swift's was thought to be a higher class worker—they got more money. Swift's had a group bonus system called the Bedaux system. After you produced so much then each person in the gang got that much more money. It's diabolical. One worker slits the throat of another. They keep going so that the group produc-tion is great enough that they can all get a bonus.

Swift and Company had a strong entrenched company union with a paternalistic system to keep people sort of quiescent and controlled. The company actually selected the representatives from the different departments. They called it an "Independent Employees Organiza-tion." Anybody who spoke up about it was a troublemaker and they got rid of him.

I went to Swift's to get a job. The personnel director said they weren't hiring but what were my qualifications, where did I work last. I told her Independent Casing. "Well, why aren't you there now?" I told her that I got a scholarship to go to the University of Wisconsin through the Y that previous summer. And she said, "Well that's my Alma Mater!" So she hired me for the casing department.

Later I got sent to the sliced bacon department which is the elite department. It was the cleanest job and you made the most money. They had this visitors' ramp where people went by and would look down. We were freezing our asses off in this cooler of about forty degrees. I wore two pairs of wool socks and a couple of wool sweat-ers under my uniform and a cap. We'd have to go every two or three hours into the washroom to thaw out and spill out.

Swift and Company had a slogan that the premium bacon was "not touched by human hands." The sliced bacon came down on this conveyor belt and we women sat three on either side facing forward, sitting with a scale in front of us. One woman would just put the plastic see-through cover on the bacon. Then we would catch the bacon with our tongs, turn it over on the scale to make sure that each package was about eight ounces in weight—a quarter ounce less or more—then we would wrap them up, put them back on the belt and on they would go to the packer at the end of the line.

The women themselves had gotten together and they would turn out a hundred and forty-four packages an hour of bacon. We were making $15 a week at 37½ cents an hour, but if we each produced 144 packages an hour we got $7 more in our pay. We made 50 per cent more than anybody else but we produced 90 per cent more than the set group rate. A new girl would come in and the oldtimers would train her. They would help her out so that gradually by the end of a certain period of time she was doing the 144. But they would never let anyone go beyond that 144 packages. They maintained that limit and they did it without a union. One smart-aleck girl came in there once and she was going to show them and go beyond that number because she wanted to earn more money: all the bacon that she got from the girls further up the line was messed up and scrappy and she'd have to straighten it up to put it in the package. She couldn't make a hundred packages an hour. (We took a loss just to show her.)

The checker would come around with the stop watch. You learned to wrap a package of bacon using a lot of extra motions because it was a time study thing. When he wasn't there we eliminated all those motions and did it simply. This was done everywhere—sausage, wrap and tie, bacon, everywhere. (It's all done by machine now.) There is always a faster way to do something, a simpler way where you save energy and time. The older women, in terms of experience, would show the new women. It was a tremendous relationship of solidarity. But they weren't about to join the union. They weren't about to put out a buck a month in union dues.

At first the women were afraid. It took quite a bit of courage to join. They were concerned about their jobs. Many of them were sole breadwinners. Also the Catholic Church said that the CIO was red: you join the CIO and you are joining a red organization. To talk about the CIO then was like talking about socialism to some people today. Even to talk union, you talked about it in whispers. You had to trust the person and know the person very well because he could be a stool pigeon.

When I was at the University of Wisconsin, John Lewis made his speech that he was breaking away the coal miners union from the AFL and they were going to set up the CIO. We set up an organizing committee for the stockyards. There were seventeen of us that met, three women and fourteen men. One of them was an Irishman by the name of McCarthy who became the acting chairman of the Packinghouse Workers Organizing Committee. We met behind a tavern on Honore Street. The organizing of these seventeen people was on Communist Party initiative and we worked through contacts in the IWO, the International Workers Order. In this group of seventeen there were some Poles and some Slovaks who were indigenous to the community.

We didn't have money. We collected money in every way that we could. A delegation was sent to the Steelworkers Union to ask them for support—financial support, organizers, etc. We asked them to send some speakers and we would have a meeting. We had this first big CIO meeting at the hall behind the tavern where parties for weddings and all kinds of community social events would be held. The turnout was so overwhelming that there actually wasn't room for all the people who came.

Among the people who came was a delegation from the Paddy Brennon plant which was in the AFL. The president was black and the vice-president was white. They had heard about our meeting and they came, ready to swing their whole local right into the CIO. They had women too and they brought in all the women. It was a tremendous thing. This little plant spurred us on.

We couldn't get the sliced bacon department at Swift's into the union because of the money they were earning. What could the union do that they weren't getting already, and they *were* organized! So I told them that it was the case that they had the money, but what about the conditions—it was colder than hell. What happens if you get sick? What happens if the foreman says that he doesn't like you and he wants somebody else to have your job? I said that the union could protect them on these real problems. But they wouldn't join. I think that I only got one or two out of that great big department.

They were all white, mostly Polish. There was one black woman who worked on scrap bacon way in the back so that no one would see her when visitors came through. The company could always say that they had one black woman in this fancy department. I raised this matter of discrimination but it didn't go over too well with white women.

One day the woman who worked in the coldest spot got sick. She didn't come to work. We found out that she had become paralyzed. The door from the cutting cooler opened as the men came back and forth. It was below freezing there and every time the door opened she would get this tremendous cold blast on her side. The whole right side of her body was paralyzed and she died. Within a week we organized that whole department. She was a young woman, probably around forty, and she died because of the freezing conditions in which we all had to work. It was easier on the company to have it this cold. There was less spoilage. But they didn't give a damn about the workers. We showed that we could handle bacon and that it didn't have to be that cold.

The National Labor Relations Act had been passed, giving workers the right to organize. But this was not easy because people were laid off. I was laid off, for instance, in the gut shanty and they tried to break my seniority. We had departmental seniority and I would be shifted all around. Besides casing and sliced bacon, I got to work in wrap and tie (hams), soap, glue, fresh sausage, pork trim, almost every department. By being shifted around I became acquainted with many more women. I kept the names and addresses of all the women because I knew that some day I would need them. When we started organizing I knew women all over the whole plant. I would call them and get information as to pro-labor union sentiment, problems and issues, and so forth. We would print it up in the CIO news—the *Swift Flashes* we called it.

The same women who had hired me at Swift's approached me and asked me if I'd like to work in personnel—they tried to buy me off. They offered me better-paying jobs.

They put me in the glue factory thinking that they could discourage me and I would quit. By that time I was down to 130 pounds. They put me to work with Essie. Essie weighed 325 and she chewed tobacco. She used to bring big pots of food to work and eat it all. She was my partner.

This is how they made the glue. (I won't lick a glue stamp for anything any more!) They had these vats where they put all the stinking stuff that they couldn't use, outside of the squeal. They put the bones and the hair, and then they'd add lime and it would deteriorate this stuff. They would cook it and melt it. They would pour it on something like a screen. It would come out of the vat looking something like liquid peanut brittle. The screens were put in something like a heating room to be dried. Then Essie and I would take the screens off the pulley, turn them over and with something like a rug beater we'd hit them a full swing to crack all that stuff which would go down the chute.

When I got through with that job the first day, I was wet with sweat from tip to toe. When I came home I couldn't move out of bed for twenty-four hours because of the hitting. I was so sore—my hands and joints were all swollen from the work on this hard job. And we'd smell from all that stinking crap. They had a public shower so we would go there and shower or we'd go to some friend's house that had a shower. But I got Essie into the union. When she saw that I really wasn't a slacker and that I would keep up my end I won her respect. You had to *earn* the respect of your fellow workers or you couldn't talk to them about new ideas or unions, etc. You always had to be a good worker.

Women often did much harder work than men. For instance, in wrap and tie department—where hams were handled, wrapped in paper and tied—it is heavy lifting a twenty-pound ham. Then you'd have to put those great big hams on a slip hook and hang them up so that they could be smoked in the smoke shed. In the sausage department women used to link sausages by hand; but the men would measure the meat and work with a pedal to shoot the sausage into the casings.

The women worked much harder and much faster but they got less pay. We were paid ten cents an hour less than men. There were jobs that men had done that women took over and they'd still get the lesser pay. I worked in a cooler cutting the fat from the lean with the guard on my thumb and the sharp knife. Work with a knife is a butcher's job, but they had a pay differential. (The union corrected this inequity later.) There was also a differential between the southern rates and the northern rates.

Women had an awfully tough time in the union because the men brought their prejudices there. The fellows couldn't believe that women in the union were there for the union's sake. They thought that they were there to get a guy or something else. Some thought that we were frivolous. I would be approached by men for dates and they would ask me why I was in the union, so I would tell them that I was for socialism and I thought that this was the only way of bringing it about.

Some of my brothers, who believed in equality and that women should have rights, didn't crank the mimeograph, didn't type. I did the shit work, until all hours, as did the few other women who didn't have family obligations. And then when the union came around giving out jobs with pay, the guys got them. I and the other women didn't. It was the men who got the organizing jobs. Men who worked in plants got paid for their time loss—women didn't. I never did. But we were a dedicated group. We worked in coolers and from there I would go to the union hall and get out leaflets, write material for shop papers, turn in dues, etc., get home and make supper, get back. These guys had wives to do this but there was nobody to do mine. Sometimes I'd be up until eleven, twelve, or one o'clock and then have to get up early and be punched in by quarter to seven and be working on the job by seven.

I became educational director of the Packinghouse District #1 because, after all, I was in college for six weeks! We had classes on public speaking and parliamentary procedure and labor history. I remember getting up on Sunday morning and going to churches to speak about our union. We got involved in activity against the southern poll taxes. We elected congressmen. We defeated people like Busby who was on the Dies Committee by 1500 votes. It was cio people who helped to defeat him.

The union mushroomed; it spread. The union had a certain vitality about it that was just tremendous. We had many problems but they were all problems of growth. We tried to make sure that there were both Negroes and whites as officers, stewards, etc., in all the locals.

There were people vying for jobs—they wanted to be leaders of this union. It was a marvelous time.

For a long time I fought dishonesty within my local. There were some guys who would pocket the dues money. I would debate them on the union floor. Many times I was the only female there.

The women felt the union was a man's thing because once they got through the day's work they had another job. When they got home they had to take care of their one to fifteen children and the meals and the house and all the rest, and the men went to the tavern and to the meetings and to the racetrack and so forth. The fellows were competing for positions and the women didn't feel that that was their role. They were brainwashed into thinking that this union was for men.

The union didn't encourage women to come to meetings. They didn't actually want to take up the problems that the women had. I did what I could to get the women to come to the meetings but very few came—only when there was a strike. I tried to make the meetings more interesting than just a bunch of guys talking all evening.

We organized women's groups, young women's groups. They liked to dance and I loved to dance so we went dancing together and I talked to them about the union. The women were interested after a while when they saw that the union could actually win things for them, bread and butter things.

We talked about nurseries. In World War II we finally did get some because women were needed in greater quantities than ever before in the factories. But the unions had so many things they had to work for—the shorter work day, improved conditions—so many things that they couldn't worry about these things in relation to women.

Later on, during the war, there was one department where I got the women but couldn't get the guys in. They hung out in the tavern and so I went there and started talking with them. I didn't like beer, but I'd drink ginger ale and told them to show me how to play pool. I learned to play pool and I got the men into the union. I did what they did. I went into the taverns. I became a bowler and I joined the league. The only thing I didn't do is rejoin the Catholic Church.

I was on the grievance committee and I was on the Swift nation-wide negotiating team. Before I left, there were a whole number of job evaluations. It was one of the things we fought for on the wage policy committees. I remember talking with Helstein (president of UPWA) in the national office one day and saying that I thought there should be a study made of jobs, especially for women, because I didn't see that a job had a sex. He said that it was a very interesting idea and that maybe I could do something about it. But I wasn't equipped to go into research, nor did I have the time even if I were. Later on they set up a Women's Department and did it.

There were only so many things that we could do and there were so many big things, we couldn't handle everything. You'd have to have socialism.

About socialism, you didn't talk about socialism per se. You talked about issues and saw how people reacted. You talked about how one could attain these things. The only time I ever heard anyone from the union talk about socialism outside of the small meetings was the head of another CIO local, a Scotsman. After negotiations and they didn't get all they wanted, the guys were turning down the contract. He said, "Look, you bunch of bastards, you're not going to get all of this stuff, not until you have socialism." That's the way he put it to them and I thought it was great. "This is a limited contract under capitalism." I think the workers got the message. It all depends what your relationship is to the people you are talking with.

If you are an honest leader, recognized and supported by the work-ers, you could raise and talk about issues. You couldn't talk about socialism and what it meant in an abstract sense. You had to talk about it in terms of what it would mean for that person. We learned that you can't manipulate people but that you really had to be con-cerned with the interests and needs of the people. However, you also had to have a platform—a projection of where you were going.

At certain times we felt that the union wasn't enough. We worked in the stockyards with blacks but when we came home, we went to lily-white neighborhoods and the blacks went to their ghetto. How were we going to bridge that? There was unemployment and people were being laid off. There were many young people who didn't get jobs. There was no concern on the part of anyone, the city fathers, the church, the union and others, about the needs of young people and places to play. What are unemployed young people going to do? There were a bunch of young people—I was twenty-four or so—and we felt that our needs were not being met by the union.

The Yards YCL group got together and talked about getting more playgrounds for baseball, basketball and so forth. One of the things that we felt we should do was fight to get blacks into professional baseball. I remember being part of the delegation that went to see Fitzpatrick, who was chairman of the Central Labor Council, about labor exerting its influence to get blacks on organized professional baseball teams. It was one of the initial things our union did.

We tried to show the community that the union was concerned about the welfare of the young people. We raised the problems of youth; we raised the problems of women; we raised the problem of inequality. We tried through the National Youth Act to get some funds to set up facilities for young people in the community. We had to find ways to attract youth and women and keep all these people within the union.

We asked the union to back us up in calling a community conference to set up a council, a Back of the Yards Youth Council, which would be concerned about these kinds of things in the community. The union said OK. They gave us their blessings. We went ahead and we did it. Actually there were three of us young women who did it.

We had a successful conference. The place wasn't big enough, it was such a turn-out—young people from about 18 to about 25 from the neighborhood.

The man who really organized some massive youth activities was Bishop Shiel. I think he was the first major churchman to recognize the CIO. The first time this bishop of the Catholic Church accepted to come to a CIO meeting, it was historic.

Remember that the CIO didn't have bargaining rights in the different plants yet. This was 1938, '39, '40. We were in the organizational stage and there was tremendous ferment. There were strikes. There were beatings. There were people being fired and laid off and there were test cases in the NLRB. There was picketing going on.

The AFL was opposing it. During the early organizing meetings they sent goons with guns to threaten individuals to scare them so they would not organize. Twice they shot at Herb March.

But you had this sense that people were ready come hell or high water to get together, to protect each other, and come into the union. It did happen that people were fired but when people were fired the whole department just closed down. People refused to work until this person was put back. They had this feeling of solidarity, this sense, because they knew that if the company could get by with doing it to one they could do it to another, maybe me.

By the 1940s, we had meetings on every issue where we would call on the workers to come out. The union would come around with their sound truck and everybody would come to the CIO corners in the Yards. The butchers would all come out with their boots and their bloody white smocks. Thousands and thousands of people would show up for meetings right there in the middle of the stock-yards at noontime. Even people who were not in the union would come out.

There would be an issue a day, just about. The Armour Plant, Local 347, would have meetings on Wednesday. Friday was payday so it was sacrosanct and there were no meetings. Tuesday was our day. Wilson's on Thursday. Then for some overall issue we'd have everybody come out. There would be so many people coming that the companies would protest to the union—we had half hour lunch breaks and we would stay out for an hour. The companies never did a thing about it because the turnout was that tremendous and massive.

The union leadership would be negotiating within a particular plant on a grievance and the agreement was that if they hadn't received word that the matter was settled by a certain time, the department would walk out. The beef kill at Armour's stopped so many times! They were the best organized and most militant. (These were blacks, by the way.) And if this department went down, the whole plant went down. The kill floors were the key floors. This was true all over. The beef kill was the most important because more beef was killed; then the hog kill, then the sheep.

We participated in all sorts of things beyond just our own industry.

At that time there were no black bus drivers. Bus and streetcar driver jobs were considered very good-paying jobs and our union promoted the idea of having blacks work as streetcar and bus conductors.

The contract and recognition were the thing that everybody wanted. Armour's was the plant with the greatest concentration of people and the union came to be recognized there in 1941. Wilson went before our plant did. Swift's had to have two elections and it was the toughest. We won there during the war, I think in '42. We didn't have the militancy in the Swift plant that we did elsewhere. The Swift Company bought off many guys. Later on we found out that some of the white leaders were paid agents because they testified before the House Committee on Un-American Activities on a lot of us. They were stool pigeons.

I worked in the yards during the war because I thought that it was my patriotic duty. It was part of the thinking of everybody within unions that you just couldn't quit. We even tried to get people to produce more in our zeal to support the war effort. Besides, I had all this seniority and all this history. Then I got frozen on the job. There was a job freeze because white workers were leaving the industry to go to higher-paid jobs in defense plants.

No-strike was part of the deal. The men in the union felt that the company was making all kinds of money on the war and the workers weren't. During that time there were slow-ups and workers who didn't join the union were ostracized. Grievances were hung up without being settled or turned down because the company knew we couldn't do anything. We knew that the company took advantage of the war in a whole number of situations.

I left packing in 1945. With recognition and with the war ending, certain changes took place within the union itself and within the union officialdom. Soon after, a whole group of radical CIO unions were kicked out of the CIO and the McCarthy period set in. I think this ended that era. It was a privilege and a wonderful experience to participate in the excitement of those times.

GEORGE PATTERSON, JESSE REESE AND JOHN SARGENT

T HIS IS AN EDITED TRANSCRIPT of a community forum on "Labor History From The Viewpoint Of The Rank And File" held at Saint Joseph's College in East Chicago, Indiana on March 24 and March 31, 1970.

Patterson, Reese, and Sargent all worked in steel. George Patterson was picket captain at the Memorial Day Massacre in 1937 and first president of Local 65 of the United Steelworkers of America (United States Steel South Works, South Chicago, Illinois). Before the formation of the Steel Workers Organizing Committee in June 1936, Patterson built an independent union of 3,000 workers at the South Works mill. In September 1936 he was fired for union activity, and from then until he retired in 1969 he was employed as an organizer by SWOC and the Steelworkers Union.

Jesse Reese, a black man and an open member of the Communist Party, went to work at Youngstown Sheet and Tube in East Chicago, Indiana in 1929. Reese was a member of the Resolutions Committee at the first national convention of the Steel Workers Organizing Committee in December 1937.

John Sargent was first president of Local 1010, USA (Inland Steel, East Chicago, Indiana). Sargent was re-elected in 1943, 1944, 1946,

and, despite vicious   red-baiting, 1964. In 1958 and 1962 he took
a strong stand against a dues increase at the Steelworkers conventions. In 1972 he was still working in the mill. Sargent is the "John
Smith" whose experience and point of view are presented in the
article "Guerrilla History In Gary" by Staughton Lynd, *Liberation*,
October 1969.

Two major themes emerge from these accounts. First is the vigor
of rank-and-file activity during the 1930s. Before the CIO was
formed, George Patterson had organized the Associated Employees
at South Works and Jesse Reese had organized a lodge of the Amalgamated Association of Iron, Steel, and Tin Workers (the old AFL
union in steel) at Youngstown Sheet and Tube. John Sargent describes how in Little Steel, because there was no contract and no
no-strike clause, wildcat strikes in particular departments continued
for three or four years after the Memorial Day Massacre in 1937.

A second theme is the expulsion of radicals after the unions were
organized, and the narrowing of goals which resulted. We wanted
the union to be a watchdog for the working class, Reese concludes,
but "Your dog don't bark no more."

These three accounts, together with talks at the same forum by
Harvey O'Connor and John W. Anderson, were published as "Personal Histories Of The Early C.I.O.," ed. Staughton Lynd, in *Radical America*, May–June 1971, and reprinted as a pamphlet by the
New England Free Press. The text as it there appears has been
slightly re-edited to conform with the general style of this book.

GEORGE PATTERSON, JESSE REESE
AND JOHN SARGENT

Your Dog Don't Bark No More

I

GEORGE PATTERSON. I came here when I was sixteen years of age and went to work in South Chicago at the South Works. I became a roll turner's apprentice and went to night school at Englewood High. I worked ten hours a day in the mill and went four hours an evening to night school: I was self-educated. I graduated from high school and served my apprenticeship all at the same time, and it wasn't easy for a young fellow.

The first job I got was in a blacksmith's shop, and we got $5 a day. That was 50 cents an hour for ten hours. But I quickly got over trying to be a blacksmith. I wasn't built for it. So I went into the roll shop and became a roll turner, and I dropped down to 29 cents an hour. That was $2.90 for a ten-hour day. Of course every six months you got a raise.

We in the roll turner's trade began to form our own union, and I became the international vice-president of the United Roll Turners of America. This was my first experience with unions. I wasn't too interested in unions other than to get more dough; I was a typical steelworker. We had just come through the Depression. Those Depression years were terrible. I almost starved to death. The reason I got interested in the union was that I got married in the middle of that Depression, and then along came my son and I didn't have enough money to buy a bottle of milk.

The steel mill people came into the mill around 1933 and handed us a piece of paper. We looked at it, and it was called "An

Employee Representation Plan.'' Now the Employee Representation Plan was the company union plan. It was based on the fact that we had the right to bargain collectively. The company drew the whole thing up, and the workers in the various departments elected representatives of their own. I looked at this paper as a young lad and said, "this thing could never work," because it said right at the outset that there would be five members from management to sit on a committee and five members from the union—the company union—to sit on the committee. I asked who settled the tie, and of course I found out management did. So you see how useless it would have been.

I talked to the fellows in the shop, and I talked faster than the others about unions. (I'd heard my dad talk about unions in the old country.) I said, "I don't think this thing is any good." So they elected me to be their representative! And the first thing I did was to begin to destroy this company union idea. I believed in the legitimate form of union. I got in touch with the Amalgamated Association [of Iron, Steel and Tin Workers, the old AFL union in steel] through my craft union, the Roll Turners, and they wouldn't have anything to do with us. Leonard was the secretary. He wrote me nice letters, but never came to see me or invited me to come down and talk over joining with them. The Amalgamated Association was lying there and wouldn't do a thing for us.

So we formed an independent union. We tried to disband the company union, and we formed what we called the Associated Employees. This was just workers like myself attempting to do something by way of getting into a legitimate union.

Then, strange things began to happen. One night I came home —I'll always remember as long as I live, it was Lincoln's Birthday about the year 1936—and I walked into the house and there were two big fellows sitting there talking with my sister. They had a wonderful opportunity for a job for me. Now I was working in the mill as a roll turner, making pretty good money for that time. When I got to talking with these fellows, I found out that they wanted to hire me as a spy. So you see I became very quickly acquainted with labor espionage. We were trying to form a legitimate union, and these people invited some of us to come spy. Of course I turned this down and told them I had nothing much to offer them.

One day we read in the newspapers that they were trying to do the same thing [form an independent union] down in Pittsburgh. So I was elected to go down to Pittsburgh and talk matters over with the fellows who were attempting to do that. And I got to talking to a man named Johnny Mullin who asked me if I knew of a certain man named Hemingway. And I looked at him and said, "Yes. What do you know about him?" "Well," he said, "I work for him." I said, "You mean you're working for that spy?" He said, "Yeah." He had been approached by these same spies down in his plant in Pittsburgh, and he was taking the money. He was giving them the reports they wanted, and then he was turning them over to Clinton Golden of the National Labor Relations Board. We found out that Frick, vice-president of U. S. Steel, was the company man in charge of the spying. Mullin and I went down and testified before Senator LaFollette's committee, and there we revealed the beginnings of labor espionage in the steel mills and in other industrial plants.

I became president of the Associated Employees, and then we heard about a man named John Lewis who was very interested in trying to organize the unorganized. I wrote him a letter and said we had an independent union that would like to join up. He wrote back and told me if I held my shirt tail in he'd be down there in the near future and he'd send a man by the name of Philip Murray. So I got to meet Phil Murray and found he was a Scot, born about a mile from where I was born, and we got along pretty well. He was old enough to be my father. He was a United Mine Worker and could tell me more about unions in America than anybody else I knew, and I began to work very closely with him.

One day he said to me, "I'd like you to come down to Pittsburgh and do a little testifying against 'yellow dog' contracts." A company had quickly signed a "yellow dog" contract with a company union that still existed—the remnants of it. So we appeared before Madame Perkins and testified against "yellow dog" contracts, and these contracts were ruled illegal and the company unions were disbanded. But I was fired for doing this. I had twelve years in the steel mills. It was the only place I had worked. Just at that time the Steel Workers Organizing Committee began their drive. I was quickly picked up, thank goodness, by the Steel Workers Organizing Committee, and for the last thirty-three years of my life I've been working as an organizer for the United Steelworkers of America. In June 1936 we started the drive to organize the steelworkers in this area. I had a lucrative place to go; I had all these company unions throughout the steel mills, and I knew nearly every one. I would go to these people and get them to start joining the Steelworkers Union. Of course, many of them were joining up at their own volition. I didn't do all this by myself. I was just an organizer.

By that time 1937 had rolled around, and we had already gotten a contract with U. S. Steel (Carnegie-Illinois at the time). When we tried to get a contract with Republic Steel on May 26, 1937, the workers went on strike because Tom Girdler [president of Republic Steel] said he would rather dig potatoes than ever sign a contract with any labor organization. So the strike was on.

I understand you want to hear just a little bit about the Memorial Day Massacre. I was there. I was there on the Wednesday night when the strike started. I watched the police march around in their military formation. They were very well oriented. And toward 11 p.m. they marched out all of a sudden and broke up our picket lines, and the next thing I knew I enjoyed being placed in jail for the first time. I was in jail many times after that, and I never found anything too wrong with jail except the bedbugs, which I didn't like. Otherwise I got along fine in jail. I always carried an extra $50 bill hidden away somewhere so I could get myself out. (You know, the Wobblies, they didn't have a $50 bill. But we young steelworkers were getting wise and saving our money a little bit by this time, because the Depression was beginning to get over with and we were working a little steadier.) So I ended up in jail on the first night of the strike with about eighteen other organizers. We got out immediately the next morning, charged with disorderly conduct.

Thursday I began to organize the picket line and we went down to picket, and they wouldn't let us picket. Mayor Da . . . Mayor Kelly—I've got to watch that, Daley and Kelly, there's no difference, you know—Mayor Kelly said at the time, "Yeah, you can picket all you want." But if we went down there the cops would beat the hell out of us. So we kept trying to picket and we got put back in jail.

On Friday night we got real angry. We marched, and we were determined that we were going to picket. We met the police again. This time they really took a swat at us, and they were beating the hell out of everybody in the front lines. If you were in the front you were pretty lucky if you could get away without being clubbed a little bit. Then they fired a few shots in the air, and that scattered us. There was no riot. We ran like hell. The cops were after us.

They always say we riot. We never riot. We wanted to picket. They won't let you picket, so they beat you up and then they say you rioted. This is the fact. The cops make you riot. They riot against us, always. I know it, I've been there too many times. I'm always well-behaved: I might talk to them, but that's about all. Anyhow, they chased us and they beat us again.

This got a lot of union people mad. They got mad over here at Inland Steel, they got mad at Youngstown Sheet and Tube, and they got mad down at Gary. So we decided to hold a big meeting the following Sunday, which was Memorial Day. We invited the public to come and hear us, and we were going to picket. We had been given the right; it was in the paper. Everybody said we could picket; now we were going to picket.

After the meeting was over we started to march, and I went down with the front group, right by the flag, and there we met about 650 cops lined up. It was getting to be kind of familiar. I was always ill at ease. I didn't like it. Don't ever think that anybody's that brave. But I was an organizer in charge of the picket line, so I walked along and saw my familiar old friends Mooney, the commander of the police, and Kilroy. They stood about six feet, six inches tall. They were big fellows, and I'm not very big. And I looked up and said, "Well, here we are. We'd like to go through. Would you escort us? We'd like to picket."

Well, he was standing there—Kilroy was the man—and he was reading a very official document asking us in the name of the people of Illinois to disperse. As soon as he said that, he put the paper down and all hell broke loose. They began to shoot us, club us, and gas us. Ten people died while sixty-eight were wounded and we don't know how many got hurt in all. It really was hell on that field. I ran back with the rest of them, and I got mad. I could see the cops there shooting away with their guns. At first I thought they were blanks—I really did. I could smell the gunpowder—I'll never forget it—and then I began to see people fall. I saw a boy run by, and his foot was bleeding. Then it dawned on me. They were shooting real bullets. This was for keeps. They didn't stop shooting and killing till an hour and a half later. They were chasing people and picking people up.

It was about a week later that I was picked up by the police, and this time I really got the treatment. I went in and was held incommunicado for four days and four nights. You know how they do it: every twenty-four hours they move you (they don't need to book you) and all the time you're being questioned. My wife didn't know where I was at. Nobody knew. I just disappeared. They picked me up on 95th Street at Torrence. I was going over to a meeting at the Burnside Steel Foundry, where I was organizing at the time. I never got there.

How did I get out of it? Well, after about the third night there was a boy in the cell next to me who had been picked up for drunken driving, and his mother came down from Joliet to get him out, and I asked this lovely lady, "Would you do me a favor?" She said, "Well, you look like a nice fellow." And I said, "Yes, I am. I've been in here for four days and four nights, and I'm trying to get word to my wife." And she said, "Give me your telephone number." And I told her. And she called my wife. When they got the information from my wife, my lawyers got a writ of habeas corpus and produced the body—which was me—and we were put out on $50,000 bond.

We were charged with exactly the same thing these seven fellows [the Chicago Seven] were charged with: conspiracy to commit an illegal act. They did it then, they'll do it next year, they'll do it any time. The police will react the same way, the mayors of Chicago will react the same way. Every time you put on a demonstration, always take for granted that this is what's going to happen. I haven't seen it change from the Haymarket days, to the Memorial Day, to

the 1968 National Democratic Convention, when the police are faced
with a plain group of citizens and are stirred up by the newspapers
and foolish propaganda. I don't know what we can do to teach
policemen that we're law-abiding citizens who are walking on the
streets, we're demonstrating for something right. My heart bled the
night of the Democratic Convention.

You know these things happen, and you'll have to be prepared
to face them. We were ready to do these things. We stood up and
we organized the steelworkers all over the country. Some people
ask, "Was it worth it?" Of course it was worth it. We got a contract
at Republic Steel.

II

JESSE REESE. You are looking now at living history: not reading
from a book, but listening to a man who took part in the history
of building a trade union in steel.

I went to work at Youngstown Sheet and Tube in 1929, and we
had a skeleton union there called the Amalgamated Association. It
had only three or four people in it. I worked down there for a few
months, and I decided to join that union and see what I could do.
The Party organizer of the American Communist Party came to my
house and sat down and talked to me for two hours. He said, "I
have an assignment for you." I said, "What is that?" And he said,
"I want you to go into the old Amalgamated Association. I want
you to build that union. You're going to meet many difficulties.
You're going to meet Jim Crow; they're going to throw it in your
face. You're going to meet racism; they're going to throw that in
your face. But I want you to stand up and throw your ring around
with the leadership. That's your assignment." I said, "Well, I have
a few things on my mind." And he said, "What is that?"
"Freedom, Tom Mooney, the Scottsboro Boys—nine young Negro
kids framed for rape in Scottsboro, Alabama," I said. "If I can
take a stand on that. . . ." And he said, "Well, you've got to go
in there with the leadership, and report to me about every week or
two how things are going."

I went in, and the first thing I met was old Jim Crow. They
intended to run me out. So they said to me, "Well, we don't take

colored people in here, we haven't been taking colored people. But since you're a steelworker and we need the trade union built, we'll give you a chance. But remember one thing. You'll have to organize to stay here." I told them, "That's my business coming here, to help organize the union." One of the secretaries said to me, "I love Negroes, but I like to see 'em in their place." I didn't say a thing, because the organizer had told me to take it cool ("Don't lose your cool, but stay there.") So when it came to my time, I took the floor. I said, "I met a brother here in this union, and he gave me something to think about and something to do. He told me he liked colored people, but he liked them to stay in their place." I said, "Brothers, I agree with him. The place of black people is in the labor movement and officiating in their place, and I'm going to see that everyone out here can be put in his place." I said, "Every working man should know his place. I don't know what place you belong to, but my place is in the labor movement. Is that the place you were telling me you wanted me to stay in?" So that went on.

A few days later, they said to me, "We heard the reds were coming in here, to take over the union. Stay away from the Communists. Stay away from them." I didn't say a word. I waited till my time had come, and I got on the floor. I said, "Mr. Chairman, fellow delegates to this union. I didn't come here to tell you how good communism is, I came here to help you build a union. I feel that if a man is in jail, and you have a piece of pie in your hand and tell him how good it is when he needs liberation, it is foolish, when you can't enjoy it under the present system that we live under." And they left me alone, and next time they said, "This brother, we're going to make him president of this local union. He's able to take care of stuff, and the rest of us don't." And they said, "We're making you president. How about it?" There were four of them. I said to them, "Well listen, you white fellows say you are free. Why do you want to put such a load on my shoulders?" They said, "Well, you're the man for it; you can do it; you can do a good job. You're president of the union—we're going to nominate you." So they elected me, and I took it.

I reported to the organizer and told him I'd done a good job, and he said, "Tell me what you did." I told him. I said, "They hit me in the face, they hit me everywhere, but I hit back. And they hit me with communism, but I told them I hadn't come there to tell them how good communism was, since they couldn't enjoy it anyway under the present society that we live under." And he grabbed me and kissed me. [It was the] first time I'd ever been kissed by a man in my life, but it was a true kiss. It wasn't a Jim Crow segregation kiss, but it was a kiss of an honest brother.

I went on there in the union. I wanted to know how I could get the people in the union. That was my next step—to get people to join the union—to get black people in there. So I kept talking to my brothers and working with them. Black folks had the key positions in the mill, the positions of the hardest jobs, like pickling. All the steel had to come through the pickles of the Youngstown Sheet and Tube tin mill. They fired our foreman, a nice fellow, and they brought over a slave driver from Gary. A white fellow told us he was an organizer for the Ku Klux Klan and said, "You all going to stand for that guy to come in here?" So I went down to the operators of the pickles and said, "Shut the pickles down." And they said, "We can't do that, man!" I said, "Shut the pickles down." And they shut them down. I went over to see Long, the foreman, and I said, "Long, you lost your job?" and he said, "Yes." And I said, "Well, give me five minutes and we'll make them tell you where your job's at." And he said, "You got all day."

I drove over to the hot strip where the white fellows were rolling hot steel, and I said, "Hey fellows, just stop a minute rolling that steel. We're shutting down over there. We're fighting for ten cents an hour and our foreman back on the job." (It would look foolish fighting for your foreman and not for yourself.) And they said, "Oh, you got it organized?" And I said, "Yes, we shut it down. Look over there. We're down, we're not moving. We want you to stop until our grievance is heard." So the white fellows said, "We'll follow you."

Before I could get to the superintendent's office every superintendent in the mill was there. When I walked in, this man by the name of Mr. Griffin said, "Hello. Come in, Mr. Reese. I heard you were coming." And I said, "Well, Mr. Griffin, you should have cooked a cake." And he said, "Well, if I had known it in time maybe

we could have had a cake. What's your story?'' I said, ''Well, I'll
tell you. You fired our foreman, and we want him back on the job
if you want any steel rolled and any tin pickled.'' And he said,
''Well listen, you boys all made a mistake. We gave your foreman
a vacation with pay and a better job.'' Nobody had ever given anybody a vacation with pay before, not in the mill, not any place.
I said, ''Did you give us ten cents an hour? Didn't you know that
we wanted ten cents an hour on our pay and an annual thirty-five
cents added onto that?'' ''Oh Reese,'' said Griffin, ''that's too
much. Oo-oo, I can't do that. You'll have to go to Youngstown
Sheet and Tube.'' One of the superintendents said, ''Give 'em three
cents.'' And Griffin said, ''Well, I'll tell you, we decided about
a month ago to give you all three cents on the hour.'' So I said,
''You can't make it ten cents?'' And one of the fellows came up
hunchin' me and said, ''Take it. Take it and let it go.'' So I couldn't
go ahead of my army; you know, if I went too far ahead of my
army I would lose my gang. I looked around, and they said, ''Take
the three cents and come on.'' And I said to them, ''If we can get
two cents more, let's fight for it!'' And I said to Mr. Griffin, ''The
brothers say two cents more, Mr. Griffin, and we'll settle with you:
two cents.'' ''Well, we'll think about it,'' said Griffin. ''Boys, I
want to tell you this is your home, this mill is your home. Go along
back to the pickles and pickle the steel, and we'll see about your
raise.''

   We went back down there, and I said, ''You asked for ten cents.
Why don't you . . . ?'' And they said, ''Yeah, we want ten cents.
But you know that's too much.'' And I said, ''That's never too
much to ask from the man. Ask for the mill.''

   I went back to the hot strip and told the brothers, ''Well, we got
three cents on the hour, and the foreman a better job with a vacation.'' And there was an iceman, whose name was Bill: Bill Anderson. He was a big, heavy, strong fellow. And he said, ''Bring 'em
on up to the union, and we're going to initiate them, every man.
We're going to make a strong union.'' So I brought them into the
union and we made a talk [about the shutdown, and the three cent
raise] and how they got it. But the hot strip didn't get anything.
They just gave to the pickle. So everything was hot on the hot strip.

How were they going to get their increase? The hot strip boys were coming into the union. They were afraid of the union at first, everybody was scared to come in. But they were going to join the union.

I had a meeting in East Chicago, in Indiana Harbor. A candidate by the name of Mr. Fred Higgins was running for Lake County judge, if I remember right. And that was my smokescreen. I could bring forth my union, what my union was doing for the politician, so I could call for membership. I think I had about 2,000. Then I was called in on the carpet. Mr. Griffin called me in and said, "Hey, I thought you were satisfied. What are you doing now? I heard you got to be president of the Amalgamated Association, and you're calling mass meetings." And I said, "My viewpoint, Mr. Griffin, is politics." "Oh, that's all right," he said, "go ahead." But I didn't tell him what kind of politics I meant.

The years rolled on. We had a terrible Depression, 1932 and '33. Evictions were taking place. Black people were being thrown out from block to block and from street to street. And we were beginning to work one day a week—one day in the mill—and the rest of the days in the street putting furniture back in the houses. Lots of people had bought property on option lease. They thought that they had a contract until their real estate agents proved that they had only leased their houses: "We didn't sell it to them." (Something like what's going on in Chicago now.)

A Hunger March came through led by a man named Claude Lightfoot. So I got my gang ready, getting some of the people in Gary ready to meet the Hunger March, all those who could go to Washington getting aboard the train. The train was moving in for unemployment insurance, social security, and $6 a day with a five-day week. Those were the demands of the Communists in that day. Arnold Johnson, the Republican mayor of the city at that time, said, "No Hunger March is coming through Gary!" Well, Claude got an average number in his march (which looked about a mile long), and stopped about fifteen minutes and said, "Arnold, we are here! And we are on our way to Washington for unemployment insurance, social security paid by the government, and five days' work six hours a day." That was the way it was.

Sure enough, they passed social security (which you pay for). And

that's what you're getting today; that's how you got it. And if anybody here doesn't know how he's getting social security, that's the
way it was got: through a struggle. The old fellows here, I know
they know. Everything that we gained there came through struggle.
And it was a hard struggle. I came up some time in the union on the
strength of the slogan, "Five days' pay, social security. We must
organize our union and fight for those things."

We had a "rump" convention of the old Amalgamated Association in Pittsburgh, but we didn't have any money to send people
there. We had to have $100. One of the brothers there who red-
baited so bad told me, "I want you to go to Communist Party headquarters and borrow $100." And I said, "No, I won't. I'm the presi-
dent of this union. I'm going to let the delegation go, and you're
going to be on the committee." "Well Reese," he said to me, "I
thought you knew [the Party organizer]." I said, "You can get
acquainted with him!" So sure enough, they went on and borrowed
$100 to go to Pittsburgh. They never did pay it back. They couldn't
give social affairs to raise money because there was so much racism
in the outfit. They were scared of a black and white social affair,
but later on they began to see that there wasn't much difference,
and they had to do whatever they could to get money.

They went on to Pittsburgh. That was Mike Tighe's union, the
old Amalgamated. They called on Mike Tighe to come and help
build a union; they wanted his viewpoint. Mike Tighe came and
expelled all of us, calling us reds. I said, "Oh my goodness, this
bunch of Catholics. All of them are Catholics but me." I was the
only red in the bunch but he expelled all of them. I went back and
said, "Hey, I thought you were going to keep the reds out of the
union, you fellows turning red all the way around in one night. How
did that happen?" And they said, "We ain't going to have no red-
baiting in this union. We're going to be in this union, and Mike
Tighe is out to break it up."

In the year 1935 a resolution to organize steel was introduced at
the AFL convention. It was a knock-down, drag-out fight. John L.
Lewis and Bill Green [actually, Bill Hutcheson] got to fighting over
the resolution, and I understand that Lewis knocked Green down
and came out with a CIO industrial union council, ready to organize.

John L. Lewis told Philip Murray that he wanted our union built in steel and to go into Party headquarters and hire all the Communists. Philip Murray told him, "I don't want to have anything to do with the Communists!" He said, "Murray, if you were going to build a house you wouldn't go to the mines and get a dust blower, and you wouldn't get a plumber; you'd get a carpenter, wouldn't you? So I want you to go and get the know-how, go and get the Communists. We're going to build the union if we have to fight the Devil in Hell!" Well, he came out to Party headquarters, hiring everybody he could hire. So the Party organizer said, "Reese, you can get a job for $8 a day." I said, "A man can hire, a man can fire. I'm going to stay in the mill and build my union where I know I'll have security." I said, "John L. Lewis with his money . . . well, he can fire, but I have no security; but if I have mass security, I can have security in the mill."

Well brothers, we rolled on, building steel. I helped to organize Youngstown, and we had a strike in 1937. Republic Steel was scabbing. So we went to South Chicago with truckloads of people, working-class people. And we started our picket line like any union would be doing, and brother George Patterson was leading the strike. And while walking along I heard guns, and I thought, "Oh-oh, they're shooting blanks." I said, "Keep moving, folks. They ain't doing a thing but shooting blanks. File up; march!" But then I began to see people drop. There was a Mexican on my side, and he fell; and there was a black man on my side and he fell. Down I went. I crawled around in the grass and saw that people were getting beat. I'd never seen police beat women, not white women. I'd seen them beat black women, but this was the first time in my life I'd seen them beat white women—with sticks. There was this woman carrying a flag in her hand, and they took the flag away from her and began beating her with the flagpole. I thought, "I'm here with nothing. I should have brought my gun." But I didn't get hurt; I got out of there all right.

U. S. Steel signed a contract. And I think the steel plant where we were working signed some kind of state agreement [see page 107.] And later on we also got a contract.

I had always said that I wanted a union that would be a watchdog for the working class and guard its interests. So I always called our union the watchdog. If I ever had a chance I was going to turn my dog loose on the steel corporation. I always looked at Mississippi and Alabama. The lynching, Jim Crow, and segregation always stayed on my mind. How could we stop it? My aim was to do it.

The first [SWOC] convention at Pittsburgh I begged to get on the Resolutions Committee, and I wouldn't tell anybody why. I wanted to draw up a resolution for Tom Mooney and the Scottsboro Boys, and I knew if I told them that they wouldn't put me on the Resolutions Committee. Well, I met a white fellow from Missouri, and I said, "How about nominating me for the Resolutions Committee?" And he did. I went in the resolution room (you had to bring the resolution from your committee onto the convention floor), and I had one of the biggest fights in that room with my own man—a black man. He was sent by the Alabama committee to keep me from bringing up our resolution in the resolution room. He didn't mean it, but he had to go back to Alabama; he had to make that fight against the resolution on the Scottsboro Boys. I said, "Listen, I'll tell you where I'm going to stand. You're from Alabama. I'm from Mississippi, but I happen to be here for a little while. I know how you feel going back, but I'm going to fight for this resolution on the floor of the convention." Well, I did. John L. Lewis called me on the floor. Yessirree, as the representative of East Chicago 1011, I had a right to speak on the resolution. I came forward and I spoke on Tom Mooney and the Scottsboro Boys, who had been framed. I said the union was the watchdog of the working class, and it must speak up on the misery of the working class of people. [Both resolutions were adopted.]

I want to say, friends, I have to give it to you like it is. The Communists built the union. After we got the union built, something happened to John L. Lewis, and Mr. Philip Murray carried out his aims: he fired every Communist organizer. He made an agreement with the steel trusts, it seems to me, that he would fire the Communists. And that's what happened, and the union's been going back, back, back ever since. It doesn't open its mouth.

Today we have in our unions a pet dog—what you might call a pet company dog—led by the caretakers; and the caretakers are the leaders of our union. And our dog is being fed red-baiting and his teeth have been pulled out (that's the no-strike clause) and your dog don't bark no more for you. So the only thing you can get to win now is a cat, and it's got to be a wildcat, organized as a blanket matter. You've got to use blanket cover to keep from being exposed.

Your so-called leaders are the leaders of the industrial pet dog. Your dog don't bark at no misery. Your dog don't bark no more. He can't hear. Makes no difference how many people they kill, your dog don't say nothing. He ain't the dog of 1937, when that dog turned loose nine boys—the Scottsboro Boys—and freed Tom Mooney. Your dog . . . what's the matter with your dog? I couldn't stay in that union, pay dues, and keep quiet. They'd have to do something about things. There's no justice, no justice! And we sit down with a big trade union, with intelligent people (people who are educated, they say), and you don't hear nothing, and you can't say nothing, and you can't see nothing. You can't see those people getting killed. They have declared war on color, and not just on one color, but on all color from the Kennedys to the Kings to the black ghettos to the Black Panthers to the mine workers.   And they're now dancing on the doorsteps of Asia, and your dog don't bark. Because you don't have anything but the pet dog of the steel trusts.

You have no leaders. Your "leaders" don't say nothing: they're scared. Freedom is in the jail house. That's the way of freedom. It ain't worth being free if you're not willing to go to jail for it.

III

JOHN SARGENT. I got in the mills in 1936, and I [was] fortunate to be caught up in a great movement of the people in this country. And that doesn't happen very often in one's lifetime, but it's an experience that I think is important to anyone who has been able to participate in a movement of this kind. It's indeed a very important event in his or her life. Because a movement of the kind that we had in the Steelworkers Union and in the CIO was a movement that moved millions of people, literally, and changed not only the course of the working man in this country, but also the nature of the relationship between the working man and the government and between the working man and the boss, for all time in this country. There are some parallels in the movement today, especially among the young people and the black people, that I won't go into. . . .

I was hired at the Inland Steel Company in 1936. And I remember I was hired at 47 cent cents an hour, which was the going rate, and at a time when there were no such things as vacations, holidays, overtime, insurance, or any of the so-called fringe benefits everybody talks about today. But the worst thing—the thing that made you most disgusted—was the fact that if you came to work and the boss didn't like the way you looked, you went home; and if he did like the way you looked, you got a promotion. Anything and everything that happened to you was at the whim and will of the fellow who was your boss and your supervisor. Now fortunately Jesse [Reese] had a good boss. Ninety-nine per cent of the people did not have good bosses. As a matter of fact, in order to get a promotion—and sometimes even in order to work—you had to bring the boss a bottle of whiskey, or you had to mow the boss's lawn, or you had to do something to make yourself stand out from the other people he saw. This was the type of condition that existed as late as 1936 in the steel mills in this region.

When the CIO came in, the people were ready to accept a change. And because they were ready to accept a change, it was not a difficult task to organize the people in the steel mills. Thousands upon thousands of them, in a spontaneous movement, joined the steelworkers' organization at that time. And they did it because conditions in the mill were terrible, and because they had become disgusted with the political set-up in this country and the old tales told by the Republican Party about the free enterprise system in this country in which any man was his own boss, and there was no sense in having an organization, and organizations and unions were anti-American, and so on. All this fell off the backs of the people at that time. They realized that there was going to be a change—both a political and an economic change—in this country, and there was.

John L. Lewis had an agreement with the U. S. Steel Corporation, and they signed a contract. Little Steel—which was Youngstown Sheet and Tube, Republic Steel, Inland Steel, and other independent companies—had no contract with the Steelworkers Union. As a result in 1937 there was a strike called on Little Steel. And one of the things that happened during the strike was the massacre in South Chicago, the Chicago cops beating and shooting the people. The strike was not won. We did not win a contract. Neither Youngstown Sheet and Tube, nor Republic Steel, nor Inland Steel won a contract with the company. What we did get was an agreement through the governor's office that the company would recognize the Steelworkers Union and the company union and any other organization that wanted to represent the people in the steel industry. And we went back to work with this governor's agreement signed by various companies and union representatives in Indiana. At Inland Steel we had a company union; we had our own Steelworkers Union. When we got back to work we had company union representatives and Steelworkers Union representatives, and we had no contract with the company. But the enthusiasm of the people who were working in the mills made this settlement of the strike into a victory of great proportions.

Without a contract, without any agreement with the company, without any regulations concerning hours of work, conditions of work, or wages, a tremendous surge took place. We talk of a rank-and-file movement: the beginning of union organization was the best kind of rank-and-file movement you could think of. John L. Lewis sent in a few organizers, but there were no organizers at Inland Steel, and I'm sure there were no organizers at Youngstown Sheet and Tube. The union organizers were essentially workers in the mill who were so disgusted with their conditions and so ready for a change that they took the union into their own hands.

For example, what happened at Inland Steel I believe is perhaps representative of what happened throughout the steel industry. Without a contract we secured for ourselves agreements on working conditions and wages that we do not have today, and that were better by far than what we do have today in the mill. For example as a result of the enthusiasm of the people in the mill you had a series of strikes, wildcats, shut-downs, slow-downs, anything working people could think of to secure for themselves what they decided they had to have. If their wages were low there was no contract to prohibit them from striking, and they struck for better wages. If their conditions were bad, if they didn't like what was going on, if they were being abused, the people in the mills themselves —without a contract or any agreement with the company involved— would shut down a department or even a group of departments to secure for themselves the things they found necessary.

We made an agreement with Inland Steel way back in '38 or '39 that the company would not pay less than any of its competitors throughout the country. We never had it so good, I assure you of that. All you had to do as a union representative was come into the company and say, "Look, we have a group of people working in the pickle line, and at Youngstown, Ohio or Youngstown Sheet and Tube in East Chicago people are getting more money than we're getting for the same job." And if that was a fact, we were given an increase in wages at Inland. In those departments where you had a strong group of union members, where they were most active, we had the highest rates in the country. We were never able to secure conditions of this kind after we secured contracts.

What I'm trying to get at is the spontaneous action of people who are swept up in a movement they know is right and correct and want to do something about. Our union now has a grievance committee of twenty-five people. In those days there were more than twenty assistant grievers and hundreds of stewards. The grievance committee set-up could handle the affairs of the people on every shift and every turn with every group. Where you did have contracts with the companies (at U. S. Steel, for example) you had a limited grievance procedure. The U. S. Steel plant in Gary, the largest steel plant of the largest steel company, had a grievance committee of only eleven. Where union officials did not take over the union through a contract with the company (as they did with U. S. Steel), you had a broader, bigger, more effective, and more militant organization that set an example for unions throughout the country. Where the union and the company got together through union contracts (as at U.S. Steel), you had a smaller, more restrictive, less militant union that provided less representation for the people in the mill. U. S. Steel has never had a strike (so far as I know) since the unions organized, whereas unions like the Inland Steel union had a whole series of strikes in order to protect their conditions and prevent the company from taking over or taking back the things they had earned. What happens to a union? And what happened to the United Steelworkers of America? What makes me mad, and what makes thousands of other people in the mill mad, is that the companies became smart and understood that in order to accommodate themselves to a labor organization they could not oppose that labor organization. What they had to do was recognize that labor organization. And when they recognized a labor union they had to be sure they recognized the national and international leadership of that labor union and took the affairs of that labor union out of the hands of the ordinary elected officials on a local scale.

Now Little Steel was not smart. Little Steel had people like the president of Republic Steel, who said he would go out and pick apples before he would recognize the union. And our own dear Inland Steel Company said they would do nothing, they would rather shut their place down forever than recognize the Steelworkers Union. Now what happened to these companies that did not recognize the union, that forced the union to act against the company, was that the workers developed the most militant and the most inspiring type of rank-and-file organization that you can have. Now when the companies realized that this was what was happening, they quickly saw that they had gone off in the wrong direction, and they recognized the leadership of the union.

We used to bargain locally with the Inland Steel Company, and we had our own contract with the company. We let a representative of the international union sit in, but we bargained right in Indiana Harbor and settled our differences right there. But soon Inland began to realize that this was not the way, because they were up against a pretty rough bunch of people who had no ambitions to become political leaders and labor representatives on a national scale. They realized that the best way to handle the situation was to work with the international leadership of this union. And today, the company and the international union get along pretty well.

The union has become a watchdog for the company. The local union has become the police force for the contracts made by the international union. If a local union tries to reject a contract in the

Steelworkers Union, the contract is put into effect and the local union acts as the police to see that the men live up to the contract, even if it is rejected by the entire committee [of the local union] which negotiates the contract.

This is, I think, the normal growth which occurs when labor unions and most other organizations become legitimate and old and part of the general situation of the country. At the same time, I think it important to realize that the growth of the union in this country has changed the bond. We no longer have many of the sweat-shops we had in the '20s and early '30s, or the terribly low wages we had before. The union taught the system—taught the industrialists of this country—that it is possible to pay decent wages and provide decent working conditions and still make a fortune. In fact the steel mills make more money now than they ever made before. They do it by paying people a fairly decent wage and by working people not nearly so hard as they were worked in the past. The union has taught the companies how to make money through recognizing the union organization. And the government and the employers have learned how to adopt, co-opt, and engulf the union and make it a part of the establishment. And in making it part of the establishment they took the guts, the militancy, and the fight out of the people who work for a living.

SYLVIA WOODS

SYLVIA WOODS' experience spans half a century of black struggle. As a child in New Orleans she took part in the movement of Marcus Garvey, which powerfully projected both the dream of a return to Africa and black pride. At the time that we interviewed her for this book Sylvia Woods was playing an active role in the national campaign to free Angela Davis.

Many black workers today believe that they must first organize as blacks, and only then (if at all) seek an alliance with white workers. Sylvia Woods, like Jesse Reese, came to a different conclusion: that only through the unity of black and white could black working people move forward. She describes in detail her gradual conversion to this point of view.

Sylvia Woods also had the good fortune of belonging to, and helping to create, a democratic local union. The UAW local in the airplane parts factory where she worked during World War II did not want the dues check-off, feeling that it would dampen voluntary participation by the membership. Local union officers worked in the shop. Like Nick Migas [see page 168]. Sylvia Woods always took the aggrieved individual with her in processing a grievance, rather than representing an individual who wasn't there. Departmental meetings at the end of the night shift made it possible for fellow-workers to form deep relationships. And education was a regular feature of the local union's meetings.

No wonder, then, that the day the plant closed down at the end of the war the members of this extraordinary local just stood around the gate, wondering, ''What am I going to do without these people?''

SYLVIA WOODS

You Have to Fight for Freedom

I WAS BORN March 15, 1909. My father was a roofer. In those days they put slates on the roofs and he was a slater. It was a very skilled job. You had to nail the slate. They used to make a fancy diamond with different colors. Every time the white guys got ready to do this they sent him for the bucket of beer so that he wouldn't learn it. But when they got ready to send him for the beer, he would find something wrong. He didn't know where his hammer was or he had to get something before he went, and in the meantime he would be watching. He learned it and he could do it beautifully. He'd say, "I'm the best. I stole it from those bastards but I'm the best." He became so good he didn't have to work with contractors any more. He could go out on his own.

And he was a union man. There was a dual union—one for whites and one for blacks. He said we should have one big union but a white and a black is better than none. He was making big money—eight dollars a day. I used to brag that "My father makes eight dollars a day." But he taught me that "You got to belong to the union, even if it's a black union. If I wasn't in the union I wouldn't make eight dollars a day."

New Orleans is a trade union town. My father had seen the longshoremen organize and they made a lot of money. Unions were not new to this city. And I mean they had unions! When they came out on strike, there were no scabs. You know why there were no scabs? Because you carried your gun. The pickets had guns and they would blow your brains out.

My father got into the Garvey movement when the Garvey movement was being born. I was about maybe nine or ten at the beginning
of the Garvey movement. We couldn't wait for Sundays to come
because we went to the big meeting in Longshoremen's Hall. The
band would be playing and we would march. Everybody had a title
and everybody had a uniform. My husband used to say that any
organization that puts a black in a uniform, that's all he needs. It
makes him something special. If you have a uniform it gives you
a little more dignity. The other thing was freedom. You want to
leave this oppression and go back to the mother country and have
some freedom. This was the beginning of my realizing that you have
to fight for freedom.

I'll never forget, there was a little woman there and she used to
speak every Sunday. When that woman got up to talk, my father
would just sit thrilled and then he'd look at me: "Are you listening?" I'd say, "I'm listening." "I want you to hear every word
she says because I want you to be able to speak like that woman.
We have to have speakers in order to get free." And then when
we got home he would say, "Now what did she say?" I could say
it just like her, with her same voice, all of her movements and everything. This would please him no end.

He was a gentle man. He believed in women doing things. He
never slapped my mother. If the housework didn't get done, he
didn't see it. There were more important things to do.

He was a very kind man. He never raised his voice. He never
wanted my mother to give us a licking and my mother was hard
on us. She really would give it to us, but he would say "No" if
he was home.

I had a grandmother who was very religious and my mother was
kind of because that was her upbringing. After she married my father
she sort of got away from it. But my grandmother made us go to
church and she would frighten us: "You're going to die and go to
Hell 'cause you're telling a lie and when I get through beating you,
you're not going to tell any more lies." I was actually afraid I might
go to Hell. My father would say, "That's a lot of crap. This is
what the white folks tell you so that you will be scared. They go
to church and come right out of church and lynch a nigger before

you can say scat. Now, are they scared that they're going to Hell?''
My grandmother used to get so angry with him. "Tom, you are
going to send those children's souls to Hell.'' He said, ''The white
folks send them to hell every day. They were sent to hell when
they were born right here on earth, Ma.'' She would pray and we'd
all have to go and pray and he'd say, "Don't believe all that. Go
and kneel down but don't be saying all that crap.''

My grandmother was born in slavery. It's a funny thing, we never
thought to talk to her about it. She never talked to us except to
say, "Scrub the kitchen,'' or do something or don't do something,
or "Come with me.''

If she hadn't had a stroke I wouldn't have been married until I
was maybe forty because she took me everywhere. When I was
twelve years old she was still picking me up from school. "You
got to watch girls. You can't be too careful with girls.''

When I was maybe ten years old, I changed schools. On the way
to school, I had to go through a park that was for white people
only. We could walk through the park but we couldn't stop at all,
just pass through it. There were swings in this park and, oh, I so
much wanted sometimes to just stop and swing a little while, but
we couldn't because we were black. I would walk through this park
to my school where there weren't any swings.

Every morning all the kids would line up according to classrooms
and we would have prayers and sing the Star Spangled Banner and
then we'd march to our respective groups after this business.

I decided I wasn't going to sing the Star Spangled Banner. I just
stood there every morning and I didn't sing it. One morning, one
of the teachers noticed that I wasn't doing it. So she very quietly
called me over and asked me why didn't I sing the Star Spangled
Banner. I said I just didn't feel like singing it. So she said, "Well
then you have to go in to the principal and explain that to him.
All of the children in the school take part and you've got to do
it too.''

OK, I went in to the principal and he asked me why I wasn't
singing the Star Spangled Banner. He threatened me with a lot of
[stuff like] I'd have to bring my mother. I said, "I don't care. I'll
tell her to come but she won't come because she has to go to work.''

I said my grandmother would come, not my mother. "Alright, then you'll have to bring your grandmother." I said, "She don't care if I don't sing the Star Spangled Banner." (I didn't know whether she would care or she wouldn't care.) He said, "You won't be able to come to school here." And I said, "So, OK, I won't come."

He says, "Why don't you want to sing it?" Finally I told him. "Because it says 'The land of the free and the home of the brave' and this is not the land of the free. I don't know who's brave but I'm not going to sing it any more." Then he said, "Why you've been singing it all the time haven't you? How come you want to stop now?" And I told him about coming through the park and if I could not swing in those swings in the park, and I couldn't sit in the park, and I could only walk in Shakespeare Park, then it couldn't be the land of the free. "Who's free?" He didn't say anything.

Then he said, "Well, you could pledge allegiance to your flag." I said, "It's not my flag. The flag is with freedom. If the land is free and the flag is mine, then how come I can't do like the white kids?" And then I told him that the next white kid I see, I'm beating him up. "I'm telling you right now, he's just going to get all beat up. I don't care." He says, "But you can't do that. You could go to Jones Home." So I said, "Well, I'll go to Jones Home. I don't care. But he'll get beat up. I know that!"

Anyway, he told me that I didn't have to sing the song and I didn't have to pledge allegiance but I had to stand in the back of the line. So who cares about standing in the back of the line? Sometimes the white administrators would come to the school and look the niggers over. (We called it that. "Well, there's the white folks looking the niggers over.") And he didn't want them to see me. But I didn't mind getting in the back of the line as long as I didn't have to sing that song. But I was so hurt and disillusioned, I would not have sung it no matter what. I'm sure that this man must have sympathized with me although he gave no indication that he did. He had said he was going to make me bring my parents but he never mentioned it again. I never sang it again from the time I was ten years old. I still don't pledge allegiance to the flag and I don't sing the Star Spangled Banner.

My mother had two children, my brother John and me, and then we had a brother Joseph. I'm eleven years older than him. She had to work and I had to take care of the two boys. Every morning when she got ready to go to work Joseph would cry, "Mama, please stay home!" She had to go off and leave him and I know how her heart must have been broken. In the evenings I would take him to meet her. We walked two blocks to the streetcar. The first streetcar would come along and she wouldn't get off. He'd say, "Where is Mama?" I'd say, "She will be on the next one." So the next one would come and she wouldn't get off and he would cry, "When is she coming?" She left him crying; she found him crying. You know she felt sorry for me her little girl, her first born, taking this burden.

She went to work in "the white folks' yard," as the blacks would say. She did the washing—and then there wasn't any washing machine—she did it by hand. This man used to have fifteen white shirts a week. She took care of the child, the house, the washing, the ironing, everything but the cooking. I think she made two dollars a day.

My mother was very strict with me. The school used to have dances for the youngsters on Saturday. I could go if John went with me (that's my older brother). He would say, "Don't dance with him. I saw him carrying on in the corner. You dance with him and I'll be telling Mama." And then, "Come on. Let's go." "But John, just one more . . ." "Let's go! I'm ready to go." I'd say, "I'll bring in your wood for a week." "OK, bring in my wood for a week. You can dance another dance." Then I'd have to do all of his chores for a week in order to dance another dance.

They were really strict and tight, so I wouldn't get spoiled, so I wouldn't have a baby. (They didn't know that I wasn't going to have any babies.) Then my grandmother had this stroke and I had to take care of her. And I had to mind Joseph. I didn't mind minding him—we were happy.

Finally, I got tired of it. Then Henry came along and he was talking about we would get married and then we would go to Chicago. I had never been on a train in my life. I would have married just to get on that train and come to Chicago.

He lived two blocks away from us. We grew up together. But my mother didn't know his parents. The first time he came he asked my mother if he could come to see me and she said, "Have your mother come up here Sunday and we'll discuss it." I was fifteen. The next winter I got married. When he got serious my mother was sorry she had let him come. We got married and my mother just hated it. My father didn't want me to get married either. My father was a skilled laborer making eight dollars a day and here is this man who didn't even have a trade. Henry was working as a porter in a dress shop. "How do you intend to take care of her?" my father asked him. "She can't cook. She is lazy. You will not find anybody as lazy as that girl! I'm telling you what you are getting. She doesn't want to do a thing in the house and her mother has to get after her to wash the dishes. She slops them up. She don't dry them. You take down a plate to eat and water drops in your face. She is the laziest thing you have ever seen." Henry said, "Yes, sir. That's all right. We'll get married."

Henry came to Chicago. He got a job and he sent me a one-way ticket. I was so happy. It took him three months to send it to me because the train fare was $35. Thirty-five dollars was a lot of money. When I got the ticket I told my mother, "I got my ticket, Ma. I can go to Chicago!" She looked at it and it was a one-way ticket. She said, "Put that thing in that dresser over there and leave it there. When your father gets enough money, he'll buy you a two-way ticket and then you'll be able to go. You're not going away from here with a one-way ticket." I cried and cried. She said, "You take your round-trip ticket and if they say your eye is black you can tell them the devil with them and you'll come home." So I had to wait. It took almost a month before she got that ticket.

The minute I got off the train and I told Henry that I had the two-way ticket, he couldn't wait until the next morning to go down town and sell the other half of it so that he would have some money, because he had lost the job in the meantime. It was in the heart of the Depression. He's a little guy and in those days they just didn't hire little guys.

So I had to go to work. I had never had a job in my life. I came from a family that didn't allow the girls to work because they didn't know who you were going to work with and you couldn't mix and mingle with anybody and everybody. All you could do is go to school.

I got this job in a laundry. The first morning I went there, this guy asked me, "Did you ever work in a laundry before?" I said, "No." He said, "Well there's no point in your coming here because we only hire people who know how to work in a laundry." I said "OK" and I left. The next morning I went back because I didn't know any place else to go. "Weren't you here yesterday?" "Yes." He said, "Well, I told you that we don't hire people who don't know how to work in a laundry." I said, "Well, maybe you'll need somebody one day. I'll come back tomorrow." So the next day I came back. When I walked in the door he said, "Come with me." He took me upstairs and he said to the foreman, "Teach her how to shake out."

You had to shake these clothes out and put them on long poles. You know how things look when they come out of a wringer. You had to shake them out so that they could run them through the mangle. Two girls put the things through the mangle. One girl did the sheets and the other did the small things like towels and pillow slips. I worked really hard. I kept those poles full. The women would say, "You mean you never worked before?" I'd say, "I never had a job before."

When I went back the next day, my arms were aching. I just couldn't lift them up. The women were angry with me. They said, "You just don't want to work." There was this one big fat woman and she said, "That kid's tired. You know it's the first time she's ever worked. What in the hell do you expect of her? If anybody else says anything to her, they're going to have to reckon with me." She was pulling those great big bags and tying them up and pitching them just like they were nothing. Nobody wanted to reckon with her. I limbered up in the afternoon and I did a little better.

So then I wanted to start shaking sheets because there is an art to shaking sheets. You pick these sheets up and—wham—if you did it right they popped. You made the sheet pop and then you threw it over that pole. This fascinated me. "Come on over here. You can shake out the sheets." I was going so fast. There were four poles and if we kept those poles full, then I could monkey around. I'd go over and watch the women feed the sheets into the mangle. One day I said to this white gal (only white feeders—black shakers and black folders, the hardest jobs—white table girls), I said, "Will you let me see if I can run this?" She said, "Sure." By the next week I knew how to feed.

So the next week I wanted to fold. I hurried up and filled the poles and they showed me how to fold. I wasn't there three weeks before I knew how to do everything.

I was working for ten dollars a week and I asked this white woman on the mangle, "How much do you make?" She said, "Fifteen dollars." I said, "You mean you're making fifteen and he's only paying me ten?" She said, "Yes, but I'm a feeder." I said, "Well that girl over there"—and she was a Negro woman—"she only makes ten and she was feeding. I'm going to ask him for a raise." She said, "Kiddo, don't do it because you'll be fired if you do." "He doesn't have to fire me. I'm going to quit. I'm not working for ten dollars a week."

The next morning I said to the owner, "Hey Charlie." "What do you want?" He never stopped walking. You had to walk behind him to talk to him so I walked right behind him. I said, "I'm not working for ten dollars any more." "What do you mean you're not working for ten dollars any more? I hired you, you didn't know how to do a goddamned thing, I did you a favor." I said, "I know how to feed and fold and stack." He said, "It's impossible. You've only been here three weeks. I don't believe it."

He came up and he watched me work. I stood at that mangle and fed those sheets in. He said, "Speed it up!" I put it up to its highest notch and ran it. He said, "All right, I want to see you fold." I snatched those sheets out of that mangle, me and this other girl. . . . He didn't say a word. He turned around and he walked out.

Everybody said, "He's going to fire you. He's going to get you." I said, "I don't give a damn if he fires me. I don't have to work here. I know how to feed and fold. I can go to King's Laundry down at the next block."

The next week he raised me to eighteen dollars. That was the top for the table girls. He said, "Now don't you tell anybody." The minute I got that check I went right back up and said, "Hey everybody, I got a raise!" "Aw, you're crazy." I said, "Look at my check! Eighteen dollars." So they called him up.and they asked, "How come she's getting eighteen dollars" instead of saying, "Give me eighteen dollars too!" He looked at me and said, "God damn you, I made a mistake when I hired you. I told you not to tell anybody."

Then they organized a night shift. There was so much work that they just couldn't get it all out. So they put all the black workers on nights. I used to work from five o'clock in the evening until three o'clock in the morning, every night. I was getting $18—top salary.

No whites. All blacks but the blacks were stealing them blind. They were wrapping sheets around them and wearing them home and taking everything. They said, "Well, hell, we are just getting the rest of our pay." The foreman would go downstairs and everybody would stop. They wouldn't do a thing.

One night a white woman was hired. "Who is this white woman?" Everybody was looking around. She was hired to watch us to see that we didn't do any stealing. The boss came up and said that this woman was going to be the forelady. I said, "I don't know what the rest of you think but I'll be goddamned if she's going to be forelady over me. We've been working nights for over a year. We've the most seniority. We're all black women here and if he has to have a forelady I don't know why he couldn't have one of us. She's got to go." So everybody got mad. They closed the mangles down.

And then the boss comes up. He walks right up to me and says, "What's going on here?" I said, "We're not working." He said, "Why not?" I said, "We're not going to have a white forelady over all black women. Until you get her out of here, we're not going to work. If you are going to have a forelady you have to get one of us. Either one of us or nobody." So he goes out and calls the cops.

The cops came in and said we had to get out if we weren't going to do any work. We really messed the place up. We mixed the bundles up until the cops didn't know what to do. They told them that I was the ringleader and they put me in the patrol wagon but the white policeman just took me home.

We went up to my house and held a meeting. It was all new to me and I didn't know how far to take it. We didn't fight any more. We just left. But they didn't put a white forelady over us!

My husband got fired that night—he was working there—and they fired my brother. I just went down the next block to another laundry and got a better job. I was making $20 a week as a table girl and all around girl.

From there I went to a laundry in Oak Park that paid 32 cents an hour, and that was a lot of money! This laundry was owned by a family and they would give us a turkey every year for Christmas and two weeks vacation with pay. This was unheard of. Other laundries were paying 18 and 20 cents an hour, their top rate was 25 cents an hour, but Brooks in Oak Park paid 32 cents.

When the union came to organize, I went to all the meetings and I was the spokesman for our laundry, for Brooks. The union said that they had negotiated with the laundry owners for 26 cents an hour. And I said, "You have got to be kidding! We are already making 32. You have to negotiate for 35."

I got mad and quit the union because the best they could get was 26 cents. I just pulled out the whole Brooks laundry. We walked out of the goddamned union.

The guy came running after me, "You can't do this. You have to come back." "I'm not coming back because you had no business to negotiate the contract. You should have brought it to us first." They had signed the contract and it was a closed shop and eventually everyone had to join the union. So I quit the laundry.

I was still in the laundry when the war came. My friend Martina and I decided we were going to go to work in a war plant, Martina and I both, so that we could earn some more money. And we were sick and tired of working in a laundry.

We went over to Wilson Jones. That's a place that made notebooks and papers. There I learned to run a punch press. Then

I heard about Bendix Aviation that made carburetors for airplanes. It was right around the corner from where I lived. They used to wear blue uniforms, pants and a blouse, and I loved it. The black gals would put on a white shirt under the blue and they'd bring the collar of it out. They'd wear white socks and they'd get blue sneakers. You really had an outfit. You had the cap. "I've got to get a job in there!"

So I went to Bendix looking for a job. I used to go about three times a day. I would go in the morning and they would tell me I was too fat. Then I'd go home and put on a hat and I'd go back in the afternoon and they'd say, "Well, we're not hiring right now." I would sit there and hear them begging white girls to take jobs, so I picked a fight with them. I said, "What do you mean you're not hiring? You were begging that woman. You told her you had a job at nights on the punch press, and nobody can operate a punch press better than I." He said, "We don't have punch presses here." I said, "Whatever you have, I can do it." But I didn't get hired. They had their quota.

Finally they wanted to give me a job. What is the job doing? Cleaning up the bathroom. I wasn't taking no washroom job! "I want to work on a *machine*." Martina took the job, which was good because otherwise I never would have gotten in there.

One day she called me up at home. "Hurry up and come on over here. There's a man here says he'll hire you." We always thought that this guy had some connection with the Communist Party. He hired everything black that came in. Martina went to him and she said, "I have a friend who wants to work in the factory and she's been coming and coming and they never will hire her." He said, "Tell her to come. I'll hire her." So he hired me. When I walked in the door of the plant I said, "I'm going to make you sorry for every day that I walked around to this shop hoping to get hired!"

I worked on the carburetors. I was on an assembly line that had two sides and a belt ran down the center and I was burring—taking all of the burrs off the carburetor. Right across from me was a young Polish woman named Eva. She was going to show me how to do it. We did about ten of them. Then I said, "You don't have to help me any more." She said, "Do you think that you can keep up with the line?" "I can keep up with the line." So I did. Eva and I became real good friends because when she got stuck I would reach over and help her.

One night she said, "There's a union meeting tonight. Will you go with me to the union meeting?" And I said, "Ahh, I'm tired." She said, "Aw, come on and go." She said, "I want to buy you a drink anyway," because I had helped her. I said, "OK, you can buy me a drink but I don't want to go to a union meeting."

So we went to this tavern and then we started talking union. I got kind of high, you know, and "OK, we'll go to the union meeting."

This was United Automobile Workers. I was the only black there. All the stewards were coming in and saying how they couldn't organize the workers: "I can't get anybody to join"; "So-and-So said the union is no good . . ."

I said, "You know why you can't get anybody to join? Because you don't have anything to sell them. You aren't selling them union. You're letting them sell you non-union from what I hear you saying here. You'll never get the workers to join the union if you let them tell you the union isn't any good. I wouldn't join a union that's no good either." A steward must sell the union, telling the workers how much strength they have when they are organized.

I looked at this guy who was the organizer and his face was just lighting up. "Union! What do you mean? I'll bet you if I was the steward I could sign them up." The next day I was elected steward of my department. Two nights later everybody in that department was signed up.

I only joined the union for what it could do for black people. I didn't care anything about whites. I didn't care if they lined them all up and shot them down—I wished they would! I had no knowledge of the unity of white and black. I had no knowledge that you can't go any place alone. The only thing that I was interested in was what happened to black people.

Of about three thousand, twenty-five per cent were blacks. Ninety per cent were women. I was making ninety cents an hour—great big money! I never thought I would live to make that much money.

When the union thought they were ready they notified the Labor Relations Board and an election was held in the shop. The union won. Then we were going to have an election of officers for the union. I was nominated for financial secretary. I didn't know how to account or keep books and I didn't want to be bothered but I accepted the nomination.

Then Mamie Harris came to me and tried to convince me that I shouldn't run for office. I said, "What do you mean I shouldn't run for office?" (She had somebody else all picked out to be financial secretary.) "Why shouldn't I run? I have been nominated and I have accepted and my name is going to be on the ballot and why in the hell should I take it off?" She said, "Well, do you know how to keep books?" I said, "No, I don't know how to keep books? Do you?" She said, "Yes." "Well, didn't you have to learn? So, I'll learn." She never got around to telling me why I shouldn't run.

Then I went back and told the guys Mamie Harris had told me not to run and that did it! "Discrimination! We got to get her!" From then on the campaign became black against white.

I probably would not have won except that everybody on the night shift was going to vote for me because I was known. I became shop committeewoman when I was working nights and I never lost a case. I settled almost every case on the first phase of the grievance procedure because the foreman knew that I wasn't going to let up. I was going all the way up to the top—arbitration, anything. We always took the worker in when there was a grievance they brought. They saw how we fought. They'd come out and tell it. "You better join the union. I mean because if you get in trouble, Sylvia goes in there and wrecks the place. You better join." So everybody knew me.

The night shift was smaller than the day shift. If everybody on the day shift had voted, they probably would have beaten me. But the day shift didn't come out to vote in as large numbers as the night shift. The night shift didn't have anything to do but go to the union hall. They couldn't go home washing and ironing and cooking and scrubbing at that time in the morning. They had plenty of time, so they all came to vote.

I won by two measly votes. Then they demanded a recount. I won by one vote. The director of the region took me under his wing.

I didn't know what to do and they were sending guys in from downtown to help me.

We had the reputation with the international for being a good local. In fact, the region gave a party for our local because we kept 90% signed up. With the turnover being what it was in those days, we still kept 90%. We were a well-organized local.

We never had check-off. We didn't want it. We said if you have a closed shop and check-off, everybody sits on their butts and they don't have to worry about organizing and they don't care what happens. We never wanted it.

One day a black guy came there looking for a job—one of the skilled jobs. Mamie was called because they were going to hire him. If they hired him, the guys said, they would walk out. But [the company] wanted to hire him because they needed him and he came well recommended. Mamie said, "Fine." So she went back in and said, "He's coming here to work. Anybody that doesn't like it if a black person comes in this shop can leave right now. Turn in your union cards and get the hell out. Go." But nobody left. The guy came and he worked. Two days later he was friendly with one, and the next day with another. Soon he was getting along very well.

So this made me take a little notice of Mamie. She wasn't so bad. She was fighting for the black people so I said, "That gal is all right."

Then another thing came up with another young woman, Selma. They were having a cutback. In our contract it said that you could be cut back to the highest skill and nothing more. The highest skill for Selma was in a department where there had never been any blacks. Selma was a fiery little thing and she was single-minded that she go in there. Here too, they said that if Selma came in, they would walk out. This was on the night shift. I went down there and I said, "If you walk out, fine. We'll fill your places before you get home." They were going to wait and see Mamie in the morning. Mamie told them the same thing. They stayed. Nobody left. About two weeks later, there was an opening for a steward and they nominated Selma to be steward. Selma was elected.

The night Selma was elected I was really tired. I was sitting in the office waiting to go and Mamie came over and said, "I have

a friend who is having a party. I'd like you to go to the party with
me." I wasn't going to go to a party with white folks! She had
to be kidding. I said, "I don't want to go." She said, "Why not?"
I said, "I just don't go to parties with white folks. I've never been
to one." She said, "But there's going to be colored people there
too." I said, "This I have to see."

We went to the party and I enjoyed it. They were writing a letter
to someone's husband who was in the Army. Everybody had to sign
it. "Well, he won't know me," I said. So Mamie said, "Put down
that you're Sylvia Woods and he doesn't know you but he's going
to know you when he comes home."

Mamie had done these few things and I had begun to like her.
She got in my good book. From then on she was instrumental in
teaching me the need for unity between black and white, who was
the enemy, because I thought the white people were our enemy
—every white worker in America. And she taught me that that
was not so. My attitude about black and white changed when I saw
what Mamie was doing.

The next year when election time came up nobody ran against
me but somebody ran against Mamie and I got more votes than she
did. Then I began to see that if I could win an election and get
more votes than Mamie with only twenty-five per cent blacks in
there, if every single black person voted for me I still could not
have won the election, no matter what. So all these white people
had to vote for me. Now this is something. I began to think "Now
why are they voting for me? Why?" And then, "They're voting
for you because you're fighting for them."

We had one guy from Tennessee who went down south and over-
stayed his vacation. He didn't send a telegram. He came back and
the company fired him. We got his job back with back pay. Then
after the union got him back in the shop, he didn't want Selma in
this department. I was for going down there and throwing him out
bodily and Mamie said, "Let's not do it like that." (We became
a really good team. I would fly off, she would rub me down. When
she would get mad, I'd say, "Just a second, Mamie . . .") Mamie
said, "I'll write him a letter." She wrote him a letter and she said
that the union spent half of whatever the arbitration cost was to get

him back in the shop. . . . Well, that guy changed and he worked
for Selma. He became one of the best union members in the shop.
We threw a party one night and he came—this southerner who didn't
want a black to do anything—he brought his wife and children. We
used to call him Tennessee. I danced with him that night. It was
really something.

We used to have a lot of absenteeism and we took the position
that you can't fire anybody for being absent. We would tell them,
"You don't have to tell any lies. You don't have to make up any
excuses. If you're tired and you are absent, you just put down
'Tired.' " The foreman would say, "But you can't say . . ."
"But, that's the only reason I was off. I was tired. I worked seven
days straight for three months without a day off, so I am tired."

Every night I would have departmental meetings. The women
were coming off the night shift at three o'clock in the morning. They
didn't have to go home, so this was some recreation for them. We'd
have beer and sandwiches and coffee and cake or whatever. We'd
sit there and eat and talk. People would voice their grievances about
the shop, home, family or whatever. They'd love to come. Every
night we met, department by department. This kept us organized.

We had good union meetings too. We would have speakers. Either
I would speak or Mamie would speak or we would invite a speaker
to come in. We would talk about trade unionism. How were trade
unions organized? What was the very beginning? How come they
were organized? We would talk about the structure of the international union, how it was set up and how it worked and why it worked
like it did, how the CIO was born. We would have a question period
where the workers could ask questions. We would discuss current
events.

We had social things too. We had a picnic and a big Christmas
dance every year. We organized a horseback riding team.

We stayed there until the day the plant closed down. I'll never
forget the day the plant closed down. Everybody came to work and
there we didn't have any job. I wasn't so worried about my not
having a job. I wondered, "What am I going to do without these
people?" Everybody just stood around the gate.

Two years after the plant closed up, we still had union meetings.

We would have full crowds. We were fighting for [unemployment] compensation. We made ninety cents an hour and some, of course, made more. You would go to get your compensation and they'd offer you a job. You weren't supposed to take a job that was less than the rate you had been getting. We would fight these cases. They would throw them out and we would go down to the arbitration board and fight the cases and win them. We could call a union meeting and bring in maybe seventy-five per cent of our plant two years after it closed down. We had representation in the international because we still had the workers together.

The main thing that I would say is that you have to have faith in people. You know, I had very little faith in white people. I think that I had faith in black people. But you have to have faith in people, period. The whites, probably a lot of them feel towards blacks like I felt. But people, as a rule, come through.

You have to tell people things that they can see. Then they'll say, "Oh, I never thought of that," or "I have never seen it like that." I have seen it done. Like Tennessee. He hated black people. A poor sharecropper who only came up here to earn enough money to go back and buy the land he had been renting. After the plant closed he went back there with a different outlook on life. He danced with a black woman. He was elected steward and you just couldn't say anything to a black person. So, I have seen people change. This is the faith you've got to have in people.

The big job is teaching them. And I was not patient. That is another thing, you must be patient. I just didn't have any patience. If a worker did something, "To hell with you. You didn't come to the last union meeting, so don't tell me when you have a grievance. You just handle it the best way you can by yourself." But you can't do that. "You better go talk to Mamie Harris because I don't talk to non-union people and folks who don't come to the union meeting. Don't talk to me." This I learned was wrong. You have to be patient with people. People have to learn and they can't learn unless we give them a chance.

MARIO MANZARDO

MARIO MANZARDO'S parents came from northern Italy. They brought with them to the United States a rich working-class culture. Among its heroes were the sixteenth-century philosopher Bruno, burned at the stake for affirming that the universe was infinite in extent, and Garibaldi, who led the nineteenth-century struggle for the unification of Italy. The family settled in the community of Pullman in South Chicago, Illinois, where the 1894 railroad strike led by Eugene Debs had originated.

In Pullman, Manzardo's father, together with his fellow-workers, friends and *paesani* (immigrants from the same region of Italy), continued to express joy and longing for social justice through cultural events of deep meaning to them personally and collectively. The meeting places of their fraternal societies often also served as headquarters for successive waves of working-class struggle. Christine Ellis, Stella Nowicki, and Nick Migas touch on the importance of this nationality group solidarity, but Mario Manzardo most fully describes the sense of roots, the atmosphere of trust, and the ready help which it provided.

Manzardo's account is also notable for its portrayal of the red-baiting in the union movement which followed World War II. He responded in a principled manner, yet without losing contact with the rank and file.

This account is drawn from three sources: two interviews we made with Mario Manzardo; an essay, based on similar interviews, by Gary Antlept; and an essay by Mario himself, entitled "For My Father—A Requiem."

MARIO MANZARDO

Liberi Cuori [Liberated Hearts]

I

I WENT TO WORK in 1927 for the Pullman Car Shops. My father and my brother worked at that plant. There I found out what it was to be a worker. Around 1880 the giant Pullman Car Works and the surrounding town had been built. The architecture was beautiful and the homes comfortable, but behind the facade of the buildings of Pullman the 12,000 people of the town were living in a paternalistic society created and controlled by George M. Pullman. He acted like a feudal baron. He selected his superintendents and foremen and also most of his workers from those ethnic groups which he considered the most desirable — primarily Anglo-Saxons.

When I worked in Pullman, there had been some changes. A few of the Polish, Greek and Italian workers had been made foremen, but one could still feel the aura of discrimination. The Pullman supervisors were still expert at weeding out the so-called malcontents.

It was the period when everybody was going for employees' representative plans [company unions]. They called it a union, but it wasn't. And I spoke up, without realizing that I was sticking my neck out: "Why don't we have a real union, from the outside, here?"

In this plant I realized what I had learned from my father, when I was a little kid. When I was young I didn't realize what was going on. But now it was beginning to catch up with me, and I had some talks with him. I began to realize that he had gone through many of these same things when I was just a youngster, four, five, six years old.

His father had been a Garibaldini. Grandfather was one of "the thousand" who had gone through all the campaigns of Garibaldi as a soldier. As an old man he'd sit in front of his door, in his chair, wearing his red Garibaldi shirt. He was senile, and he'd have tobacco juice and what-not on the shirt, but he wouldn't take his red shirt off—he was so proud of it. And he taught all his sons to be ardent fighters for freedom and equality in the spirit of Garibaldi, the great Italian emancipator. This was the tradition my father came from. I remember my grandfather in Italy, but I was only four years old.

My father worked in the paper mill in our town in Italy as a boy of twelve. He was a rag sorter. Later he worked with my uncles in his father's vineyards, and when *nonno* [grandfather] received a contract to haul the big heavy rolls of paper to Vicenza, Verona and Padova in the horse-drawn two-wheel carts of the period, my father then eighteen or nineteen became a regular driver.

A few years later he married. Mother, his childhood sweetheart, had also worked as a rag sorter at the age of eleven. Before leaving for America, my father was working at a small hydroelectric plant on the Astigo River. The pay was low. Times were bad. He dreamed of the New World and its promise.

In Chicago, Father worked in shops as a laborer, hauling material and sweeping floors; later, as a night watchman, and still later, an apprentice in a forge shop. Summers, often he would leave the shops and work "outside" in the building trades as a cement finisher. Sometimes he would leave home, joining a gang of Italian workers who spent a season or two working for contractors in Iowa or Minnesota paving the streets of an entire town. One time I went along as water boy. I will never forget the adventurous summer of 1920 in Pomeroy, Iowa: a boy and his father.

Eventually he settled down in the forge shop of the Pullman Car Works, a worker with three growing children, a mortgage on a Pullman house, a golden voice and a great love for opera.

Most of our *paesani* and friends were music lovers. They had formed amateur singing and dramatic groups, and performed in the local halls for over a quarter of a century. Often the proceeds of the singing and dramatic "festa" would go to labor causes: the Ettor and Giovannitti [leaders of the Lawrence, Massachusetts textile strike of 1912] defense; Sacco and Vanzetti; Tom Mooney, others. Father sang baritone, a sweet, lusty voice. He could sing the entire role of Rigoletto and performed duets with his friend, Gildo Padovan, a tenor. They sang from the music of Puccini, Donizetti, Verdi. Also I recall the clamorous applause received for the operatic or popular arias the other singers rendered. Together they sang beautiful stirring Verdi choruses as well as melodic mountain tunes of the Veneto [in northern Italy]. How well I remember the glorious workers' songs they sang: the "Inno dei Lavatori" ["Workers' Hymn"] and other union and Socialist anthems, the old patriotic "Inno di Garibaldi," "Fratelli d'Italia." These, my father sang together with his *paesani* and friends.

But more often they would get together in a home—many times ours—on cold winter Saturday nights. There were songs, new and old; chestnuts roasting in the oven; the Zinfandel wine flowing; black bitter coffee laced with *grappa* [grape brandy] and often a surprise: *Spaghetti al olio e sardella* at midnight.

My father was part of a vocal and organized minority in the Pullman community. Even the priest had to respect them. In the pre-World War I days, and during and for a little while after the war, the local church used to have a church feast every spring. This included the carrying of the saint on the shoulders of the devoted ones in a parade through the town, with the priest in front, and with firecrackers, and with all the sinners following, some of them walking on their bare knees to do penance. And my father and his bunch used to scoff at this. They would stand in front of their hall and hold up a big portrait of Giordano Bruno as the parade went by. The priest's face would show annoyance and anger but he didn't dare say anything, because this was a significant section of the community. My father and his friends didn't mind certain things about the church but they were anti-clerical. I remember my father being invited to sing a requiem in the church. He accepted, but he didn't like that which was medieval and out of touch with reality.

It was a period of struggle and change. My father and most of his friends were workers and trade unionists: a few apolitical, some religious, some Socialists, some anarcho-syndicalists, and later, some Communists. They had witnessed much history together. On the issues growing out of this history, my father and his friends did not always agree. In fact, they often argued vehemently. Sometimes they were split into several groups, each supporting his favorite cause with time, energy, and money. However, there was always general agreement on support of labor struggles in the United States. On one question there was no disagreement: *Noi siamo antifascisti* ["We are anti-fascists"].

In the spring of 1936, on the first day of May, my father joined the Italian chorus on the stage of the Venetian Hall in Kensington. On this gala occasion they sang:

> *Vieni, o Maggio; t'aspettan le genti,*
> *Ti salutano i liberi cuori,*
> *Dolce pasqua dei lavatori.* . . .

> [Come, oh May Day; the people await you,
> The liberated hearts salute you,
> Sweet Easter of the working class. . . .]

This was the last time my father sang in public.

It happened at work in the shop just before the noon whistle. They carried him home on a litter. "Cerebrovascular hemorrhage," the doctor said. "Keep him quiet. Don't waste your money on a hospital. Nothing can be done." We propped him up in bed to make him comfortable. His mute mouth attempted a twisted smile.

We rolled the old victrola to the door of the bedroom. After winding the old spring motor I carefully placed the needle into the groove. The record was a favorite operatic aria. Tears welled up into his eyes. We turned off the disc fearing we had caused trauma. He moved his good arm up and down, beating against the mattress. His intelligent eyes became opaque as with anger. I placed the needle back in the groove and the music started again. His eyes cleared. His lips attempted to form the words he had sung numberless times. But no sound came out of his mouth.

II

During the early 1930s, I was part of the time in Wisconsin and part of the time in South Chicago. My parents had first sent me to Wisconsin during the summer when I was a boy, to improve my health. They sent me to a part of Marinette County where there were other Italians with whom my father had once thought of buying land.

The farmers set up roadblocks on highway G between Loomis and Marinette when there was delivery of milk to the condensery. The family I stayed with was not involved because they made cheese out of their own milk. But I would go along with the other farmers.

You had this kind of situation. When I went up there I had some stickers which said, "Save the Scottsboro Boys," and I put them around in different places. They condemned this. They didn't want anything to do with it, or with some of the other things that were going on in the cities. But when it came to their own struggles even the most conservative were militant. They would have their meetings in the Grange Hall, or one of the other halls. And they would discuss the problem of stabilizing or increasing the price of milk, because in some cases they weren't even making the price of the feed which they gave the cattle for the milk.

They formed a very loose organization, but when it came to setting up these roadblocks, they were there. They even brought guns. They were that serious. They had cars and trucks by the side of the road, and when a milk truck came by it was "Stop! Where are you going? What are you doing?" If the driver didn't turn right around and feed the milk to his hogs, it was dumped on the road. In a majority of cases they turned around.

This only lasted a few weeks, because the government began to respond. Traditionally most of the farmers had been followers of LaFollette but now they supported F.D.R. and the New Deal.

When I came back to Chicago I got involved in the unemployed struggles in South Chicago. All over the area are halls which had been the headquarters of many organizations, many struggles, which the unemployed now used. At 8743 Buffalo Avenue is Linnea Hall which Foster used as his headquarters for U. S. Steel South Works during the 1919 steel strike. In the '30s it was in turn a headquarters for the unemployed, and a headquarters for the Steel Workers Organizing Committee until shortly after the Memorial Day Massacre. Right now it's a Baptist black church. Then there is the famous Turner Hall, where Debs spoke, where Carlo Tresca spoke, where Elizabeth Gurley Flynn spoke, where a whole series of people spoke up and down the history of the last hundred years of labor. Right across the street from it used to be the headquarters of the American Railway Union during the Pullman Strike of 1894. That's gone now, torn down.

Then there's the SFBI hall: Societa Filarmonia Bel' Italia. They sponsored a brass band. We had parades in Roseland in '32, '33, '34, '35, '36, five years of parades on May Day, and they were always led by this band. It's now reduced to a coffee club of a few old-timers. But in its day it was a very important organization among the North Italians and the headquarters of many other smaller organizations, mutual aid societies from each area of Italy. The Italians were organized in the form of these societies, 200 to 300 persons, 50 to 60 families, which would give out a little money when they were hospitalized, maybe a little money when they died. About half a dozen of them met in the SFBI hall.

The largest of these modest organizations was the Liberty Club. Later on, some of the members of this club formed the Matteotti Society which was Socialist-dominated. However, the giant among the mutual aid societies was the Venetian Union. In the 1920s they built their own large hall. With 2000 member families it dominated the area. They even rented space to a rival organization which had national ties, the Order of the Sons of Italy in America. Both were apolitical though some leaders were openly pro-fascist.

For a few years in the 1930s there was also formed the Centro Operaio di Roseland (Worker's Center). This became the anti-fascist headquarters, uniting workers under the influence of Socialists, Communists, and anarcho-syndicalists.

Through their language organizations, the workers donated halls for meetings of the unemployed. Some of the halls were even soup kitchens. The one at 104th Street and Michigan Avenue, headquarters of several Lithuanian workers' cultural societies, became a soup

kitchen, where, through the administration of the language organizations and the unemployed councils, surplus food from the government was distributed to hundreds of people every day. Whole
families would come over for their main meal of the day.

That's how we got to know people, including the people who later
became the leaders of the Farm Equipment Union out that way, and
the people who got on the staff of the Steel Workers Organizing
Committee in that area. One fellow in particular was very active
in the Public Works Administration. They were paving streets, a
government project. He and others led a strike of the workers for
better conditions and better pay. The strike was won. His name
became quite famous. He was a left-wing radical. Later on he got
on the staff of the swoc, and he was one of the fellows that got
hold of me and put me on the staff, too.

III

There were about twenty or twenty-five locals of the Steelworkers
Union in the Roseland-Harvey-Chicago Heights sub-district, just
west of South Chicago, I helped organize during 1936, 1937, and
part of 1938. There was the Pullman Manufacturing Company where
I had worked in the 1920s. There was Acme Steel in Riverdale;
Buda; Bliss and Laughlin; Brassco, and the stove works; Western-
Austin and Perfection Gear; and some others I can't remember in
Harvey. Also Calumet and Inland in the Heights; International Har-
vester's West Pullman Parts plant, Chicago Malleable Castings,
Allied Castings; these are some of the shops and I could name a
dozen or so more around Blue Island, Roseland, Pullman, and so
on.

I remember those mornings in the spring of 1937. Three, four
cars would start from the old headquarters on Michigan Avenue in
Roseland. There would be about six organizers from the union and
six volunteers. We broke open the bundles of *Steel Labor*, inserted
the leaflets and retied them with twine, placed the bundles in the
trunks of the cars and off we'd go to the plant gates to catch the
day shift going in.

We'd park on 155th Street and after a short consultation among
ourselves we'd go to the gates, two at the stove works, three at

Bliss, three at Western-Austin and four at Buda. We'd catch a few
going out and the main shift going in. Most would smile and take
the literature. A few would look angry or cuss and say, "Keep it,
we don't need you," but most of the fellows were eager for it and
would holler, "Good work, boys!" Volunteers never distributed in
front of the shop where they worked. That way the company men
could not report them. When all the literature was distributed, back
to the cars and breakfast at the Swedish restaurant in Roseland.

We followed up the distribution of literature by meeting with key
workers from inside the plant. Naturally the very first meetings were
secret. Maybe only five or six people from a department met to discuss how to get the whole department to join the union. We would
get together in homes, basements, in the back of taverns.

We designated certain key workers as officers of a new local.
They then asked for, and signed, a charter. Then we began to coach
them on how to conduct a meeting, how to keep track of their
records, how to send in their reports, and so forth, just the servicing
work of an organizer until they stood up on their own feet.

The local to which I later belonged was called Security Lodge
of the Amalgamated Association of Iron, Steel and Tin Workers of
North America. How do you like that for a name? I might explain
that in the early days of the swoc we used the old Amalgamated
Association's charters, also their recruiting cards and meeting manu-
als. In those days, the meetings had to be conducted according to
the ritual in the manual. Everything was stiff and formal. The meetings were called to order by Jordan Perry, the first president. He
wore a derby and often would forget to remove it. I got a big bang
out of watching Jordan up there, flustered and embarrassed and
stumbling over the words. One time, he put the manual down, glared
at all of us in the room, turned to the sub-district leader and said,
"To hell with this crap, this meeting's open."

With all our inexperience with unions, locals were organized,
officers were elected, and dues were collected. The stewards did
that job once a month and, by George, most fellows came across
with their dollar. A few would give us trouble, but the great majority
saw the benefits the union brought into the shop with their own eyes.

Where the locals had people who had been apolitical in the past or who were interested strictly in what was going on in the shop, their activities were restricted to that. But in some cases locals had within them people from the various language organizations that had been influenced by radicals. They would sing labor songs. One of them wanted the union to learn how to sing "The Internationale." We had to tell them, "Look, let's keep that out of here." But they sang "Solidarity Forever," "Hold the Fort," and a lot of other union songs.

Local leadership was coming forward. A few of us attempted to get hold of some of these leaders and give them an idea that what we were trying to do was not just build the union, but build a movement of the people—a movement that affected all aspects of their lives, and also their whole outlook, their philosophical outlook. In short, we tried to radicalize some of these people, to a greater degree than union life had radicalized them.

In this we weren't too successful. We had a few successes. Some of them remained honest, sincere workers who knew what the score was for the balance of their lives. But some of them would not go along with this kind of thinking and would go back to their narrow, trade union, bread-and-butter type thinking, and looked upon trade unions as a stepping stone to personal success. Our main concern was to make radicalism, or progressivism, or whatever you want to call it, a way of life for these union people.

We would have, let's say, a half a dozen of these people together in a circle. On a couple of occasions I thought that the people who helped me organize these things would back me up, but they didn't, they backed down, which left me holding the bag as the alleged theoretician of the outfit, which I really wasn't.

I think one mistake we made was in trying to disillusion them with existing status quo politics, at the same time not pointing out clearly the steps that you could take from status quo politics into a more progressive kind of politics. Instead we said, "You've got to jump from one to the other," and people didn't know how to make that jump. You've got to have highways, you've got to have bridges, from one point of view to another point of view. The bridges have to be well laid out, so that people can walk over them calmly, without too much emotional strain, without feeling that they are getting into something where the Un-American Committee would be after them and the FBI would start chasing them. "Yes, at a certain point there is a chance that, if you become a well-known leader, some of the monitor groups may try to see what they can do. But don't be frightened. This happens all over." We could have talked to them this way. But somehow we didn't do it right. I think that if we had it to do over again, we could find better ways.

I was laid off by the Steelworkers Union after the Little Steel strike. During the next few years I had many jobs. For instance, a young man got me into a book bindery, on 13th and Michigan Avenue. They were all kids in there, young men and women. We learned how to bind books with the bone, and the glued paper. I ran the paper through the glue machine, let it lay there until it hardened and got tacky, and they used it to cover the boards of the books.

They were ripe for a union so we contacted a union in Chicago, the United Paperworkers Union. I got into a little trouble with those union fellows. Right away they wanted dues. I said, "First let's organize, then we'll talk about dues." So we got in cards and about five of us organized the place in two weeks time. At the end of the two weeks I was fired. They made a Labor Board case out of it and I won the case. I got something like $350 back pay, and the right to go back to work in the plant. I had already gotten a job so I didn't go back. But the Paperworkers Union sent me a bill, for dues! I was still paying dues to the Steelworkers. So I wrote to them very scathingly and said, "How about organizing pay?"

Then I had some experiences in organizing Campbell Soup for the Cannery Workers. There were a lot of women working there. They had a lot of wildcats before the plant was even organized. I was in charge of getting out their bulletin. And I remember one particular issue where I made a big article on "Sweat-Sweetened Soup." When they opened up the big pots they made the soup in, the workers were so hot the sweat would go from their brows into the soup. And the workers told us that when the tomatoes would go through the belt line, they couldn't clean out all the bad tomatoes: they could only do it now and then. As a result, many worms, and bugs, and even mice got into the soup. So Campbell's Soup was not the pure soup that you read about. Shades of *The Jungle*!

In 1940 I went back to work at the Buda plant. This was a Steel-workers local which I had helped organize back in 1937. I remained there until I got out on pension in 1970. I was financial secretary of my local, I was recording secretary, I was on the grievance committee, and often on the negotiating committee. I was among the leaders of that local since its inception, as an organizer, then servicing it and later as a worker in the shop. In those thirty years I've seen executive committees come and executive committees go.

During the war, I was a delegate to the state CIO convention. It was 1943 and I was elected to the state executive board. They wanted two people from steel. Four people were nominated; I was one of them and I accepted. Somehow the forces representing the district leadership got confused and I won. The district leadership was mad as hell. I only served on that board about four months and then was drafted into the Army where I remained for two and a half years. What happened right after the war was already laid down in the minds of some of the people at that time.

After the war, against the advice of my family I went back to the plant. I had the opportunity to do other things: go back to school on the G.I. bill; or go into business with some wealthy relatives. With my eyes wide open I chose the role of a worker in the plant and playing there a part in the local union.

We had a progressive local. At that time we formed a council of Steelworkers locals in Harvey, but they would allow only one council for a county so the Chicago council took over. We had a strong womens' auxiliary, which played a strong role in the strikes of 1946 and thereafter, and there were also women in the plant. It was a local that would send delegates to many things that other locals wouldn't. For example, I went a couple of times as a delegate to get-togethers of the National Negro Congress, which was a forerunner to many of the present organizations.

Of course, later we ran into trouble. I ran into personal trouble, too, where I was brought up on charges for being too far out in left field. The staff man assigned to my local—it was the same man who had led the sewer workers' strike and recruited me for the SWOC—put me on trial for running for office in the local when the constitution of the Steelworkers Union says that no Communist, fascist, or what not, can be an officer in this union. He said, "You can't be." I said, "Why?" He said, "You were in the YCL [Young Communist League]." I said, "But you were a well-known member of the CP." "Yeah," he said, "but I am no longer." "Well," I said, "you want to know if I'm still in the YCL? I'll tell you. I'm too old." Anyway, he put me up on charges and we had a trial. The executive board supported me. In fact, I became financial secretary of the local.

But aside from the question of our political outlooks lay the deeper question of what was going on in America. My father's generation had gone through some rough times, especially during the Sacco-Vanzetti days and the Palmer raids when immigrants who subscribed to socialist or other radical papers or who voiced anti-capitalist opinions were hounded; some were deported.

In my generation we often faced red-baiting, but the creation of second-class citizenship for radicals within the unions and the signing of non-Communist affidavits were no ordinary "contratempo," as the Italians would say—not ordinary bad times, but a time for clear thinking.

As I saw it, unionists should reject the whole idea of two types of membership, one from which leadership would be chosen and one that could only pay dues. Also, the charge that radicals were working against the interest of the unions had to be rejected. When John L. Lewis formed the SWOC he hired the men and women necessary to do the job regardless of their political background. All made many contributions, some of them at great personal sacrifice. The Communists were among the most dedicated. As I saw it, neither the Congress of the United States, nor the union leadership through a steamroller at a convention, had the moral right to pry into the political philosophy of workers.

This is an inalienable right which my friend, the organizer, couldn't see. He figured he had cleansed himself by washing his linen in public. Cleansed himself of what?

It seemed to me further that union leadership should be judged on the basis of work done to promote the welfare of the union membership, and not on the basis of an individual's politics.

I remember how within three, four weeks the atmosphere changed. A delegation of CIO leaders led by James Carey came back from a trip to the Soviet Union for the CIO, and put out a report. They didn't say it was a workers' paradise but presented it as a country that was doing something for the people. They had some good words to say about the unions there. We distributed the report in our local union meetings. And then, about a month later, we had a banquet and Van Bittner from the Steelworkers Union got up and attacked the Soviet Union and every one gave him a big hand. The climate changed overnight. This was in 1948, when [Henry] Wallace ran for president.

Then came the Taft-Hartley Act. It required that the officers of trade unions, including local trade unions, sign non-Communist affidavits. I was an officer of my local, and had been active in the Wallace campaign. I felt that none of us should sign and I got some of the other officers to go along with the idea. But they changed their minds later. Only the top officers were required to sign: if it had extended to grievance men and stewards, there were plenty that would not have signed, and would have gone along with me. The district laid down the law that it had to have the signatures of the three or four top officers. "We're waiting for them," they said. "We've got to have them. Send them in." And I was delaying it.

Finally, I said I wasn't going to sign. It was just stubbornness. I made a statement to the executive board of the local, which passed it on to the membership, that I wouldn't sign a Taft-Hartley affidavit because it was impinging on my freedom of association, my freedom of thought, that I would be tying myself down because I think certain ways and I would have to sign that I wouldn't think those ways, and I can't control my thoughts. Thought control I wouldn't go for, and that's why I wouldn't sign. I said, "I have nothing against those who will sign, because they're doing it for the practical purpose of maintaining a consistent leadership in the local union." I said, "I feel that leadership is a good leadership, and at this point, if I have to sign something against my conscience to remain in this leadership, I'd rather not remain in the leadership and play a role lower down in the organization." They accepted that.

I assumed the leadership at the lower level where I didn't have to sign. The officers invited me to all executive board meetings, and I played a role among the stewards. Later on the Taft-Hartley affidavits became unimportant and were no longer enforced, and I ran for office and became part of the executive board again until I retired.

IV

The leadership of the unions today is not the same type of leadership as in the 1930s. In fact the union turned out to be the training ground for some of the supervisors and some of the superintendents and some of the foremen and even some of the engineering people. They first worked, and they became stewards and grievance men, and then later on went on to jobs with the companies. Many times the companies will take aside the strong members of the union and say, "Look, we've been watching your progress and we think if you keep it up you'll make foreman or superintendent within a year." Now, this offer of personal advancement many times can affect how hard this union member will, let's say, push a grievance. After all, the company may not give him this job if he fights too hard. Many times the company will do this to weaken the union.

You come across workers who will say, "You know, we ought to eliminate the dues check-off because dues check-off puts the burden of collecting dues on the company, and the steward doesn't go around and talk to the people and find out their gripes."

My answer to that is, you should have stewards at a departmental level always available to the workers. In the plant where I worked we never had more than twenty-five or fifty workers without a steward. Each shift had a steward for each particular line or group of workers. When you had 1500 workers and you had thirty or forty stewards you had enough to take care of the situation. So that a worker couldn't say, "I can't see a steward for days at a time." You could see him.

And we had a separate steward body that ran independent of the officers. They used to call their own meetings at their own time. We requested grievance committeemen to volunteer to attend the meetings of the stewards, not to dominate, just to listen and to answer questions whenever called upon. But the chief steward and assistant chief steward ran their own meetings. They would meet once a month or sometimes more if necessary and they would order their own refreshments and sometimes even have their own little stag party.

Capitalism has a way of influencing people and buying them out, whether they're bought out with cash or prestige. There is an English movie, "Fame is the Spur." It's the story of an English labor leader [Ramsey Macdonald] who was an honest labor leader until he started rubbing shoulders with the elite in the country, and he ends up being given a lordship and having sold out workers all the way down the line. He became isolated, his wife left him and his children hated him, his friends he had no more. What did he have but a peership and the love and admiration of the lords of the clubs? He didn't have anything else, his life was empty. And he became aware of it. In the end he realized what caused it. Most of them don't.

Take David J. McDonald, the second international president of the Steelworkers Union. He was an assistant to the first president, Philip Murray. Murray was quite an honest guy, a good leader. Unfortunately, near the end of his life he fell for the red-baiting business, too. That was the way of the times and he went for it. Well, David J. McDonald took over and the first thing you know McDonald started developing what we called "tuxedo diplomacy": rubbing shoulders with the big corporation owners, visiting in steel mills together with the president of U. S. Steel. They voted him out of office. Everybody did.

But David J. McDonald went on to write an autobiography that was out of this world. He claimed everything in the first person: "I did this, and I did that, and I did the other." He didn't do any of these things. It was all done by other people, mostly local leaders, rank and filers, radicals among them. He didn't single-handedly organize. This is history twisted around, history which is written from the viewpoint of: "I walked into the room and I looked at these corporation heads and I had anger in my eye and they saw it. And they then knuckled down and signed this contract. I went out of that room and I went to the workers and I announced, 'They signed. They gave in.' " Is this history? He went in and terrorized them and they gave in and signed. That's not history, that's egotism. History is where you show that workers through their militancy, their picket lines or their demands or their continuous agitation, forced an issue.

I was just a guy at the level of the local union or at the level of a staff organizer, and briefly on the state CIO council. But I think it was guys in the position of myself, hundreds of thousands of guys in the position of myself, who helped establish these unions. For that I take a little credit, but only to the extent I was able to, not any more than that. I don't want to exaggerate my role or that of any of the people I worked with.

BURR McCLOSKEY

B
URR McCLOSKEY came to the conclusion that workplace organizing around economic issues could not in itself produce a
political movement for comprehensive change. In 1946 he
joined with John C. Green, an elderly agitator who had been a delegate to the founding convention of the IWW, to form the United Labor
Party.

The United Labor Party was based in Akron, Ohio, where the first
sit-down strike took place in the rubber plants in 1936. The party ran
working people for City Council and Congress on a platform which
opposed racism and the Korean War, and called for nationalization
of basic industry. At its height it received about 10,000 votes in
Akron. It had branches in several other communities, and had given
a certain impulse to a national movement for libertarian socialism,
before it died in the early 1950s.

The ULP is described by John Barbero, Ed Mann and others (pages
265–284. John Barbero and Ed Mann were members of the ULP).
The present account describes Burr McCloskey's personal development.

There is a good deal of kinship between the approach to action
of Burr McCloskey and his friends, and that of the New Left of
the 1960s. The ultimate value was not to be pushed around: to take
shit from no man, as Burr McCloskey puts it, or in the language

of sds, to participate in the decisions that affect one's life. Central both for McCloskey and the New Left, as for the iww before them, was the notion that the best way to communicate an idea is to act it out.

BURR McCLOSKEY

I Appeal the Ruling of the Chair

SOMETHING MAKES A RADICAL, in every time and place. You can't be for any kind of a program different from the prevailing main stream unless you have the capability to resist the status quo. You don't have the right to a dissenting point of view unless you're prepared to fight for it. That was the main thing in our militant history. I think it's mostly a matter of chemistry, but the chemistry, of course, is stimulated by specific events.

I learned how to fight as a wee boy because my name is Burr, and my father's name was Burr. The popular cant is that Aaron Burr was a traitor, and my lovely chums in grammar schools across the country used the cant to malicious advantage. I had to fight because I knew better. In my family the saying around the Sunday dinner table was that the only mistake Burr made in killing Hamilton was that he should have done it twenty years sooner. I still believe this. There was a national debt, an Eastern establishment: it all goes back to Hamilton. He was a pimp for Washington at Valley Forge. He should have been killed twenty years sooner. American history is so distorted that it still isn't nice to say this in polite society.

Akron, Ohio is a very important part of the story. It represents one of the mythologies of America, the melting pot. Nothing ever melts, you see. Because of its hillbilly tradition, Akron had the strongest, most militant, unadulterated strain of Protestant Anglo-Saxon whites in a very, very difficult industry. I've worked in rubber and I've worked in steel, I've worked in the Teamsters and I've worked with District 50 of the Mine Workers, and nothing touches the rubber shops in those days for what we used to call "rawhide" labor.

I grew up with an uncle who was treasurer of the Goodyear Tire and Rubber Company until it was reorganized, and the banks took over, about 1924, and I resolved never to go into the gum mines. When I ran into the (what I considered) middle-class radicals in the early '30s, who almost idolized the working man and whose goal was to get into industry and become proletarianized, I said, "Bullshit!" I couldn't stand the smell of soapstone. I vowed when I was eleven years old that I'd never go into a rubber shop. Never wanted to. Never saw any great distinction in it. But I did. The current of the times pulled me in, just as it was going to pull me into the infantry later on.

I went into Goodyear. As I say, my uncle had been treasurer of Goodyear. My uncles, my father, my mother, my sister, all worked at Goodyear. So I ended up at Goodyear.

But my feeling toward Goodyear was not the same feeling that the hillbilly kids had, coming in from out of town and standing in line to get a job, making a dollar an hour for the first time in their lives. I was full of contempt for it from the very beginning. I knew, for example, that my mother never could keep a clean table because Goodyear was burning its filth and blowing it out its smokestacks right into our kitchen. I can't get excited about the newfound discovery of pollution because I grew up in it, and I knew who did it, and I knew why they did it, and I knew what it was doing to me, and my mother, and our food.

Goodyear, like all basic industry in the '30s, was waiting to be blasted out of medieval baronialism and my particular "sense of awareness" gave me a different point of view, for better or worse. Have you ever heard of the College of Complexes here in Chicago? I used to make it a practice to debate there once a year. And on one occasion my topic was "The Day American Labor Died." My oversimplified thesis was that American labor died the day the check-off went in, that once we lost the voluntary principle we were screwed like a Christmas goose. No way out. Unionism became an adjunct of the company, lock, stock and barrel, once the automatic check-off went into effect. During the session, the priest with whom I was debating, who had been working with the Chicano fruit pickers out West and was very much enamored of the class struggle as he was engaged in it, stopped in perplexity and said, "I have never met any one who was as disaffected as you are." Well, my alienation has always been the same since I was a small boy. The thing I believed in, and the reason I've been in the anti-Communist Party faction from the time I drew a political breath, was the old American "Don't tread on me" tradition. My Uncle Charley was an alcoholic follower of Gene Debs in Canton, Ohio. He rode the Red Special [the train Debs used in campaigning for president of the United States]; he had the greatest socialist library in Canton, which was a Socialist town. He was a reporter there when Debs made his famous speech which led to his imprisonment for opposing World War I. And Uncle Charley was always a hero of mine. The big thing about Uncle Charley, and about Debs, and about that whole tradition, was that you took shit from no man. And when the monolithic political movements came along, and you had to take a party name, and you spoke only when the chair recognized you, and you had to follow the party line, and you had to worship the shibboleths that they pre-fabbed for you, I was again alienated. There was no place for me in such a movement. It didn't matter to me whether it was Goodyear telling me how to vote or the break-off faction of the CP telling me how to vote.

My grandfather had run for councilman during the big Socialist upsurge of, I think, 1916. He ran as a Democrat and was defeated by a Socialist. And he was the kind of man that when the Ku Klux Klan marched down East Market Street, and we stood there watching it, all of them with their sheets on and the burning cross, he'd say, "Look at the shoes." I said, "What about the shoes, Granddaddy?" He said, "They're riffraff. You can tell by their shoes." So I was alienated even from that kind of proposition.

My father, who was crippled and alcoholic, wouldn't go on WPA. He was too proud to go on WPA. He didn't believe in taking help. He had been a salesman; he sold tires. He was a good salesman but he was pushed into the sales mold because he had a club foot. Alcoholics Anonymous started in Akron, and my father was one of the early recruits—prominent in AA until he died. He always regarded the Depression as his own personal fault, and refused to lump himself into an abstract statistic. We fought industrial fingerprinting at the beginning of the War for exactly the same reason.

My rebellion, if you want to call it that, began against the schools. I believe in nine-tenths of what Ivan Ilyich says about deschooling society. It's a horribly manipulative institution. And I led two school strikes before I was fifteen. I could do it because I was in a position of leadership, editor of the school newspaper, and so on. I confess that we used the fire alarm bell to get everybody out. We figured that once we got them out, we could keep them out. I was expelled. In fact, I was expelled several times. I wrote an editorial on syphilis, because a young freshman girl in our school developed syphilis when she bought an apple from an old vet in front of the school who was spitting on his apples to make them shine. I devoted the school paper to the signs and symptoms of syphilis, opening the door to sex education, and demanding that it be established as part of the regular curriculum. They wouldn't publish the paper. So I went down to the print shop—it was a contract shop, not a school print shop—and got the paper out, and bootlegged it.

One of the demands in our high school student union was, "Ask your teacher for his union card." I was a delegate to the Central Trades and Labor Assembly, representing a student union.

I joined the Young Peoples Socialist League. As a result, Akron was to have the largest YPSL group between New York and Chicago. I was recruited by a school teacher, Chalmers Stewart. He was one of three—another was B. J. Widick, who wrote the Reuther book and is a kind of mouthpiece for the UAW—who were very active in educating the first group of Akron labor leaders, when the CIO was first formed. They were the young intellectuals who went in and gave them classes on the labor theory of value, and the class struggle as the locomotive of history and so on. Along with Cannon and Shachtman they helped to set up the Socialist Workers Party in 1938. They were the so-called adult group in the Midwest. They got me, and I got the rest. Our membership was very bright, very brave. They came from a variety of family backgrounds—hillbilly, foremen's children, Jewish—the whole spectrum. High school, university, and dropouts, too.

I got the rest on the basis of militant activism, because we were going to do things. For instance, we agreed with the ıww in its free speech fights that the way to fight for free speech was not to talk about it but to do it. We did things in our own smart-assed way. The American Legion was sponsoring the head of the Un-American Activities Committee in Akron. We wanted to picket against it. The police refused us a permit. They said, "Look, the American Legion will crack your skulls, and after they get through the Akron cops will crack your skulls." We said, "Do we have a right?" They said, "Yes, you've got a right, but we're not going to give you a permit." So we said, "All right, we'll picket." We got our heads broken a little bit.

I was a senior in high school when the sit-down strike of 1936 happened. It was winter, Akron's coldest winter up to that time. They had shanties set up along the "longest picket line in the world," built out of waste wood. They each had a name: "Mae West," or "Orphan Annie," or "Toonerville Trolley." We used to sit in the huts and drink Dago Red and coffee with the guys on strike. And they held a mass meeting in Central High School auditorium. This was in my high school. And I'll tell you, watching them pour into that auditorium was like watching the storming of the Winter Palace. We had a lot of physical evidence to make us accept the doctrine of the class struggle. The only catch was that we wanted it to be *our* class struggle, not the property of a commissar.

And when they came down the street for a collection for the striking rubber workers, they went to the pool rooms, they went to the butcher shop, they went to my grandfather's store, and they went to the whorehouse. Everybody chipped in. Everybody knew, "These are our boys. If they don't make it, we don't make it." The idea of community solidarity was pretty well impressed on me at that time. In those days, when somebody carried the title of "committeeman" it had all the weight, in our neighborhood, of "councilman" or "alderman" today.

The big riot, where we took the bad licking, occurred in 1938. It happened on a Sunday at the Rialto Theater which was right across from Goodyear's one entrance. My father, my mother, my sister, and I were driving in from the country and when we got to the stop light we saw all these women running, with their heads flopping, because they'd all been billy-clubbed. My father and I got out of the car. We both were teargassed that night, badly. The battle was waged all night. Three were killed and hospital arrests numbered something like seven hundred. I did a couple of things that night that I'm quietly proud of. When we found out that fire engines were being used to bring in more tear gas and ammunition, we set up a barricade and stopped the fire engines. All through that night, my father said it, I said it, and I could hear all these rubber workers saying it: "This can't happen in America."

At that time there were men marching and drilling in basements all over Akron. We believed there would be armed civil war. You made no long-term plans. You never worried about family, you never worried about retirement. There was no point in thinking about college.

We didn't even worry about war. We knew the war was coming. From the time that the gunboat, the *Panay*, was sunk on the Yangtze River in 1937, we were saturated with a sense of inevitability about the second World War. There was no way to do anything but make a hopeless, desperate protest against it, because you knew it was a juggernaut that could not be stopped. We felt—I'm speaking for my peer group—that it was important to be your own man, to believe what you believed and speak out when you felt like speaking out; that in this terrible, suffocating cul-de-sac it was important to find something meaningful to do, that you planted your own garden even if the bombs were coming.

I decided to go into the rubber shops but I had a hard time getting in, because I was pretty well known. Since we believed in "open struggle," not conspiracy, we always had a good press in Akron and my file was voluminous. I got into the tire department at Goodyear by a fluke. Our whole fight then was to hold the meager advances that had been made. The six-hour day, for example—this became our major battle, lasting right into World War II. They put us on an eight-hour day without consulting us. We went in at the beginning of the shift and left two hours early. The next shift came in two hours late, so that there was a four-hour gap when the factory was open and nothing happened. Then they locked us out. So we set up our picket lines: "When one is locked out, everybody's out until everybody's in." In the papers we were Hitler's agents.

Along with trying to hold on to the six-hour day and these auxiliary privileges, I had another problem because they came around and wanted to solicit for war bonds. They got the union to be their collection agents. And I said, "I don't buy war bonds." They said, "We're going to have one hundred per cent." I said, "Well, you can lie about it but you're not going to have one hundred per cent." All my friends took the same position. "Are you a Jehovah's Witness?" they asked. "No," I answered, "I just don't believe the government's going to last." It was more than ironic when my own union brothers formed a "gate party," using goon squad techniques to try to force me into buying war bonds. They failed.

Finally Goodyear refused to let me work. They insisted that the union put me on trial, under the clause of the contract that read that the union will not open its membership to any "Nazis, Communists or others." I was an "other." I had to stand trial. The executive committee tried me without permitting me to appear in my own defense, and found me guilty. So I had to get the tire room out to the mass meeting which would ratify or overturn the executive committee's ruling. And they did overturn it. But by this time, because the executive committee had expelled me from the union, the company shut me out. And that night the draft board called me and said, "We understand you're not working." I said, "That's a contentious point. The company says I'm not, but I say I am. If you take one side or the other you're interfering in a labor dispute." That held them up for about four months. But the union bureaucracy failed to follow the membership mandate and refused to negotiate sincerely for my re-employment. So I was "out for real," and shipped for cannon fodder without as much as an Army induction physical. On a small scale, it reminded me of what happened earlier to a good buddy of mine, Clark Culver.

Culver was Canadian-born, a strong, laconic man. He had a massive forehead, inset eyes, and a muscle-clamping jawbone. He was a tire builder.

He was building passenger tires when Roosevelt's Section 7(a)
came along. There wasn't anything like a union at Goodyear at the
time except the company union, the Goodyear Assembly. Culver
happened to know Stanley Denlinger, an Akron criminal lawyer who
later went on John L. Lewis' staff. They got together and Culver
said, "Stan, tell me what this 7(a) means." Denlinger studied it
a day or two and then he said, "You can organize, the government
wants you to organize." So Culver rented a basement hall on
Goodyear Boulevard in East Akron and put out a call. Something
like a hundred tire builders showed up. Denlinger was there to tell
them what he had told Culver. They signed up.

The union kept multiplying, until finally they held a mass meeting
and elected Sherman Dalrymple as president, and Clark Culver as
secretary. In those days the secretary ran everything. The secretary
took their dues, had their names. The president just opened the meetings. Culver quit the plant because it was a full-time job. He was
the first full-time officer in the Akron rubber union. He gave up
ten years' seniority because the boys voted him to take a full-time
job with the new union.

After a few months the rubber workers felt ready for their own
international union. A meeting was called in Indianapolis to consider
getting out of the AFL. Culver was the delegate from the Goodyear
local. The local paid its per capita tax direct to William Green and
he loved all that dues money coming in from thousands of rubber
workers, so he said, "No, you can't have your own international."
The meeting in Indianapolis was supposed to be secret but all the
wire services were there, and when Culver got back to Akron the
shit had hit the fan.

Green sent a hatchet man named Coleman Claherty into Akron.
A mass meeting was called in the very hall where Culver had set
up the union and Culver was expelled for having been a delegate
to Indianapolis. The same men who had stomped and hollered when
they made him full-time secretary packed the hall to hear Green's
motion to expel him. Claherty said, "Clark Culver is as far out
of the American Federation of Labor as a Chinaman walking the
streets of Hong Kong." Culver waited for his chance to speak. He'd

stayed up all night planning his speech in self-defense. His wife, who had been to high school, helped him. But they ruled he couldn't say a word. A vote was taken with none dissenting, and he was out. After the meeting the guys were still coming up to Culver to pay their dues. They didn't know what had happened.

Because he was expelled he was out of work. He sold insurance for a while, and he didn't get back until the latter part of 1937. Because he was a new man, and had no seniority, he worked the night shift. His second night back on the job he heard that there was a big strike at the city waterworks. A CIO committeeman came down the line and said to him, "All union men at the waterworks first thing in the morning." The committeeman didn't know him from Adam. He was saying the same thing to everyone.

Culver hadn't been signed up yet in the CIO but he thought, "Well hell, I'm a union man, card or no card." So he drove up to the waterworks. It was still dark, but he could see a mass of men already there. A voice yelled, "CIO?" Culver yelled, "Yeah." They broke his nose, four of his ribs, shattered his collarbone, gave him a rupture and concussion of the brain. Only two CIO men had showed up, Culver and a man from National Rubber. The rest were all sheriff's deputies.

They took the two men down to the station and Culver demanded medical treatment. They said, "Sure." So two cops ran him up and down the three-story stairs of the city jail until he blacked out.

Then they brought down Denlinger, the same lawyer Culver had gone to about Section 7(a). The lawyer sprung the other guy, and then he said, "Clark, I can't touch you because you're not a member of the union."

He was one of my best friends in the Rubber Workers. I kept nominating him for president and he kept declining. He kept pushing me for president and I kept declining. Neither one of us would take the top job, or even run for it. When Clark and I went to union meetings we'd sit alone, because every man who had been in the union in the early days and knew what had happened to Clark, just didn't know what to do about it. He's not in labor's history books as a hero of any kind. He's just one of the anonymous guys who got every bone in his body broken. And his own men wouldn't help him. Clark died a premature death, the delayed effect of the awful beating he took at the waterworks.*

There was not the maturity in the CIO for any ideological organiza-tion, that I can see. Industry was so highly organized, and the human-kind involved were so not-ready-to-be-organized, yet we were forced into it. Union meetings were absurd. I can't tell you how many times I've appealed the ruling of the chair. Some stumpjumper would be up there shaking a gavel like every bureaucrat that'd ever preceded him, and people would be saying, "Isn't this a lovely meeting?" And I'd say, "I appeal the ruling of the chair." This wasn't always a safe thing to do. On one occasion the president came roaring down the aisle to attack me with the presidential gavel.

The real militants like Clark Culver ended up on the grievance committee. They were the job stewards, shop committeemen. The few, such as C. V. Wheeler or Ike Watson, who became local union presidents, were eventually torn apart by the tensions of an adminis-tration it was impossible to administer. With their help, however, we tried a good many thrusts to keep the union structure democratic. For example, we advanced the concept of rotation of officers: that you couldn't be out of the shop for more than eighteen months, because you'd forget what it was like unless you went back in. It failed utterly. The rank and file said, "What the hell! We train a man to be president, he might as well stay there. Why bring him back?"

To give you another example of the things we fought for, there

*Clark Culver is in labor history books but what they say about him is so incom-plete that it is actually misleading. Harold S. Roberts (*The Rubber Workers*, pages 108–109) and Irving Bernstein (*Turbulent Years*, page 102) tell the story of Culver's expulsion, and then state that William Green restored him to full membership privileges in his local. This statement leaves out the fact that "Culver was accepted into the union and promptly suspended again by the executive committee." (Federated Press dispatch, Feb. 15, 1934, Special Collections, Columbia University.) The state-ment also fails to consider that Culver had given up his job at Goodyear in order to work full-time for the union. Even had he been restored to membership in the union, unless he had also been restored to his position as secretary of the local he would have been out of work. As it was, having lost his seniority he was not called back to work (says McCloskey) until late in 1937.

was no smoking in the shop. I worked in the fifth floor tire room, and you had to go all the way down the stairs and walk about two city blocks to a railroad siding, where you could smoke. And we were all on piecework. The only way you could afford time for a smoke was if you had rates good enough to allow you to take the time off. You had to pay for your own sins. They sent around chow wagons, packaged foods. We never touched them. We'd shut our machines down, wash our hands and faces, go out of the plant and across the street and have a meal like a human being. We were allowed twenty minutes, but we took fifty and paid for it.

It was at that primitive level. You could talk to them about a lunch wagon, but on the political end of things, the sociological end of things, there was no dialogue. The night of Pearl Harbor, Sunday, December 7th, I was so goddamned mad that I said, ''Remember the Maine.'' And my boys turned on me and almost killed me. When big guys like that get mad at you, you're in trouble.

I'd argue economics. I'd say, ''I'm building the goddamned tire and the salesman that sells it will never see it and he's going to make more than I do. Something wrong with the set up, that's all.'' They'd say, ''You're making enough, you're making more money than the guy down on the other end.'' I could never get it beyond that level. Later, we'd bring scores of the best men down to the United Labor Party hall for a beer party, and we'd have a hell of a beer party. But the ratio was about one to a hundred in making a ULP-er out of them.

From this experience, I came to the conclusion that the Trotskyists were wrong in thinking that everything was going to be solved by economic organization. I and my confederates said, ''No, it's going to be solved politically.'' We hoped for a populist organization with a labor-anchored base. That was our theoretical platform. But it takes independent politics. You can't do it by a Political Action Committee. We pushed and pushed within our local unions for independent political action. Finally we decided it was like the free speech fights: there's no use talking about it, do it!

After the war I went back in the plant, at Firestone Steel. At the same time that we set up a credit union we demanded a sliding scale of wages and hours: as the available hours of work were reduced, the work force should be divided into those hours. We regarded this as a transitional demand. But Jesus, this threw you in the face of seniority. Our battle cry was "Solidarity Versus Seniority!" They said, "You youngsters don't have obligations. We gotta work more hours." We said, "Piss on you, we got the credit union for you. If you can't pay it back, we'll pay it back." But it didn't work. It was too divisive, too stratified, but we tried it.

I always knew in a fight—a picket line, or a union meeting, or a political faction struggle—whether somebody was on my side or not. You learn to recognize the cohorts who will be there when the chips are down. The chips were down about all the time. I'm proud to say that my closest friends today are men and women who were with me in these struggle situations thirty-five years ago.

They always said that anybody from the radical movement in Akron had a certain look around their eyes. We were mavericks in the radical labor movement. We were intellectualized activists. We fought every battle there was to fight. Student fights. Unemployed fights. Anti-ROTC fights. Anti-conscription fights. Anti-Legion fights. Anti-management fights. Anti-Union-boss fights. Anti-CP fights. Anti-Jim Crow fights. You name it. We were there.

NICK MIGAS

I N HIS AUTOBIOGRAPHY *Union Man*, David J. McDonald (then secretary-treasurer and later president of the United Steelworkers of America) gives the following account of the climactic incident at the 1948 Steelworkers convention:

> That convention was kept in an uproar most of the time by a handful of left-wing radicals who were angry with Murray for deserting Henry Wallace. They badgered Murray constantly from the floor until some of the Murray supporters finally took matters into their own hands. A delegate named Nick Migas made a vicious attack on the union leadership, and as his language became steadily more violent, a group of angry members formed spontaneously on the floor and began to move menacingly toward Migas. Several ushers got there first and removed Migas for his own protection. In the scuffle, a .32-caliber revolver fell to the floor. Migas was escorted to the door and turned loose on the street. The next morning I read in the newspapers that he had been beaten up a few blocks from the convention hall. Feelings were running high among the steelworkers.

This is the view from the rostrum. The following account presents the view from the floor mike. It includes the text of the leaflet which Nick Migas and his supporters circulated during the luncheon recess after Murray had refused to recognize Migas during the morning session. Circulation of the leaflet obliged Murray to recognize Migas when the afternoon session began, although Migas was continually interrupted and unable to present his point of view fully.

Nick Migas was an open Communist with deep roots in the union movement and strong support from his own local. This account makes clear why he had that support. Unlike many other locals in the steel industry, Local 1010 at Inland Steel in East Chicago, Indiana was organized by the men in the mill and had to struggle for years to achieve recognition. It had a tradition of departmental wildcats and aggressive handling of grievances (see, in addition to Nick Migas' account, the account of Local 1010's first president, John Sargent, pp. 105–110). As a grievance committeeman for the open hearth, staff man, and local president, Migas had won the respect of his fellow-workers. The demands he presented at the 1948 convention were demands he had been instructed to make by the membership of Local 1010.

As Migas explains, the confrontation at the convention was part of a larger process through which the international union took over and tamed a vigorous local. The same process took place in many CIO unions during the years after World War II.

Late in 1948 Nick Migas left the mill and settled on a dairy farm in Wisconsin, not, he states, because he had been driven out, but because he had always wanted to own a farm of his own.

How the International Took Over

I WAS BORN in McKees Rocks, Pennsylvania and raised in the coal fields of West Virginia. My dad was very active in the union and especially in control of the union by the rank and file, by the members themselves.

Before Dad came to the coal mines he worked in Pennsylvania, in the mills there. He was in a big strike there [the McKees Rocks strike of 1909]. It was a vicious strike. I remember him talking about the police on horseback and the Pinkerton detectives. In fact, he was blackballed and that's why he had to go to the coal mines. He couldn't get a job anywhere in Pennsylvania.

My dad was a member of the United Mine Workers. This was a small mine. They had their own small local there. He was a pit committeeman. He was looked up to as a good representative because of his position for the rank and file, for the average miner. I listened to him discussing grievances with the miners who came to our house: Poles, Italians, Ukrainians like ourselves. He would always stick to the men's version of the grievance. There was a no-strike clause in the union contract but that didn't prevent the men from striking when they had to. Some safety violations were settled that way. I know of a number of occasions when the miners came right out of the mine with my dad in front of them, walked into the superintendent's office and got a grievance settled.

There was a big coal strike when John L. Lewis became head of the union. Many miners were in a pretty tough position because the coal companies imported scabs and especially Negro people, to try and break the strike. Many of the black people were not aware of this until they were brought in and then, to the amazement of many white people, the black people supported the strike, would work with the white miners and help them out. That's where we gained the experience of labor and of the control of unions by rank and file.

My dad was a member of the ıww way back and then he joined the socialist movement, and I guess he went with the left wing when the Socialist Party split up. I remember him talking to me about Debs. One of my big heroes was Big Bill Haywood. I heard him speak in Rockford, Illinois when I was attending workers training school. He was a wonderful man.

In the early 1920s the mine closed down and we moved to Hammond, Indiana. Quite a number of relatives from the old country lived there. There was a big car shop in Hammond, and in corresponding they told him that jobs were available, and so we moved. He got a job at the Standard Car shop in East Chicago. I was fourteen.

When the Depression came, my dad was laid off because he did not have much seniority, and went on wpa. We almost lost our home. My brother and I got jobs after school in a bowling alley, setting pins. My mother went out to do housework among the rich people in that area. That way we were able to pay interest on our loan. In fact, I was involved in an accident which enabled us to pay off the mortgage. I had just pulled out of a neighbor's yard where a Serbian orchestra I belonged to was practicing. I was coming out of the yard across some railroad tracks, and another group of kids were trying to beat a train. There were no blinkers. As the train came by they had to pull over to my side to avoid the train and we crashed right in the middle of the tracks. The cowcatcher picked up my car and slid me for about three hundred yards. My wheels collapsed. I tried to get out of the car but the cowcatcher caught the door and my leg, and crushed them up against the car. We settled with the railroad and were able to pay off the mortgage. We were lucky. Many people lost their homes, their bank accounts and life savings.

My dad was active in the unemployed councils at that time. There were meetings at the little red house which was owned by the Hungarian Fraternal Society. The ıwo and the ycl also used the Hungarian hall. I remember parading in Hammond, going from store to store, asking for donations to help the hungry people. Most of the grocers would give small donations, although they were as bad off as the rest. There were demonstrations in Indianapolis, and I remember one time the police and fire departments in East Hammond tried to break up our car caravan as we were getting ready to go to Indianapolis.

After graduating from high school I thought of going to college. But financial conditions being what they were I was unable to go to college. I could probably have worked my way but a job came in the offing at the steel mills and I thought, "Well, I'll make some money"—get started, you know. So I took this job at the Inland Steel as a stocker in the scrap yard, loading scrap on little pan cars and hauling them up to the furnaces. That was in 1933.

From stocker I was promoted to switchman, and from there to conductor. That's when I became involved in union activities. I was a steward in my department, the No. 1 Open Hearth. That was the stronghold of the independent union. The president of the company union was a first helper in No. 1 Open Hearth. And so the fight against the company union wasn't something remote. It was right there.

When I saw how the company worked against the workers, especially against the foreign-born workers who were in no position to defend themselves, it kind of roused my feeling about those people not getting a fair deal. At that time a foreman could easily say, "You don't like it? Go on home. Take three days off. Take a week off." And there was nothing you could do about it. And so when the Steel Workers Organizing Committee came in to organize the CIO, we were pretty ripe for organization. I suppose being connected with labor unions through my father pushed me right ahead.

We had a lot of Mexican workers in my department where discrimination was practiced. They were constantly kept on small, menial jobs—scrap yard, labor gang, furnaces—dirty, menial, hard work. And no chance of promotion. That's why the union swept like a wildfire through the steel mills. Every place you looked you saw, "CIO, CIO, CIO," in spite of everything that the company would try to stop it.

During these early years Johnny [Sargent] was president, we had
a progressive leadership, and that made a world of difference.
We were encouraged to work with the rank and file, with all
the people that we represented. We organized departmental meetings. Every month the department would meet at the union hall
and discuss their immediate problems, work things out, and decide
what to do about it. You had a sympathetic leadership to work with
you. Whereas now, departmental meetings are discouraged, you're
discouraged to put out [departmental] newspapers reporting to the
membership what you're doing as far as their grievances are concerned. A man will file a grievance, the steward will take it up,
and that's the end of it. If it goes to the international, the member
himself doesn't know what is happening.

In those days, the man who had the grievance came right along
with me. We discussed it right in front of the foreman. He went
with me to the next step, the superintendent. We discussed it there.
If we couldn't settle it there we went to the industrial relations
department, the third step. He was always involved, he was always
there, he knew exactly what his case was, he knew exactly what
position the company was taking.

There were times, I remember, we'd take a man into the superintendent's office and the superintendent would try to browbeat the
man involved, give him a little scare. It was then that the union
made its position felt, by blasting the superintendent for his attitude.
We slammed the table. You'd be surprised at the results that would
bring. Then they'd say, "Nick, how would you like to be a foreman?"

There was one time when they wouldn't settle a grievance for
the charging car operators. They had increased the tonnage on the
furnaces without increasing the rate. We discussed this question with
the superintendent: nothing doing. So that night it started to slow
down, and by the next morning there were two furnaces where they
had to shut the heat off. By that evening there were six furnaces
that had to shut the heat off. They settled the grievance in a hurry.
Nobody told anybody to strike. There was just that close relationship, working with the people, where they knew what was necessary.

It was nice. It was good work. We set up promotional sequences in every department where it made no difference if you were a Mexican, if you were a Negro, what you were. Every step of the way you were entitled to the next position if your seniority permitted. So as a result, my first case was of a Mexican worker promoting to a crane operator. This was unheard of. It happened to be one of my stewards, Merced Velasquez. He was very intelligent. The grievance was taken up, and he became the first [Mexican] to get on a crane.

Same thing on the open hearth. You never had Mexicans as helpers. "First helpers? That's ridiculous. No Mexican can be a first helper." Well, it wasn't too long after that when we had a regular procedure. There was no chance of any real opposition, because that was the procedure, that was the way it was set up, and every person had his rights.

We had a strike in No. 2 Open Hearth when a Negro fellow was refused permission to become a second helper. There were many Southern people who had come in at that time, and were working as third and second helpers. This thing broke out: management refused to give him the job and [management] was supported by the other workers. We held a meeting inside the plant. Gillies, the superintendent, spoke first. He was wishy-washy: "Well fellows, you know what's right and what's wrong, but we can't force you." Then I spoke after Gillies got through. I told them in plain words that this was wrong, that the union would never support them, that this man was entitled to a job regardless of his race. I pointed out to them that discrimination starts, maybe, with a Negro, but next it will go to the Mexican worker, and that it hasn't been long since Mexican workers could not work at this job (and there were Mexican workers there listening), and then it'll go to the Kentuckian, the hillbilly. I said, "Then a so-called hillbilly won't be able to work in a steel mill. And where will it stop?" After that the man was given his job.

Women were brought in during the war and immediately the company began to pay them less wages. The first case I took up was a woman by the name of Delgado who was working in the labor gang, and was getting less wages for the same work. It took about six months but the arbitrator ruled against the company. That set the precedent. The women in the tin mill struck over the same issue.

During the early days, the international wasn't too much of a question. People were involved with their immediate problems in their own localities, their own local unions, and they felt that here was where they had to settle their problems. It wasn't until the international came in, and dictated a contract with a no-strike clause, that it became a matter of what kind of leadership you had in the international.

When swoc became the Steelworkers Union, it became a top-heavy organization. Before that the local union leadership did its own negotiating. A contract would be read clause by clause at the local union meeting, and then voted on, and adopted or rejected.

How did the international take over? It was very much like the political situation now. Look at the trend in this country with Nixon. He goes into Cambodia, he goes into other countries, doing what he pleases, and people feel that they can't do anything about it. It was just the same way when the international came into the local unions. Hedging here, hedging there, getting people under their influence in the local who were ambitious to become foremen or to get on the staff, spending money just before an election: that way progressive leadership was broken up in the plant, in the union.

It was a gradual process. You had elected representatives in the different departments. Maybe for a period of time they were sincere, and they worked hard to get grievances and problems settled. But generally, they did not work closely with the membership. They didn't report to the people they represented. Eventually, maybe some people broke away, got disgusted, and new people were elected. Or, if you had a good man as grievance committeeman, and the international didn't settle his grievances at the third and fourth steps, then the people involved thought it was the grievance man's fault [and voted him out of office]. That's how the international took over.

I was a staff man myself for a while. They wanted Sargent, and he turned them down, but he urged me to accept it because it was a position from which I could help the rank and file. It was good work. You got into contact with more people that way. Even as a staff representative, when a grievance man had a grievance that was perplexing him I would go with him into the department and discuss it with the men. And while I was a staff representative wage increases were received throughout the whole mill. Every time there was an increase I wrote a personal letter to the grievance committeeman, listing the amount of increase each job was affected by. He had to post that letter on his bulletin board and this brought me almost directly in contact with the people in the opposition's departments.

While I was a staff man, George Patterson [see pp. 89–97] decided to run against Joe Germano [for district director of District 31 of the United Steelworkers of America, including Chicago and northern Indiana]. I immediately supported George. I was the only staff man who did, at least the only one who did wholeheartedly. And at Inland, which was the only place we were in a position to ensure an honest election, Patterson carried the local. But Germano was declared to have won the election and the day after the election I was fired.

[Nick Migas went back into the mill. In June 1945 he was elected president of the Inland local, Local 1010. In 1946 and 1948 he was a delegate to the Steelworkers convention, although no longer president of the local.]

As a delegate to the 1948 convention I was instructed by my local on every one of the issues I raised. Many of Germano's delegates were out playing cards all night. They didn't give a damn. They didn't care. I went up to Murray [Philip Murray, president of the Steelworkers Union] and asked him if he would permit me to get up at the front mike. Murray refused. He said, "You have a mike on the floor," and he said, "If I want to I shall recognize you, and you can speak on any issue that is at that time on the floor." So I walked off.

After Murray refused to recognize any of us who wanted to speak, we put out a leaflet. We didn't want to disrupt the convention. We did it when the convention was not in session, when it was recessed for lunch. I'll never forget the look on the face of Dave McDonald [at that time secretary-treasurer of the union] after he read that leaflet. I was standing there in the hallway and McDonald walked by me. The look on his face was pure hatred. He never said a word to me. Normally he would have said, "Hello," or something, because I'd met him a number of times at conventions in Pittsburgh. I knew something was up just from the look on McDonald's face.

The leaflet challenged Murray's position and Murray being the exalted ruler, no one had dared to do that. It said he was working with the company. That was the sharpest point, that he had acquiesced in the company's position. The international's position was no wage increase.

[The text of the leaflet was as follows:]

FOR A 25 ¢ WAGE INCREASE NOW!
STOP THE NO-FIGHT POLICY!

The officers' report shows that the Steel Companies were never in a better position to grant unions' demand for a wage increase.

—Workers need it—higher prices make it mandatory.

—It is clear that prices are *not* dropping, that they will rise more.
So—we can't wait until next year or until Steel Companies feel like granting wage increases. Nor can we sit by with mouths open to take what companies want to give us.
This convention should adopt a stand that:

—We want wage increases NOW!

—We want 25c an hour increase NOW!

President Murray revealed that the Steel Trust did not bargain in good faith in the wage talks. Not only that: We now see the companies didn't bargain in good faith when they signed the present two-year contract.

On the other hand, our leadership has done almost everything it could to please the trust and the powers-that-be:

—It influenced our union to go easy on beefs in the mills.

—It stopped or discouraged departmental stoppages, slow-downs and other actions against departmental beefs; it permitted staunch union men to be fired without benefit of union defense for simply fighting speed-up and other beefs.

—It supported the Marshall Plan.

—It condemned the Third Party and the only Presidential candidate who supports our wage demand and opposes Taft-Hartley— Henry Wallace.

—It carried on more and more anti-Communist, red-baiting activity. This is how our leadership proved its good faith and its confidence in the company's good faith! Only the good faith of the rank-and-file was forgotten.

And for all this, the pay-off wasn't even a wooden nickel pay raise. We got taken in; we got speed-up; we got a weakened union; we got laughed at. We pleased the Company and hurt ourselves.

Never Again! Never again must our union be made a laughing stock! Never again must we be taken into camp by the wily steel trust and a gullible leadership! No more 2-year contracts! No more no-strike clauses! No more free hands for the company and bound hands for the union!

The bad faith of the companies in these wage negotiations is clear. In the face of the companies' bad faith—in the face of a crying need for a wage increase—we cannot let the talk about "sanctity of contract" replace our responsibility for working out a policy to carry on the fight to **win a wage increase now!**

The miners too, have a no-strike clause in their present contract, and a few other rotten clauses. But when the chips were down these clauses didn't stand in their way. It was found that they had to be "willing and able" to work. It is widely known that the miners had good reason to be "unwilling and unable" to work, for certain reasons. AND THEY WON! THEIR FIGHTING POLICY PAID OFF!

The same goes for us: Either we are a fighting union every inch of the way or we go down the road to company-unionism! Let's show some good faith in our membership! Let's respond to their good faith in electing us to this convention. They expect a fighting wage policy—not weasel words, from us.

The Wage Policy Resolution now offered to you by the Resolutions Committee should be sent back to be amended as follows:

1. That we make clear that our demand for a wage increase is 25¢ an hour retroactive to April 30.

2. That in addition to the advertising campaign to win the public there shall be an all-out drive to win the solid support of the steelworkers for this demand. That we shall set aside one day for union rallies in every steel center to show the rank and file support for the demand and to express their determination to win it.

3. That we shall establish closest possible unity with all other
unions which are in struggle or negotiations for wage increases.
Statement of Delegate Nick Migas, Local Union 1010, USA-CIO.

Because of the leaflet, Murray had to call on me. When I got
up to the mike I felt, as I was talking, that the people were listening.
I could have swayed the people. But the damn staff representatives
wouldn't let me. They started hooting. They were there for a purpose: they wouldn't let you talk. And half of the delegates were
staff representatives. So how can you do it? If it had been just the
membership, the rank and file, I could have carried them right along
with me.

Germano took this opportunity to bring up every personal slander
he could think of, to tear me apart. I was escorted by three big,
husky staff representatives right out of the convention, and thrown
out of the door. There was a group standing there, I don't know
who they were, and they started after me. I got across the street
and as I stepped on the opposite gutter I slipped and fell down, and
one of these guys caught up with me and kicked me in the ribs.
Then Ralph and a couple of other friends came up and things quieted
down. We went into a drugstore. Then the police came. I stayed
hid for about three days in a friend's house there in Boston.

Upon returning to our locals we continued to press this issue, and
finally, the wage increase came across. Bill Young got up at the
local meeting and said that it was thanks to me that it had happened.

Elections in our local came up a month later, and I ran for grievance committeeman in my department. I was unopposed. The international had their people in the local prefer charges [because under
the Taft-Hartley Act, a Communist could not hold office in the
union]. A trial committee was appointed by the president: Bill Young
and Merced Velasquez from my department, Max Luna who worked
with the Trotskyites, and Don Lutes and Pete Calacci representing
the international. During this trial, the Trotskyites contacted me
several times and said that they were going to support me because
this was a political persecution. And they did. They supported me
during this trial, so the majority on the trial committee voted in support of my position. The majority and the minority gave their reports

at the local union meeting, and the local union supported the majority. Then the international overruled the local. That's the way it happened.

But I was never removed as a grievance committeeman. I had bought a farm. I had always wanted to own one. While this struggle was going on in the local, my family had moved to the farm. My wife was having problems. She was trying to run the farm with no water, no electricity. She had a refrigerator, a washing machine, an electric stove, but she had no electricity. It was overbearing for her to take care of the two little girls and all this as well. Our political activities, our union activities, had nothing to do with this decision.

I wouldn't change a thing if I had it to do over again. A lot of people feel that the progressive group isolated itself in the steel union by supporting Patterson. I don't think so. We supported a progressive man, and we had to show opposition to a fellow that wasn't doing for the union what he should have been doing.

STAN WEIR

D
URING MORE THAN TWENTY YEARS as an industrial worker, unionist, and organizer among seamen, auto workers, teamsters and construction workers, Stan Weir became impressed by the importance of informal work groups. The informal or primary work group is

> that team which works together daily in face-to-face communication with one another, placed by technology and pushed into socialization by the needs of production. It is literally a family at work torn by hate and love, conflict and common interest. It disciplines its members most commonly by social isolation and ridicule, it has a naturally selected leadership, makes decisions in the immediate work area, and can affect the flow of production.

Searching industrial relations libraries, Weir found much literature on primary work groups but only one study that was partisan to workers (Loren Baritz, *Servants of Power*), and he learned for the first time of the Hawthorne experiments. Weir sees the informal work group as the only organizational form opposed to formal bureaucracies which cannot be captured by them.

This account does not present the cumulative life experience of Stan Weir, being highly condensed and ending in 1956. In the late 1950s, Weir went back into maritime as a San Francisco Bay Area longshoreman. Together with a thousand others hired in 1959, he was part of a new class of registered longshoremen called B-men. B-men paid a special form of dues but were not permitted membership in the union and were allowed only the work that was left over after the union members or A-men took the work that they wanted. As one of the elected leaders of the B-men, Weir became involved in a sharp and protracted dispute with the leadership of the International Longshoremen's and Warehousemen's Union (ILWU) headed by the union's president, Harry Bridges.

After four years of agitation and after a large number of A-men had retired, the union and the employers decided to take the 1959 B-men into what almost amounted to full membership. All were investigated and all were promoted but a group of eighty-two which contained those who had taken the lead in criticizing Bridges' policies affecting the B-men. The eighty-two, Weir among them, were fired after a secret trial which was opposed by the local union. Accusations against them involved late payment of dues for which they had paid fines, and chiseling in accepting work assignments out of turn. Ten years later a number of those who were deregistered were still attempting to get a hearing and reinstatement to their jobs via the courts.

Stan Weir is at present an instructor at the University of Illinois. He has written several influential essays based on his experience, including "USA—the Labor Revolt," first published in the *International Socialist Journal* (Rome, Italy), April and June 1967 (reprinted in *American Society, Inc.*, Maurice Zeitlin, ed., 1970, and in *American Labor Radicalism*, Staughton Lynd, ed., 1973); and "Class Forces in the 1970's," *Radical America*, May–June 1972. His articles on longshore have appeared in *New Politics*. There are substantial similarities in the life events of Stan Weir and Harvey Swados' fictional character Joe Link in *Standing Fast*.

STAN WEIR

The Informal Work Group

I

THE WHOLE EARLY PART of my life was dominated by the idea that solutions to all that's wrong lie in individual morality. But my life experience, like that of most people, sent me messages which constantly contradicted this idea. I came to have a different idea, that you had to have a cause that was bigger than you because that was the only real freedom—living at one with a total society rather than just for oneself. It's impossible to know precisely where one gets that idea, but I came to know that the corruption of individual humans is the result of corrupt and outdated institutions.

My grandmother was a scrubwoman in office buildings in downtown Los Angeles. My mother quit high school in the tenth grade and became an apprentice dressmaker at fifty cents a week. She met my father when she was working at the Post Office. A year later they married and I was born a year after that, in 1921, the year that women got the vote.

I didn't know my father. That marriage lasted five months after my birth. Both my great grandfather and grandfather died in the early '20s. That left me with a family that was female-dominated. My uncle was an important member of our household, but due to the Depression, his unemployment and resulting alcoholism, he was constantly held up as an example of what not to be. My block in East Los Angeles was made up of close and long-time neighbors. They worked hard. They were poor, generous, warm and at the same time petty and suspicious of anyone not like themselves; that is, not of English, Scotch, Irish, or German stock. Most of all they wanted the happiness they felt could come from obtaining "a steady job." When two Armenian families moved in at the bottom of the block there was a temporary but noticeable resistance. Real socialization and integration did not materialize. In 1944, a freeway cut through and made the separation of the lower part of the block permanent.

All through school there were not more than three teachers who related to me on my own terms—really only one, a young Armenian substitute teacher. I was to give one of the speeches at the graduation ceremony from junior high school. My speech was called, "Our Flag, the Star Spangled Banner." In rehearsal, I walked up onto the stage to give the speech in a very sloppy manner. The teacher in charge of the ceremony had a fit of anger and in front of everybody told me off and said, "If ever I see you walk up there like that again, that's the end. You're not going to give the speech." One of the big tough ball players on the team that I played second base on came to me at noontime and said, "Mr. Dingilian was talking about you. He said you did that because you didn't want to lose touch with us regular guys."

In the first year of high school I completely stopped attempting to participate in official school activities that were connected with the administrative establishment. I began to see that they were part of a system of favoritism and I was one of the beneficiaries of that system. However, I was opposing it individually, without organization, not effectively. I can remember I cut school one day, left the school grounds in my '29 Model A Ford with five others. We drove to the beach and spent a great day body surfing. The next morning I had to face up to the fact that I had been seen ditching. I walked in to get my demerits with everyone else and I was told by the registrar to report immediately to the vice principal's office. The vice principal explained to me that he couldn't give me, one of the leaders in the school, demerits like anyone else. That was impossible. "Just watch your step and don't get caught like that again. Get back in class." That had a great deal to do with opening my eyes.

Out of 323 seniors graduating in February 1940, the same man (who thought he was doing us a great favor) invited the five boys who were known to be going on to college to his house for dinner. He explained to us how to get a commission in the Armed Forces when the U. S. finally got into the war. He told how he had gotten a commission in the Army as a young man in World War I and how we could do the same, that we should not get caught being privates in the Army. He told us how to work the angles through Congressmen.

It was very oppressive for us to know that the war was going on in Europe. I think this is one of the reasons why we threw ourselves into the "swing era" so hard. That was a big part of my life. Dancing and listening to the swingbands, and the security of the group that was doing it, was a way of putting behind the thought of that oncoming war. We all knew one another and all the males wore suits that were at least slightly zoot.

I always thought in grammar school that it would be different in junior high—we'd start learning the truth. In junior high I thought it would be in high school. And in high school I thought it would be in college. I went to Los Angeles Junior College in February 1940, and it appeared to me that that was finally going to be so.

I had a professor of English named Richard Lillard. He was a liberal from the John Dewey tradition and he provided an analysis of society and the world around us that made sense to me. It was liberating and I listened hard to every word he spoke. But toward the end of the semester I asked him, "This is all fine but where does one go to put into practice these ideas?"

The following semester I went to UCLA. I was in the Westgard Co-op. It was a co-op eating group. I was introduced to it by a friend of mine I had gone to high school with named John Slevin. He was a Molokan, a member of a fundamentalist Christian pacifist sect from the Ukraine near Armenia. His pacifism hadn't had a great effect on me until the war got very close. Then it became apparent that he was going to be a conscientious objector. He was in conscientious objector camps for four years and he led a strike as a CO. That made him a felon and for life he has literally been blackballed out of any career because of it—and he is a great human.

I didn't finish my third semester at college. I could see no point in it. I had had a philosophy course in which the professor effectively tore down what he called the metaphysical temple and philosophically destroyed any basis for my belief in God, and I went with

Professor Piatt every step of the way. But he had nothing to supplant it with. At this point I was developing a lot of cynicism about the world around me. I was despairing about ever finding a way to pursue a good life.

I seriously considered being a CO myself and I went and talked to Richard Lillard about it. He said, "Well, there's just one thing about being a conscientious objector. With your particular bent, your personality, it seems to me that you would like to live the social experience of your generation. And if you become a CO you won't, not directly." I wanted to find a way to do that without at the same time becoming a victim of the discipline in the Armed Services. It appeared to me that while the risk to life was greater on merchant ships during the war, if I became a merchant seaman I could then get the best of both worlds.

I became an apprentice seaman in the Merchant Marine. I was then accepted as a U. S. Merchant Marine cadet and midshipman in the Naval Reserve, went into training, and went out on a merchant ship as a deck cadet.

Living with the officers topside, I saw that this was an aristocracy. The contempt that the officers had for the men in the foc'sle (forecastle) was a fact of life. The first day on that ship I appeared on the boat deck with my midshipman's uniform on. The deckhands looked up at me and I saw in their faces that look of pity for the worthlessness of the contribution that anyone could make who would be wearing such an outfit. To them, that uniform symbolized useless activity.

They knew something about the ability they had to make that ship go from port to port with or possibly even without officers. They were a highly conscious group of men from the strikes of the '30s, an experience which was still fresh in their minds. They were involved, even on that ship, in job actions from time to time. Several among them were ex-iwws; they believed in direct action.

Within three months, I was working on deck with them as a seaman, wearing the same clothes they were wearing which I got out of the slop chest. They saw that I was interested. They went out of their way to teach me all of the skills, the wire and line (rope) splices, the knots and hitches, and to make a deck sailor out of me.

They wanted to win me away from the "topside" for good. So they started telling me the history of the strikes to win the hiring hall, the fights to destroy the "fink hall" and the "fink book," which had been parts of the government-employer controlled hiring system. Prior to 1934 on the West Coast, when you got off a ship, if the skipper wrote anything other than "VG," very good, in your continuous discharge or fink book, then you were marked and couldn't get another American ship. Carrying the continuous discharge book meant you carried your own blackball in your pocket.

So they pumped all this history into me. And then they would quiz me. "What happened on such-and-such a date?" "What's Bloody Thursday?" "What were the big demands?" "What was the 1934 award?" "Why were we able to win victories before getting a collective bargaining contract?" "Who's Lunchbox?" (That was Harry Lundeberg, the secretary-treasurer of the Sailors' Union of the Pacific.) "What's a Lunchbox Stetson?" (That was the sailors' name for the traditional white cap of the West Coast maritime workers.)

On that ship I had finally found a cause and a vehicle for pursuing it. These guys were involved, day to day, in establishing dignity for themselves and thousands of others, and policing all the things that they had done to obtain that dignity. I saw the boatswain tell the chief mate on that ship, "Get off the deck while we're working. Come and see me before 8:00 in the morning and tell me what to do. Come out here after we quit at 5:00 in the evening and find out what we didn't do right, if you think so, and tell me what's wrong. But don't come and stand on this deck while we're at work. Get off the deck and back on the bridge where you belong." I was very impressed with that power. He got away with it. I was amazed he could do that. I knew I wanted to be able to do that too. And I did! The time came when I sailed boatswain and I told the mate, "Get off this deck. Don't stand around us and watch us or else there's going to be no work going on while you're here. Hold everything, fellows!"

When I left that ship I had learned the loophole in Naval Reserve law on how to resign as a midshipman without any penalty, just to get out. So I did that and I went immediately to San Pedro and reported to the port agent at the Sailors Union of the Pacific hall. (We didn't have "presidents" in the Sailors Union—it was a syndicalist tradition—they were "agents.") I went with a letter from the boatswain saying, "This here is to introduce Red Weir. He wants to come up through the forecastle like a regular and he knows the work. Give him a trip card." So I was in the foc'sle as opposed to the "topside" where the officers bunked.

Within a year's time I became a person who was usually elected the deck delegate on any ship that I would hire onto. They don't have union stewards on deck crews because the word "steward" means the person who is head of the food department. So you have "delegates" from the deck gang, black or engine room gang, and steward department. I was extremely and youthfully militant against the officers on every ship, to protect the gains of 1934 to 1937, like I'd been taught on my first ship by that gang of strike men and ex-Wobblies. When the food was not good or the mattresses were bad, and the ship got ready to sail, I several times had the crew standing on the docks and saying, "Until those mattresses come aboard . . ."

We were being trampled on because of the no-strike pledge. We were losing the gains of the 1930s because of the war, and that in particular kept me in political opposition to the war throughout the war. World War II was being used by employers to wipe out the gains made by labor a few years earlier and the democratic gains previously won by the general citizenry. When I finally became political it was through the only socialist organization that maintained political opposition to World War II. This was the Workers Party, later renamed the Independent Socialist League, whose leading personality was Max Shachtman.

One day, still early in the war, I came out on the deck of a Moore-McCormack ship on which I was deck delegate and I spotted a small broad man walking down the dock under a seabag that almost hid him from view. We were short one skilled deck hand [AB] and I figured that had to be him, the last man to fill out the crew so that we could sail. He came up the gangplank and I asked him, was he the AB from the hall? He said yes. I introduced myself, learned his name, showed him where to stow his gear and took him forward and introduced him to the whole gang by name. That kind of impressed him because he was a Jew and there weren't many Jews sailing, on deck in particular, and he had expected a little harder time. We rapidly became close friends. Within two weeks after we left port, he was the authority on almost all subjects in arguments on almost any question.

This man, who introduced me to socialism, was a visionary and had created in his mind a vision of a better society. He was a developed intellectual. He knew music, art and literature and a lot about natural sciences, and he was able to apply all those things to a vision of a better society. That was very attractive to me and many of the men on that ship.

When we got to Australia, he visited one of the famous rank-and-file organizers of the Australian labor movement. From that old man, who was retired, he got a number of copies of *The New International, The Fourth International, The Militant,* and *Labor Action.* He told me to read them, see what I thought. So I read them. I wasn't tremendously impressed with any of them, but there were some good things in them I thought. Trotsky was raising the whole question of democratic ideas and the necessity of democracy, which I was very much interested in. But the Russian experiment did not seem important to me at that time.

It was in the Sailors Union and while going to sea that society at least in part began to become understandable to me. Marxism facilitated that. The term "cause," instead of just being an emotional and simplistic thing where you got an identifiable enemy figure in "the boss," became part of a whole world view. I could see that the great contribution of Marx was that he was paying attention to what people were doing rather than trying to impose a utopia upon them. He had analyzed the French Revolutions, the communes and the forms that people themselves had produced and was trying to systematize it in some democratic way so that they would have some control of their own destiny. Being a militant delegate began to take on new meanings.

I began to understand that the reason why merchant seamen were often in the forefront of militant labor activity or revolutionary activity throughout the world was because, as citizens of a ship after it left the dock, they were really citizens of a molecular state, a total state in which the captain is the dictator. There is the middle class—licensed officers. And then there's the "lower class," the unlicensed seamen. It's a reflection of a class society. Once one can make an analysis of a small state like a ship, one can transmit that analysis to the larger state without even fully realizing it. There's a carry-over. At first I thought that merchant seamen were militant because they travelled and read a lot. But later I was to see that the informal social groups that develop on a ship at sea are in the main created by the formal and official division of labor which operates the ship; that is, the informal and formal work groups are identical so that the social and technological powers of the seamen are merged, thus revealing to them the importance of their role and enlarging the consciousness of their strength.

One of my deepest concerns when I first met a Marxian socialist was the whole question of violence and terrorism, sabotage, all those things I'd read about that radicals are supposed to be "guilty" of. The answers given me were that there is nothing radical or revolutionary about terrorism or any kind of super-militancy. It's essentially a reformist activity in its attempt to change society without changing institutions, merely by removing a person or group of people or terrorizing people through violent methods. Someone who is revolutionary, in the literal sense of the term, is someone who is for changing society's institutions. Socialism, if it's good, is finally for everyone's benefit. A way of saving the souls (if I can use the term) of all, including those who are managers or owners of the forces of production, is to create a society in which no one ever has to make that terrible decision to exploit others.

The question then came up to me immediately, well then why aren't we pacifists? It was explained to me that we cannot be pacifists because at a certain point that is irresponsibility. One has to be prepared, if attacked, to fight to defend oneself, and maintain the right to meet, to talk, to picket, whatever, and carry one's rights as a citizen to full conclusion. But if one ever has to do that, one should be as thrifty as possible, for not only do you want to not take a life but you want to create as few bitter enemies as possible. Those in power always have more arms than you. Those who work, who operate society, make it move, whether they dig coal or write poetry or keep books or file bills, have to be the answer to that brute force. Because that brute force can't stand up finally against the threat of the withdrawal of labor and economic and political power by those who, "from below" so to speak, operate and make the society function in all its ways.

In late '43 or early '44, the Sailors Union of the Pacific, in conjunction with the Seafarers International Union, decided to organize the tankers belonging to Standard Oil of California. [The Seafarers International Union was an industrial union founded by the Sailors Union of the Pacific which was a craft union. The SUP then became an affiliate of the SIU.] The only men who could get hired by Standard with any ease were those that looked young enough not to have had union experience. I was easily hired and I went out to Point Richmond, to the dockside refinery, to get on a ship. The practice was to hire seamen and let them work on the dock, servicing incoming ships, until they were assigned to a crew. I became a member of the relief gang and I was made assistant dock boatswain. That put me in a key position and I soon became head of the campaign on the job. I would assign rank-and-file SUP organizers so that they were not all concentrated on a few ships.

At a point midway in the campaign SUP men began to appear at work who were giving Jim Crow messages to the seamen we were trying to win over. Our opponent was the National Maritime Union (NMU).Their organizers were preoccupied with winning the war, Russia, and maintaining labor's no-strike pledge into the post-war period, rather than improving conditions for seamen in the here and now. We had been doing a good job by openly comparing our contracts with those of the NMU. I could prove to anyone who was white that we had the best union because we had the best contract. I hadn't thought through the whole racial issue but I could see that I couldn't give uncritical support to either [the SUP or the NMU] and neither side would abide criticism of any kind.

The men coming out now from the Sailors Union were saying, "We got to get a white union in here." On that dock, the messmen in the cafeteria and the room stewards in the hotel were Filipinos who were bitterly anti-union because of the experience that they'd had in the original union organization campaigns years before when the union had rejected them as members. I grabbed one of the men who had made some Jim Crow statements and pulled him behind a shed and demanded to know, who sent him out? It turned out that he had been sent, not from the Sailors Union hall but from the siu tanker office in Richmond, headed by Hal Banks, a man who was later to get into the news as a strikebreaker in Canada for the American siu. He was open about his bigotry. Some among those he worked closely with said he boasted membership in the Ku Klux Klan and was often armed. I phoned the head of the sup, Harry Lundeberg. He had been challenged about Banks before and to me, like to the others, he said, "Well, Red, the man's doing a good job for us over there and we have to overlook some of his faults you know."

I immediately got myself shipped out on one of Standard's tankers. Two months later the NLRB representation election took place. I piled off the ship the same day. Eighty-five per cent voted for the SUP-SIU. Lundeberg signed a contract allowing Standard to hire forty-nine per cent non-union seamen, but by that time I had been sent to Canada as a special representative to the British Columbia Seamen's Union to clear up a bad situation created by the man heading it up.

I hit all the ships as they came in and organized the ranks to take control. After several months I learned that Lundeberg had armed the British Columbia union's president with a telegram stating I was a "Trotskyite," with the idea in mind that this could be used to keep me from cleaning house too thoroughly. I had learned a lesson about how control is maintained by bureaucracies. I stayed on until I had maximum insurance that the ranks could sustain an opposition. I returned to the states and got the first ship available to the East Coast.

I would no longer be a staff organizer for the Sailors Union. I could no longer see my official union as a viable instrument for qualitative social change. I was now a militant but without legitimization from the union. In 1945, when it appeared that the war was going to be over, the Coastwise Committee in the Sailors Union of the Pacific held a meeting and came up with a post-war program in which they said that, "This union does not checkerboard ships," in other words, ship blacks or accept blacks into the union, "because checkerboarding causes racial friction. But we are still a democratic union because the day the membership wants blacks in we will allow it."

I took the floor of the meeting and pointed out that the report of the Coastwise Committee "solved nothing," that it was true that the unions that were in any way Communist-line did utilize blacks as political footballs by patronizing them and then using them, but that no member of the Sailors Union could tell that to a black man and be heard because blacks were allowed some kind of citizenship in CIO unions and not in the AFL unions on the waterfront, and were totally barred from the Sailors Union. And therefore the crisis continued for us as long as we were an all-white union. (We had minority groups in the Sailors Union with darker skins than many American blacks. To this day I believe the bar against American blacks is more political, in the small "p" sense of the word, than it is racial. Confrontation with guilt is feared.)

I was interrupted by the chairman who said, "What would you do, Brother Weir, if you were on the Coastwise Committee . . ." but he never finished his sentence because I believe he realized it would be opening up a discussion on the floor about the whole basis of racism to the ranks present. They had visibly shifted during even that brief exchange on the floor of the meeting.

I think most people were seriously pondering the problem in that key meeting. But bureaucratically the discussion was avoided. One did not pursue questions after the gavel had come down. In those days it meant having to face up to violence and unless you had a caucus or organized muscle going you couldn't stand up to it. I had no caucus. Like all the other dissenters in those war days, I was very much an individual, isolated and alone in that union at that time.

I decided after the war was over that I no longer wanted to go to sea. I no longer was able to do what seamen do when they first start going to sea and that is to "ball it up" in foreign ports, carousing in bars and whorehouses, because finally one sees that the women are only there because of their abject poverty. As a man of twenty-five, and like most seamen, I had become divorced from mainstream shoreside society and I wanted a broader social life. I remember one night I was in Port Avila on a tanker and the moon came up over those California foothills in the east. It was New Year's Eve and I realized how many guys my age were ashore having a good time and here I was with my ass on a cold tank top watching nothing but the moon come up. So I got a ship, a Grace Line run, and paid off in New York. That was the last time I ever shipped offshore.

II

I went to the national office of the Workers Party and Max Shachtman asked me, "What are you going to do now, Red?" I said, "Well, I'm going to go to San Pedro and I'm going to spend three months on the beach in the sun on the sand and in the surf, see my friends, get a job longshoring, work three days a week and do what I want to do."

Shachtman said, "Red, we don't want to miss the boat in auto. A lot of important things are happening. You could do a lot of good in auto." That wasn't what I wanted to do but I realized that I would no longer have legitimization in the Party if I didn't do that. So I went back to the Bay Area, got myself a little apartment in West Berkeley, went out to Point Richmond to the Ford plant, and got hired on the assembly line.

It was chaotic. In those early days after the war they couldn't keep anyone working there. People'd hire in in the morning and quit by noon. Some of them never even got far enough down the line to report to the foreman when they saw what it was like. So every day you'd start off with almost the full complement of personnel and by noon you were already taking over half another man's job. The work was really oppressive. Those who worked any length of time on the Ford line called the place "the prison." I would come home every night battered by the violence of the work.

Every day at quitting time, at the five-minute whistle for clean-up, the men would all line up waiting for the second bell to ring, like at the line in a race. When the second bell would ring they would *run*, as fast as they could go, down the aisles to the time clocks.

During the first few days I thought they were out of their minds. A week later, I was butting them out of line to get my place at the starting point too.

We were always in the hole on that line. One of my operations was to put two bronze screws into the frame of the car that would hold on the hydraulic brake linings or tubings that run to each wheel brake cylinder. One day I was so far in the hole (the man next to me couldn't complete his task because his partner on the other side had put him in the hole) I couldn't reach my electric wrench. And so, not wanting the inspector to spot loose screws, I hit them all the way in with a ballpeen hammer and learned that they would stay in. No one would suspect. I had found a shortcut in the work. Those brake linings would stay on the frame of that car probably for several thousand miles without loosening. But I quit looking at Fords after that when they drove down the street past me because of my guilt and because I knew everyone in that plant was taking shortcuts in some way.

One day they transferred me to another job. A man working near me lifted the motors off the motor line on a hoist and then lowered them into the chassis of the car. He couldn't lift the motors high enough into the air to clear the other men's heads if he was going to make the drop into the car at the right time, so he had to move them horizontally over the men's heads at about a five foot height. He had to yell constantly, all day long, "Watch your head . . . Heads up, heads up." The man was a nervous wreck. He would say after work, talking to himself, "Well, I only hit three men today." "Why don't the dummies get out of my way? They know I have to do it this way to make it on the job."

But then came the day when one of the pneumatic air wrenches hit me on the side of the jaw, because of a faulty clutch, and knocked off half a tooth. I walked out. That was my last day at Ford's.

There I was without a job in auto. The very next morning I went and got a job at Chevrolet in East Oakland where I stayed for two years. Most of the people in that local were Portuguese-Americans from East Oakland. There was a great deal of Jim Crow amongst them because American society was constantly trying to put them in the position of the American blacks. Their way of avoiding that situation had been to say, "Look, we're not American blacks. We're American Portuguese. We have our own Latin culture and we're proud of that culture." So for both good and bad reasons, to express their own culture, they were Jim Crow. The East Oakland, California plant and the Atlanta, Georgia plant of Chevrolet were the last two all-white GM plants in the country.

I pushed a resolution on the floor of the union that we should go to management to bring blacks into the plant. There was opposition to it in the rank and file and the leadership of the shop unit (which was mostly from the then dominant section of the left) went along with those Jim Crow sentiments in order to maintain their hold on the leadership. But then they were in the position of being in violation of the United Automobile Workers constitution. That couldn't go on for too long and I realized that it would come up again.

When I was transferred to another department, everyone in that department was Jim Crow and they wanted me to be the shop steward. I had the choice of either rejecting them because they were Jim Crow or accepting them and dealing with a life situation as it came up. I chose the latter.

We won a lot of conditions in that shop. As a matter of fact, we had a sit-down strike in order to retain the right of having gloves supplied by management. We wore out three pair a week on that particular job. We won gloves in a grievance and then management began to renege on the supply of gloves. The men came to me and said, "We got to do something about this," and half of them were going to the time clock. I got them all back and said, "Look, any man who clocks out . . ." I didn't get to finish my sentence because someone else in that group of about forty men said, "We'll never get back in the plant again." And someone else said, "But if we stay here . . ." and someone else said, "Available to work when they supply the tools to work with, we'll be OK."

It was an outcrop of an idea I'd laid on them very early. They came to me saying, "Look at the holes in our gloves. They're reneging on the supply." I said to them, "Well, gloves are tools, aren't they?" and walked away. I learned that an efficient agitator is not one who talks and lectures a lot, but who simply throws out an idea and sees if that idea is workable and acceptable. We won that sit-down. We were opposed by the leadership of the local for doing that, and they tried to get us for it but we survived.

In all this I was learning from and being counseled by an old-time fighter who had led the sit-down strike at the Richmond Ford plant in the early '30s. His name was Luis Guido. He was one of the greatest men I have ever met—a true yet unsung hero. He would never take a union administrative job. For over thirty years as shop committeeman he fought the Ford and General Motors corporations to create a better life for himself and others. Who will ever record his name as a maker of history?

The second time the question of hiring blacks was going to come up, the men in my department said in effect, "We've got to forgive Red for his strange ideas," and "He needs help on this resolution." The speakers in favor of bringing blacks in were mainly Portuguese from my department and that won the rest of the Portuguese: "If you don't want to do it on a moral basis—the fact that everyone's got a right to eat and work—you damn sure better do it because if we have a strike they'll recruit scabs in West Oakland." It was only a matter of time after that that blacks were on the line and working everywhere in the plant.

I got married while I was working in auto. My wife came out of a West Virginia coal mining family and we had a lot of basic values in common from the first. In addition to developing a career and family, she found no insurmountable problems living a life whose routine was regularly broken by job crisis and economic insecurity.

It was in that period right after I met her that the Oakland general strike occurred. The Oakland general strike was called by no leader. It was unique, I think, in general strikes in this country. There was a strike of women who were the clerks at Kahn's and at Hastings' department stores and it had been going on for months. The Teamsters had begun to refuse to make deliveries to those department stores and the department stores needed commodities badly.

Not many people had cars right after the war and you took public transportation to work in the morning. You had to go downtown to the center of Oakland and then out in the direction of your workplace. So thousands and thousands of people travelled through the heart of town every morning on the way to work, on public transportation. Very early one morning, here were the policemen of Oakland herding in a string of trucks, operated by a scab trucking firm in Los Angeles, with supplies for these department stores. Some truck driver or some bus driver or street car conductor asked some policeman about the trucks (this is now part of the mythology) and the policeman told him, "This is a scab trucking firm coming in from L.A. to take stuff to Kahn's and Hastings'." Well, that truck driver, that bus driver, or that street car conductor, didn't get back on his vehicle. Truck drivers got off their trucks and that increased till those trucks and those buses and those street cars just piled up and thousands of people were stranded in town.

In a small way it was a holiday. The normal criteria for what was acceptable conduct disappeared. No one knew what to do and there were no leaders. No one called it. Pretty soon the strikers began forming into committees on the street corners. Certain shopkeepers were told to shut down and drug stores to stay open. Bars could stay open if they didn't serve hard liquor, and they had to put their juke boxes out on the sidewalk. People were literally dancing in the streets in anticipation of some kind of new day. Soon the strikers began to direct traffic and only let union people into town and keep out those who it was feared might be against the strike. It lasted fifty-four hours.

I'll never forget an incident in that strike. Some Army recruiting truck came in town through that mass of strikers and the lieutenant on that truck said over a P. A. system, "Why aren't you all out fightin' for your country instead of striking?" Most of the bus drivers still had their Eisenhower jackets with the hash marks on because they could use their Army uniform as part of their bus driver's uniform. And some big ex-top sergeant said, "Where do you think we got these?" With that he sang out, "Fall in!" and about a hundred men lined up and he put them through close order drill. Pretty soon there were several hundred going through this close order drill. They marched on City Hall and demanded to see the mayor. He wasn't in, of course.

It was that vision and the experiences in that strike that I experienced and which my wife saw, the vision in actual life of people determining their own destinies that sustains one and makes one stand fast for a long, long time. You don't have to so often go through all those doubts about, "Are the fundamental ideas of Marxism sound?" if you've been fortunate enough to have had those experiences. It's a matter of being advantaged or disadvantaged through your own life experience that sustains or drives one away from those basic ideas.

In 1951, my wife and I lived again in East Los Angeles, right near the high school where I had gone. I was in the Teamsters Union, freight handling. Some old friends of mine that I'd gone to school with and were from my neighborhood were officials in those unions. I was making a pretty good living. Then I began to realize I was getting a lot of work because the dispatchers were instructed by my friends to give me a lot of work. I went to them and I said, "Look, I want to shake square like anybody else." I immediately started getting only two days work a week. I quit and got a job driving a truck steady.

In that local, which was a local for industrial laundry wagon drivers, there was a terrible situation. The working conditions that had been built up by the membership of the local were slowly being sold each year, bit by bit, for nickel and dime wage increases. Rebellion in that local developed, which I led, and I became chairman of the Negotiating Committee. The secretary of the local, it turned out, colluded with management and I was fired on a flimsy pretext that couldn't hold water. While I was awaiting the arbitration, the men in the local, through collections each week, paid my full wages. What we didn't realize was that even the arbitration had been rigged. Instead of utilizing the American Arbitration Association, they got an arbitrator who was an employers' representative in the culinary industry and I went down the drain.

At first the men were going to strike to protect my job. I was part of the reason why they didn't strike, because I was agreeing to go through the mechanics of the grievance procedure. I really participated in my own undoing, and of the men, because I was simply a symbol by which to break the back of militancy in the union. It was an extremely bitter experience for me. I learned that one does not always use official procedures in circumstances like that if one is going to survive.

This rebellion took place early in 1954, when no spotlight was on the labor movement on this question. I have an honorable withdrawal card from that union, however, because twenty members of that union walked into the secretary-treasurer's office and demanded, right then and there, that an honorable withdrawal card be given me. Their instincts told them that I would need it in the future.

I had at least a dozen jobs within the next year. I'd get a job and two or three days later the management would come to me and say, "We didn't know you were in trouble with the Teamsters Union. We have to let you go." I finally got a job as an apprentice grocery clerk for Safeway Stores. I made about $1800 that year. I had one child and my wife was pregnant. I needed and wanted a steady job.

I saw in the newspaper that they were hiring at the General Motors plant in all departments. They hired me immediately and I was spray-painting again, like I had been for a time at Chevrolet. This time, instead of going into industry in part for political reasons, it was just for a job. The McCarthy period had disintegrated my political movement considerably. The people were not interested in doing anything much but surviving. So there was no movement telling me what to do. I was "just a worker."

I began to discover the subculture in the factory and that I was working in an informal work group with a life of its own, its own informal leadership, discipline, and activity. A whole new world opened up to me. I began to see that to approach any situation like this with a whole set of preconceived slogans was way off the beam. One first had simply to learn what the subculture was so that one's actions were understandable to everyone else, and not to violate what had been created. Because if you couldn't understand the individuals and the groups that they formed, you certainly weren't going to understand anything else.

Then it occurred to me that, by and large, the radicals' conception of the masses was a metaphysical one, an average, which didn't exist except in our minds. Really, the mass was a conglomerate of millions of workers in their subcultures, and rarely were there issues which were real mass issues. One had to try to find common denominators but, even more than that, had to speak to the reality of the people's lives as individuals and in their groups and in the subcultures, in each place of work.

I made friends with the people around me the way you normally do. Most of them were Chicanos from my side of town. We soon had a ride group going. We were on swing shift and one night we'd go to the black community where part of our work group lived and have ribs and the next night we'd go up and have tamales, enchiladas, tacos or burritos, and the next night we'd go and have spaghetti—here and there to each one's house. One guy's mother'd make a big feed and my wife'd make a big feed and so on. We created our own social life, which you have to do on the swing shift, when you work from four in the afternoon until midnight. And the politics that I injected into that group? I didn't even have to try. It came in the natural course of life.

One night when one guy stole something fairly big (from the plant) I told him off. By stealing he was risking his job and he risked us losing a valuable member of our group. And that was irresponsible not only to his family, but to *us* who were his family-at-work. It was the most meaningful kind of politics that one could talk and be involved in. Because we were into that kind of politics we could very easily get into other kinds of politics. Just being *me* was being political. I was helping politicalize those around me without trying to design anything special for a mass.

In 1955, our plant struck against the contract the minute its conditions were announced and before a meeting could be called to ratify that agreement. I'll never forget. I was in the men's locker room on my break. One of my friends up the line came in on his break; he was livid with rage. He had heard the conditions of the contract announced on a news broadcast and he was saying, "Man, he must have really got us something!" I said, "I don't understand. What do you mean?" What he meant was that the settlement must be damn good, for Walter Reuther had sacrificed an opportunity in which the ranks were willing to give their full energies to a fight for working conditions, just to get that improvement in the economic package.

In 1956, I got laid off in a cutback of 1700 men because the boom in auto was over. And by the time they called me back on the basis of seniority I was already back in the Bay Area. But it was in that period, 1955 and 1956, probably the biggest auto years in the postwar period, that some of the insights into the future began to occur to me. I knew from my experience in auto at this point that the next outbreak would be about the nature of the work, the oppressive nature of life in the plants, about the humanization of working conditions.

III

Rank and file revolts today remain isolated and localized. They'll begin to develop to a new plateau once it's discovered how to create an organizational vehicle whereby they can merge and no longer be isolated. But that means a new form of organization, and if that new organization doesn't change existing institutions, particularly of unions and collective bargaining, it will re-bureaucratize rapidly. Rank-and-file movements are already having the experience of sending good rank and filers into the bureaucracy and losing them as fast as they send them in, because the institutions aren't being changed. And, if we don't find a way to avoid rapid bureaucratization, we'll merely create more cynicism.

The only organizational means that I know of that cannot be taken over by a union bureaucracy are the informal work groups in the workplaces. The greatest enemies the groups have are unemployment or any change in the technology that destroys the group's life continuity, internal relationships and group-culture. Industries that don't have these groups, like the teamsters who drive alone on a truck, are at a natural disadvantage. But if informal work groups are the only form of organization that can't be taken over by a bureaucracy, then anti-bureaucratic organizational vehicles have to be based in them. The only way I have been able to think of it is to obtain a ratio of stewards or committeemen representation of about 1-to-15 or 1-to-25. That would mean that every steward would be a working steward, working within the vision of, in direct contact with, these informal work groups—something like the way it used to be in Chrysler before 1955 when Reuther allowed that corporation to adopt GM patterns. In effect, the work day is a full day of meeting within each one of these groups. And if the representative gets out of line, he or she is on the job and can be disciplined by the threat of chill-treatment, ridicule, and worse. If stewards' committees at that representation level were to be pyramided into councils on an area level and finally into congresses on a national level, then the people involved in that pyramiding would still come under some kind of disciplinary hold of people on the job. If the American working class could get an appreciably shorter work week, which is technologically possible, then no matter to how high an office a person went he or she would still be working representatives. The representation time it would take would come out of leisure time as well as work time.

The labor movement in this country has never done a thing with the whole primary work group concept. And that's where the muscle of the workers is and where the union's strength should be. A workplace isn't a collection of individuals so much as a collection of informal groups. Until you recognize that, you're not really into utilizing the power of people in the workplace.

At no time in our society has there ever been a serious discussion of work. The workplace is where most of a human's waking hours are spent. For the first time we have to examine the total oppressiveness of the individual's life. Workers in large numbers can have a fairly good life economically. But the total life experience is a very oppressive one and this goes for all levels of the working class in this country. People seek new solutions to that oppressiveness each day of their lives rather than just in terms of the next union contract or the next strike, and that is not being spoken to, whether it be in terms of heavy industrial, white collar, or professional work. I recently quoted a humorous Big Bill Haywood story to a carpenter with the remark, ''Nothing's too good for the workers.'' He answered, ''Yeah, until they get on the job.''

The combination of a long period of relative full employment and automation has to a considerable extent destroyed the old values and work ethic at all levels of our labor force. In their desperation to lift morale, eliminate sabotage and increase production, employers are doing dabbling experiments involving piddling amounts of worker control. The official labor leadership fails to grasp the opening this provides to win some real controls. Their piecemeal approach looks to earlier retirements rather than humanizing the work. For the rank and file, life is supposed to begin with pension qualification in the autumn of existence. The view "from below" is quite different and that is the only place where real force generates to bring satisfaction, dignity and creativity to the work process.

GEORGE SULLIVAN

GEORGE SULLIVAN is a member of FASH (Fraternal Association of Steel Haulers), an organization of rank-and-file truck-drivers. He has lived for many years in Gary, Indiana, where FASH originated.

The steelhaulers who belong to FASH are owner-operators. They purchase their own equipment, pay all the cost of operating it plus fines and other incidentals, but are not allowed to haul for hire. They must lease their trucks to trucking companies on terms which are decided by the companies, although subject to bargaining by the International Brotherhood of Teamsters.

In 1967 the steelhaulers had not had a pay increase for eleven years. The Teamsters Union told them there was nothing it could do to increase their rates. After repeated protests, in August 1967 a small group of steelhaulers in Gary began to picket the headquarters of the Teamsters local. They were rebuffed. An even smaller group then set up a picket line at the gates of U. S. Steel Gary Works, one of the largest steel mills in the United States. Drivers began turning back and by nightfall steel shipments in the Gary area had halted.

For three weeks the men in Gary picketed alone. Then a group from Wisconsin came in and asked if they could help. The strike spread to Pennsylvania and other eastern states. In the seventh week of the strike the governor of Pennsylvania called together representatives of seven states, management, and labor. Agreements were reached providing pay increases amounting to eleven per cent over the next three years, and pay for loading and unloading trucks. FASH was born from this successful spontaneous strike.

George Sullivan has told the story of this strike in "Teamsters In Revolt: The Birth of FASH," a pamphlet published by the Writers Workshop in Gary, and reprinted by *Liberation* magazine in May 1971 under the title, "Rank and File Rebellion in the International Brotherhood of Teamsters." He also wrote an unpublished book-length history of FASH from which a few portions of this account were taken.

Here, George Sullivan describes the experiences which formed his ideas. He portrays himself as a small boy, raising and lowering the flag each day day at the schoolhouse, as an ex-serviceman taking part in the beatnik movement, and as a scab during the FASH strike before he joined FASH in 1969.

Since 1970, George Sullivan has been active in the Gary community. He was chairman of the Crime and Corruption Committee of the Calumet Community Congress, founder of the Calumet Action League, and assistant coordinator of the 1972 McGovern campaign in Lake County, Indiana.

GEORGE SULLIVAN

Working for Survival

I

MY FATHER was from southern Illinois. His parents were born there and lived on a little farm. My father went into the service, came out and got a service-connected pension, something wrong with his lungs. He acquired a little farm, too. He could do almost anything he was pleased to.

Dad wouldn't take anything from WPA. We had a relief program which people could get. (I remember because I used to sneak off to a neighbor's house and get me half a grapefruit or something like that.) He always talked about anybody who was on that relief program or welfare [as] some kind of a bad individual, to take something for nothing and not working for it. He had a pension and he would get $50 a month and that's what he fed us on.

There were fourteen children in the family. Two died but there were twelve survivors. We were just one year after another until there were about six or seven of us. Unfortunately, I was the first one of the second group. I was at the wrong age to get any clothes handed down to me. I had less than the others because of that.

I had one pair of overalls and I would wear these all week to school. And then on Saturday I'd have to go around the house wrapped up in a sheet while my mother washed them and hung them on the clothesline to dry. That was a very uncomfortable kind of thing. We used to wear tennis shoes all winter because they were the cheapest shoes you could buy. And my feet were always cold.

My father had a lot of attitudes that I haven't seen in other parents. He didn't seem to feel pain very much and for that reason whenever he punished his sons he would overdo it. I think he thought we couldn't feel it, either. I don't remember ever seeing him act as if anything bothered him, and I've seen him in situations where he should have. If he hurt himself it just didn't seem to harm him. We weren't ever allowed to cry around him. He stressed that boys don't cry.

I never knew that other kids sat on their parents' laps. We never did that kind of thing. I don't blame my parents for that. There were just too many of us.

The only one of my grandparents I ever knew was my grand-mother. She was always harassing my mother about something. They were always arguing. I never did even know why. She died when I was probably six or seven years old.

My mom and dad didn't go to church but they made us go. Dad kept a Bible in the house and he used to read it a lot and he always justified things by making comments or quotes from the Bible.

Reading was the first thing I can remember that I felt aggrievec about. My sister used to read the funny papers to me every Sunday. She'd get the paper and read it to me and I would watch as she was reading and follow all the action. Buck Rogers was my favorite. I'd spend half the day with the paper just going over what she'd been reading to me and trying to identify the words. If I didn't know I'd go back and ask her. This was before I went to school.

So I reached the point where I felt competent that I could read the newspaper. I got up real early one Sunday morning and went and got the paper before anybody else. I read it over first to make sure that I could understand it. When I took it in I announced to everybody that I was going to read the paper that morning, which I did. They said, "Aw, that's nothing, your sister's already read the paper to you and you memorized it." She said, "No, I haven't read it." Everybody denied that they had read the paper to me. At that time I really expected to get some credit for being able to read the paper without anybody reading it before I did. They just wouldn't believe it or they acted like "so what?" (Now I'm wondering why I didn't get any credit for being able to read it *after* someone else had read it to me!) That's one of the paradoxes that I ran into early.

Reading *Tom Sawyer* is almost like reading about my own childhood. I didn't have a river but we had creeks. I played in or around water all the time. I spent a lot of time in the woods. We played cowboys and Indians. We carved pistols out of wood that looked almost real. We even used to make our own holsters out of possum hides. We rode horses a lot of the time we were playing cowboys and Indians. Everybody had horses. We didn't have saddles. (If you didn't have a saddle you had to be one of the Indians.) We made bows and arrows that you could actually kill small game with.

I had a hearing problem but I didn't know that. I thought people didn't talk loud enough. In school I was doing very badly in classes where you had to have a lot of instruction from the teacher. I think my parents really thought I was lazy, but they always just referred to me as being stupid. I was barely passing in some of the grades.

I was in fourth or fifth grade when the school nurse came along and gave us all inspections. She told the teacher and my parents that I was hard of hearing. I had a blockage in my tubes. After I got that problem taken care of I never had trouble in school again.

Our school was back in the woods and often the roads were so bad you couldn't get in. The teacher had to drive some distance. If he couldn't get in he might have to walk, he might be late. So he asked for someone to be at the school every day to build a fire in the furnace, sweep the schoolhouse out and put up the flag, and he said he'd pay five dollars a month for that. So I took the job. I was only six or seven years old at the time. I did that for ten years.

I'd always have the flag flying before anybody got there. It was a point of honor with me that I had to have the flag up before anybody got to school. I didn't want them to be at school with the flag not up.

Taking the flag down was the same way. I never did let that flag get down on the ground. It was a pretty big flag too, or it seemed big to me at the time. Sometimes it would get all over the place when I was trying to get it down but I never did let it get on the ground. I would always fold it in a cocked hat like you're supposed to do. We had a little shelf where I put it away. I was really proud of that flag.

I liked to read a lot so I was always reading about American history and the flag plays a great part in the early years. The flag meant all the things I was reading in the books. Everybody is a hero. We were fortunate in never getting a bad guy to be president. We never had a louse in high office. America has always managed to get enemies who were evil. I don't think I ever read in school about us being in conflict with someone who wasn't of a very evil nature. I was just proud of the fact that we as a nation were able to be so selective in our enemies.

When you read about other nations who have been aggressive, the world is full of bad guys. There's always nations that are ripping off other nations and in some cases they're both mean people. In religions, the Moslems and Hindus and so forth . . . I just felt great to live in a nation where we were Christians and we didn't make those kind of mistakes. I can't ever remember feeling that America had attacked someone who didn't really deserve it.

I can remember very well the feeling I had for that flag. I knew what it meant to me. It was not the same as it is now. That's what gives me the feeling that I was cheated as well as lied to. I read the books that talked about indentured servants at the same time they praised the glories of America. I read the books that talked about our great cotton production in the South and the greatness of the nation at the same time that they talked about the slaves. And when I read *Uncle Tom's Cabin* I didn't read any indictment of America into that. I feel stupid. It's like I was sitting there watching someone deal from the bottom of the deck but I didn't even pay attention to it. Why didn't I see it? You feel like an idiot.

Maybe part of it is that I was too young when reading the books to understand what was being said. When I read books about Indian wars, the way the Indians would do in the woods and the things they could do, I related to that because I spent a lot of time in the woods, too. I tried all that stuff, trying to make arrowheads out of flintstones, building a fire with a stick (which I never was able to do). But I could still accept that they were bad because they didn't believe in God. Their god wasn't explained the way ours is. They

were here trying to keep this land away from us and it should right-
fully have been ours because we were smart enough to find it. [The
books] didn't go into the fact that [the Indians] found it a long time
before we did or that they were already here. Naturally when you're
young you don't put those ideas into context.

I read every book in our school library and I was having my sisters
bring home books from high school, but some kinds of books I never
got to see. None of the people in my type of background read a
book like *The Wind in the Willows*. If anyone around had read it
I would have heard of it so that I know that that book is not a part
of our culture. The people who have read it are middle-class or
upper-middle-class. It is not a working-class fairy tale.

In all the fairy tales that we had, one thing came through loud
and clear. There was always the squirrel that wouldn't work, that
wouldn't do anything in the summer but play games. He was stupid.
And he either met eventual death or suffered through the winter on
someone else's charity, was a welfare case you might say. And after
that one miserable experience he then learned his lesson and worked
hard and industriously for the rest of his life. The transgression of
the law may be slight—in an animal story it is always slight, like
an old bear stealing the honey—but the punishment that befalls those
who break the laws is terrible. In my fairy tales I never encountered
an unjust judge or an unfair policeman.

And when I [recently] read *The Wind in the Willows* it was so
opposite. The rat and the mole get together, the rat runs down into
the hole and comes out with a picnic basket packed with a thousand
goodies. It was just there: he probably had a servant. But had I read
that fairy tale [as a child], there would first have been a description
of the work that went into the preparation of that picnic basket and
where all this food came from. There would have been a big difference in the way he acquired it, and the way they acquired food all
through the summer. And never once was there a mention that they
must worry about the winter that was coming. Somehow they were
going to party through the winter or just sleep it off. Like the badger,
when they went into his house after being caught out in the snow,
here he was with this huge larder, well-stocked, and the badger did
nothing but diddle around all summer too. Their greatest fear was

the stoats and the weasels. I immediately related that to us. The stoats and the weasels are those low-class groups out of the woods who might want to take some of the goodies. It made me mad.

There never was any question in my mind that niggers weren't any good. I knew that, but it didn't necessarily mean they were bad people because everyone knew that a nigger's a coward and that he won't cause you any trouble. The one thing I never knew anyone to worry about was problems with the niggers. There weren't any around where I lived.

One did come to the house one time, scared me to death. I saw him at the door, there he was, and I didn't know what to do. Any time we would be doing something wrong, one of the comments my mother would make was, "I'll have some big nigger come and get you if you don't stop that." So I went to the door and there was this big nigger. I just knew that he had come after me. But that's the only association I had. I wasn't taught to hate them. It was like the feeling about animals. It's OK but their place is not in the house or it's not where *you* are. Animals live in the woods. Niggers live somewhere else.

My first association with black people was when I went in the service. They were following the policy of integration. We were in a barracks with three black guys, seventy or seventy-five white guys. The blacks were not hard to get along with. It would have been kind of foolish if they were.

The first real association I had was in England. I transferred to a new base. I got there in the middle of the day. They told me what barracks I was assigned to. I went into the barracks and no one was there. Everybody was out working. I put my gear all in, made my bed and everything and went to the canteen and came back about 3:30 or 4:00. I walked in and I didn't see a white face. It was a barracks full of black people.

I knew, of course, that the sergeant had made an error, put me in the wrong barracks. So I went to the headquarters and told him he'd made a mistake. "No, we've been having some problems about not integrating enough. As new white guys come on the base they're going to be put in there. You just happen to be the first." I said, "But you don't understand. I'm the only guy. You don't put just one white guy in with all those black people." He made me to understand that they did and that's the way it was to be. I wasn't very happy with that.

The first couple of days I didn't talk to any of them. They didn't talk to me. I restricted all their conversation, that was obvious, because they were having a real good time and when I walked in everything just quieted down. It was their first realization that they had a white guy in the barracks. They didn't know how to deal with that any more than I knew how to deal with all of them.

I was a meat-cutter and I got a bit careless. I cut three or four of my fingers. I had them all bandaged up. I had just been promoted to sergeant but I still wore my corporal stripes. I was sitting out in front of the barracks and the sergeant came by and he said, "Sullivan, aren't you a member of the first class?" "Yes." He said, "Well, get your stripes on." "I can't sew with one hand," I said, "and I don't have any money to take them over to the PX." They charged something like fifty cents a set to put them on. He said, "I don't care. You'll have stripes on your uniform by tomorrow or we'll just take the stripes away from you."

I was stitting there by myself just wondering what to do. One of the guys in the barracks who'd heard it, he came out and said, "Have you already got your stripes?" I said, "Yeah, I bought them already." He said, "Well if you go get them I'll sew them on for you." So that was the first thing that really broke the ice. He sat and sewed those stripes on my uniform while we got to know each other.

I was in the service for four years. It was my first experience being in other countries. I was in France, Denmark, Germany and England.

When I got to England I just went wild—I thought I was in the land of my books. Robin Hood had been one of my heroes. And the knights and King Arthur's Round Table and, boy, it was all there. When I first saw Ely Castle I couldn't believe it, still the old castle with the moat around it, the drawbridge. I went to Nottingham, Sherwood Forest . . . I just couldn't stop. From the time I went to England until I came back I was going where my books were.

When I used to read all the time about England and Richard the Lion Hearted, he was mine. So was Robin Hood. It almost felt like these were my people. I felt like that was the mother country. Maybe I felt like it was part of our ancestry or something. But other guys over there didn't have that feeling at all. They treated the English as though they were beneath contempt. It used to anger me, some of the tricks they would pull.

Even before I went to England I had some admiration for the bobbies in England. And after getting there and watching them operate I had even more. I had already been instructed in America by the police to move on or get out of the way a time or two. It's unbelievable, to have a bobby come up and say, "Sir, if you'll excuse me a moment, you are blocking the sidewalk. Please move on." They spoke so polite that for a moment you weren't sure they were serious. They were very serious and when they asked you to move, they intended for you to move. American cops have the attitude of "get the hell out of the way" and start shoving. I never saw London bobbies do that.

When I went to France and other places I would search out someone who was a civilian there, find out what he had to tell me about where he lived. The only time I was in a problem, I was in the Bastille area in France and although I wasn't wearing my uniform I was immediately spotted for an American. It was all Communists there and they started a terrific uproar about "Yankee go home" and all that stuff. But even at that point, when they were doing it, I understood what they were angry about because I had already seen what the GIs were doing to the people over there, the way they treated them, and I knew why they would be yelling "Yankee go home," so it didn't make me angry. I would always go out and look for what was going on and hear the other side of the story. I thought the Communists were a bit silly but I liked to hear what the *people* were saying. I liked to talk to them.

I came home with a different feeling than I had before. I no longer felt as proud to be an American as I had in the past. I just didn't feel that sense of we were unique. I began to have more the idea that we exist and they exist.

I lost a lot of my ideas about what you should and shouldn't do. I began to feel like maybe in America you'd just as well go ahead and do what you felt like doing because nobody really gave a damn about it anyway. Before I went into the service, to do something against the law, to do something you're not supposed to do, was a bad thing. When I came out I didn't have the respect for the law that I had had before because I felt that the law itself was a cheat. I guess I lost my sense of right and wrong.

In the service in the early fifties I had the experience of meeting people from all over the United States. Most of these people were not gung-ho Americans who had enlisted to be heroes for the country. They were guys who had done exactly what I had done. They had joined the Air Force to escape being drafted into the Army and going to Korea. Most of us had older brothers coming out of World War II who had the experience of going to war and they were all giving the same advice: "Man, get into the Air Force. You don't get your ass shot off." So I think that the Air Force was the recipient at that time of what is today the draft dodger.

I came back into civilian life in the mid-fifties. That's when the beatnik thing was beginning, the idea of "let's just get out of it and not be involved." Disillusionment was what was taking place, but the action was to just set down and do nothing, not be a part of what you considered a very phony world.

When I came out of the service I worked for just a little while and then I didn't work any more. I felt that it didn't serve a purpose. It wouldn't lead anywhere. And the idea of being forced to work just for survival—it seemed to me to be degrading that you should have to work simply because you are a human being and you are here. I started wondering, who made those kind of rules and why?

I remember meeting an old guy who said he refused to work because he'd never been able to find a job where someone else didn't make a profit off his efforts, and he was looking for a job where he was the recipient of all he produced. I wasn't looking for that kind of job. I just wasn't looking for a job. But neither were a whole lot of guys at that time.

I think the beatniks were political by being apolitical. They were the ones who were just beginning to set down and say, "I don't want to participate." It wasn't like the strikes in the thirties when people would set down and strike as a demand for something. They just didn't want anything. They wanted to disassociate themselves. And I can see now how it would be really dangerous [to the system] for working-class people to do that.

I met them all over the country when I was going around, and nearly all of them were from working-class families. They had a mom and dad and a small home somewhere and everybody in the family worked but them and they were considered the bum or the outcast of the family. They didn't feel guilty about it. They just felt, "Why the hell should I work if I can do something else?" It wasn't a welfare attitude. I never signed for unemployment or did all that. I somehow scuffled my own living and I did things that were illegal as well at times to get some money or to get survival, but I didn't feel guilty about that because I could have shown a policeman doing something illegal to match what we were doing that was illegal. So, I felt, fair is fair.

I remember jokes that you could very easily relate to at the time. You may remember the attitude of the beatnik when the guy was laying in the street, got run over by a car, and was saying, "Call me an ambulance." And the beatnik says, "OK, man, you're an ambulance," his attitude being, I'm not a part of whatever's taking place and I don't want to be. There were a whole series of them. They called it the beat generation or the cool generation because they were totally unruffled by whatever was surrounding them.

The beat generation made a thing out of saying everything very slowly and very drawn out—no fire, no snap—even in conversation they were saying "I quit." They always stressed the same thing, their disinterest in what was taking place.

Another one of their expressions was "no sweat." That's an expression from the fifties, no sweat. Don't get excited. Don't worry about it. And they didn't sweat about anything.

I had very much the same sense myself, and I'm sure a lot of other guys had it, that everywhere I was at I was a spectator. I remember an incident in Ohio sitting on a hill, looking over the town and just watching what the people were doing and thinking,

"This is ridiculous." I remember hearing a door slam and it's in the evening and a mother calling her kid to come to supper and I was thinking, "She's worried about the kid. He's out playing ball and he doesn't want to be bothered. She's worried about his not coming." I knew other mothers who used to be that way at home and I thought, "Isn't it silly? People all over the country are out now yelling for their kids to come for supper and they're all worried about where the kid is and when he's coming." It's just like a whole big issue over nothing. Everything I saw I was putting into the context of, "Why is everybody getting excited? It's not important." You would see a squad car roaring up and down the street, answering a burglar alarm or what-have-you, and your thought would be, "So what's the hurry?"

Throughout that whole group of guys that I knew there was the feeling that nothing is worth [worrying about]. They weren't bad people and most of them finally got married and I guess most of them are back within the system and working. I don't think they care that much now about what is going on. But somehow or another you get forced into working for your survival.

I knew how to drive and that's one of the things I used to do when I was drifting around. If I got really hard up for money and didn't see any other way to acquire it, I'd go somewhere and drive a truck for a short time. Also I could drive a taxicab. A lot of the guys I knew did cab driving as an odd job, whenever they needed a few dollars.

I got into driving a truck seriously in 1960, drove for a while. . . . Then the guy asked me if I'd go to work in the office. I did and in a short time I was running the terminal. I got bored with that and I quit, went back to doing nothing for a long time. . . .

I went downtown and got involved with some poker games, working for the house joints. I did that until '65. Then I went back to driving a truck again and I drove a truck most of the time up until the FASH strike [in 1967].

Trucking is a job to which a man soon becomes addicted. The young people have been insisting that there is more to life than money and though the average trucker may not know how to express it in words, he feels the essence of this belief deeply. I will not attempt to speak for everyone but, as for myself, I have a weakness for the late hours of the night.

Running late at night through small rural towns I often have the feeling that I am the only one awake in the whole world. Things appear different from high in the cab of a truck. The trees along the road make a tunnel through which your headlights illuminate a semi-circle of green. The limbs across the road are so close that at times I can reach out and touch them. Mailboxes seem to rise up from the ground as my lights pick them up. The dashlights glow softly in the dark and the dials are constantly keeping me informed that all is well with "my horse." The easy snick-snick of the stick as I change gears and the sound of the tires singing in the cool night air, all combine to make my truck seem like a living thing that is keeping me safe and protected in its shell. Oncoming trucks blink their lights in a friendly hello as we pass in the night, or maybe flash them to warn me about the local cop in the next town who may be still awake trying to make another fine before he turns in. Another truck overtaking me comes around and I see the same soft glowing lights in his cab as he lifts his hand from the wheel to wave. I signal him in and he fades off into the darkness leaving me alone with my thoughts again. There is a soft glow in the East and then the rising sun comes up on a new world for I am four hundred miles from last night. These are the hours that compensate for the rest of it and for me they are the best part of trucking. Although the hours are long and hard and the amount of money earned is often less after expenses than in other skilled trades, most truckers will not trade places with anyone.

Truckers who have taken the time to talk to the young have learned to their surprise that they are in agreement on about ninety per cent of the discussion. The two major differences are that the truckers believe that the establishment should not be overthrown as it would only be replaced by another rule that might be harder to handle. They prefer instead to give City Hall the same treatment as the proverbial mule.

The other major difference is in the area of tactics. In spite of all the publicity, the students are far too mild-mannered and don't have enough "clout." A reporter for *Iron Age* has researched the matter and stated that, "The revolt of the truckers has made the student rebellion seem like a Sunday school picnic by comparison."

II

I did not become a FASH member until August of 1969. Along with many other steelhaulers, I had thought that their original protest in 1967 would be a waste of time. They were fighting with the Teamsters Union and I felt that they did not have a chance.

When the protest of 1967 began I was working as a dispatcher for Artim Transportation Company in East Chicago, Indiana. Throughout the protest this company never stopped operating. As trucks began coming in with bullet holes, busted windshields and shattered radiators, I started to wonder what made the drivers keep going out. The clerk typing out the bills thought he had the answer. "They're nuts," he used to say over and over. "They don't know those bullets can hurt you."

Along about the middle of the strike, I started driving again and so began my first experience as a scab. I thought I was missing all the fun but I soon learned that it was the other side that was having the fun. A truck strike is unlike any other because you don't just go through a picket line and have only one danger point. All the time you are on the highway, you are a target and you never know where it is coming from next. The scabs may not like to admit it, but when they reach their destination they all breathe a little bit easier.

I have never met [a scab] who could give a sensible reason for trying to prevent his fellow men from gaining a better way of life. All scabs refuse to discuss the issues at stake or go to strike meetings to hear what's going on. Knowledge is a dangerous thing to a scab's existence for once he learns what it is all about, he ceases to be a scab or else exposes himself to be the kind of no good bastard that some scabs are.

There are many reasons why a scab is such a hated man. There is much more to it than the mere fact that he is working. There is often a long history of injustice behind the man who is aiming the rifle. Just how long that history is and how much effect it has

had on him is what determines whether he aims at a tire or the driver.
For myself, there had been very little direct injustice. I had won
only one grievance while with the union which should have paid
me about a thousand dollars or more. The business agents had told
me that I would have to take four hundred dollars or shut up about
it. I hadn't thought I was getting a fair deal but the drivers who
were old hands told me that it was par for the course and I was
lucky to get that.

I joined FASH because I saw that it was a good thing for the owner-
operator. When I first met Tom Gwilt, president of the Indiana
chapter of FASH, and Paul Dietsch, who is president of the Wisconsin
chapter, I was not very impressed. They seemed like a couple of
nice enough guys but they were not what I had expected the officers
of a growing organization to be. They acted just like truck drivers.
We had been complaining for years that no one else understood the
steelhaulers' special problems and that what we needed was our own
thing. We wanted our own people to run it. Now we had exactly
that and here I was thinking to myself, "What are these guys doing
in charge? They don't know any more than I do." As I got to know
them better, I found out that they knew a hell of a lot more than
I did and they had learned it the hard way.

I had never felt any inclination or impulse to change the world
around me. I felt in any situation I went into that it was that way
before I got there. And if I didn't like it or couldn't make it with
that situation, I would just leave it and find another one. For all
I cared it could stay that way forever, so long as what was happening
didn't infringe on me. I really didn't want any conflicts. I'd done
a lot of scuffling earlier and I didn't want to do it any more—unless
it involved money or something I was really trying to protect. I had
developed the attitude of not bothering anyone who didn't bother
me, not trying to take something that wasn't mine, but because of
that, I had to make very sure that what was mine was not touched
or not bothered. On the street there are certain things that are yours.
Your car is a valuable possession, your girl friend is a valuable possession, and your money. Anything else is not really worth so much,
if you don't own a house or property. If someone is bothering your
girl friend and she doesn't like it, you tell him not to. And if he

keeps on, you really make him to understand that he is not to do that. If they're trying to take your money or trying to do something to your car, those are what you have outlined as your rights. I never would have gone out of my way or gotten involved to protect someone else's rights. It had to be mine before I would do anything.

The incident with the Teamsters involved one of the three things that you never surrendered to somebody else. Money, perhaps because it's so necessary to survival, perhaps because the only reason you're going through a lot of things that you are is for that money, is the one thing above all that you never let anyone take away from you. You just don't let that happen. I didn't get into it because I felt that it was up to me to change what was taking place in the union. I was going to fight them because my money was involved.

Really, the only reason I was involved with it was that I was trying to get myself uninvolved, by saying, "Give me what's mine, stop doing what you are doing wrong, and then we'll get along with each other." So [I began] to look around for allies, somebody to help, and the problem kept growing. I knew in the back of my mind all the time the way the whole system was but I just never cared. Somewhere I began to realize this: the only thing to do is to change the whole system or you got to go through this the rest of your life. And I expected that when I was done with this argument I'd be back trucking so while I was at it I might as well get the whole problem cleaned out. So it was for very personal reasons that I was trying to change the Teamster system, because I planned to go back to driving a truck and I didn't want to be harassed later.

At the time that I joined FASH, they had been fighting an unpublicized war with the union leaders for two and a half years. They were preparing to distribute a magazine called *Teammate* which told about the Teamsters officials' nefarious activities with the members' money. As far as the Teamster officials are concerned, it is an unwritten law in the Teamsters Union that what is done with the members' money is not to be discussed.

After reading the first issue of *Teammate*, I was sure that somebody was not going to like it. Just as I expected, about a week after we had started distributing the first issue of *Teammate*, trouble arrived.

I was at the terminal working on my truck when Don Williams, a long-time friend of mine, came speeding up in his car. He jumped out and said, "Hey George, I just heard a radio broadcast that said that Tom Gwilt's house was bombed." "Is anyone hurt?" I asked. "I don't think anyone was home when it happened," he replied. "Come on, let's get over there and see if there might be something we can do."

When we found Tom, he was at a neighbor's home who had been kind enough to give him and his wife Betty a place to stay. Paul Dietsch was there also and he gave us a rundown on what had happened.

Tom and Paul had been in Pittsburgh and Betty and their two children were visiting a relative when their house was bombed. We assumed that our enemy had known this and so the bomb was simply their time-honored method of giving a warning that FASH was getting out of line.

There were several other drivers there and more came in while I was there. Most of them had been with FASH since its beginning. I noticed that Tom was having a disagreement with some of them and I walked over to them to see what was going on.

The men were planning to take action against the union officials in Local 142 and Tom was trying to discourage them. "No! No! you guys," he was saying. "There wasn't anybody hurt so don't do anything foolish. Let the police handle it."

"Police, hell!" exclaimed one of the drivers. "They wouldn't arrest one of those sons-a-bitches if they had watched him set off the bomb."

"Listen to us, Tom," another driver said. "If we let them get away with this there will be more trouble later. I think they are testing us to see what we will do."

Then another driver spoke. "Just one will be enough," he said. "We'll just get one of them and that will be enough to show that we mean business," and he named the man that he thought we should hit.

Tom was adamant, however, and he refused to give in. "This is just their way of harassing us," he said. "As long as they don't kill any of our people, we won't kill any of theirs and if you get

carried away now it might cause a lot of unnecessary bloodshed.''
We had no proof of who had bombed the house, of course, but there
wasn't a man there who thought it was anyone other than the Teamsters Union. Tom managed to cool things down and went inside to
prepare a press release for the newsmen who were on their way over
for an interview.

I went up the street and looked at the remains of Tom's house.
Whenever we hear about gun battles and bombs and other kinds of
violence, we don't usually think too much about it. That sort of
thing always seems to happen to strangers and doesn't make too
much of an impact unless a lot of people are killed or hurt. When
it is someone you know it changes things. No one had been hurt
but that explosion had been a message. Someone was trying to tell
us something and I didn't like it. I had grown up believing that I
was lucky to be born in a country where men had a freedom to
choose their own destiny, and terrorism was something that I had
not experienced. I had been happily helping to build an organization
that would be our own thing and, in my innocence, I had thought
that we had every right to do so. And now, I was looking at a message that drew the line of freedom loud and clear. To me it said,
so far—and no farther.

During the next few days as I watched Tom and Betty trying to
clean up the mess caused by the blast, I did a lot of thinking. Betty
Gwilt had been extremely helpful to Tom in his work with FASH and I
thought that if she were to become afraid to go on, it might cause
Tom to quit also.

The Gwilts had only recently redecorated their home and, like
most wives, Betty had been rather proud of their new furniture and
the new wall-to-wall carpet in their living room. I was thinking about
the carpet because they used the house as sort of a second office
and since steelhaulers usually have their shoe soles impregnated with
oil and grease, Betty always made us take off our shoes before we
walked on the carpet. So now, most of the furniture was destroyed,
the carpet was a mess and Tom didn't have any insurance.

I could see that Betty was having a tough time controlling her
emotions. We didn't have any trouble in removing the damaged furniture because the entire front of the house was gone and we could

just walk from the front yard into the living room at any point we wanted to. Betty was trying to sweep up the rubble that was lying all over the place and once I saw her pick up a broken object from a pile of rubble and she stood there turning it over and over in her hand and looking at it for a long time. The expression in her face was one of deep sadness. I don't know what the object was or what it meant to her, but she didn't seem to want to part with it, even though it was destroyed. She finally laid it back in the pile of rubbish and walked away.

There was only one time when I thought she was going to give up. The carpet she was so proud of was split in several places and had also been scorched where the bomb had exploded. Tom was holding up the edge of the carpet and inspecting the damage when he said, "What do you think, Betty? Maybe if we sewed it up it wouldn't look so bad and we could still use it." She looked at him as if she were about to cry and said, "Oh, Tom," in a very quiet sad voice and then sat down and put her face in her hands.

I suddenly had the feeling that there were too many people in the house so I walked outside. Betty toughened up after that though and never once did I hear her mention the possibility of quitting. I wanted to tell about this incident because afterwards someone was trying to spread the rumor that Tom had blown up his own house for publicity.

After the bombing of Tom's house I began to realize that the FASH leaders had knowingly laid their lives on the line. They had also placed their wives and children in danger. It was not for money because any driver with a steady job earns more than a FASH officer. I am not the hero type and my good sense was telling me that we weren't playing with kids.

There were some other things going through my mind also. I have had the experience of talking to people who talk in glowing terms about the great freedom we have and in the next breath say to me, "You had better not do anything those people don't like or you will get yourself hurt." I think a newspaper reporter summed up the whole situation when he said, "We are not restricted but we know what we should not say."

I don't like to admit it, but I had always belonged to that rather large part of the population that prefers to let other people do the fighting while we set back and wait to see what they win for us this time. After thinking the matter over I decided that I would stay with FASH and if it led me to danger I would face it in the best way that I knew how.

KEN TUCKER

A T THE TIME of the events described in this account, Ken Tucker was the secretary of an independent local union of chemical workers at the Du Pont Chemical Company plant in East Chicago, Indiana.

The situation of workers at Du Pont is like that of many workers in the early 1930s. When Ken Tucker became a union officer the Du Pont union had never been on strike. For all practical purposes it was a company union. Tucker and his fellow-officers bargained militantly and finally led the union on strike, only to find that as a single local union confronting a national corporation their position was very weak.

Before going to work at Du Pont, Ken Tucker had started an underground newspaper for servicemen in Korea. But as he candidly explains, when he first became involved in union affairs it was as a stepping-stone to a job as a foreman. His experience as a local union officer changed his mind.

Ken Tucker is one of a group of younger workers at the Du Pont plant who, like younger workers elsewhere, want not only material benefits but a voice in decision-making. When they went on strike they raised pollution as a strike issue so as to win community support. As an unintended result, Ken Tucker himself became the first president of a multi-issue community organization, the Calumet Community Congress, formed in December 1970.

KEN TUCKER

It Got My Back Up

I STARTED WORKING at Du Pont in 1963, after I got out of the Service. I was single at the time and didn't care especially where I worked. I was just knocking around, looking for a paycheck. My family had a past history of working at Du Pont. My foster father and my uncle had worked there for a total of more than eight years. So it was natural that I had a little pull to get in.

In fact, it wasn't until I was elected secretary of the union and went through the records that I realized my foster father had been secretary years before. I hold him responsible for a lot of the problems at the place!

Du Pont screens very carefully in hiring. One of the first questions you are asked is how you feel about international unions, and how you feel about unions in general. And of course, someone coming off the street and looking for a job is not going to take a militant union stand. At the time, being twenty-three years old and not really caring about people's problems, just caring about myself, I was pretty honest with them when I said that an independent union was fine with me, no union was fine with me, the only thing I wanted was a job.

So I got hired in. After working there for a while, and getting married and having a family, just like anybody else I started to think about ways to move up the ladder. Our plant has a simple way for a working guy to advance. All you had to do was get elected to a union job, work closely with management and show some potential for leadership, and inside of a year or so you'd get a nice job as a foreman. About ninety per cent of the supervisors have come off the union board.

Recognizing that this was the way to get a better-paying job, I decided to run for union office. This was in 1968. I had been there five years and was known only in my own department, where I had been a steward and had raised some hell, done some rather militant things. They were really done for my own self-interest, as a way to get attention and to move up.

I was elected by two votes. For three or four years prior to the election our union had been starting to flex its muscles, trying to become a union and really represent the guys. Those of us running for office attacked the incumbents for failing to communicate with the grassroots and failing to allow decisions to be made at union meetings. Just before the election there was a union meeting at which the president said that a wage offer had been made to the union, and the membership could vote on it if it wanted to, but it didn't make any difference because the offer had already been accepted. Being a politician, I took him on strongly and this probably got me the votes I needed to win. I was twenty-eight years old and the next to oldest man on the new board of the union. John Smrekar, the new president, was twenty-six.

During the years I've been in office my viewpoint has changed, obviously. I've had two offers to go into supervision. The first was a sincere offer, I think, but the last was just to get me out of there.

It's a simple thing that happens. Even though I was still looking out for Number One, I did have the responsibility of protecting other people and they had grievances and complaints. It put me into a head-on battle with the company. It's a tragedy that every wageroll guy doesn't have that experience. Because it didn't take me very long of being involved in a confrontation with the company over a legitimate grievance to begin to see what we were up against. Being on a union board, and doing this an average of once or twice a day, my whole outlook changed. I had worked in one department where I saw maybe one guy get messed over a month, and now I had the exposure to the whole plant, and saw what was happening everywhere.

They were very reasonable demands. A contract is in effect, it's been agreed to by the union and the company, grievance procedure and everything else, and the company refuses to honor it—just completely ignores it—depending on how they feel. When you run up against this enough, you begin to get angry. You start feeling a little bit different about things. You sit down to bargain, you believe that you're supposed to be the bargaining representative of the people who elected you, and the company just puts up a pretense of bargaining so that they won't be liable under federal law. It got my back up.

Du Pont has traditionally been a very paternalistic company. One of the problems that we faced, and other Du Pont unions faced, was that for years Du Pont did take care of their employees. That was at a time when the chemical industry wasn't very competitive and Du Pont was the kingmaker. Every time there was a war, Du Pont expanded and made a lot of dough. That's not the situation today. Today everybody's into chemicals. There's a very competitive market, and in many cases they even try to withdraw the benefits that you already have. I've seen the company slip from a position of being tops in the area in wages to a position of being fifth or sixth. It's gradually falling back in every area of the contract. And Du Pont's whole language changes. When I started in it was, ''We will maintain the best pension plan of any industry in the United States.'' Their policy today is, ''We never said that. We said we'll give you one of the better pension plans.'' In a couple of years it's going to be, ''You guys have got a pretty good pension plan.''

There's also a split within the union membership. Forty-seven per cent of our employees were hired before 1958. They were there when Du Pont was the best. Many of those guys will tell you that they worked every day of the Depression. For them Du Pont can do no wrong. The rest of the guys, like myself, began hiring in around 1962 or 1963. They don't feel this loyalty, and they don't see this paternalism. Even if it was there they wouldn't want it, because their attitudes are different, they don't want things doled out to them, they want to start making decisions and they want to be involved.

We don't want to bargain on a local comparison basis. If everybody in Lake County got a $10 raise tomorrow, Du Pont would get it, too. That's not what we want. We want to have something to say about our own destiny. Our whole philosophy is that we don't

even want to compare. Our position with the company has been,
"Look, open up your books. If the East Chicago plant is making
a twenty per cent profit this year, we want a twenty per cent wage
increase."

As secretary of the union, I had possession of the records. I started
studying the history of our union a little. I found out, for example,
that in the five years before 1968 there had only been forty grievances filed. With three hundred guys in the union, that breaks down
to eight grievances a year. I found it hard to believe that the company
made mistakes only eight times a year. The first year we were in
office we had to learn what the contract was, what the grievance
procedure was, getting our education the hard way. We filed forty
grievances the first year. Now we've gotten to the point where I
myself last year filed two hundred.

In 1970 we led the first strike in the history of the union. Between
1964 and 1968 there had been three strike votes, but the union had
never gone through with it. We felt we had to.

What our strike amounted to was a strike for recognition. We had
started to bargain four months before our contract expired, and we
had been working without a contract for eight months, so we had
been trying to bargain for a year. We were unsuccessful, simply
because Du Pont refused to recognize us as a union. They didn't
believe that we would really shut them down. They had always managed to evade a strike threat without making a change. So we were
very honest with our people. We took the strike vote in January,
and we told the members: number one, if you give us the strike
vote we will use it; number two, if we strike we won't win. We
said there was no way that we could bring a corporate giant like
Du Pont to its knees, that they could spend any amount of money
to defeat us in a strike, and that from the minute we went out until
the minute we came back, we would be looking for an honorable
way to come back. But we said we had to strike to let them know
we were serious. What we were striking for was the same thing that
unions struck for in the '30s, recognition as a union.

We had no experience with strikes. Du Pont, on the other hand,
will go to fantastic lengths to win a strike. Du Pont in Niagara was
on strike for six months. The company was close to the mayor and

the City Council, and within four hours of the strike they had a court injunction guaranteeing them ingress and egress at the plant. The union wasn't even notified of its right to appear in court. They had a second exit which went out through a power company and when the union tried to picket it, they called it a secondary boycott. They organized a dissident group within the union which took the union to court on the ground that it was violating its constitution. Du Pont will use tactics you wouldn't believe. In our plant, for example, they ran trucks in and out with nothing in them, to give the impression that the plant was doing just fine. They were paying wages and everything else just to run trucks through our picket lines. They fly in scabs from all over the country. There's a law against that, but the way they get around that law is that those people all work for the Du Pont company. They tap your phones: my phone was tapped during our strike. They will hire lip readers, will you believe? They will hire lip readers who stand on top of the plant with binoculars and read what's being said on the picket lines.

We began to look around for support for our strike, before we ever went out. We raised the pollution issue at the bargaining table. We hadn't been able to move the company on anything, so we began to talk about pollution as a health and safety issue, and then we realized that we were talking about a community concern, a social problem. We thought that maybe we could move them off dead center by beginning to bargain about this. And we also thought that, if we were forced to go on a strike, we would be the first union in the country to go on strike over pollution, and possibly would pick up the support of people from the community. That's exactly what happened.

We met with the federal mediator in Chicago and he asked us what the issues were. We said, "Pollution, of the water and the air. That's the only thing we're striking for." He said, "I don't believe it. I've just come back from two weeks at a conference in Florida with people from labor, management, government, and we all agreed that one of the issues that had to come to the bargaining table was pollution. Here I am, my first day back, and that's all you guys are talking about." We went on strike the next day.

We didn't really push for press coverage. But people started to stop by and ask, "Are you really striking about pollution?" It was interesting. Our own people, when we started handing out the picket signs about pollution, would say, "What the hell are you doing?" To them we would put it that this was a major issue and maybe we could get community support on it. It really was a tactic. But as we got into it, and a citizens' support group was actually organized, it opened up a whole new world.

There was a union board, a leadership, there were union members, that were willing to come forward and testify to the public or anybody else that was interested, about what they knew about pollution. No matter what Du Pont said or did they could say, "Look man, I work there and I'm telling you what's happening." We are the only Du Pont plant that's ever been on strike without being punished, by the company shutting down facilities and moving jobs elsewhere, or something like that. And the reason was that we had community support.

The company called us and asked to meet with the union. They offered us a contract. The contract wasn't much: there was very little change that would seem meaningful to, say, the Steelworkers Union on strike. There were some things in there that I felt were important enough to strike about. For example, we never had the right to arbitrate a discharge. We won that. We never had the right to say anything when the company brought in outside contractors to do mechanical work or electrical work. We won that, too. Monetary gains were very slim, amounting to perhaps $5 a month. But the important thing was that for the first time in its its history Du Pont had changed what they call their "firm and final offer."

We went back without settling the pollution issue. But the community group did manage to negotiate a very strong agreement with Du Pont. It created an altogether different situation. Our people became aware of pollution. Our people would call me and say, "Hey, the company told me to dump something in the river last night, and I didn't do it, and they're going to give me a hard time." I'd call the company and they'd send me a written report on the investigation of the pollution incident.

It was very successful. It changed some attitudes. It helped to get our plant manager transferred, which was another reason for our going on strike, and I think that was a first, too. We managed to get a company representative to come to a meeting at Bishop Noll High School and debate the issue. I've never been so scared in my life as to be there confronting my own plant manager, calling him a liar. But I did it. The board members were there with me. I did speak up. That was one of the experiences I went through where our union could never have won anything until we tied in with the community. At the same time the community won a major victory because it had the support of the union, both the leadership and the rank and file.

The next year, when contract time came, we tried to look into Du Pont's taxes. We tried to contrast the taxes of a white employee with those of a black employee, and the taxes of Du Pont with those of a homeowner living across the street. We were going to ask Du Pont to pay its fair share of taxes in the community. I'm sure Du Pont got wind of this because the first day of contract negotiations they said, "We've really got a package for you this year." It was head and shoulders above anything we'd ever gotten before.

Being president of the Calumet Community Congress gave me some new ideas about my union work. For instance, a way to deal with problems that aren't covered by the contract. I used to think, "If it's not covered by the contract I can't file a grievance." Now I began to think of a grievance simply as a statement that you're unhappy with something. I started to say, "If there's anything you don't like, file a grievance on it. We'll interpret it as a working condition." That way, when you go into contract negotiations you can point to all the grievances that have been filed about a particular problem, and you can say, "If the contract doesn't cover them now, let's change the contract so that it does."

However, there was a limit to what we could do at a local level, no matter what we did. We had to find a way to cope with the power of Du Pont as a national corporation.

It's been an educational process that's still going on. Our independent union belongs to a federation of fifteen or twenty independent Du Pont unions. This organization has been in existence for twenty-four years. Its original idea was very good, but very limited. It was brought together on the basis of exchange of information only. Over the years, the independents around the country tried to put some muscle into that and what developed was a very severe split. There were some unions whose only purpose was to come to Atlantic City three times a year, find out what the guys in each place were doing, and then go back. The other unions that wanted to do something more tried to work within that structure, but they were doomed from the outset. Just the name itself, "Federation of *Independent* Unions," excluded some fourteen Du Pont unions that were international.

In our bargaining, the fringe benefits—vacations, pensions, holidays, military service plan, insurance—come down from Wilmington and are put into effect at every Du Pont plant whether there's a union there or not. Locally we bargain over wages and working conditions. We wanted to have some say-so in the pension, the vacation plan, and everything of that kind. After we were elected to local union office in 1968, we tried to make the Federation a more militant organization. But we met with little success.

We decided in East Chicago that the Federation was an obstacle to progress and had to be destroyed. Once there was no vehicle there, people would have to look in another direction. So people from the East Chicago, Cleveland, and Toledo plants got together and decided to go to Wilmington, the corporate headquarters. We wanted to confront the president and chairman of the board of Du Pont, Mr. McCoy. There was to be a union convention in Atlantic City that weekend, and we timed the trip to Wilmington to go there just before. We knew we wouldn't accomplish anything with Mr. McCoy. But we had suggested earlier to the Federation that they send delegates to Wilmington to meet with Mr. McCoy over a strike situation, and they voted that down. They said they could never get in. So we wanted to show that they could get in. We felt that if we could prove this, other unions in the Federation might decide to pull out.

To make a long story short, we went to Wilmington and did very well. The night before we managed to get on radio. So we hit the front page of the morning paper: seven employees in Wilmington,

which is Du Pont land. When we got to Mr. McCoy's office the
TV cameras were waiting for us. We got into his outer office. We
tried to get into his inner office, and were stopped. There were security police all over the place. Vice presidents were running around,
trying to get us to go to another room and talk it over. We said,
"We're not leaving." We sat down. They threatened to put us under
arrest. We said, "Fine, we'll be bailed out. We've looked his house
over. He's got a nice front yard. We'll camp on it."

We got in to see Mr. McCoy. He promised us fifteen minutes,
and we spent three and a half hours. Afterwards we had seven
minutes of prime time on ABC television, and when we hit Atlantic
City that evening every one at the convention was well aware of
what had happened.

The first thing that was placed on the floor the next morning was
a motion to dissolve the Federation. It failed by two votes. So East
Chicago got up and called for a walkout of all those interested in
moving toward a real organization. Ten of the fifteen unions represented walked out. We held our own convention, and invited representatives of the internationals which had organized Du Pont plants
to speak with us.

Initially we in East Chicago felt that we would like to put together
our own international, to do it ourselves. The finances were there.
We felt that even though we might not have the skills which internationals possess, it could be done if people were willing. But unfortunately we got voted down on that. I still feel that would have been
the better way to go. The vote in our coalition of local unions was
to affiliate with the International Chemical Workers Union.

However, when we voted on affiliation with the ICWU at my own
plant in East Chicago, the membership voted to remain independent.
Thinking it over, Smrekar and I concluded that we had let ourselves
become the union, just like the board that we defeated in 1968. We
had let ourselves deteriorate. From now on, board meetings will be
open. Stewards will be mandated to be there. In a way, I'm glad
we lost.

White working-class guys aren't together yet, the way blacks and
Latins are. They say, "Why do I need a union?" I did the same
thing. When they see someone get stepped on, or get stepped on
themselves, they change. But it's a long process.

WAYNE KENNEDY

W AYNE KENNEDY is an organizer for the rank-and-file movement in the American Federation of Government Employees (AFGE). He has been a chief steward for the union of Office of Economic Opportunity (OEO) employees in Chicago, Local 2816, AFGE; a delegate to the Chicago Council of AFGE Locals; and president of the National Council of OEO Locals.

Kennedy believes that public employees should ultimately belong to the same organization as the workers, consumers, and community groups which they serve. In this account he describes the experiences and influences which contributed to the development of that belief.

At the time the interviews on which this account was based were recorded, Kennedy had just been discharged from his OEO job for taking the side of Chicago's urban Indians in their struggle for homes and jobs. The AFGE locals in Chicago issued a joint supporting statement which called on their own agencies to make available to the Indians surplus federal land "that we not tolerate a new form of broken treaties with the Indians." Wayne Kennedy's fellow-workers declared:

WHAT HAS OEO COME TO, WHEN AN OEO EMPLOYEE IS BEING FIRED BECAUSE HE IS ALLEGED, AS AN ELECTED REPRESENTATIVE FOR FEDERAL UNIONS, TO HAVE CALLED ATTENTION TO THE NEEDS OF SOME POOR PEOPLE AND REQUESTED THAT THE VARIOUS

234 Wayne Kennedy

FEDERAL POVERTY AGENCIES TAKE ACTION? HAS IT
BECOME SOME KIND OF CRIME TO THINK THAT MORE
OUGHT TO BE DONE FOR THE POOR AND SAY SO?

On October 24, 1972, a panel of three federal judges reinstated
Kennedy with full pay. The panel ruled that OEO had proceeded
unconstitutionally in failing to grant Kennedy prior hearings before
suspension or removal, thus depriving Kennedy of his rights to due
process under the Fifth Amendment. It also held that Kennedy's
First Amendment free speech rights had been violated because OEO's
rules regarding public speeches by employees are too vague. This
decision may apply to all public workers, not just federal workers.
(For further information see Staughton Lynd, "The Wayne Kennedy
Case," *The Nation*, January 24, 1972. The case is *Wayne Kennedy
et al v. Phillip Sanchez et al*, No. 72 C 771, in the United States
District Court for the Northern District of Illinois, Eastern Division.)

As the account explains, Kennedy gained exposure to the frustration of workers in unresponsive unions through working for five
years in the railroad yards of western Chicago. Here he found that
the memory of the strike of the American Railway Union against
the Pullman Company led by Eugene Debs in 1894 was still vivid
in the minds of railroad workers. The crushing of that strike by
federal troops and a court injunction left railroad workers in a state
of demoralization which persisted more than sixty years later, Kennedy discovered.

WAYNE KENNEDY

An Absolute Majority

I

I GREW UP in a suburb of Chicago—Western Springs. My father taught at Wilson Junior College for about thirty years. He was very active in the teachers union. He was always in opposition to the union leadership because it was in political collusion with the Kelly machine.

My mother was a very, very gentle person. The whole atmosphere was very unrealistic: if you are honest every one else is honest, if you're gentle every one else is gentle; every one should be democratic. Then you go into the real world and you're totally unprepared. I think what I do is largely conditioning from the early years. The older I get the more I want to live it out regardless of the consequences, but when you first get going you have all kinds of problems.

I met my wife in high school. We decided to wait to get married until I graduated [from college]. I was to graduate in '58 and I wasn't even close to it. So we got married anyhow and then she got pregnant so I went to work.

I worked at the railroad yards in Cicero for five years while I was going to school. I was a railroad clerk. I would line up the switchmen for their assignments. If you made a mistake they could put in a claim and collect a day's wages. The management was trying to put them where it wanted and the switchmen were, of course, trying to exercise their seniority. You were kind of in the middle. You could get involved in intrigue right away. The yard master, who is the boss of the yard, he'd tell you, "Oh, skip that guy. I don't want him. Go on to another guy." So you'd have to tell somebody, "Hey, the yard master wants to skip this guy. You'd

better get word to him." And then somebody would call the yard
master and get on him about it. But if he knew you were involved,
you'd be in trouble.

The first time I joined a union was at the railroad. I belonged
to a very corrupt union, the Railway Clerks Union. I went to some
meetings but my interest was more with the switchmen. I got in
with the natural leaders there. I was in a strategic place because
all of them had to go through me. I got along with them well so
I got involved in talking about union problems.

The switchmen also had a very controlled union and the union
wouldn't support them in anything. They were always electing a new
rank-and-file guy to be the union spokesman for the men in the yard,
and then as soon as he was elected he would be going against them.
So they would put up another opponent who would say, "When
I get elected, I'm going to do what you guys want. You know this
guy (our representative), he's taking orders from the bureaucracy and
not from us. When I get elected I'm going to do what the switchmen
want and tell the bureaucracy to go to hell."

They would elect the new guy. But as soon as he got elected
he'd turn on them. He'd take orders from the bureaucracy and from
the rear door of management. They would take a vote at a membership meeting instructing him to do something. He'd check with the
union bureaucracy and go in and make an agreement with management that was just the opposite. So they would never have control.

There was one guy who was always denouncing the union and
the union representative, and he was always right. He would say,
"Yeah, we're going to put you in there and you'll do the same damn
thing." And sure enough that would happen. But he had an in with
the management downtown. Even though he was a switchman he
could call downtown to this big shot he knew and get things reversed
out in the yards. We had a funny situation where the union would
go along with the yard management, and here was a rank-and-file
switchman who could call a big shot downtown and get something
on behalf of the workers. The union was more reactionary than the
top management—at least this one guy.

We were captured in this union. But we used to talk about, what
were the alternatives? We would talk historically. I read a little bit

about Debs. I think he has a fascination for anyone that's connected with the railroad.

A lot of personal hatreds were based on railroad history. The workers had started at different periods. Some workers there had come in as scabs. They could tell you, ''So-and-so, he's a scab who came in in 1920.'' If the guy was a scab back in 1920, he'd be a scab the rest of his life. One group of scabs would have nothing to do with the guys that came in as scabs at another point. Personal relationships to each other were largely defined by the work circumstances that they hired in at. They'd try to work with people that had the same history in the railroad. And this was very important because they were dependent on each other for their lives. You had to be able to trust the other two switchmen or you'd get killed.

You'd think the Pullman strike was yesterday, the way the old-timers would talk about it. Their whole history was the various conflicts and strikes — management tried to pull this and we tried to do that . . . the day we had that last strike you walked out or not — this defined who was buddies with who. They hated the engineers because historically the engineers never supported the other workers. Class conflict just dominated everything — major conflicts.

A lot of these guys had come into the railroad business when it was considered the highest skilled craft. When you were a railroad worker in the 1910s or '20s or early '30s, you were the most skilled workman and you were getting the highest wages. That was when they started out. Now when I was there they were virtually reduced to unskilled laborers who could be replaced with the next guy walking by the yards. There was a tremendous downgrading in terms of wages and in terms of how they were looked at. For most of the white switchmen it was a further humiliation to have blacks, unskilled blacks, coming in as switchmen.

Really to make it they had to work overtime. That's why the seniority system was so important to them. They could get on crews where they would make overtime and work their rest days, and they'd pick their rest days by seniority. A lot of them, to make a living, would try to work ten to twelve hours a day seven days a week. Here they had very responsible, in a way very skilled jobs, and they were reduced to having to work long hours like common laborers.

The productivity of the railroad worker had gone up tremendously. It's measured in ton miles. They'd see these charts showing the tremendous increase in worker productivity and they felt grossly robbed over the years. Had there been any kind of corresponding increase in real wages, the railroad men would have been earning a tremendous salary.

They realized that where you had corrupt authoritarian unions there was more and more pressure to prevent them from striking. It was harder and harder to get their unions to respond. So they felt a destruction of any feeling of importance or having anything to say about their working conditions, even though they recognized how strategic they were.

I think that the failure of the American Railway Union, at least among the oldtimers, was the big tragedy of railroad history. You wonder if it was possible, because of all the tremendous pressure there was to divide the railroad workers, but had that pulled off the railroad workers would have had the upper hand with the industry, I think. Instead, just the opposite happened.

It was obvious to me that the workers knew better how to run the railroad than the management. If the workers had had any say-so about the railroad, it would have been one hell of an efficient operation.

They all drink. They ride on boxcars and go out on ice where you can hardly stand up, and I don't think people can work on that job in that cold weather without drinking. One of the big things for the yard master or the train master was to catch a switchman drinking. Especially the switchmen they didn't like, they were always trying to nail them drinking. They'd have the gumshoes waiting for them or trying to hide on them. (The gumshoes were special agents, plain clothes armed policemen, employed there. They're really labor spies.) It was nothing for the gumshoes to be deliberately spying on switchmen, just waiting for them to make a false move. So there was a constant battle between the gumshoes, and the switchmen and the other workers.

There was also the constant battle of the bosses trying to get each crew to do more work than the crews thought they should be doing, or to do it without enough people around the engine or on the train. They'd want them to move the trains faster and take more chances moving the trains than the crews wanted or thought was safe.

It is a hell of a hazardous job. When I was there some guys got badly hurt and I think a couple got killed. It was just a fact of life that you would get injured. It was a question of how badly, or would you get killed, but it was inevitable that you would get hit. This was the thing that made the guys who worked together feel very, very close. Even away from the yard they socialized a lot together.

Everything they do is an act of defiance. The bosses are trying to get them to do one thing and they don't want to do it. It's a continual struggle between the two. When your physical life depends on your making the right moves and you can be fired on the spot if you're caught breaking the rules, it's an extreme situation.

One thing that used to bug them was that the railroad associations, the management, were always putting on a big campaign about featherbedding—all these unneeded jobs. These guys, here they were risking their lives, they felt they were shorthanded as it was, and they were being accused of featherbedding.* They would react very hostile about it and they wished they could strike back.

*Several months after this interview, on October 30, 1972, a crash involving two Illinois Central trains at South 27th Street in Chicago took forty-five lives. A spokesman for the United Transportation Union, AFL-CIO, to which the crewmen involved in the crash belong, made the following statement (*Chicago Tribune*, November 1, 1972):

. . . The UTU had warned I. C. railroad officials and the Illinois Commerce Commission nearly four years ago of the possibility of a catastrophe because of the dispute over crew sizes and responsibilities.

A dispute in 1969 which led to a weeklong strike by the UTU erupted over the railroad's attempt to cut crew sizes on its commuter runs.

At the time the union insisted a flagman be added for "safety reasons." The I. C. cited its safety record and sophisticated signal system as reasons that the addition of a third crew member was simply an example of featherbedding.

"We won the strike when they agreed to the extra trainmen," Stuckey [the spokesman] said. "But to prove they weren't needed they would not allow the crewman to flag oncoming trains at unscheduled stops and gave them conductors or collectors duties."

The day-to-day reality there was so bad, the job could become so humiliating, that aside from all the intrigue the number one topic of conversation was retirement. Their whole lives, in terms of satisfaction, were postponed until retirement. To me it was unbelievable to have guys in their twenties and thirties talking about, "The first thing I'm going to do when I retire is . . ."

I think if there was any democracy at all in the railroads you'd have one hell of a militant situation. There was certainly a willingness to talk about some kind of direct action. They admired the black movement in the early '60s which was the sit-ins and so on. Even though they were racist, they thought the blacks were doing the right thing and they respected the power that they were developing. Some of the guys now have the Right-to-Vote reform movement going. The big issue is being able to ratify their contracts. There are elements in the railroads like everywhere else that I think will change things.

I think one whole area where there needs to be some very serious thought is, how do you overthrow a corrupt union situation? I am convinced that the reason you have these corrupt unions is that you have a lot of situations that are inherently militant and if management and the government didn't impose a corrupt union apparatus you'd have a very radical development. I'm sure that if there was any kind of democracy in the railroads you'd have left-wing industrial unions. I'm sure that's true of other industrial situations where the militancy is right there so it's just a question of giving it an outlet, some kind of mechanism to express it.

II

After I left school, I went and took a job as a caseworker at the Cook County Public Aid Department.

You had a very depressing situation at the Public Aid Department. The caseworker was taught that a lot of these people were cheating. "They could be working," and "they're getting too much," and it was your job to crack down on them. They would actually count your cancellations per month. The more families you cancelled off aid, the better caseworker you were. They'd want you to look for any pretext to cancel people out. A person might have the promise

of a job and so they'd want you to cancel him out right away and
it might turn out that the job didn't work out. So he'd have to go
through the whole procedure of applying again, maybe not have aid
for a while. Any pretext at all, they'd want you to cancel the families
out. And yet you could see there really were no jobs for them, that
it was a hopeless situation in terms of getting off aid.

They weren't getting the benefits that they were entitled to.
They'd be entitled to furniture and some supervisors would just say,
"Well, I don't give out furniture!"—just arbitrarily would say that.
I had a supervisor that didn't believe in birth control and wouldn't
authorize any costs for birth control. The supervisors there were typically matronly middle-class women who were very bitchy and petty,
and hated the people they were serving, and it just completely
dehumanized people.

The supervisor would give you a rough sketch of every family.
It was always negative: this one is just plain lazy, we got to get
after her, she ought to be out working, you got to get after her to
get a job. This was what you were supposed to do, just follow this
negative sketch that the supervisor would give you.

You come there, you're told that casework is a profession, but
they didn't want you using your own judgment with the families.
It didn't mean anything to hire you; there was no screening at all.
We used to say they'd hire Jack the Ripper if he had a college
degree. It was very frustrating for people who were trying to be
professional caseworkers, to use their own judgment and to act inde-
pendently with the families they came in contact with. That was
not permitted. We were openly told to violate what the people were
entitled to.

Also, the caseloads are so heavy that if you don't become callous
you have an impossible caseload. The ones who make the adjustment
there are the ones who are able to tell them, "I'm not talking to
you today." Because if people on your caseload find out you are
listening to them, you're trying to do something, you just get
swamped. Most people try to fend this off. They stay with the system by becoming very cold and hostile. It is very common there,
if a recipient calls up and the caseworker hasn't told him to call,
they just hang up on the recipient. It gets to the point where unless

the caseworker wants to talk to him he better not bother him. The caseworker has the choice either to become the enemy of the recipient, very hostile, or to leave the system because the workload is just ridiculous. You're continually fighting to get what they're entitled to and being turned down and you inevitably get in trouble with your supervisor and get a bad evaluation.

Before Welfare Rights got going, there was talk and there were some attempts to organize recipients. There was an eccentric guy, I think his name was Jackson, who believed in anarchy and free love. But he would individually take up the cause of recipient families. I worked at the Englewood office, which was the largest Public Aid office at that time, and he would come and picket the front office over some woman not getting her check or something, or he would walk in and raise hell with one of the supervisors or the director of the office. He was something of a threat, not that he had any political power, but it was disruptive and embarrassing to have this guy marching with a picket sign out in front.

Another thing was happening on the West Side. Rev. Mitchell, who was a black minister, was trying to organize the recipients on a right-wing basis: that if they would clean themselves up and think about working and go to Christian ways, that the state, the society would respond, they would have more money and so on. In contrast to Headstart, he had a program called Rightstart. Congressman Crane was very big on that, thought that this guy really had the answers for the ghetto. So those were the two influences. Other groups in Chicago might have been doing things but the only thing that you heard of was this lone anarchist guy and this right-wing minister.

Local 73 of the Building Service Employees was the union for the Public Aid employees and it was corrupt but it didn't have much control over the workers. The young people tried to take it over. Eventually, after my time, the independent Public Aid union was formed by people like Alan Kaplan and Paul Bloyd.

A few years later we all ended up at OEO in the poverty program. The organizing at OEO is basically an outgrowth of people who organized either at separate times or together at the Cook County Public Aid Department.

What I look for in public organizing is two major elements. One is where the professionals cannot, are not allowed, to do their job, where they cannot honestly do what they are supposed to do with some kind of dignity and independence. And the other thing is where you have a large number of clerks and even professionals who are trapped in low grades and low pay. When you have the combination of professionals who are not permitted to be professionals and a mass of clerical workers who are trapped in low grade jobs, to me you've got the two ideal elements for organizing in the public sector. I know it is true throughout the federal government. If you harp on career development for the clerks, and protection of the professional, you've got two basic issues there that people will respond to.

No bureaucracy that I'm familiar with is taking their professionals seriously. Professionals are there to endorse the system. At OEO you are really there, like a commercial, to say that OEO is ninety-nine and nine tenths pure. "We're out there helping the poor. The government is concerned. We're really providing services to the people. We and the government are doing everything we can to take people out of poverty." As long as you have that attitude toward the system—it's wonderful, it's working, we're really concerned about poor people— you have no problem. You can be completely incompetent. You don't even have to do your work. If you give your endorsement you will be OK, you won't have problems. Really, to work there you have to give up your self-respect and go along with the system.

Even the people who do give up their self-respect, if they see a chance of an alternative, they'll come back. I feel that there's no problem with getting people involved, even in the federal government where people are basically conservative and very, very intimidated. I am more and more convinced that there's a lot of inherent militancy everywhere and particularly in the public sector where you have these two elements, where you have a mass of people trapped in low-grade jobs and you have more and more obvious prostitution of the professional people.

In some ways, at OEO, we're the elite of the federal system. We've got people active in the union who are making over twenty grand a year—and they are discontented. I think more and more people are realizing that there's no real satisfaction for anyone. No matter how high the salary you make, people get turned off by the phoniness of the work. They want an alternative.

And no matter how much money you have, no matter how high you go in the system, you're still not reaching what the advertising says you should be doing and, even materially, you're still failing. The advertising standard gets more and more out of reach of even people getting good money. So public employees are being grouped with a large mass of workers that have no job satisfaction, that are trapped in a bureaucratic life, and can never really feel satisfied with their material standard of living. You're going to work, you hate what you're doing, the pay is good compared to other people but you're still not an American success and you see your life passing away. You're treated like a child, you're given no credit for independent judgment, and the more that we bureaucratize the more people hate what they're doing and hate their circumstances and are looking for an alternative.

The American Federation of Government Employees was an old fraternal group until 1961 when [President] Kennedy issued the first executive order giving federal employees some right to have some limited unionism. Federal employees in large numbers took advantage of it and the AFGE was the only available union so there was an enrollment of employees on their own without any real leadership coming from AFGE. We have the right to bargain over personnel policies and working conditions. We can't directly bargain over salaries or fringe benefits. We are restricted to very simple things.

Our belief is that there are so many damn restrictions on federal employees because there is so much potential power here. They want federal employees to be very, very restricted because if they aren't they are going to be a tremendously powerful group. The restrictions have exactly the opposite effect: we have so little to bargain over that we have to be much more aggressive where we can bargain or we wouldn't have any kind of credence among the membership.

Federal employees are at the point where they want a real labor union and the current leadership is a holdover from pre-executive order days where it was a fraternal and an insurance thing. It was traditional that you could get ahead, move into management ranks, by being a local union president. The whole emphasis was on writing your congressman and lobbying with congressmen and showing how loyal and deserving federal employees are in terms of periodic pay raises and some fringe benefits. Our present leadership has developed a pretty fair lobbying operation. There is no belief in direct action or economic sanctions or developing political clout except by knowing congressmen and asking them for things and publicizing their good works and so on.

Our conservative union leadership does not advocate the right to strike for federal employees. But there have been the postal workers and the air controllers and the government printers and others who by actually striking posed the whole question. I think that federal employees are more and more willing to resort to strikes and it is a question of the law catching up with the realities. The postal workers really have won the right to strike; even though they can't legally strike, they have won that right and no one doubts it.

The rank-and-file caucus [in AFGE] is trying to develop in the form of a local officers' organization. We hope to establish an organization controlled by those people who are still in the shops and still on the payroll and trying to service the members at the workplace. This is in contradiction to the professional bureaucracy in our union.

There is a group in Washington called the Washington caucus. They want to develop the political and economic power of federal workers, especially in Washington, D.C., which is just a colony and will never be anything else unless the federal workers make it something. In Washington, the people got involved in social issues like the grape boycott and the anti-war movement. Now they are getting down to the grievance areas and trying to develop a trade union approach.

We started out with a trade union approach and feel that the social issues are just an outgrowth of the working conditions. If you back members on working conditions, they have no problem getting into social issues. If you try to attack social issues without laying your emphasis on working conditions, you're not going to get anywhere. I think that most employees here are for the black movement. They're against the war. But they are very leery of being used in things like this. If you win their confidence on working conditions, they want to participate in the broader social issues because they

know that they are not going to be used. You're not working with
them primarily to end the war but you are working with them primarily to change their own human situation.

In the Department of Defense agency you have a problem with
the war issue because of the job factor. But even there, the DoD
employees would like to be out of the war machine. They would like
to have better jobs in the social-economic agencies but the way [the
union president] is operating, he has presented no alternative to being
involved with the war budget. They don't want to be eternally
trapped in war jobs. But unless you develop an alternative, they
have to be for the war. That represents the only job they have. I
agree. It is immoral to make rank-and-file employees the victims
of cutting back on the military.

I think that we subscribe to the philosophy of André Gorz and
others who are after democracy in the workplace. The government
treats federal employees like children in school—they have a lot of
petty rules. They treat us so that we will obey orders without question, so we won't resist orders and will carry out whatever the government wants. This is very dehumanizing, especially to the young
people. They rule by fear. There is a big fear that if you don't act
like a child, there will be very serious reprisals. So our job is to
break down that fear and get employees to insist that these petty
rules be done away with, that they be treated as equals and have
some real influence over their working conditions and the purpose
of what they are doing. We have a lot of low-grade employees where
the problem is just a decent income. But more and more we get
young people in who want some dignity and self-determination.

Government is planning and controlling resources. And OEO is all
about comprehensive planning to alleviate the causes of poverty. A
lot of people who never thought about it before are getting the
rhetoric that we have got to have public planning to control some
social problems. The more that people work for government, the
more I think they get indoctrinated in public control. Even though
it's just rhetoric—it's not serious and it's not intended to work and
it's even destructive—at least the rhetoric is there. More and more,
it's becoming part of their thinking.

The old bureaucrats who run these agencies are completely unresponsive to their constituencies or to their employees. Special inter-

ests tend to control these agencies. The bureaucrats' own mode of conduct is to do the least possible and to make no waves at all, so that they can't be criticized for doing something. This is in direct conflict with the young people who want to see the bureaucracy work, and respond to the people most concerned—not just dish out patronage and contracts.

The bureaucracy is so highly centralized and bureaucratized that it cannot really respond. It is deliberately put as far out of reach of the people as possible. We think that it has to be strongly decentralized and moved out to the regions where the constituent groups can have a much more direct control over these programs.

OEO is the most decentralized of all federal agencies. Its constituency is also the people on the lowest rung of society. This is what I think attracted people to OEO: it is the most decentralized and it is trying to speak to the most oppressed economic class. The structure and the rhetoric of OEO are very conducive to actually trying to respond to people who have traditionally not had any power. In some areas, OEO has enabled poor people to achieve political power.

I started at OEO in 1968. Kaplan and Bloyd started in 1967. Once we got in here, we had to organize for our own self-protection. As professionals we would go out into the community to try to use our influence to see that the program was carried out. We would develop conflict situations in the field and, without the protection of a union, we would immediately be re-assigned or given a desk job. We organized the union to give us some protection in the field as professionals.

At the same time, we were shocked to see what a strong class system there is within the federal government between the clerks and the professionals. We were shocked to see the hostility toward minorities even within the federal government. Our other motivation was to see what we could do to break down this class system and the discrimination toward minorities. If they can be broken down within the federal government, which is the largest employer of all, that would be an example and a base for doing it within the society as a whole.

Our Washington local won in their contract a day care center for their members. In our national negotiations we are trying to do it throughout the agencies. Our theory is that if we can get the federal government to pay for day care and become the leader in day care as an employer, then this will ensure its becoming general throughout the economy. The private sector will follow the federal government. Our salaries have been tied to the so-called comparability of the private sector. There can be a reversal. We can win things like day care and then the private sector will have to duplicate it.

The more we get into it the more we see the implications of the public worker for the whole society. Rather than just [organize] on an occupational basis, if we can do it in terms of the people we serve being in the same organization then I think we'll go a lot further than the other, corrupt unionism ever did. What I think is so interesting—where it's got to be different from anything else in labor history—is that if we do it on a worker/client basis, we're talking about an absolute majority of the country. The constituency consisting of every one on public payment now reaches between 60 and 70 million people, which is a political majority of the country. Just the public workers and those on public payments organized into a collective bargaining unit—the implication is a change in the whole economics and politics of the country. It goes beyond an industrial union. It goes into organizing every one who is dependent on public payments of one kind or another.

I think that organizing just along job lines is not going to carry the society as far and it will corrupt much sooner. Fifteen million public workers getting strong enough where they can demand and have a salary of fifteen to twenty thousand a year could be done sooner and have less impact on society than if you're trying to get the sixty million people to organize. That will definitely change the society and take much longer to corrupt.

The thing that we have to harp on is identifying with the sixty million rather than the fifteen million. When you look at it, like at OEO, our salary is really a form of welfare. We call it middle-class welfare. All you have to do is show up and endorse the system every day. You don't have to do any real work. So you feel like, well, you got this degree so now instead of being on ADC you're on a public payroll. I think people will recognize it's really a payoff. You're not getting rewarded for the job that you're doing. You are basically in the same situation as public recipients. Get away from the idea that we're different than the recipient. You're in the same boat. Your money's coming from the same source. To get your share you've got to get together with these other people. Otherwise, you just get pitted off against each other. In terms of changing the economics and politics of the country, you've got to have the broadest possible base. As the public sector movement you can have a hell of a lot more impact than just federal employees or white-collar federal employees, professional employees, or some such thing.

The attitude now is that these welfare mothers are getting something for nothing. But you turn the question around and say, look, they're getting underpaid for what they're doing. Raising kids is the hardest thing in the world! We've got to get them a decent salary and we've got to recognize them as day care people and we want to pay them enough so that they'll care for other children, too. You'd already have all the natural child or day care centers you'd want if you'd just recognize it and pay the people. When I worked at Public Aid, a number of the recipients I had would tell you, "Look, I'm here to raise my kids. I never got anything out of society and so they're going to pay me to raise my kids." They would tell you that.

I think the basic problem is to get a real shift of money into the public sector, for every one in the public sector, as that's how every one in the public sector will get a decent income. At Public Aid, the money for the salaries for caseworkers is pitted against the benefits for recipients. You're told, we can't raise your salaries because look at how the cost of public aid has gone up, we can't even handle the applications for aid. And, of course, the recipients are told, we have all this administrative cost and the caseworkers want more money. So you're always pitted against each other because of the underfunding of the whole public sector. The only way you can overcome that is to get together and gang up on the sources of taxation, to get the taxes from where the wealth is to finance the public sector.

We are in an ideal position for worker/client organizing because federal employees represent every occupation in the country and they come into direct contact with almost every constituent. There is no movement or reform situation that we are not in contact with because the federal government is involved with everything. I don't think there's any more nobility among the public workers than the private workers, except that the public workers are in contact with the constituency.

The classical situation has been the meat inspectors where they are exposed to a very corrupt industry and they have also had the good influence of the Packinghouse Workers. Single-handedly, through their own union, they upheld the integrity of the federal government in meat inspection. Without their being unionized, very strongly so, there would easily be a corrupt situation. Because of the pressures of a corrupt industry, they have become not only a union, they are really an extended family. They do everything together. They socialize together. They have financial institutions together. They tend to be a very small and very closely-knit group of workers. They are mostly white but they don't have a racial problem (any more than the agency imposes on them). The ones I have had contact with are mostly working-class whites. They are certainly not college-educated professionals. In terms of integrity, they are the ultimate civil servant.

The mine inspectors are more of a potential situation. I don't think that they have developed the unity that the meat inspectors have. They are for strict enforcement but so far they have been controlled by a corrupt industry. Real integrity in the inspection force would interfere with the operation of the whole industry.

One possible way I see public sector organization coming about is for recipient groups to come into a bargaining position, like the federal employees have, by executive order. I think that it is politically very possible to get some kind of executive order that would give the military the beginning of collective bargaining, give the men in the military the right to bargain over marginal issues like their food and their housing. That's all the federal workers have now, other than the postal workers, is the right to bargain over personnel policies and working conditions. But the marginal bargaining is the starting point.

I think that an executive order could be issued that would permit representatives of the government and representatives of people on old-age pensions to sit down and bargain about marginal things.

They've already done it in the area of tenants and public housing. HUD has already issued guidelines that give them some marginal bargaining power.

I think you could issue an executive order giving welfare recipients the right to marginal bargaining, like maybe they could bargain over how their budget would be allocated. Initially, they are not going to let welfare recipients bargain over the size of their welfare budgets. But it could be marginal things like, would more go for rent or more go for furniture? or what about a clothing allowance? What about treatment in the welfare office? I think you could begin to get marginal bargaining going. To me, Welfare Rights is primitive unionism. Where they have been able to force concessions, they have actually engaged in collective bargaining, but it needs to be legitimatized before you can get a real union movement going.

I think the thing that got the CIO off the ground was the indication from President Roosevelt that the government approved of this. The accounts I ever read, workers would say, "FDR wants us to unionize, the government says it's OK." This gives a legitimacy. Maybe we don't like to believe that legitimacy has to come from the establishment, but generally it does have to get a mass of people aroused.

The way I see it developing is, the government consents to very marginal bargaining, so that groups will get organized and begin to sit down collectively with government, and then as that happens there will be more and more pressure for real collective bargaining, till you reach the point where public benefits as well as public salaries will be negotiated.

Our union is the largest in the federal government. I think the most immediate thing is to get the federal unions into a situation where they can merge and have one strong federal union. As this develops, we've got to push harder to get marginal bargaining powers for the military. We have a direct interest in the military since they're employed by the federal government. And then the next thing would be to get marginal bargaining rights for welfare recipients— redefine them as federal employees and bring them into a merged federal union. And then try to do the same for the people on pensions. The National Council of Senior Citizens claim they have two million members. That could be merged into a federal union and you'd have two million people right there.

As I see it, the whole solution to poverty and public services in this country is to get those people who *are* poor and *are* dependent upon public services into the collective bargaining process and develop enough joint power where they can demand that the government pay adequate salaries and benefits. Until it comes from their own power, their own self-developed power, we'll go on not having public services and having welfare and pension budgets that are totally inadequate.

JORDAN SIMS

J ORDAN SIMS is former chairman of the Bargaining Committee
for Local 961 of the United Automobile Workers, and co-chair-
man of the United National Caucus in the UAW. His account presents a view of black struggle different from that of Jesse Reese and
Sylvia Woods (pages 97–105 and 111–129). Like many black
workers who became active in the 1950s and 1960s, Jordan Sims believes that blacks should first get themselves together and only then
build broader alliances.

Toward the end of his account Sims refers to the following incident, which happened in the plant where he worked.

In July 1970 . . . at 4:55 on a Wednesday afternoon shift, a
thirty-six-year-old black employee of the Chrysler Corporation, James
J. Johnson, Jr., walked into the Eldon Avenue axle plant, pulled an
M-1 carbine from his pant leg, loaded it with a thirty-round banana
clip, and went on a wild killing spree. "He's firing at everyone in
white shirts," a worker cried. It is the foremen who wear white shirts.
Within minutes, three men were dead: a foreman who had suspended
Johnson for insubordination an hour before, plus another foreman,
and a job setter. Johnson told the UAW committeeman who captured
him, "They took me off the job I had held for two years and put
a man with less seniority in my place."

The sequel was this:

> Johnson's defense attorneys, members of a radical Detroit law firm,
> contended during a three week trial that the pressures of being a poor
> black from the rural South, combined with the strain of working on
> the assembly line, had made Johnson temporarily insane at the time
> of the shootings. The jury members, two of them factory workers
> and three of them the wives of factory workers, toured the plant,
> which had been cleaned and painted for the occasion. The jurors also
> heard testimony about harsh treatment of workers, violence, and poor
> working conditions at the Eldon Avenue plant. In May 1971, in a
> stunning decision, the jury found Johnson innocent because of tempor-
> ary insanity and committed him to a state hospital. "Did you see
> the cement room in that plant?" one juror cried during deliberations.
> "Working there would drive anyone crazy." (William Serrin, *The
> Company and the Union: The "Civilized Relationship" of the
> General Motors Corporation and the United Automobile Workers*,
> pages 233–236.)

This account is an edited version of a talk to an International
Socialists Educational Conference, at the Chicago Circle Campus
of the University of Illinois, on May 13, 1972.

Going for Broke

B EING BLACK TODAY, forty years ago I was born a Negro, and this makes a big difference in the way I look at things. I happened to be born in a little famous town called Hamtramck. The Negro population was very minute and segmented rather distinctly. If you know anything about Hamtramck you know I got a good, full-fledged, white, all-American education. I didn't necessarily sit at the back of the class because our numbers were so minute that people weren't really concerned about integration at that particular point in time. This doesn't mean that I wasn't affected by my status, even at that time, although definition wasn't really clear. You were always on the outside looking in. The average American Negro, no matter how far back he was born, always has this basic, fundamental attitude. If one ever tells you something different he's lying like hell. There is no way of masking your color, nor your identity, in being an American Negro.

This was my attitude. I played with my little white brothers every day until they b.s.'d with me a little bit, and then I became "black boy," and we fought. I was called "sunshine." We fought. Don't know why, Momma said that was the thing to do. In a white environment you can't get much black history. The only black history I got in Hamtramck was Little Black Sambo, and the tiger chasing him around the tree who turned into butter. That's one of the unfortunate things about being raised in a place like Hamtramck. You never learn your own history or who you really are.

Well, I grew up like that in Hamtramck. And in most endeavors, maybe inadvertently, my family and most others that stayed in Hamtramck earned their own degree of self-respect in their own particular way. We had a basic understanding with the white race in Hamtramck. They knew that if you used derogatory terms like "sunshine," or "Sambo," or "coon," you better have at least twenty pounds on the guy or you caught a bit of hell.

Upon graduation, most of my fellow-students were white and about fifteen of us went down to Dodge Main, the Dodge Main plant in Hamtramck. All got hired but me. This didn't surprise me too much. Disappointed me some, yes, because they made some beautiful speeches at graduation about "the grand, glorious opportunities opening up in America for all you graduating students," and the major contributions that you would make to society today. It took me three months to finally land a job. That's how I wound up at the Eldon plant.

Now we get into the union aspect of it. When I first got hired at Eldon, they didn't teach unionism, not even back in those days. No such thing as an orientation program. No one told you what the union represented. No one told you what the struggles were. One cat came by—I used to call him, in later years, the "white pimp"—and he hustled your dues, because they didn't have the check-off system at that time. He told you that "the union is here and you must pay your dues." That's about all he told you. If you looked around and tried to ask someone else, everyone would give you the same thing: "Oh, you gotta pay your dues, but we do have a union." Never told you what the hell it was.

So we paid our dues like that, until they got dues check-off. In my estimation, looking back, there was the major sell-out. That's what bureaucratized our unions, made them big business, and completely dissociated them from the rank and file, because they no longer had to come down to you and hustle your dollars, and your nickels, and your dimes. From that point on, I think, we got a no-strike clause in our agreement.

At Eldon, in those early days, working with a majority of whites, I noticed there were many gentlemen's agreements, past practices, previous understandings on seniority rights, promotion, upgrading. There were also certain basic understandings. The average black was only qualified to wield a mop, a broom, or a dust cloth. I was one of the luckier ones because the times had just begun to change, a little, and since blacks were graduating from public schools I guess they felt blacks had become a little competent. They could at least run machines. This is the kind of introduction I got to Eldon. Because of my educational background, and I appeared to be an intelligent young man, I was going to get a golden opportunity: they were going to put me on machines.

I got a 5-10 classification. Never forgot it, still can't forget it. Because 5-10 meant drill press. Now it did seem complicated the first time I looked at it, because I didn't know one damn thing from another. That's a hell of a world to walk into, from playgrounds, and football fields, and institutional facilities. I got lost the first three or four days, just walking around looking at all those smoking machines and people milling around. There's not a great hospitality. Maybe there was a great degree of brotherhood between the white workers, because they established the whole thing. There was no welcome mat laid out for me—I never found it. Friends were hard to make. I wasn't too particular about that kind of friend anyhow, because I never liked the factory and still don't.

So I got in there and locked my mind up and put in my eight hours a day and got my money and ran like hell to have a good time. It was the first free breath I'd had off the welfare. My family was on welfare ninety per cent of the time that I was a youngster growing up. You just couldn't get jobs in those days unless you had the money to buy them. If you had fifty dollars, a hundred dollars, you could go to the employment office, didn't have to stand in line, somebody would call down ahead and say you were coming. You were hired. It was quite simple in the early days because they would fire somebody else to make room for you. They changed things around just as they pleased.

I see great, significant changes in unionization. More working people getting together. But it depresses me today, the state the unions have gotten into. To me they're no longer unions. To me they are as much like General Motors, and Du Pont's, and Ford's, as they are themselves. I do not think that they can relate to the problems of the worker any longer, since they've gotten a dues check-off program, and they've tied workers' hands with a no-strike clause in most agreements. There are ways of getting around no-strike clauses if they wanted to. In my estimation, much like the corporations, the UAW has taken a back seat in the corporate houses and they do business with you from that posture, from that position. I have never seen a person who could represent me that had to sneak in somebody's back door and sit down in the damn kitchen.

I've tried like hell to get myself out of this predicament. Put yourself in that position, and when I say "a union"—that's supposed to represent me and be so much more—tell me, "Look up to it, respect it, idolize it." I just can't do it.

I didn't know who the steward was at Eldon. The chief steward wouldn't dirty his hands going around collecting money. He was the central agent. They were bureaucratic even at the plant level back in those days. I never saw a contract until I had been there almost ten years. They said they didn't have contracts for rank-and-file people. I was there eighteen years before I saw a union constitution. My president told me, "You don't want to read something like this. It'll just mix up your mind and get you in trouble." He was right.

We had an administration there where the president had been in office fifteen to twenty years. We were "democratic": we had a vice president, who was half colored, who had been in there twelve or fourteen years. We had a little more colored recording secretary who had been there eight to ten years. So you can see, racial barriers were slowly breaking down, and there was a tolerance that was slowly being developed for the Negro. But only for a certain type of Negro. That's something that used to amuse me.

Our rank-and-file program at Eldon started roughly in 1966. It was a secret thing, like in the old days. Becoming a chief steward took me six years, from 1960 to 1966, running every two years. One thing about whites back in those days, they were honest. They would say, "A colored man can't represent me." And I would say, just as honestly, "One day I will." Well, the day came.

In 1963 we hadn't had a change in our plant for ten years. From 1953 to 1963, that's how bad off Chrysler was and that's how bad off the whole country was: we didn't hire a soul. With ten years' seniority I was the lowest man on the seniority list. But we had a big boom coming up then. Things were on the rise. Jobs became plentiful. Everyone started hiring. The younger whites started quitting, going to better-paying areas. Jobs that were heretofore completely white became mildly integrated. Back in about 1964, we even got a colored inspector at Eldon. In 1968 we got a colored job-setter. About the same time they finally gave us a colored supervisor.

During this period between 1963 and 1966 or 1968, with the white exodus from the hard jobs in the inner-city plants, it opened the door for all of us poor folks. We moved in and took all these good jobs. We became lathe operators, couple of us got into the skilled trades. We completely dominate the inspection department now, books, papers, figures, graphs and all. And one thing you have to say about it, you don't hear about Chrysler calling back as many cars as GM or Ford.

All this black tide moving in there, I started practicing racism—by practicing democracy. I would tell all the whites how beautiful and democratic America was, land of golden opportunity, how great it was to be benevolent and kind and sharing, how blessed it was to give rather than continually to receive. They couldn't deny this American heritage that I was setting right there before them. They had to agree, ''Sims, that's the right thing.''

I would tell the blacks just the opposite. ''You come out of the alley, you've never had a damn thing in your life. Until you get together and support a black program and show The Man that you are here, you will never get any further than you are.'' You know, that was the most difficult thing I had to do. That's what hangs me up. You've kept the race you've locked me into so well subjugated, so well oriented, that the last thing many Negroes want to be called is racist. And in my estimation, until the black accepts the identity forced upon him by the white American society, accepts his blackness, he will never establish his identity because he'll never have any strength as an individual.

And I preached it. And I got to be chief steward. I beat out an itinerant hillbilly who could neither read nor write by thirteen votes in a plant that was predominantly black and in a servicing department that was about eighty-five or ninety per cent black. And my margin of victory was thirteen damn votes. I was happy to win but I was sick of the way I had won. Because it was indicative of the attitude still held at that late date by most American Negroes, that their own kind aren't competent enough to lead them any damn where.

. . . The average worker is not intricate in his thinking. You're going to have to drop your fancy speeches. You go too far out some times. You're going to have to relate to exactly where that worker is, and educate him. And in many cases you're going to lead him. Most workers today, white included, would rather be led than lead themselves. Grumbling all the way, "Yeah, that's the thing to do, but when you going to do it?"

The same thing applies to political parties, just like it does to local union leaderships, just like it does to this black jacket I'm wearing: United National Caucus. Some people are going to have to assume some degree of responsibility, and take a position of leadership. You're going to dictate situations and circumstances sometimes in this turbulent rank-and-file or workers' force you've got in America today. You're going to be ruthless in the way you set up programs to get that worker involved. Even though some may be hurt. You have never won anything without paying a price for it. And if you've got the idea today, that there's a smooth easy way of accomplishing a workers' program, then you are really swept away with the American dream.

I liked *The Godfather*. Blood everywhere, but the devotion that was there, goddamn! That really impressed me. If the blacks had that much in organization, deep family ties, and downright guts, we wouldn't have to have anybody crusading for us, speaking for us. There's no way you can kill all of us, not at this late date. Waited too damn long. If we had just that much of what they had in *The Godfather*! I liked the composure of the young man. I liked the way he went from the orthodox all-American, who was averse to the ways of his family—the old family ways, and the old culture, the old strength and the old ties—but when push came to shove he got his hard lesson. He rolled over and did his thing.

Workers are going to have to do the same thing. We no longer owe our allegiance to our leadership because they don't respond to us. They haven't in the last ten, fifteen years. It's getting decidedly worse. In my estimation, workers are up-tight right now. The basic things we had twenty years ago no longer exist today. Simply to refer to dignity, there is no dignity in the workplace today. You're not as much as an IBM typewriter, or a nondescript lathe operation. And you don't even compare to the importance of a piece of automated equipment. If you damage one single tool in many of their automation projects, that costs you your job. It shows you how significant you are in industry today.

The Man is saying some of the same things he said thirty years ago. "We don't need you. As fast as you go, there's another man waiting in the streets to take your place." We have really digressed back to the origins of when our unions were built. We are having to struggle again for recognition, and just plain downright dignity. And we've sold all these things we used to call precious, like our seniority rights, for things like unemployment compensation, sick and accident benefits, annual improvement factors, cost-of-living increases. They tell you about all these but they never tell you how to keep your damn job, and they won't help you to keep it, even though they're supposed to be obligated to represent you in this capacity.

I wonder where workers are going to be going in the next five or ten years. I'm optimistic, though. We had a few pleasant things occur in our plant. One worker was taken off his job, improperly. He tried to assert himself and ask about his seniority considerations. He was arbitrarily fired. He couldn't believe it. He didn't beg The Man but he asked him rather specifically, "What do you mean, fired? Just for asking about my job?" And The Man said, "That's right. You don't ask. You do what you're told. You're fired!" The brother went out and he got his gun and he did some firing.

Many people thought this was a very deplorable situation. I don't, I think it practical, because we have forewarned that corporation. We warned them years ahead of time that they were deteriorating to just this kind of state. They told us in no uncertain terms, "This is not a sociological department. This is a factory. This is industry, and we're here to make money. We're not here to take any guff from any workers and no goddamn labor rep." That was their whole attitude. This worker knew this.

They have gotten to the point of treating us all the same way, black and white. It's coming down to that dollar-and-cents thing now. That's what it has always come down to in the past, that dollar-and-cents thing. In my estimation, that's the cause of most of the trouble in our country today. That dollar and cents, the way it's always centralized, the way they fight to keep it centralized.

You're going to have to broaden the base of how that money is distributed, how everything else is distributed. You're going to have to learn how to play a major and significant role, not only in industry as a worker. I disagree with GM. I don't believe, "As GM goes, so goes America." I believe, "As working people go, so goes America." I believe that as working people prosper, so does America. I believe that as they grow, so will grow America, to all forms of stature that are relevant to a country that is supposed to be so goddamn great.

In my estimation, workers have been lulled into a sense of security and apathy by good times they've never had before. Not being accustomed to them, they went off the deep end. Many of my white brothers I've seen who twenty-five years ago wouldn't have thought of buying a Buick, or a Chrysler, or a Cadillac. Hell, today I can't tell who the upper class is. I find more industrialists driving small cars than I do workers, nowadays. He has attained a great deal of affluence, monetary affluence, and he's reluctant to give it up.

This is another thing that separates the rank-and-file programs. A man with fifteen or twenty years, who takes advantage of his seniority and takes advantage of his brother being laid off, to make twelve, fourteen hours a day, and says, it's not his responsibility. You're going to have to think about things like that. You're going to have to organize the unemployed. You're going to have to go after a few cats in your own unions, who work the overtime. You're going to tell them, "No overtime."

Human nature is a very peculiar thing. Most people, given a choice, will sit up and think, talk, rationalize, for hours, for days, because they don't have to make a decision. They don't really want to. You've got to make people get off dead center in the working class. You're going to do it by education, by provocation, by force in some cases. I find all these ideas very tolerable, very acceptable, to win an ultimate goal. Because I believe, if your end is justifiable, and you've pursued all reasonable and rational courses, and met with utter defeat, you take any course that's open to you. And you go for broke. Because broke is exactly what you'll be, I believe, when the '70s come down, if you don't get together.

JOHN BARBERO,
ED MANN
AND OTHERS

J OHN BARBERO AND ED MANN are members of the Rank And File
Team (RAFT), a national caucus of the Steelworkers Union with
headquarters in Youngstown, Ohio. They work in the Brier Hill
mill of the Youngstown Sheet and Tube Company there.

John Barbero has worked at Brier Hill since just after World War
II. He has used the thirteen-week vacation which steelworkers with
long service receive every five years to travel around the world,
including visits to the Soviet Union and Japan. John's father is
Italian, his mother is Czech, and his wife, Miyo, is Japanese. He
once told an anti-war meeting that he is against war because in any
imaginable war he would be fighting against a cousin.

As members of Local 1462 at Brier Hill, John Barbero and Ed
Mann fought for honest elections and to upgrade the position of
blacks in the mill. As members of the international union, they supported the Dues Protest Committee of 1956–1960 and its candidate,
Donald Rarick, who ran against David J. McDonald for president
of the Steelworkers Union in 1957. And as members of the United
Labor Party, a local labor party in the Akron-Youngstown area, they
agitated for racial equality in the community, peace, and the redis-
tribution of wealth.

Bill Litch, another member of RAFT, has run against I. W. Abel for president of the international union. RAFT's program includes rank-and-file ratification of contracts, and election, rather than appointment, of staff representatives. It also asks that "each officer return to his home plant and perform one year of uninterrupted work at his old job at least once every four years."

This account combines an interview with RAFT as a group and a second interview with John Barbero. A condensed version appeared as "Conversations With The Steel Mill Rebels," *Ramparts*, December 1972.

JOHN BARBERO, ED MANN
AND OTHERS

A Common Bond

E D MANN: Our union was created from the top down. The Steelworkers Union came from the Mine Workers. It was financed by the Mine Workers, and the hierarchy and staff all came out of the Mine Workers. And they said, "Here's a union. Now you get people to join it." The Auto Workers Union was different: it came from the bottom. I think this is why we've been saddled with a "Big Daddy will take care of you, we'll make the decisions, pie in the sky" sort of thing.

This is shown specifically in the rough time we had with honest elections. Fifteen or twenty years ago the man who was running picked the man counting the votes. We can overcome this now because each side gets its own tellers, which was unheard-of before. We feel an honest election is no longer a battle.

But it sticks in our craw not having the right to ratify contracts. The smallest union created today in the city of Youngstown—for example, firemen, nurses, nurses' aides, garbage men—*everybody* ratifies their contract. If your staff man or your international representative doesn't do a good job you send him back to the god-damned bargaining table and say, "We want something better." Steelworkers don't have this right. We don't have a right to OK anything. This isn't my union: I'm just working for a staff man who tells me, "Sorry boy, you don't have a grievance."

We have to learn how to say "No." The average guy in the mill thinks he can't say "No," he's got to go along with the big shot. The company has a boss over him. The union has a boss over him.

The politician's his boss, and even his wife's probably his boss when he goes home. So where do the people show any fight any more? They've got to learn how to do this all over again. They've got to say, "No, *this* is the way I want it: do something about it."

JOHN BARBERO: I saw the union start. There was a lot of hope in this valley when it started.

My father worked for Republic Steel. He was not political at all, but like many Italians he had a very strong sense of independence. All during the Depression he worked maybe a day, two days a week. He had one superintendent who sold used cars on the side. If you bought a car, he saw to it that you worked for the next six months to pay it off.

Almost every one in Campbell was foreign born. The only people who had American names were the school teachers and the mayor and people of this sort. So everybody felt sort of discriminated against. But they also were people who came here with the American dream.

When the union came to town it was red-baited. Nobody knew what the words meant. I remember one incident where two Communist organizers came to my house and asked them, "Do you want to come to a Party meeting?" My mother said, "Where is the party?"

It was a wonder, the difference the [Little Steel] strike made in our house. My father was one who didn't like to butter up people, but before the strike, there would be a foreman and maybe a girl friend coming to the house. The joke is still around the mill. They would eat, spaghetti and various things. After the strike this never happened again. If somebody came to the house, it was because he wanted them or they were friends. I thought that when it was all over they were actually both better off, both that foreman and my father. There was a new relationship.

I have never seen anything like it in America since. A whole town achieved dignity. It surprised me during World War II that whenever I ran into somebody from Campbell he had this psychology. He was always fair in a question of discrimination, whether to blacks or whites, because the whole little town was this way. Even to this day, when I run into that generation of people out of the city of Campbell I automatically know how they are going to feel.

During that strike, my father was arrested. Then he was black-balled. After four years he went back to work as the result of a Supreme Court decision. He never lost faith. Neither did my mother. Everybody told them that the union was all over with. Everybody said, "Give up. You're never going to get back." But he did get back. After that, even though he was a union man, I sensed that he did not attend meetings regularly or make a big deal of it. There was an objective to be won and they won it.

I had a taste of what unions were like before the war. I worked for nine months in Sharon Steel, the only plant [besides] U. S. Steel that had signed a contract. I started out in general labor and wound up in their blacksmith shop as a helper.

But the big taste I got of what the union was before the war was what I saw at our house. It just changed the whole life of the house. The family was more secure. Our parents got along better. Everything.

Then World War II came and I was affected like everybody else. I actually wanted to go in. I had to go down and sort of sneak in because my mother wouldn't sign the papers; I had to go to the draft board and tell them to draft me. All I can say is that throughout that whole period I believed that what Hitler was doing to the Jews was wrong. We had to get in and had to get in early and stop it. But you wonder. You get into the Service and overnight you sort of sense that you joined the wrong outfit.

Another experience that may have changed my life is that I was sent to Japanese language school. Somehow, when you go to a language school you lose a lot of your hate. If you can talk to the soldier you are supposed to be fighting, you no longer hate him. I remember my experience with the first two prisoners that I had to interrogate on Guam. My Japanese was so poor that they must have laughed at me, except that they were so scared. This guy had a bundle of rags that he had been carrying. He asked me if he could throw the bundle away. He used the word in Japanese which means,

"May I throw it away?" I didn't know. I used the same word back
and said, "Yes, you may throw it away." After he threw it away
I picked it up and handed it back to him.

I was lucky in World War II. I came through all of it without
having to kill anybody. All I had to do was fire my rifle three times
in the air and I was sore because I had to do that. One day I acciden-
tally captured eleven Japanese. I was coming around a big boulder
and the Japanese were coming around the other side of it. I disarmed
them. Before the war was over, I had eleven more. But other soldiers
behind us shot and killed people.

We had a Korean that we captured on Guam. Our colonel liked
him and never turned him in to the PW camp. So he lived with me
in the same tent for the next eighteen months. He was sort of my
instructor in Japanese. We used him because the Japanese had a lot
of Koreans. When we ran into Koreans we always had a three-way
interrogation going.

After the war I worked in Japan for two years. I gravitated to
people who had the same sort of experience in unions. I met a
Japanese-American—at that time, we had none in this area—who
knew all about the organizing on the West Coast. He was a union
leader.

After getting married in Japan I came back here. The law was
that [my wife] had to be here before the year was out; otherwise,
there was the Oriental Exclusion Act.

MIYO BARBERO: Congress had to pass a special law that it was OK
for us to get married. I went through a complete physical. They
take your picture with numbers—you feel like a criminal.

BARBERO: When I came back in 1948, I started right in to look
for a job at the Campbell plant. That's where I lived. They sent
me to Brier Hill which is about ten miles away. So that is how
we happened to move up to this area.

MIYO BARBERO: He told me that he was a steelworker and was
going to work in steel, so that I would know what to expect. When
wives came from Europe they had a dream of a wonderful land.
Many of them were disappointed so their marriages didn't go well.

BARBERO: When I came back I also went to school. Ed Mann and
I took everything that they offered at Youngstown [State University]

but never once did I dream of being a businessman, or anything else. I always knew which side I expected to work on. Just the experience of seeing what happened in our own family was always enough to make me say, "This is what we want for everybody." Later I found that people who were active in the union, who participated in that first dream and knew what they wanted, were not against the students at Kent State. Like Bob, whom we hadn't seen for years: automatic good reaction on Kent State and he got into a lot of trouble in the plant over it.

I intended to work for the union when I got out. But the union was already in when we came back from the war, and the union was no longer the union we expected. The president of our local was named Danny Thomas. The man had at one time been a very good unionist, very militant, a very effective organizer. He was for the people he was serving in the beginning. Many people were pushed around on the job, terrorized by informants. Danny Thomas was somehow able to counter, to put foremen up against the wall and say, "You don't push that old man around again." But somehow, somewhere, that wore off. He became a tyrant in his own right. Not only that, it was just the way you read about in the Teamsters. The local paid all his expenses, even bought tires for his car; and everything voted automatic because of his earlier record.

At every meeting you went to you were "out of order." No matter what you brought up, he had such a well-organized machine it was "sit down and shut up"; and he had the goons in the hall to enforce it. An opposition candidate who asked for the right to speak would be thrown out of the hall. Many times I was the only man who stood on the floor. Then Ed finally came. And we'd raise this point: "Give that man a right to talk."

MANN: We had a running battle with that group all through the years.

BARBERO: All through the years. I thought in some ways I was a catalyst. I talked to guys—some of them to this day don't forgive me—broke them away from the machine. I broke up what had been a very tight clique. "A man has a right to speak." I told them how brave they were. "You got a right to stand up and talk in your own union. We've got to have a better system than this." And we put that first caucus together. It took guts on the part of people, because they were part of the machine, they were getting a little bit of a dole.

Talking about it several years later I heard the statement that when the Danny Thomases came in, all they had to worry about was the company. They didn't have to worry about the men. But when people like me and Bill Litch became active, you had to worry because the union could get you fired every bit as fast as the company. You had to watch both sides. You were always accused of being anti-union when you got up and made a motion, like on an honest election.

One of the ideas we came in with was to work with the blacks who were interested for the advancement of black workers on the job. The open hearth department, on the floor end of it, was traditionally all white. But after World War II, many of the returning GIs felt like I did that we fought certain things we didn't like in Hitler and the Japanese, and we didn't like them here either. We were willing to make this fight here. This got to be the beginning of the Cold War on the union floor. Anybody who would do anything of this sort was immediately suspect as a Communist. The labor gang that I was in was almost all college students at that time. It was called the Red Labor Gang. There was not one Communist in there, but this was the automatic reaction.

Jesse Cavaleer with whom I worked at the open hearth belonged to the Socialist Party. He was a theological student, a Phi Beta Kappa from Union Theological Seminary. He wrote on church-labor relations. He came to Brier Hill because he needed a job. He worked there for several years. His primary interest in life was the end of discrimination. In Brier Hill he was one of the first to eye the lily-white departments and to start talking to the blacks about "let's give it a try." He himself was white.

He was the first one to talk to me about patterns of discrimination—how, in every recession, the discrimination somehow reasserts itself. When times are good, blacks can move into jobs very easily. I have seen it many times. But as soon as there is a recession they are squeezed right back out. You can see past discriminatory hiring practices reflected in how men walk up the floor in gangs. The same people who did jobs twenty years ago are doing them again now because there has been a cutback in operations.

Somehow through all this were some permanent gains. Jesse Cavaleer did break a few people into going slagging. One quit because he received such a rough time. Another fellow stayed but finally left for a better job. The third who went was at Youngstown University with us. At the open hearth furnace we tap the heat at something like 2850° F. and the slagger's job is that he goes up to this and throws what looks like road gravel making up all the banks. As he was going up to the furnace one of the whites opened up the furnace door completely and just burned the man. Now you hear, "Where's the discrimination?" Somehow everybody forgets.

In the open hearth we didn't work successfully to end discrimination until the Kennedy years. Somehow, the same people who harassed the blacks in the Truman and Eisenhower years, under Kennedy their sense was to do the decent thing, accept it, and no struggle at all. Our department was desegregated and blacks moved into all the jobs. I didn't hear any complaints at all. This is maybe where the tone of the nation helps. But now, with the recession again, it is an all-white department for all practical purposes except for the few blacks who got in at the early breakthrough. People are getting bumped according to seniority. How do you break in and become a black machinist's apprentice if the youngest machinist has thirty years in the plant? Everybody with twenty-five years or less is either laid off or is doing some other job and has rights to go back to the job of machinist's apprentice first. How does a man get into the skilled trades?

Through Jesse Cavaleer talking to him, Harry Hurtt came to town. I'm not sure any more how they met each other. Harry Hurtt was a rubbber worker. He had been an officer in World War II, and he was from the Akron group of the United Labor Party. It seems to me that the United Labor Party was the sps of its day, very democratic, very free in attitude. They had run Harry Hurtt for Congress, but before that they had sent him to England to study at a school run by the British Labor Party. He married an English girl and brought her back. She thought that we really had a labor party here. At that time the United Labor Party in Akron had five halls.

I think that the United Labor Party came out of the old Independent Labor League which I don't know too much about. All of them looked to Trotsky. The United Labor Party added one other thing that no other left-wing party had: where Marx didn't fit, Freud did. Marie Wagner is an old rubber worker in Akron. And every time a question came up, she would say, "OK, what does Papa Freud have to say about this?"

The people involved in the United Labor Party around Akron were in high school in, say, 1936: they were of the age of the sitdowns. They came out of high school together and went into the rubber shops. Somehow, in Akron, high schools were organized by the Socialist Party and all sorts of independents [see pp. 154–155]. These people all had a history, you know, father, son. They were practically all Anglo-Saxons, or Irish; it was said that Akron was the capital of West Virginia. But they turned out pretty much like the people in Campbell, who were from Europe.

The United Labor Party was the set of decent people we met here. They took Miyo in, they helped Miyo with her English. It was the one group I was in in my life where everybody seemed to trust each other. It was a free group. Ideas weren't discouraged. In fact, they had a slogan in the United Labor Party, "The only left party that treats a member as well as a non-member." But members got to be scarce.

The United Labor Party functioned until the first Eisenhower administration. [Its candidates for Congress and City Council] got a vote of about 10,000 in Akron until 1950 or so. But after that, it just became impossible. We had an anti-war pamphlet on the Korean War that we wanted to distribute at the mill gates but [the atmosphere] was just too hostile. It never got out.

The FBI came around. One of our party chairmen turned out to be an FBI agent. He was the only one who paid dues. Nobody else in the United Labor Party ever paid dues. Every time we would get together, he was taking pictures. He even took Ed Mann's childrens' baby pictures. It wasn't until years later that everybody put it together.

We had something like four basic demands. "Basic industry should be nationalized" is the one that stays in my mind.

I went to the Soviet Union on a thirteen-week vacation. I wondered, how do we get the fifty different can openers that we get in America from private or free enterprise and the job security that you would get in the Soviet Union (except maybe if you are political)? How in America do we introduce job security and still keep democracy?

The United Labor Party considered itself part of the American movement and wanted to get away from Marxist language. We would put the question this way: You have a government in America which is almost like a sideshow. Business really runs its own area and government doesn't interfere. So then, government decisions are nullified on the job. How do we bring the Constitution into the plant? Sure, Eisenhower could say, "Hire more Korean War veterans," or, "Hire more blacks." But he wasn't sitting on the board of directors to say, "OK, let's bring them in." How do we introduce democracy on the job?

We wanted all these things within our union, things that we thought were very natural in America. So all of our literature has always been, "Get for America what everybody is supposed to have." You can talk all your life that the system you want is socialism or job security or on-the-job promotion rights. You say the same thing but you don't use the words that trigger people. Most of the demands, like on-the-job promotion rights, everybody wants. If you get a department that is shut down, a man out of that department coming into a department that is operating has all the problems that the black has always faced. You are not saying, "Give it to the blacks." You say it for everybody. And you could sell it, that this is the American dream.

But then I had a problem wondering about that. Say you are for socialism, but you're selling it as "democracy" or "fairness." The fact that you don't sell it openly means that no education goes on in the process. The problem for rank and filers is that in every election you say, "We can do more for you than the other guy." Somehow there is no education: just appealing to the selfish interests of the individual, primarily economic. I've seen Trotskyists and Communists who when they got to be union officers actually were very good because they could read the contract better. They did a better job servicing their locals. But they never sold Trotskyism, they never sold Communism. The only people who knew that they were Communists were the FBI and not the people. Nobody was ever educated in the process.

But getting back to the early days, one of our earliest fights was to be able to elect our on-the-job stewards. When the machine was built up every steward was appointed by the president. We felt the man on the job has the right to choose his own representative. I won that fight many times. After I had done some groundwork for a few years, I had about as many friends in that local as the president did. I'd get in the meeting and I'd sense the mood of the crowd and I'd get up and make my standard motion that we be allowed to elect our representatives, and carry it. The next meeting, if he was organized better, he rescinded all that. Now it is standard practice. Many times it doesn't mean that we get a better representative, but at least if we make a mistake it is our own.

We knew that we had a corrupt union on our hands. We thought that it was just our plant but it turned out later in the McClellan Hearings that everybody had pretty much the same experience throughout most unions in the country. The corrupt politician also became the patriotic politician. The opposition was always "Communist," even though nobody knew what one was or what they stood for. There may have been one or two Communists hired. But accusations went on forever with us.

We thought that somehow we could force an honest election. With Archie Nelson we put a whole coalition together. Archie Nelson was probably the best speaker we ever had in our local. A black, he was from Alabama and the vice-president. Archie had a knack. Sitting around a table with twenty guys, each with an individual grievance, he could focus them. Instead of everybody fighting each other with different ideas, Archie could refine it and when he got through speaking, people both black and white were saying Amen. He was in a department that was more white than it was black, the scarfing yard. Once Archie Nelson became active and tried to change it, he was forever the grievance man of that department. The white who ran against him once got only two votes.

It was the most effective group I ever organized. We got a man from every department. I never was a spellbinder but I could talk to the man who was on the grievance man level or the steward level.

In the first meeting we must have done something right because the whole red-baiting thing came down on us. Our literature countered that we had the right to choose our own stewards, that the right to have an honest election is the American way.

I remember one of those meetings, the largest I ever saw at our local. We were choosing an election committee. In those days getting nominated was no problem, the whole fight was getting your vote counted. Like Huey Long once said, "If you ain't smart enough to get 'em counted, you ain't smart enough to get elected." This was our reason for getting everybody out. That night they had St. Anthony's Hall, which was an old Italian church right in the Brier Hill area that seated maybe two thousand people.

The whole place filled up. Of the 2,500 people working at Brier Hill, it seemed everybody working there came. Archie, the vice-president, was sitting up front with Danny Thomas. Archie tells the story that the hall kept filling up and Danny looked them over and said, "These people aren't here for me."

The meeting had been going on maybe two minutes. There must have been a space of about ten feet in front of the platform. It was so crowded and there was so much commotion, everybody picked up their chair and they moved up those ten feet. They wanted to hear.

At that point Danny Thomas adjourned the meeting, using the excuse that these people had picked up chairs and were about to attack him. "Don't you lay a finger on me," Danny Thomas said to me. There was no intention of hitting him.

Everybody milled around. Nobody got hurt but the police were called to disperse the two thousand or so people. The regular union office was about a block away and people wouldn't go home for a long time, insisting that we had a right to have our tellers.

Danny appointed all the tellers. We asked for a commission of the international union to hold a hearing on the right to choose tellers. The district was on our side because Danny was a potential candidate for district director. We were told by our staff man, "Come tell your side of the story. You'll get justice here." We figured that if the district director was out to give justice, we had some chance. It turned out that Danny's connections were with David J. McDonald [president of the international union], so the commission was David J. McDonald's people not the district director's people.

A complete set of minutes was written up for a meeting that never happened. Then two hundred people were paid a day's lost time to come down and swear to the fact that the only reason we didn't know about any of this is that we were making too much noise and didn't hear them.

So the commission acted as though nothing had gone wrong. A Steelworker staff man who was sitting on the commission supposedly told this friend of mine, "[some people] can lie more skillfully than the rank and file can tell the truth."

MANN: I think this is where we first got raped and realized it. Two hundred people at the hearing held by the commission perjured themselves for a day's wages.

BARBERO: All the people who came down were his appointed stewards. It's strange. The money was so little. But a lot of these people picked up a day's lost time out of the local's money. They were white; they were black; they were Catholics; they were Protestants; they were Baptists; they were Methodists. It seems that the people who perjured themselves were everything—some were preachers. You just wondered what was this stuff you read about in American history books, that there was a fair system here.

MANN: This is where we woke up. We could no longer believe the international that we would get a fair shake. To get a fair shake we had to take it. If you can't take it, you don't have any right to it. That is the way it is in the Steelworkers Union.

BARBERO: But that didn't stop the fight. They held the election and it was a crooked election. Archie Nelson had put his whole career on the line by testifying at the commission about what really happened at St. Anthony's Hall. Archie should have been a shoo-in but an unknown became vice-president. For years, Archie was out in the cold. In fact, he is now out of the union and has become a foreman. Many times when they needed a black staff man they went and got someone who would toe the international line. These things finally disillusioned Archie Nelson, who had done a great service for our union. Finally, a few years ago they offered him a foreman's job, and he took it. I understand that he is running the department now, except before he ran it as union chairman.

The Dues Protest movement grew out of things like this. Many people suffered the same frustrations in every other Steelworker local. Dishonest elections and absolutely no rights on the job, people being fired: this was general in the Steelworkers. After Rarick ran against McDonald, about twenty people from another local were sitting around a table in a cafeteria. They found out that every man at the table had voted for Rarick. The local had reported more than 2000 votes for McDonald and ten for Rarick, less than were sitting at the table. We were ripe for going into Dues Protest, and we just joined with everybody else from around the country that had similar experiences.

The issue was strange. The dues went from $3 to $5 a month. This happened at the union convention in Los Angeles, and on the train coming back from California—they didn't travel by plane in those days—Rarick started agitating for rescinding the dues increase. He came back to the Pittsburgh area and started there. We picked it up here.

MANN: We had membership cards and petitions in the Dues Protest.

BARBERO: We signed them up like hot cakes. They just came in looking for you to sign this thing.

MANN: It was as if it was payday. You might have been a laborer and black, and I might have been a first helper making $40 a day, and hey, we were buddies. I don't think it was a greedy thing. People resented the international union asking for more money. We don't have the right to strike; so why build up a big strike and defense fund for the international union, when local problems are not being taken care of?

BARBERO: The thing that impressed me was that the dues increase itself was not the issue. The frustration tied everything together. Dishonest elections, no on-the-job representation, no voice: everything that everybody felt.

I recall [a friend] said to me, "What you need is to go back into your plant and have outlaw stuff." It was no longer reds. Our fighters now were outlaws. This was the year of "Gunsmoke." We were the outlaws. "Get your big mouths, your big guns, your outlaws out on the union floor."

BILL LITCH: The international union tried to blackball Rarick as a dual unionist.

BARBERO: Anybody in labor who decides to run against the incumbent immediately becomes a union buster, a dual unionist.

LITCH: The fact that he started another organization . . .

MANN: The membership cards . . .

BARBERO: Even without all that, every time five people got together it was dual unionism. You were creating an organization within an organization.

MANN: Maybe we haven't made it clear enough. I don't think we're cranks, and I don't think we're anti-union. I think we're more pro-union than the people who are representing us.

I believed what I heard about unions before I came to work in steel. We believed the stories they told us, and the literature they put out. Today Joe Hill is a great man but in 1950 you wouldn't dare say you even knew Joe Hill. Now they have a Debs Award in the Steelworkers Union. We're trying to put these things into practice, and there's just no room for it. We believe in justice on the job; and this puts me in a dilemma, because I'm fighting the company on one side, and the union on the other.

We've had some hard times here in Youngstown and the results . . . well, we got a district director elected. This is the group that did it. And he never looked back. We've elected too many people who never looked back. We get a guy in, we have no control over him. This is a fault of ours: we can't keep control, or we're not instilling in these people that there's some kind of an ethic involved. Or, Big Daddy can just do more for them than we can.

BARBERO: I want to emphasize some of the victories won by the Dues Protest. McDonald was taking us down quite a road. The Dues

Protest is the whole reason why the Steelworkers is a little freer organization today. We were part of the same pressure that was building up within the Teamsters, within the Mine Workers, every place else, for democracy.

Through it came the Landrum-Griffin bill. I don't know, maybe the labor bureaucrats are right in saying that it's anti-union like the Taft-Hartley, but as far as on-the-job democracy is concerned this is the first breath of fresh air that came into the trade union movement.

MANN: Right. Especially in elections.

BARBERO: It was a nationwide problem that some locals never held elections. The Landrum-Griffin Act said an election at least once every three years. The union bureaucracy studied the bill to find out exactly how far they could go and stay within the law. So the Steelworkers amended their constitution away from the two-year to the three-year term [for local union officers]. It said that ten per cent of the locals have to nominate, so this is what they did. Actually, they tightened up our union and made it difficult. But the Landrum-Griffin Act [also insured] an honest election.

It didn't mean that rank-and-file groups won—the machine was still better organized—but the rank and file is beginning to feel its oats. We're getting a little more honest guy as a local president, a little more independent. The level is rising. But they are not yet standing when it counts. They are like those shop stewards we had. They are still at the point where they won't stand if there isn't somebody in their ranks who will stand.

MANN: I can give you a good example of rank-and-file action not connected with elections. We had a man killed in the open hearth three years ago. He had seven days to go to retirement. Two or three months before that I'd filed a grievance, requesting that certain safety features be adopted. The grievance was rejected out of hand. He was killed by a truck backing up. One of the items on the grievance was that trucks backing up have a warning system.

The guy gets killed. Everybody liked him. He'd worked there . . . how many years? . . . you know. All right, I led a strike. I had to scream and holler, drag people out by the heels, but I got them out, shut the place down.

We went right to the union hall. We appointed a committee immediately. Every area—pit, cranes, floor—was represented. I said, "I want three men from every area to be on this committee. Now, what is wrong in your area?" Before the company could call us, in two hours, we had a list of thirty demands. When they called, we didn't just say, "Goddamn it, Tony got killed and we're shutting it down." We said, "This is what we want."

The company met with us. They bargained for three days. We got what we wanted. We kept the committee in force. Our local president cut this committee out about three months later but it worked for the time it existed. They still talk about it.

BARBERO: Murray [Philip Murray, first president of the Steelworkers Union] was not for the right to strike. But in the early days, if you talk to any of our people here—and even in our first five years in the plant—we had many shutdowns. If we had an incentive problem, we settled it right there on the job. We had a no-strike clause in the contract. But Pittsburgh would be called by the company, and they were always told that Murray would be out of town for two or three days: just enough time for you to settle your problems. But once McDonald came in this was no longer true. Strikes stopped in Youngstown with the firing of one of our union presidents, at Republic Steel.

LITCH: We had a wildcat when I was fired in 1960, but that was the last until Tony got killed.

BARBERO: Let's go back to the walkout over Tony. We had the men out, we were meeting almost continuously in our union hall. The company had finally agreed to every demand we could think of. We couldn't get the guys back to work! This was strange. You know everybody says, "Labor will strike at the drop of a hat." What I notice is, it's hard as hell to get them out but once they are out . . .

KEN DORAN: You know what happened? After they'd been out for three days they agreed, finally, to go back. Then the company announced that the accident was "human error on the part of the worker."

LITCH: They were going to go back at 3 o'clock that afternoon. Everybody was getting ready to go back. When they heard this, they all came back to the union hall and stayed out another day. Finally the company retracted its statement.

BOB LEWIS: I came to work in 1950. We had a lot of strikes, walk-outs in individual departments. Now I think the average steelworker *feels* that he can't strike. It's in his mind.

MANN: That he'll be fired, that the union will see to it that he'll be fired.

RED THOMPSON: My plant walked out about a year and a half ago. There were only two people who got time off: our president got thirty days and the steward got thirty days. The reason they got time off was because the steward and the president have got to stand there [because of the no-strike clause in the contract] until the last man walks out and say, "Come on back to work! You can't go!" They walked right out with the men!

MANN: I think we've got too much contract. You hate to look back, you hate to be the guy who talks about the good old days, but I think the IWW had a darn good idea when they said, "Well, we'll settle these things as they arise." I think we've got to get back to a little workers' rights. Let's say I'm in the research department of the international union. How can I say what's good for that guy shoveling his ass off in the open hearth? First of all, I probably don't know what that open hearth is all about. Secondly, if I ever did work there I've put it out of my mind, because I've got it made now. One of John's points is that anybody who works for the union, on a staff level or any level, must work in that mill at least once every four years, to find out what it's all about again. Because, like I said before, nobody's looking back.

LITCH: Doesn't it go back to the old saying that the union is to rise with you, and not above you?

MANN: I don't know, from being in it all these years, there's a lot of things that I think I might rather do; but I feel that the union is still the best place for a man to express himself. You can talk to people. You can put out leaflets. You can agitate. You can start an organization like RAFT. I can get up on a soapbox in the washroom and say whatever I please. I still have this freedom. Whether it gets much results or not, I don't know. But I still have this freedom, which I don't see white-collar people having. I see that workers still have a hell of a lot of freedom, if they would exercise it.

BARBERO: When Burr McCloskey and I get together we always kid each other, "My fellow failure." Many of our friends have gone on to the U. S. Steel office, or the NAACP, or, of course, the union bureaucracy. What first brought us together is no longer in the picture. You ask the question, have we done anything?

I look over racism. I told you about the city of Campbell. We were the first of the children of the foreign born who went at least through high school. We suffered discrimination, we said we would do better. But racism may be worse in our society today than when I came out of high school. It's more open, deeper. I wonder after all these years. I am sure that we will keep working at it. But other forces, the divisive forces, are much bigger and have done a better job.

Still, Bill Litch, I, Eddie Mann, are lucky. The other Sunday we were down in Akron talking to Marie Wagner because she is sick and we figured that we better see her. She asked me, "Do you have another person in the local that you talk to?"

It turns out that we are lucky in our local. Ed has always been there. He fights things. You wonder where the commitment comes from. Our local had a fighting tradition before we came there. Even though we have had our layoffs, somehow we have forever had a rebel group coming up in our local. She asked me, "Do you have one other person?" I said, "We have twenty."

It goes back to the honest election fights. You could recognize them as they came up to vote. You knew that, despite all the red-baiting, they were working for you and for the local. Somehow this has formed a common bond.

BILL WORTHINGTON, LEE SMITH AND ED RYAN

I N THE 1930s the United Mine Workers under its president, John L. Lewis, spearheaded the formation of the CIO. But the UMW was an undemocratic union and Lewis ran it in an arbitrary and often violent way. Rank-and-file members did not have the right to ratify contracts, nor to elect district (regional) union officials. When Lewis passed on the presidency to a hand-picked successor, Tony Boyle, conditions became worse. America's most dangerous industry had one of its least responsive unions.

In the late 1960s an insurgent movement appeared. Health and safety were part of the reason. Mining disasters like that at Farmington, West Virginia in 1968, which killed seventy-eight men, came to seem intolerable. As Bill Worthington relates, Black Lung was found to be an occupational disease and the demand grew that its victims should at least be adequately compensated.

Union reformers ran on a program of making the union more democratic. In 1969 Jock Yablonski, a member of the international union's executive board, ran against Boyle for president of the UMW. He was defeated, or counted out, and soon after he, his wife, and his daughter were murdered. Miners For Democracy was organized at Yablonski's funeral. Finally in 1972 Arnold Miller, a retired miner who himself suffers from Black Lung, defeated Boyle in an election closely supervised by the United States Department of Labor.

The following accounts were presented by three participants at a public meeting in Gary, Indiana in February 1973. Speaking with enthusiasm of Miller's recent victory, they also stressed the miners' tradition of refusing to work when their safety is endangered. A distinguishing quality of these union reformers is that rather than relying wholly on elected leaders, they expect new leaders to give "backing" to their own rank-and-file action.

BILL WORTHINGTON,

LEE SMITH

AND ED RYAN

Miners For Democracy

I

BILL WORTHINGTON: I was a coal miner for thirty-three years. I left the mines in 1969 on account of an injury, as well as Black Lung. I'm going to talk a little bit about the beginning of the Black Lung Association, of which I'm president, and how we got our things together.

For years while I was working we were all told that when you see a miner walking around, wheezing, trying to get his breath, he had "miner's asthma." We were also told that inhaling coal dust was really good for us, it was healthy.

About 1953, I believe, a doctor by the name of Dr. Donald Rasmussen who did research for the Appalachian Regional Commission began to study miners. He found out that we didn't have "miner's asthma," or walking consumption, or any such thing, but we were suffering from pneumonoconiosis. We cut the term short to say, simply, Black Lung, a respiratory disease.

Finding out from this crusading doctor what was actually going on, we began to get pretty angry. Our people were dying. They weren't getting benefits. Coal companies were making millions of dollars off of us, and then, when we got too sick to work, they said we had "miner's asthma" for which there's no compensation. You were just out. You went to the poor house or started begging.

Upon finding this out, we began to get together. We began to do some serious thinking about what we could do. The whole movement started in the state of West Virginia. We found out that the first step was to get state legislation passed that would compensate for this occupational disease. We began to lobby, talk to our legislators, congressmen and so forth. We got state legislation passed, and we got the federal Coal Mines Health and Safety Act of 1969.

We thought that this was the answer, that a lot of people would be paid, that something would actually be done. We did what so many other people have done, what we did earlier, back in the '30s: we thought we'd won a victory so we relaxed.

Then it dawned on us that something was wrong. There were not enough people getting paid. There were too many sick people, walking around, dying slowly, and nothing being done about it. The federal Social Security Administration was not following the law. If they had been, more people would have been getting paid.

So we had to think of something to do to make more people aware of what was going on. We began to study that law closely. We began to do training sessions with disabled miners, widows, as to what the law was all about, and how to make that law work. It's one thing to have a law, something on paper, but it's something else to make it work to our advantage.

We began to inform people of their rights, what steps to take, what bureaucracy could and could not do. Our tendency was to get people to do things for themselves, to say [to the bureaucrats], "Look, man, you *can't* do this. The law says so-and-so." They were able to quote sections of the law.

Such a low percentage of people were being paid, so few of us were off in one little corner doing what we could do, that we decided to combine forces. Instead of one little group over here, fighting the law, being put off, harassed with one harassment after another, we decided that we needed state organization. We managed to get three states working closely together, doing training sessions. And we decided that some of the old law, the '69 law, just wasn't right. We had to do something about that, too.

We got together with congressmen, doctors, lawyers, and what not, and we asked that amendments be made to the 1969 law. These were called the 1972 amendments.* We practically negotiated those amendments with the Social Security Administration. We were also successful in getting them to let us help write the regulations [under which the amended law would be enforced]. This was something that to me was a first-time happening. We had never been able to sit down and work on our own problem. By doing a lot of demonstrating, picketing the Social Security offices and so forth, we got to do that.

As you know, they always try to give you the runaround. When we were in the Social Security offices in Washington we had pickets out at every district office in the coalfields. So the commissioner said, "Look, Bill, get on the phone, tell those people to leave the district offices. We'll let you people help write the regulations." I said, "Put it on paper. Put it on paper and sign your name to it. *Then* I'll pick up the phone." And we accomplished that.

What I'm really getting at is this: it's very possible for people to work together. When we formed a three-state organization we also formed what we called a board of that organization. We kept up communications. Everybody was working toward the same thing. And so there was no more denying of what we wanted, of what we needed. We became a strong, political movement. We have bar-

*The best known provision of the Black Lung Law of 1969 (P.L. 91–171) was the benefit program. As of January 1972, there were 350,000 claims filed and 145,000—less than half—had qualified for benefits. The Black Lung Benefits Act of 1972 broadened both the coverage and the definitions contained in Title IV of the 1969 act and made the amendments retroactive to 1969. The amendments broadened the coverage to include surface miners; provided for relatives who had been dependent on the miner; broadened the definition of total disability to an "inability to continue working as a miner"; and broadened the definition of "Black Lung" to include any "respiratory or pulmonary impairment which occurs after 15 years work experience in the mines."

The Social Security Administration estimates that at least 135,000 more claimants will qualify under the new regulations. Approximately two billion dollars will be paid to claimants by mid-1973 and 96 per cent of this money will be given to the residents of Pennsylvania, West Virginia and Kentucky.

However, the program lapses in 1974 and new claims from then on will be paid by the states and mine operators. The state governments are still largely controlled by the coal operators. ("Coal Mine Health and Safety," *Peoples Appalachia*, Winter 1972–73, page 35.)

gaining power. The Black Lung Association board became a bargaining power, a bargaining agent, for the whole Black Lung movement.

Arnold Miller, who is now the president of the United Mine
Workers, was the first president of the Black Lung movement. I
was proud to stand shoulder-to-shoulder with him. This is why we
have him as union president now.

This is how we formed a movement that right now has recognition
in Congress, recognition from the Social Security Administration.
We thought about all the pros and cons. We planned the thing, I
think, fairly well. We asked ourselves, What will we do if we fail
with this effort? We looked all around the ball instead of just looking
at one side.

Every rank-and-file member of a union ought to know what's
going on. This is the purpose of our training in the Black Lung
Association: that everybody knows their rights, everybody partici-
pates. We feel that everybody ought to have a right to participate
in anything that concerns their lives.

II

LEE SMITH: I'm chairman of the health and safety committee
at the Federal No. 2 mine near Morgantown, West Virginia. I can
tell you some of the things that have happened with the Miners For
Democracy. I was with them at the time Jock Yablonski ran, and
was murdered.

The company I work for, Eastern Associated Coal, is one of the
biggest. And I went in and talked to them about safety. One particular case I mentioned was over a pillar plan.

In the mines they drive headings up on the advance, and when
they come back they take all the coal out. There's a plan made for
this so that the roof will fall behind the men, so that they'll not
be under or near the fall when it comes down. They get in a hurry
for coal—more production—and they deviate from this pillar plan.

About 1969 I went in on a pillar plan for Number 9 Section of
our mine, Federal No. 2. They had deviated from it, they were completely off of the pillar plan.

I met with the company for approximately two hours before going into the mine. I went into the mine on the afternoon shift, my regular shift. I worked over on the midnight shift. At two o'clock in the morning I was coming back out of the mines and the dispatcher stopped me and said, "Hold it. There's a fall in Number 9 Section." I said, "Anybody hurt?" He said, "I think there's a man under it." So I waited a little bit, and he called back and said, "No, there's four men."

This was the section where the pillar plan had been deviated from. I went up. There was one man who could talk to us, underneath the rock. Finally we got him out and he died the next morning at seven o'clock. There were two more men that were killed instantly. The fourth man had arms and legs broken, but finally got all right.

Tony Boyle was president of the United Mine Workers at the time. I tried to get hold of Tony Boyle but it was just like me trying to call President Nixon. Same thing: I could have gotten just as much. The district headquarters for our local sent out a Tony Boyle-picked man. To start with, the man had only worked a year in the mines, and it was not in a union mine. This was back in the early 1940s. The man didn't know what a continuous miner looks like. Mining today in these big coal mines is modern, it's not pick-and-shovel, it's modern machines.

We got nothing from him. The state and federal mine inspectors said right at the bottom of their report that the company was at fault. But they weren't going to do anything. So we had to take it on: the union had to do it.

We fought for Arnold Miller and we got him in. And since he's been elected we revised the whole pillar plan. Now, the way the procedure goes, I go to the district. It's taken care of, or if it's not, I can pick up a phone and call Arnold Miller direct. I have done it on one occasion. And when I call him, it doesn't bring out mine management, it brings the presidents of these companies down. And they talk with me as if I was their equal, which we should be, we're working in there.

I'm real pleased with our election. We have backing now. We don't have to worry about the company pushing us off to one side.

Before Arnold Miller I was fired four times from our mine, for safety reasons. I shut their mine down. That's the only power whatsoever I have, is to stop their production and withdraw the men. And they fired me four times. But since he took office, it seems they don't have any more of those slips.

When I started in the mines safety was preached in the paper, was preached in any printed material that you got from the mines. There was a big buildup. Everything sounded beautiful. But then when I went to work in the mines, all those pieces of paper were left outside. The more you read, the more people got killed.

I'm a member of the Mines Rescue Team, the ones that go in and try to rescue men after they're trapped, which is a terrible job. And that's the only reason I used to go in. I got in trouble at Blacksville No. 1* over this particular thing. After we couldn't get the men, they were trying to get us to go back in when the mines were about to explode. They were trying to get us to save their coal mine. The president of that division of the Consolidated Coal Company tried to get us to go back in. I said, "There's no way of getting the men. The men are lost." They knew this. Everybody knew this. The men were burned up. I said, "You started the fire. You put it out. Only reason I'm here is to get those men out, alive if possible."

The mine where I work is new. When the company started it they hired all young men. The company took the position, like in the '20s or '30s, "We're going to put these men in there. They're young men, they don't know any better because there hasn't been a union or anything. We're going to train them to do as *we* want them to do." This went on till they got the mine filled with men.

But they made a mistake! These men that they put in there were able to read. Every man that was making a living at this mine had his own opinion. When the company did something that was wrong, each miner knew it. They went to their committeemen.

We have three safety committeemen and three mine committeemen. The safety committeemen take care of safety, the mine committeemen take care of contractual. They are elected in the local.

*On July 22, 1972, Consolidated Coal Company's Blacksville No. 1 mine in northern West Virginia caught fire and resulted in the death of nine miners.

For instance, I am elected in the local. I might add that I'm a mechanic in the mines, and work my eight hours the same as the others. I do my safety work extra, unless I have an imminent danger, when I report off my shift or any shift and go in the mines at union expense.

We have nobody to answer to other than the men we represent. So we take it on our own to make our voice heard, and if management doesn't listen, then we shut them down. That's all there is to it.

III

ED RYAN: I'm from Morgantown, West Virginia. Lee and I work in the same mine. I'd like to tell you about some of the things I've run into, from my standpoint of being a younger miner.

Our national union conventions, a lot of times, were called in places pretty far away from the coalfields. What miner could get the money together to go to some of those places, to go to the national convention? And the ones that could, they couldn't afford to take the time off from work, anyway.

If you were fortunate enough to get the money together, and have the time off to go, a lot of times you went to the door and you didn't get in, because of so-called strongarm men at the doors, with the Roscoes stuck inside their coats which they pull out and flash at you if you want to say anything. Or else if you got into the convention and stood up to propose something, you got beat on the head. "Sit down! If you don't sit down, I'll hit you."

Now we've got us some good leaders. Arnold Miller is calling the next national convention in Charleston, West Virginia, close to the heart of the coalfields. And one of the first things on the agenda is where in the coalfields to move our new national headquarters. It's not going to be in Washington D.C. any longer. Get it down there in the coalfields where it belongs!

There isn't going to be any more of this nonsense when you come to the door. Those doors are going to be open. The only people that are going to be standing there will be saying, "How are you doing, brother? Come in here and have a seat." There isn't going to be any more, "What are you doing here? Oh, you're one of those rank and filers. Sorry, you can't come in. This is a closed session.'' There isn't going to be any more of that.

When I first started in the coal mines in 1967 I did some reading on my own and found out a lot of things about the leader of our union at that time, Tony Boyle. So I started talking to people, informing them of some of these things. "Aw, you're crazy. You're just one of them long-haired hippies. Don't know what you're talking about." "Well," I said, "you take it for what it's worth." I told them, "Now, Jock Yablonski is going to get in there, and he's going to give us some reforms."

I got drafted and had to go to the Army during a good bit of Jock's campaign. My heart was with it, but unfortunately I couldn't be.

During Arnold Miller's campaign I did a lot of talking to a lot of people. A lot of the younger people have the attitude, "It doesn't matter. I've got me a good job, I'm making big money. I don't want to be concerned with this union." A lot of the older miners feel, "Let's see, I have only five or ten years to go. I'd better just sit back here and be quiet. I don't want no change to come about. I might get fired and lose my pension."

You can't say that these people are dumb, you can say that they're ignorant of a lot of facts. After you sit down and talk with these people a little bit—and that's what it takes—then if they don't pick it up, and realize it, then you can call them dumb, because they aren't ignorant any more.

In the union, solidarity starts with your local. A chain is only as strong as its weakest link. All right, your local is where that chain starts. From there you can move up to your districts, and then to your international. This means talking to the people in your locals, informing them of things which, because you are concerned individuals, you'll research and find out for yourselves—because no one else is going to tell you. After you find some of this out, tell your buddy who works next to you. If he's a good enough man that you can call him "brother," then tell your brother who works next to you. That's what union is all about. That's your brother working right there next to you.

I remember one time I was working on a pillar line. I was a miner's helper. So I had to go in and help drill stumps. That's what's left. That's the only thing holding up all this rock that's ready to fall. And I was told by the boss to grab that butterfly drill and hurry up and drill them stumps because she was about ready to come in. I said, "You're crazier than hell. I ain't going in there." Up jumps another man and says, "I'll do it. I'll do it. I'll do it." Off he goes running in there, nothing but a goddamned scab.

You can't have that. I know whenever we take our initiation into the union the pledger says, "I will not take my brother's job." Now that's part of your organizing, that's part of your strength. I'd say the mine I was working in at that time was about 90 per cent scab and 9 per cent who didn't care one way or the other. That's why I was considered a long-haired radical hippie.

IV

SMITH: I want to say something about this being together. On our big strike, there were some mines in Pennsylvania which were sneaking coal in. They were non-union, little "dog holes": pick-and-shovel. But between them they could produce enough coal to hurt the strike.

Morgantown is not a very big place, but there were enough pickets to shut down Morgantown, a complete town, just going through it. We went out there and they came down in their trucks, hauling this coal. So we told them to dump it out. They dumped it out and called the Pennsylvania State Police.

The police came out and looked the crowd over, called back in, and told the State Department of Highways to clean the coal off the road. A trucker came along in a big truck which could haul maybe thirty tons of coal. This guy knew he was in the wrong, that the pickets were going to get him. He looked down the road and saw all these guys. He laid the brake on that truck, set the emergency brake, jumped out, and took off back down the road. Left the truck and all.

We didn't have to go out there any more.

RYAN: Let me tell you one thing, about coal mines. Maybe it's because it's awful dark down there, maybe it's a psychological factor. I don't know. But when you're underground, by God you'd better be a brother. Coal miners are close. They are brothers. That's what a union's all about.

SMITH: You're either company or union, there's no halfway between them. Here recently they offered me a safety division manager's job for Eastern Associated Coal, which is a *fabulous* job. I mean, $50,000 home, maybe not a Cadillac but pretty good. And I asked the man, "Is it a company job?" He said, "Yes." I said, "I don't want it." He said, "Well, think it over." I said, "I did. I don't want it."

I would think that people in all unions ought to be brothers, also. I would think that if you're working for a living the same as I am, and your goal is to make a paycheck at the end of the week, then we all ought to be brothers. The coal companies, the steel companies, they're not only brothers: it's all one thing.

RYAN: You don't usually see a picket line in a mine strike. If one man stands in front of the mine and says, "No work today," and gives a good reason, no one goes in. It's just not done.

A lot of unions have to have picket lines when they strike because you do have people who work when their brothers are out there not working. You just can't have that. Rank and file, that's where your strength is.

VICKY STARR

FTER APPEARING in the film *Union Maids*, Vicky Starr no longer
used the fictitious name "Stella Nowicki" as in her "Back of the
Yards" account above. In *Union Maids*, Vicky Starr speaks of her
impatience with some women who come from an economic base where
they have choices and who cannot relate to working women: "When
you've got to work for a living in factories or in homes or in offices, you
have a whole different concept of life—what is needed and what is required." The big industrial unions of today, she says, have not organized
the unorganized: "There are tremendous numbers of white collar workers that should be organized," and, in addition, "the union should become more involved with things outside the union," such as
consumerism and ecology. She says at the end of the film: "There's some
tremendous potential in people, in labor people, in working people, and
in union people. . . . They are very democratic. . . . There is a tremendous
militancy that's below the surface and that will rise and come up. I don't
think the American working people are going to let this country down."

In this account, she describes a second career as a rank-and-file organizer of clerical workers at the University of Chicago. The National Labor
Relations Board (NLRB) election of November 1978, in which over 1,800
clerical employees chose to be represented by Teamsters Local 743,
"was the largest . . . involving white-collar workers in the academic field"
as of that time (*Chicago Tribune*, Nov. 20, 1978).

Two kinds of organizing are evident in this account. There was a traditional top-down style, represented by Teamsters Local 743. Underneath that top-down process, however, something very different developed. Acting stewards were elected *before* the NLRB election, almost all of them women. Complaints were pursued and resolved in an improvised manner even *before* the election.

During the interview with Vicky Starr in October 1997, her former co-worker Charlotte Podolner dropped by and joined the conversation. Vicky Starr's papers, on which we have drawn for footnotes corroborating her account, may be consulted at the Chicago Historical Society.

VICKY STARR

Organizing White-Collar Workers

MY GRANDDAUGHTER Robin asked me to speak to her second grade class about my experiences in the stockyards. I asked her, "If you want me to speak to the children in your class, what do you think would interest them?" And she said, "Tell them why you had to change your name!" When I worked in the stockyards and was organizing, if you announced in any way that you were interested in a union you were put on a blacklist. You couldn't get a job. So you tried to get a job under another name. Again and again and again this happened.

After the stockyards, I married and we had four children. As soon as I could I looked for work outside the home.

I had learned typing in high school, and bookkeeping because I was Secretary-Treasurer of my local in the stockyards. I needed a job where I could sit.

When my son Steve was about two-and-a-half-years-old I got a job working in an office. It was horrible. The people I worked with were anti-Semitic, they were anti-Black, they were anti-everything that I stood for. This was around 1950.

I took another job where I worked four days a week and had Thursdays off, so I could go to my PTA group. This was after the twins were born. By the time I got through paying for child care for the twins, gasoline for driving to work, and minimum maintenance, I came out with zero dollars.

I went to a vocational service and was tested as to the kind of work I could do. The social worker said, "You should work at a place where you will be involved with other people. An educational institution would be fine." So I went to the University of Chicago and filled out a job application. I used my real name, Vicky Starr. I left "Stella Nowicki" and "Vicky Kramer" in the stockyards. But I lied about my age by about ten years. They told me I could have any of three openings. I thought I would like to have a job at the School of Social Work. I was offered the job of clinic coordinator, but that would have meant working Saturdays. I took a job as a secretary.

UNION

There were different attempts at organizing the clerical workers. One that came to my attention was by a professor named Curtis McDougal. This was the United Office and Professional Workers of America (UOPWA). In that union part-time workers were paid *more* than full-time workers, because they did not get benefits. Then, later on, District 65 of the Distributive Workers of America sent in people to organize.* I was involved in that. We got out a bulletin.

[Charlotte Podolnar, Starr's former coworker, joins the conversation.]

PODOLNAR: Then the Teamsters came in, and unlike any of the other groups, they had the money and the clout to do a big job. We were not so happy with the Teamsters because we didn't like their reputation. They assured us that Local 743 was different from the national union, that they were good people. It took two years. This was 1977, 1978, 1979.

STARR: The clerical workers in the hospital had a union, with which they were dissatisfied. Some of them had friends who were connected with the Teamsters. So these employees approached the Teamsters about coming to the University. And the NLRB decided that the bargaining unit should include not only clerical workers at the hospital, but also clerical workers throughout the whole University.† There were more than 1800 people in the bargaining unit.

I was very hesitant about becoming involved with the Teamsters. Before I signed up, I called Jessie Prosten from the Packinghouse Workers

*Newsletters in Vicky Starr's papers indicate that District 65's effort took place in 1972-1975.

†The NLRB ruling in November 1977 was sought by the University. While it represented a temporary setback for organizing clerical workers at the University hospital, the ruling paved the way for "unionization of clericals in the entire campus." *Union Report*, v. 8, no. 1 (Sept. 27, 1978), a publication of the Faculty Association of the University of Chicago Laboratory Schools.

Union. I asked him about Don Peters, who was the president of Local 743. He said, "They're tainted, that's true. But in Chicago, if you want a good union negotiator, the best is Don Peters."

I talked with Peters. His salary had been in the newspaper. I said, "You're head of a union, and you earn over $200,000? Come on!" He said, "Why, you think that's too much?" I said, "Sure is!" He said, "How much do you think I should get?" I said, "At most $40,000 or $50,000." He said, "I put in a lot of time." I said, "So do a lot of other people." He said, "I was at a meeting in San Francisco and they decided this is what I should have." I looked at him and said, "That's hard to believe."

THE CAMPAIGN

By that time I was in the Department of Education. It was one of more than eighteen buildings that had to be organized.

The Teamsters sent a lot of organizers. There was leafleting all over the place. There were meetings on the lawn. There were free lunches at the Center for Continuing Education. The Teamsters had a script, they invited people there, and they talked union.

Acting stewards were chosen before the NLRB election, on company time, by secret ballot. Of the twenty-one stewards, I was the oldest one in years, and I had the most years working at the University. Eighteen were women.*

A lot of the women felt that they should not belong to a union. They were not union people. They were beholden to the professors for whom they worked. It took a lot of convincing and personal attention to break down these negative attitudes.

We broke down these attitudes by pursuing grievances, and taking actions, even before the election. In the library they started to organize before anywhere else. One of the women was fired. The reason given was that she was overweight. The woman who headed the activity in the library pointed out that there was a supervisor who was much fatter than

---

*A memorandum from Edward C. Coleman, University Director of Personnel, July 5, 1979, lists Charlotte Podolner as steward for the Center for Continuing Education and Industrial Relations, and Vicky Starr as steward for Rockefeller Chapel, the Divinity School, and Social Sciences. The memo indicates that there were twenty-three "acting stewards" as of that time.

the woman who'd been discharged. She argued that this was discrimination. The employee was rehired with back pay. This was *before* we got our contract.

There was a rumor in my department that there was going to be a layoff, because the department had not received certain grants. People were demoralized. I got together with an employee at the Lab School and a social worker who had been involved in the UOPWA organizing. We decided there should be a bag lunch meeting. We invited all the secretaries.

At the meeting, we said that we should take a position about what was going on, and why. We should know if there was going to be a layoff. If there was to be a layoff, how big? And people affected should have a chance to go to the University employment office and check out job postings.

We circulated a petition. We walked into the supervisors' meeting and filled up the whole office. We had a spokesperson. It was beautiful.

Even before the election, we had a big meeting to discuss what we should ask for in the contract. I'll never forget a young man who got up and said, "I work in the bookstore twenty-four hours. Then I go to work in the warehouse twenty hours. And I don't get time-and-a-half." And then Louise Dennis got up and said that she had worked at the University for a number of years, got pregnant, and asked for a leave of absence for a year. And when she came back they couldn't find her record!

Going to work became a pleasure. We were stewards. We were stimulated. Helping our colleagues became our mission.

THE FIRST CONTRACT

The election was held in November 1978. About seventy-five votes were challenged. We were ahead by only fifteen or twenty votes. It was April or May, six months later, before we were recognized.

The stewards then became the bargaining committee. Let me tell you, when more than twenty of us were sitting at the bargaining table, and they had about ten on the other side, they didn't know what was what. They'd make a statement and we'd counter it! I can remember telling one of them, "Sir, you have the wrong information." I didn't call him a liar. And I remember Maggie would say, "You know what? We can run this University better than you can."

Another thing I'll never forget was said in negotiations, after we won the election. Someone in management mentioned that [the University of] Chicago was a "prestigious" university. And we responded, "When I go to the store to buy a loaf of bread, they don't ask me whether that dollar is from a prestigious outfit, or from Woolworth's. We can't live on prestige."

PODOLNAR: I think one of the factors that made the Teamsters effective was that we did a lot of research. We knew what the problems were at the University. The wage scale was very, very low. Working conditions were not good. The place had about a hundred different departments, and every department was like a little fiefdom, with a director who determined whether you got a quarter raise or not. It was so uneven.

STARR: I remember that when we petitioned for an election the University brought in over 2,100 job descriptions for 1,800 jobs.

PODOLNAR: I think the greatest contribution that we made to the union, and to the people there, was to classify all those hundreds of jobs. We gave each job a price, we gave it parameters.

STARR: We reduced the number of job classifications to something like 300. There was one steward who felt that because she had a degree she should be able to get a job that she wanted, that was higher paid. But the job description did not require a degree. We debated that. We decided that she had no right over anyone else. I remember talking about it on the basis of experiences I had in the Packinghouse Union. Our jobs in the stockyards were manual. So it didn't matter how much education you had.*

I raised the question before negotiations that our contract should not only prohibit discrimination based on race, religion, and all that, it should also prohibit discrimination because of sexual preference. We had a big debate amongst the stewards.

PODOLNAR: So many things were left undone. For instance, we talked about day care, but it never really materialized.

STARR: One of the things I suggested and that we got into the contract was that when a new person came to work, and the secretary had to

*Just before the NLRB election in November 1978, a leaflet was issued entitled "University of Chicago Employees Speak Out." The first employee to be quoted was Vicky Starr, who said in part: "After 11 years in the same department, I am still sixty cents below the maximum rate . . . . Further, most jobs haven't been re-evaluated in years, and job duties have been added with no raise in pay."

train that person, the secretary would get fifty cents an hour more for doing it. It wasn't carried out.

I was there for another ten years after we got the union. I was able to take a personal leave of absence for six months to travel with the film *Union Maids*. I came back to a job at the same pay rate.

The faculty are glad that the union is there. They now have a stable office staff. People want to stay. What would happen before is that women would come to work there, they would learn the ins and outs of the job, learn to operate different machines, and in no time, take off: go downtown and get twenty percent more.

PODOLNAR: But I think the University has been successful in taking away the power of the union. Our original union was all clerical workers. Now they've divided it, and that always diminishes the strength. And I don't think the Teamsters have done such a good job in the last few years.

STARR: Our initiation fee was fifty dollars. All of a sudden we found that it had been changed to seventy-five dollars. We didn't know about it. Even the stewards didn't know. We asked for a meeting with Don Peters. We went down there, we fought, and actually won! People got money back.

PODOLNAR: I don't know how you keep that spirit alive.

STARR: We have some complaints about union policy. But this should not diminish the great contribution the union made to University of Chicago employees. Charlotte, remember how you and I went down to the hospital recently on medical business and talked to the secretaries? We asked them how they were doing. We said, "You're a union member. Well, we helped to organize the union." And they said, "Thank you, thank you, thank you."

MARSHALL GANZ

M ARSHALL GANZ grew up in Bakersfield, California. In 1964 he
went to Mississippi as a volunteer in the civil rights movement.
He stayed until the fall of 1965, registering black voters in dangerous Amite County as a field secretary for the Student Nonviolent Co-
ordinating Committee (SNCC). He recalls that he learned a lot about
listening, about paying attention to what was going on around you, and
that he learned how to operate in a culture very different from his own.

From 1965 to 1981, Ganz worked with the Farm Workers as an organizer, organizing director, and national officer. Unlike the typical trade
union, the Farm Workers under César Chavez required equality of sacrifice from leaders and those led. During a strike its officers and organizers
were paid no more than strike benefits. The Farm Workers did not view
the "service model" and the "organizing model" as alternatives. For them,
servicing individual needs was a form of organizing. And because federal
labor law does not cover agricultural workers, the Farm Workers were
free to use the boycott and ordinarily had to strike for union recognition.
Self-appointed committees, and boycott campaigns staffed by rank-and-
file volunteers, made possible a series of Farm Worker victories.

This account is drawn from an interview conducted with Marshall Ganz
in September 1998. The narrative has been enriched by consulting Marshall Ganz, "The Paradox of Powerlessness: Leadership, Organization and
Strategy in the Unionization of California Agriculture (1959–1966)," an unpublished paper, and the transcript of an interview with Ganz recorded by
Frank Bardacke in April 1996.

MARSHALL GANZ

Organizing Farm Workers

FROM MISSISSIPPI TO CALIFORNIA

EVEN THOUGH it was a union, for me, the Farm Workers was a California version of SNCC. It was almost incidental that it was a union. It was an extension of the Movement. It was "more than a union." The bridge was a very natural one.

The Farm Workers was about economics, and we had already come to the conclusion in the South that that was really important. And it was a way to keep going. This was a time when a lot of people were dropping out of the Movement. I count myself really lucky to have wound up in the Farm Worker setting.

In the Farm Workers, I re-learned grassroots organizing. In SNCC, I had learned by osmosis. In the Farm Workers, organizing was taught as a discipline. There was a method, and you could learn it, and be good at it, and then you could teach others. That consciousness of organizing as a craft, and an art, was something special to the Farm Workers.

When I first went to work with the Farm Workers, I was assigned to Bakersfield, where I had grown up. Even though the strike was going on in Delano, César wanted me to begin by learning how to do personal service work. I opened a little office. César sent his cousin Manuel to train me in holding house meetings. I held house meetings in which everybody spoke Spanish. There was always a local rep with whom you would work, the dues collector for that particular community.

It was all built around a lot of personal service. These were immigrant communities, and they had all kinds of problems: on the job, with drivers' licenses, with the Immigration and Naturalization Service, with this, that, and the other. You made the organizing credible by beginning to do something about those problems.

In the Farm Workers, people paid $3.50 a month dues for a family membership. A kid six months old got a union card. In return for their dues, the family got a death benefit. They got a newspaper, *El Malcriado* ("the upstart"). They got help with personal services and they could join the credit union. It was the Asociación de Campesinos, an ethnic community association.*

By the end of the year I got involved in the Delano grape strike.

THE DELANO GRAPE STRIKE

The strike was begun by Filipino workers, not by Mexicans. They struck in the Coachella Valley, which is where the grape season begins, and won an increase from $1.20/hr. to $1.40/hr. Then they came to Delano and struck. César had been organizing for three years in Delano, mostly among Mexican workers. He had been planning to organize for two more years without striking. But he was confronted by the strike. There was a crucial choice to be made as to whether to join the Filipinos. César had the foresight to see that if the strike had been allowed to turn into a racial thing at that point, the union would never have recovered.

The Farm Workers decided to test support for the strike among the 2,500 Mexican grape workers by holding a strike vote meeting. It was held at Our Lady of Guadalupe Hall in Delano on September 16, Mexican Independence Day. The people were very enthusiastic, because there had been a long period with no wage increase. But César wanted to be sure that if they got into it, they would not just play with it, they would come out the other end.

So he put out three conditions. One was nonviolence. That was a new thing. Nobody had ever heard of that before. It was a condition that people

---

*In "Paradox," pp. 11–13, Ganz compares the Farm Worker approach to that of the AFL-CIO Agricultural Workers Organizing Committee (AWOC) which functioned in the first half of the 1960s. "AWOC's timing was short term, focused on visible results.... The intent was to produce immediate membership growth." Farm Worker leaders believed that a critical error of AWOC and similar efforts was trying to strike and organize at the same time.

had to accept, or the Farm Workers would not lead the strike. The second condition was that the strike would not be just for a wage increase, it would be for union recognition, and people would agree to stick it out, whatever it would take. And the third one was that there would be shared sacrifice. He explained that there was no strike fund, but everyone would share the same level of sacrifice.

There were about 1,200 Mexican grape workers at the meeting. They unanimously approved a strike with these conditions. But as time went on, it became more problematic. Lots of people went on strike and then went elsewhere to work. We had a relatively small group of highly dedicated people, farm workers and non-farm workers, a hard core of about 150.* We had to learn how to turn that into a capacity to affect the growers. We had to learn how you manage the internal politics of a group in struggle, how you sustain morale. We had to keep coming up with new ideas. Nonviolence isn't not doing anything. Nonviolence is constant action. Inaction will produce violence.

We had to work in a multiplicity of cultural settings. Mexicans were the largest group, but there were Chicanos, there were Filipinos, there were the Anglo volunteers. The Farm Workers were grounded in a deep sense of cultural pride. Mexican identity was very important, and a source of tremendous commitment and courage. But César was determined that it would not turn into an anti-white or anti-Filipino or anti-Black attitude. If it did, there couldn't be a union.

Of course there were tensions. Volunteers came in. There were farm workers and students. There were young men, young women. At one point the wives of a number of young farm workers were very upset about the white volunteers. So César had a meeting just with them.

There was a lot of history between the Filipino and the Mexican communities. There was a lot of potential for feelings to boil up. To his great credit, César wouldn't give an inch on that. It was put out in the open that people were different culturally, but we had to work together. Otherwise there wasn't going to be a union. The union was able to articulate itself as having a powerful cultural identity, yet at the same time maintain

---

*The core of about 150 activists devised the "roving picket line" tactic to compensate for their numerical weakness. Ganz, "Paradox," pp. 18–20.

a balance between different groups. Filipino-Mexican joint committees were formed, and eventually a joint board was formed and leadership was drawn from both groups. The Filipinos were actually over-represented on the merged board if you compared their seats on the board to their proportion of the workforce.

MONEY OR INDEPENDENCE?

When the grape strike began in September 1965, it was clear that you couldn't have a strike without money. The Farm Worker leadership, including César, who had been getting $50 a week, received only strike benefits during the strike. The strike benefit began at $1 a week, then went to $2 and eventually to $5. Everyone lived in the same way. The idea was that if there was no money, you couldn't pay your leadership.

But the union couldn't sustain a strike without getting help from some place beside workers. There had to be some compromise with the idea of being self-supporting. We drew support mainly from churches and student groups, who organized caravans. These were Protestant churches and some Jewish groups, not many Catholics until later. There were a few maverick labor groups.

César had applied for an OEO (Office of Economic Opportunity) grant three months before the strike. It was to set up service centers. This was an alternate future that could have happened. César was known to the Kennedy people. They tried to recruit him for the Peace Corps in 1961. The grant came through a month after the strike began in the amount of $270,000.

César turned down the OEO money. Two things were evident. First, you couldn't take the OEO money and continue the strike. If all the energy went into setting up service centers, there wasn't going to be a strike. It had to be one or the other. And secondly, taking the money would have tied the hands of the strike leadership.

In December 1965, Walter Reuther came to town. The Filipino group was affiliated with the Agricultural Workers Organizing Committee, AFL-CIO (AWOC). We were an independent association, in loose coalition with the Filipinos. Reuther had the sense to see that the Farm Workers had the potential to put out a different idea of what labor was about.

We did some very intense lobbying. The word was, Reuther was going to give a pledge of support from the UAW to the strike. We wanted half the money, even though we were unaffiliated and independent. We got that. Reuther announced at a big meeting that there would be $5,000 a month, half for AWOC and half for us.

That was a big victory. The labor movement had recognized that we were real. But that night, we got a bottle of Christian Brothers wine and went over to the house of César's brother, Richard. We sat there drinking. And César said, "Tonight we lost something that we'll never get back." "What's that?," we asked. He said, "We lost our independence."

I think it was the right choice. We were able to maneuver by avoiding dependence on any one source of funds. It was an alternate strategy for maintaining autonomy. We had labor over here, we had the churches over here, we had liberals over here, we had Chicanos over here [pointing in four different directions]. Any one group could only get so pissed off at you. If they cut you off, they pushed you into the hands of the others. The original strategy had been, depend only on yourself. This strategy was multiple sources of support.

THE SCHENLEY BOYCOTT AND THE SACRAMENTO MARCH

The first boycott, the Schenley boycott, began in December 1965. It was almost accidental. Somebody thought the Kennedys owned Schenley. They didn't, but it turned out that Schenley owned 5,000 acres of wine grapes in Delano and distributed highly boycottable products, including Cutty Sark whiskey.

I recently found the phone list that we used in the Schenley boycott. The first boycott calls were to friends of SNCC and SDS (Students for a Democratic Society) offices around the country. The boycott featured a march in Harlem organized by CORE (Congress of Racial Equality) to get Schenley products out of Harlem liquor stores.*

---

*Ganz points out that because farm workers are not covered by the National Labor Relations Act, Farm Worker boycotts were not subject to legal prohibitions against "secondary boycotts." The Farm Workers asked consumers not only to boycott Schenley *products* but also not to shop at *stores* being picketed until the stores removed Schenley products from the shelves. Ganz, "Paradox," p. 24 and n. 17.

I was assigned to coordinate the march to Sacramento, which took place the next spring. The march grew out of a concern to keep workers from returning to Delano in the spring when work in the grapes resumed. Chavez gathered a leadership group at a supporter's home in Santa Barbara to spend three days figuring out what to do. According to my notes:

As proposals flew around the room, someone suggested we follow the example of the New Mexico miners who had traveled to New York to set up a mining camp in front of the company headquarters on Wall Street. Farm workers could travel to Schenley headquarters in New York, set up a labor camp out front, and maintain a vigil until Schenley signed. Someone else then suggested they go by bus so rallies could be held all across the country, local boycott committees organized, and publicity generated, building momentum for the arrival in New York. Then why not march instead of going by bus, someone else asked, as Dr. King had the previous year [in Selma, Alabama]. But it's too far from Delano to New York, someone countered. On the other hand, the Schenley headquarters in San Francisco might not be too far: about 280 miles which an army veteran present calculated could be done at the rate of 15 miles a day or in about 20 days.
  But what if Schenley doesn't respond, Chavez asked. Why not march to Sacramento instead and put the heat on Governor Brown to intervene and get negotiations started? He's up for re-election, wants the votes of our supporters, so perhaps we can have more impact if we use him as "leverage." Yes, someone else said, and on the way to Sacramento, the march could pass through most of the farm worker towns. Taking a page from Mao's "long march," we could organize local committees and get pledges signed not to break the strike. Yes, and we could also get them to feed us and house us. And just as Zapata wrote his "Plan de Ayala," Luis Valdez suggested, we can write a "Plan de Delano," read it in each town, ask local farm workers to sign it and to carry it to the next town. Then, Chavez asked, why should it be a "march" at all. It will be Lent soon, a time for reflection, for penance, for asking forgiveness. Perhaps ours should be a pilgrimage, a "peregrinacion," which could arrive at Sacramento on Easter Sunday.*

The march was timed for March 17, when the Senate Subcommittee on Migratory Labor was to hold hearings in Delano. The AFL-CIO wouldn't join us in the march. It was led by a farm worker carrying a banner of Our Lady of Guadalupe, portraits of campesino leader Emiliano Zapata, and banners proclaiming "peregrinacion, penitencia, revolucion" (pilgrimage, peni-

---

*Quoted in Ganz, "Paradox," p. 25.

tence, revolution). The eighty-two original farm worker marchers reached Sacramento accompanied by 10,000 farm workers and supporters.

During the march to Sacramento, we won the first agricultural workers' contract, with Schenley. It was an incredible breakthrough. It showed that it was possible to get contracts with growers. There was a substantial wage increase, hiring halls to replace labor contractors, medical benefits. It went right to the heart of what the abuses were. It happened just four days before we got to Sacramento. All of a sudden everything was possible.

What we learned in the Schenley boycott was that we weren't going to win boycotts in Delano, we were going to win boycotts in New York and Boston. As long as the struggle was local, there was no way we could win. Farm unions had always been destroyed by fighting it out on local turf. By re-defining the struggle as national, then we had the leverage, because the growers couldn't do much in New York, or Boston, or Chicago, but we could. They could run the police and the courts and everything else in Delano, which they did, but we could get Stop and Shop in Boston to cooperate.

It was exactly the same thing the civil rights movement did: to re-define the arena of struggle. Gandhi did the same thing. South Africa did the same thing. Power is often a lot more unequal locally than it is on a broader scale.

DiGiorgio Farms and the Teamsters

Then we got into a fight with DiGiorgio Farms. This was a big corporate farm that had done in an earlier effort to organize farm workers in the late 1940s. We threatened a boycott of Tree Sweet Juices and S & W Fine Foods, which were owned by DiGiorgio. We pressured Pat Brown, the governor, who was up for re-election, with the help of MAPA, the Mexican American Political Association. He intervened, and mediated, and DiGiorgio agreed to have a representation election.

In the midst of that organizing, the Teamsters appeared. DiGiorgio had contracts with the Teamsters in food processing and trucking. One night we were out making house visits, and people all of a sudden had cards from the Teamsters.

DiGiorgio supported the Teamsters, so we had to out-organize the Teamsters and the employer together. This drove us closer to the AFL-CIO, because we needed their support.* One of the results was that we negotiated a merger with AWOC and became the United Farm Workers Organizing Committee (UFWOF), AFL-CIO. That was in August 1966. We remained an organizing committee until 1972, when we became a national union.

One of the DiGiorgio ranches employed about 1,200 workers. The other had about a thousand. The whole campaign was like a school. Except for Fred Ross, who was in charge, all the organizers were new. There were a lot of young farm workers. We probably trained fifty to sixty organizers during the DiGiorgio campaign. And we beat the Teamsters in DiGiorgio.

The wine contracts took us all over California. By July 1970, we had signed 200 contracts with the grape industry, covering 70,000 workers. We got contracts in 1970 with grape growers of whom we had never heard. We swept away the whole industry.

We went from a membership of 3,000 to 70,000 overnight. That was High Point Number One, no question about it. By 1972, we had expanded into Oregon, Washington, Arizona, Texas, Florida. We had citrus workers, hop workers. We had a contract with Coca-Cola in Florida. The boycott put the fear of God into a lot of employers.

THE TEAMSTERS AND THE VEGETABLE INDUSTRY

On the eve of our signing with the whole grape industry, the Teamsters went over to the Salinas Valley and signed up the lettuce growers. We didn't even have our victory party before we had to deal with the Teamsters, once again. We had gotten them out in 1967. They came back into the picture in 1970.

We wound up having to do two things at once. We had to bring all the grape workers under contract. Many of them had never been on strike. They weren't unionized workers. There was no culture of contract en-

---

*At this time the International Brotherhood of Teamsters was not affiliated with the AFL-CIO.

forcement or hiring halls. At the same time we were in a battle with the Teamsters over the vegetable industry. This led to a strike of 7,000 workers in Salinas in August 1970 and to a lettuce boycott. It was a whole Second Front.

One issue with the Teamsters was race. There was economics but there was also a lot of racism. The growers thought that César was a crazy Mexican. The workers wanted their "own" union, not run by Anglos.

Also, the vegetable industry was much more commercially organized than the grape industry, and much more vertically integrated from harvesting to processing. Grapes take seven years to grow. The grape growers were mostly Armenian, Italian, Croatian. The vegetable growers were Anglo business people. They had contracts with the Teamsters in processing operations like canneries, in trucking, in coolers. A lot of it was covered by the NLRB, because these businesses were defined as commercial operations that shipped for multiple growers.

The vegetable growers had a friendly relation with the Teamsters. The Teamsters had made their reputation in California agriculture as the responsible union, pro-private property and anti-Communist. The background was in the 1940s when a Communist-influenced union had tried to organize the California canneries. The Teamsters made common cause with Del Monte and the cannery council and they had a series of Red-baiting elections and the Teamsters took over 40,000 workers in the canneries. So the Teamsters had a way of operating in which they benefitted from the existence of a more militant union by providing an alternative.

Another factor was that a lot of work that had been in the sheds was moving to the fields, to a field-packing, field-production operation. These had been Teamster jobs. The Teamsters didn't want anybody representing field workers other than themselves.

In 1970, the Teamsters and the growers in the vegetable industry signed a five-year contract. Lettuce workers were getting thirty-two cents a box. The contract gave piecework workers an increase of half a cent a box per year, with no benefits and no representation.

We had begun organizing lettuce workers along the border in 1968 by opening a service center in Calexico, across the border from Mexicali, and beginning to do medical and other services on a small scale. These workers followed what was going on in Delano. A delegation had come in 1969, wanting to strike. We said No, we had to win the grape strike.

In 1970, the lettuce workers figured it was their turn. And when the Teamsters signed their contract in Salinas, and the growers went out to the fields and told the workers that they had to become Teamsters and have dues deducted, the workers said, "What Teamsters? What do they have to do with us?" The Teamsters were white. The Teamsters were with the boss.

We organized a meeting for lettuce workers. We had leaflets printed. We went on the radio. We had contacts. We had the use of the upper floor of a poverty program office. Two hundred people came from all over the Salinas Valley. César explained what had happened in Delano, and what the growers were trying to do with the Teamsters. He said they could have their own union but they would have to fight for it. They said, "Yes!"

We didn't quite believe that, so the next thing was a series of marches that were organized to converge on Salinas and protest the Teamster contract. About 5,000 people showed up in Salinas.

The talk in the rally was, "OK, what you need to do now is to form committees. Every ranch, form your *comité*. Every crew, form your *comité*. When you have formed your *comité*, come to the office." We had set up temporary union headquarters on the main drag in the Mexican part of Salinas. We asked the committees to come in and get cards to sign up with the union.

All these committees started arriving! "Hello, we're from so-and-so. What do we have to do?" It was one of those moments. It was a combination of the pent-up discontent from years without a pay raise, and the grape strike, which showed the possibility of victory.

We rented an old post office with a huge open space. We started to have meetings there every evening. Only committees were allowed in these meetings. What it did was to create a community among the grassroots leaders in the vegetable industry. There were people there from tomatoes and strawberries as well as lettuce. The resistance to signing with the Teamsters was sustained by these meetings.

Then three lettuce crews were fired for not signing with the Teamsters. We called everybody on strike from that company, a subsidiary of Purex named Freshpict. That was Strike Number One. The next day we went around announcing through loudspeakers, "Don't work at Fresh-pict. Freshpict is on strike." There were about 300 workers at Freshpict. There was also a huge strawberry company in the area named Pic N Pac. It had 1,200 workers, who lived in a big family camp called La Posada. They heard the announcements and they thought "Freshpict" was "Pic N Pac": they thought it was them. And so we got a call at about eight o'clock in the morning. "*Aqui estamos. Donde estan?*" ("We are here. Where are you?") "What do you mean?" "*Estamos a huelga.*" ("We're on strike.")

So we hustled over. There were several hundred workers milling around the big trailer park. We elected a committee, and pulled out the rest of the workers in the fields. Pic N Pac was the second strike.

About two weeks later, August 24, 1970, we took a big strike vote. On Friday, the committees voted to recommend a strike. The strike vote was to take place on Sunday, in a big field.

It was decided that to go on strike you had to take a vote of the people on your ranch, and report what the vote was at the big meeting. Secondly, you had to have your own flag that identified what company you worked for. One of the male lettuce workers stood up and said that "*tenemos un prob-lema*" ("we have a problem"). What is it? "*Nosotros no podemos coser.*" ("We don't know how to sew.") At that point, some of the women from the family camp of strawberry pickers said, "We have lots of women. We're great sewers. Just bring us the cloth and the pattern, and we'll sew flags." For the next three days you'd see little delegations of *lechugeros* (lettuce cutters) going into the camp with cloth. The camp became a flag factory.

On Sunday they voted to go on strike, and the next day it began. It was over 7,000 people, the biggest strike we'd ever had. Really, it was a gen-eral strike, from north of Watsonville all the way south to below King City, a coastal area of about 120 miles. Companies were going on strike that we didn't know existed. People would come and say, "We're the brussel sprouts workers. Help us strike." "We're the radish harvesters."

It was led by committees of workers, and we were trying to coordi-nate it as best we could. Harry Bernstein of the *Los Angeles Times* drove in and said, "I've never seen anything like this. There's a hundred miles of red flags."

The very first day the growers got injunctions, claiming it was a juris-dictional strike. We figured we had to turn a strike, which could be enjoined, into mass discharges, which could not. We picked Mann Packing, a broccoli company. The workers decided that they would force the company to fire them. They decided they would all go to work in the morning, and at ten o'clock the leader would jump up on the broccoli machine. He would pull out a flag. And then everybody would sit down and refuse to leave, which would cause them to be fired.

So they went to work. At ten o'clock we were all at the edge of the field. We couldn't see what was happening. We kept waiting, and eventually we saw a yellow spot in the distance. (They wear bright yellow rubber suits, because broccoli is very wet in the morning.) It was all these guys marching out, waving their red flags.

There were pickets and counter-pickets. The Teamsters brought goons to town. The AFL-CIO brought in members of the Seafarers. The workers would say, "*Los gorillas han llegado! Por favor, mandenos los gorillas buenos!*" ("The gorillas have arrived! Please send us the good gorillas!")

At the end of the first week we got our first contract. Inter Harvest was the largest employer in Salinas. It was a subsidiary of United Brands, owner of Chiquita Bananas. We threatened a boycott of bananas. Inter Harvest rescinded its Teamster contract. They signed with us. There was a thirty percent wage increase. Instead of half a cent we won twelve cents.

At the end of the second week we got a contract with Freshpict, the Purex subsidiary. Then a final injunction issued on the 16th of September. Again we faced a choice.

Since it was the 16th of September—Mexican Independence Day—we took the whole strike to the seashore. We had a big celebration. We decided we needed to focus on the boycott, end the strike but sustain our organization. People went back to work, but it was an organized workforce.

Within a month we'd gotten two more major contracts. One was with Pic N Pac, owned by S. S. Pierce. The other was with D'Arrigo Brothers, an outfit that had outlets in Boston, New York, and Chicago. By November we had four major contracts.

A NEW STATE LAW

In 1971–1972 the growers tried to pass legislation to take away the boycott. We went through a series of defensive legislative battles, in

California, in Kansas, in Oregon, in Washington. They got it on the ballot in California as an initiative, Proposition 22, but we beat them in November 1972.

We went back to the boycott. We put everything we had into reorganizing the boycott of grapes, lettuce, and Gallo wine in 1973–1975. We took the strikers to the boycott in a big car caravan across the country. We took about 300 people. We went to Phoenix, to Albuquerque. We had a mass at Ludlow, Colorado. We went across to St. Louis, up to Chicago. Every place, we would drop groups of people, members of farm worker families, who were going to launch this second boycott.

Then in 1974 Jerry Brown was elected governor of California. Up to this point we had resisted any legislation, because we knew that so long as Reagan was governor any state legislation—no matter what it said—would not be what we wanted. We didn't want federal legislation, either, because it would take away the boycott.

By 1974 we were beginning to make a lot of headway. The summer of 1974 we had short, disruptive strikes all over California. There were strikes in melons, tomatoes, you name it. By 1975 there was a great deal of pressure for legislation. National supermarkets came to Sacramento and said they wanted legislation, because they didn't want boycotts. Law enforcement in California wanted legislation. We were demanding jury trials for all our several thousand arrests and literally bankrupting rural counties. The Teamsters thought that legislation would confirm their contracts.

So we negotiated the California Agricultural Labor Relations Act and got it passed in June 1975, to go into effect in August. It provided for elections in seven days. Brown appointed a board that included Leroy Chatfield, a longtime supporter of the Farm Workers, and was chaired by Bishop Mahoney, presently cardinal in LA. The Board agents that they hired were like what I've read about the first NLRB people. Many were Chicanos, young lawyers. They were all for us. It was our law.

During the summer of 1975 we did intensive organizing. The law went into effect in late August, and within about a month we had 300 elections. I was still working in Salinas. Every day we had ten, six, eight elections. We learned a hell of a lot about how to win them and how to lose them.

The Teamsters won some elections. Every election that they won we objected to. Our attorneys organized a massive free lawyer consortium to pursue all these hearings. The Teamsters were paying through the nose for everything. We were able to use the law to make it uneconomic for the Teamsters to stay in the field. We also had launched a major anti-trust suit against the Teamsters and the growers, which was costing them lots of money.

The law worked so well that by the spring of 1976 the Board ran out of money. So it was shut down, and the legislature refused to renew its funding, because the law had turned out to be a pro-farm worker law. We had to put an initiative on the California ballot in 1976. We lost the initiative, but the struggle removed the resistance and the Board was re-funded and went back into operation. So, we had a law.

We had built the union back up, not to 100,000, but to 40–50,000. The first peak was 1970–1971. The second peak was 1977. We were all set, ready to go again.

WHOM THE GODS WOULD DESTROY

It took four years to undo what had taken almost twenty years to build up. I think there were several factors.

In the spring of 1977, we negotiated a five-year jurisdictional agreement with the Teamsters. They got out. I think the situation turned a corner when we signed that pact. Until then, we had to compete with the Teamsters. And in retrospect, it was a damn good thing. The competition between the Teamsters and Farm Workers meant that a lot of farm workers got organized, and wages went up, and conditions were improved.

Second, in 1972 we were chartered by the AFL-CIO as a national union. We never developed regional structures. Power always remained very concentrated, within the Board and, particularly, with César.

Every ranch had its ranch committee, every crew had its steward. But there wasn't sufficient concentration, such as a regional entity would have provided, to make the committees and stewards a power base. No ranch was strong enough to be a power base. You would have had to have regional local unions. We never created that.

César used to resist creating locals, because as he liked to say, "Once there are locals there is politics, and once there is politics we won't be able to continue the struggle, because we'll consume ourselves in politics." There's some truth to that. But institutionally, we never created enough diffuse points of power to have real accountability.

Further, as I think often happens to charismatic leaders, César became isolated. César was an amazingly gifted and talented person. But the more his aura grew, the more people told him what he wanted to hear. César knew that that was happening. From one standpoint, the distrust that he came to feel was rational. On the other hand, there's a line between distrusting what you are told and thinking that everyone is lying to you. By 1975–1976 it was as if he had lost his confidence. It's hard to describe. He became very inward, much more reticent, and began to lose his sense of humor. It was a whole personality change, a kind of breakdown.

There had always been the danger of agents. But by 1976, there started to be unreal stories about agents, about Communists, just very bizarre stuff. The first people started to be purged. I didn't fully grasp what was going on. It seemed that something very strange was at work, and I kept thinking that César would get on top of it. I was close to him, as you are with a mentor and a teacher. It was hard for me to accept what was happening to him.

About this time, the secretary treasurer of the union got on the road and said to different ones of us, "We need to do something." Nobody quite believed him. César had governed with a spoke system. There was more connection between you and him than between the people around him. There wasn't the kind of trust that it would have taken for us to respond.

Finally, people began to want to get salaries. All this time we had been functioning as a strike community. When we got the contracts in the 1970s, we immediately wound up in this other fight with the Teamsters, and everybody continued with no salaries. You got $5 or $10 a week. You got food stamps. We didn't pay rent, you could put gas in the car, and the union took care of medical problems if you had them. Basically it was a subsistence deal. We did pay our lawyers something like $7,000 a year. We had a couple of doctors to whom we paid $12,000. Some of the field staff began to want salaries, too.

César felt really threatened by this. He thought that once you started to pay salaries, you lost your community, you became professionalized and bureaucratized. There's an element of truth to that. But on the other hand, how were we to stabilize the organization? Is there a point at which people need to be able to live whole lives?

The effort to make the Farm Workers into a total community became a year-long campaign. Along the way, the union got rid of its lawyers. The Board split for the first time over whether to abolish the legal department. We had a 5–4 split, with the four younger members, including myself, voting against César. People started leaving.

We had no tradition of legitimate opposition. A group of workers I helped to organize in the late 1970s tried to run their own candidates for the Board at a union convention. They were run out of the convention.

By 1981, the capacity that we had created over the years for leadership at all levels was gutted. It was just gone. By 1982, the union leadership was mostly César's family.

FIVE SMOOTH STONES

I call the doctor's dissertation that I am writing about the Farm Workers "Five Smooth Stones." The Farm Workers are like David when he fought Goliath. When David volunteered for individual combat with the Philistine champion, the king of Israel armed David with a helmet of brass and a coat of mail. But David put off the king's armor, because this was not the style of fighting natural to him. David was a shepherd. He fought lions and bears to protect his father's sheep, but he did so with a shepherd's weapons. And so "he took his staff in his hand, and chose him five smooth stones out of the brook, and put them in a shepherd's bag which he had, . . . and his sling was in his hand." Thus armed he went forth and conquered (I Samuel 17: 4–51). So it was with the Farm Workers.

MIA GIUNTA

MIA GIUNTA (pronounced "Junta") grew up in a working-class community in eastern Pennsylvania. It was a union family, the kind of family that formed the backbone of the emerging CIO. As a young adult, Mia Giunta went to college in Connecticut and became an organizer for the United Electrical, Radio and Machine Workers (UE).

To be hired as an organizer for the UE at that time you had to come out of a factory. Mia Giunta started organizing as a volunteer. And in the UE the organizer took part in negotiations at the place that he or she had organized. This was because the organizer stayed in one community, putting down roots. It was a practice consistent with what Mia Giunta calls "women's style of organizing."

Among Mia Giunta's memorable experiences was a factory where women workers insisted on sharing the work equally during layoffs. Later, she was present at the scene of a building collapse, waiting with an Italian immigrant family for news of a family member who didn't make it. She believes that this event gave rise to Workers' Memorial Day, now celebrated each year on April 28.

MIA GIUNTA

Sharing the Work

HOW I WAS RAISED

BOTH MY MATERNAL grandparents came from the southern part of Italy. My father's family came from Sicily. I never met my father's father. My grandfather came to this country in the 1890s because of the Ethiopian War. He came not to be wealthy, but to be free and independent, and so as not to fight in a war in which he did not believe. He peddled fruits and vegetables and olive oil from door-to-door. He died of influenza in 1918.

My father's mother worked in a cigar factory after her husband died. When I was in college and opposing the Vietnam War, my grandmother loved the hippie movement, because it brought out something in her that she remembered as a young girl. She told me that my grandfather didn't want to work for anyone because he didn't want to be a slave. And he didn't want to employ anyone, and have them become a slave. The only thing that suited his temperament was to go door-to-door.

He couldn't read or write, but he kept a notebook in which he drew pictures to keep track of his accounts. My grandmother and my aunt say that he would throw a pocket change purse to the children, and let them play with the money, because he hoped that some day there would be a world where people didn't have to have money, and didn't have to work for it, because everything would be provided.

He was a man of contradictions, though. He wanted his family to have absolutely the best, and worked very hard for that. My father and his brothers were very proud that they were the first family on the block to have an inside toilet and electricity.

This was in Scranton, Pennsylvania, which is the anthracite coal mining region. I became aware of unions at a very early age. My father was a plumber, partly because his older brother was a plumber. While working at the trade as a teenager my father found an old, old plumber, who was a member of the Knights of Labor. He learned about the labor movement from this old man.

It was part of the family tradition not to trust the boss, to be suspicious of authority. My father wanted to join the plumbers' union. He was not allowed in because he was an Italian-American. The story my father told me is that one day the plumbing inspector, who was also president of the union, came to my father's work site to inspect a job. My father waited until the guy was in the bathroom, met him at the door, and said, "There are three ways out of here. One is the window. One is over me. And the other is by letting me in the union." My father joined the union that day. When he passed away last year, he had been in the union fifty-eight years.

He was a building tradesman, so there was a certain elitism. But there was also an understanding that the union should be open, and he saw to it that other people who had not been allowed into the union were admitted. His nephew became business agent for the same local in the 1970s, and my cousin fought to have women admitted and also recruited African-Americans.

Once my father got into the union, he was upset that everything was so secret. He found out that there were some other guys who didn't like it, either. You never knew how the money was spent, you never knew what was going on. So he was part of a rank-and-file movement. As a kid I didn't know what was going on, but I knew it was deadly serious. They met in my parents' living room or in the basement to talk about how they could get rid of the corrupt officials. There was such energy there! You just knew it was good stuff.

I got addicted to it. Once when I was only three or four I was listening intently, and at the same time, shaking a ginger ale bottle with a stopper in it. The bottle suddenly went "boom!" They all hit the floor.

They won. My father went on to be treasurer of the local, and representative to the Labor Council and the Building Trades' Council.

My uncles were coal miners. They went into the mines when they were eight years old, and were put into spots where grown-ups couldn't fit. They never learned to read. I remember with great sadness how I came to realize this. I had begun to figure out words and when I went to my uncle and asked him to read a story, I found that he wasn't reading. He was making things up.

My mother's father was a stonecutter. He eventually left stonecutting because he developed silicosis. And he opened up a grocery store. That was something that a lot of people did, because they were blacklisted, or became disabled. When my grandmother died a few years ago, someone came to the funeral who said he wanted to thank her, because during the Depression she and her husband had helped their family to stay alive by giving them stuff to eat. Nobody knew that but my grandmother.

My father had a little cottage somewhere near the Poconos. There used to be a lake there, but the lake went during a hurricane. We still used to go up there. The whole Giunta clan would come. You had coal miners. My aunts all worked in garment factories. There were people who worked on the railroad. You had the whole AFL-CIO represented.

Naturally when anybody came the first question was, "Where do you work? Who do you work for?" My grandmother used to say you can always tell who somebody is by what kind of work they do. So one time they asked a man, and he said he worked for a certain company that was on strike. So they said, "Oh, you poor man. You've been on strike all summer," and they really laid the food on him. And he said, "Oh no, not me, I go to work every day. I'm in management." They took the food back! Nobody would speak to him. They fed his wife and daughter, but not him.

Then there was another time I got a Judy Bond blouse with a little bit of money I had saved. It was all I could afford. This blouse had the Peter Pan collar, and the little buttons, and all the things that blouses were supposed to have in 1960. But Judy Bond was on strike. My father made me take it back, and apologize to everybody on the picket line. I was mortified.

That's how I was raised. I don't think my background is anything special. It's part of a working-class experience that can make us very strong. But in the process of becoming Americanized, we run the danger of forgetting who we are and what our families taught us.

BECOMING A UE ORGANIZER

I hated Scranton. I felt so confined. It's in a valley, and there are all these mountains, and I used to have fantasies of flying over the mountains to the other side.

I was encouraged by my father to think for myself, to look beneath the surface. Somehow I couldn't do that in Scranton. The world was too rigid. I wanted to get out. And school was the way to do that. I went to the University of Bridgeport and studied sociology. But the reason I went was not to study sociology, it was to get out of Scranton.

I found out about the UE [United Electrical, Radio and Machine Workers]. I met some wonderful UE organizers. I found that rather than say, "Oh, you're a woman, you can't do that," they were happy that I was a woman because as a woman, I could reach other women and help them to organize.

I didn't go to work for the UE right away. I used my social work background and in 1975, got a job with the Bridgeport Labor Council, to help unemployed union members during the recession. Then a big strike hit one summer and I said, "Striking members are unemployed members!," so the job became doing strike assistance. I became known as the "food stamp girl." I would show up at a picket line and they'd say, "Oh, you're the food stamp girl!" It became more than helping people to get resources. I was helping people in one factory to get in touch with people in another factory, encouraging people to go to each other's picket lines.

One strike was at the Bullard machine shop. Racially and ethnically it was a very mixed shop. So during the strike they had different kinds of nights, when they would show films. On "Hispanic Night" they showed *Salt of the Earth*. When people were on strike there was a different kind of community. People were on the picket line together, day in and day out. At Bullard they got a very good contract offer but people didn't want to go back to work!

I did get in trouble with some of the Labor Council officers. They didn't think it was right for me to be doing this. But the people on strike got wind of what was coming down, so they showed up en masse and it didn't go very far.

I knew I wanted to do organizing. But the UE wasn't hiring college kids. You had to come out of a factory. I was willing to go into a factory, but by that point, no one in Bridgeport would hire me. My picture had been on the front page of the local paper. There was a very long strike at Jenkins Valve, and the company was bringing in scabs. John Del Vecchio, a member of Steelworkers' Local 7528, and I showed up one morning to try to dissuade the scabs from going in. There was one really young guy who just didn't know what was happening. John and I were talking to him. We weren't being nasty or threatening, but we were both Italian, and we were talking with our hands. The photographer took a picture of us with our hands in the air! Eventually I went to work for the UE as a volunteer. It was no more than $50 a month.

F-DYNE ELECTRONIC

There was a place I had heard about when I worked for the Central Labor Council, an awful, awful hellhole. Its name was F-Dyne Electronic. The plant made little products, less than an inch long, which held electrical charges. Most became parts of a razor or a pencil or a tape recorder.

I told the international rep that I wanted to organize this factory. He said, "Well, go ahead and do it. But please understand that places like this can move out very quickly, and it's a tough workforce to organize, because of all the different nationalities."

The place was fascinating. There were African-Americans who had lived in the city a long time. There were African-Americans who had come from the South fairly recently. There were people from Africa, from Puerto Rico, from Portugal, from Cuba, from Mexico. There were people from countries like El Salvador, who didn't want you to know they were from Latin America. There were over two hundred hourly workers, and less than a dozen were men. In Bridgeport at that time there were trucks that would come around outside the plants and serve breakfast: awful coffee, awful chile. People would get that cup of coffee before they went into the shop. I would go and ask questions. "What's it like working here? Are they hiring?" People started complaining. I met one Portuguese guy whose name was Manny, and asked him, "What's it like here?" He said, "It's terrible. We need a union." I said, "Oh. I'm from a union." He said, "One minute please." He came back with a bunch of women, and said, "I go now."

I took the women's addresses and said, "I'll meet you after work." That's how it started. Some of the people weren't interested, but you ask around, and you find out who the organizers and the leaders are.

In the process of organizing, by department and by issue, the barriers started to break down. Many of the women could not read and write in their own language. Certainly many of them could not read and write in English. As they got to know each other, they found they all had something in common as working women. They were willing to take a chance together to better their lives.

The women had different political experiences. The women from Portugal said about elections, "Oh sure, you get to vote Communist, Socialist, whatever." But you also had women from Cuba who were anti-Castro.

There was a woman in the factory named Marguerite. She was a Cuban immigrant. Marguerite's goal was to become a citizen. She was terrified she would be sent back to Cuba. One day Marguerite, who was very active in the union drive, was suspended. She was upset because she thought she would not get her citizenship. She left the factory in tears.

An African-American woman put out a leaflet about what had happened to Marguerite. She wrote it in the voice of Harriet Tubman. The leaflet more or less said, "Harriet Tubman rides again." At that time Jimmy Carter was president and he was talking about human rights. The leaflet said, "Mr. Carter is talking about rights, but not rights for everybody. Mr. Charley is in the North and won't let us have our union. Harriet has to come again, and organize her people, and help Marguerite!"

People loved it. Harriet began to become different people. Harriet was Puerto Rican. Harriet was from Pakistan. The woman who started this was not a political woman. She had stayed home, raised her kids, found herself with a husband who didn't love her anymore, divorced, went on welfare, and then worked at the plant. Her name was Louise.

After the union came in, and we got our first contract, some of the women went to college, got better jobs, ended abusive relationships with husbands and boyfriends, and I think it was because the collective experience had transformed them.

I get really angry when it is said that working-class people don't have culture. They have a very deep culture. It's a culture that's based on solidarity and trust and helping each other, and a dream for a better life for your children. These people were tired of the way they were being treated.

SHARING THE WORK

We won the election. People were jubilant. People got caught up in thinking that they had transformed their workplace.

It took us most of a year to get a contract. There were all kinds of legal delays. I was a part of all this, because at least in my day in the UE, the organizer took part in negotiations at the place that he or she had organized. This was because the organizer was viewed as part of the community. You could be transferred within the same community, or asked to work on special projects, but you had a base. I was a better "organizer" because I was also a "servicer," and a better "servicer" because I was also an "organizer." I can't imagine not doing it that way.

We came very close to striking. We would have lunchtime meetings, to inform people what was going on in the contract negotiations. Sometimes the meetings lasted a little longer than the half-hour lunchtime. People wore stickers, buttons, T-shirts. Workers spoke to organizations in the community about their struggle for a first contract. We formed a strike committee.

Finally, we had a lunchtime meeting and people voted not to go back to work. The company told them they were all suspended. They let in only a few people who didn't go to our meeting. We acted just as if it was a strike, and the company settled shortly afterward.

It was an interesting contract. The company claimed they didn't know what they were signing. We got voluntary overtime. We got a year's maternity leave. While you weren't paid during the leave, you accrued vacation and seniority and your health benefits continued. The average age of the women in the shop was about twenty-five.

Then came the day that the contract was all typed up and we were going to have the signing. The company wanted to reneg. People walked out of the factory, with signs that said "Mr. K. [the company president] won't sign the contract." He signed.

There was a clause in the contract that provided a cost-of-living clause in the third year. The company said they were not going to pay. The women were furious. They created such an uproar, the bosses went to the only place they could think of, the men's room. The women wouldn't let them out. Finally the bosses came out and the women said, "You broke the contract!"

So we filed a grievance, and the company had to pay a lawyer, and before the arbitration hearing the company settled. The average worker got maybe $75 a few weeks before Christmas. People went out and bought a winter coat or whatever, and said, "This is my union coat."

People in the shop were very supportive of each other. I remember when the local was going to get its charter as Local 210, UE. A woman in the shop was going to go to a meeting to pick up the charter. She was embarrassed, because she didn't think her clothes were dressy enough to go. The women were all making minimum wage at the time. They took up a collection and got her a whole new outfit.

One woman had a horrible absentee record. We went in and said, "She has children, and it's very hard when you have children that you're raising by yourself." We got her job back.

The company had an operation in Florida. Mr. K. was from New York, and as long as he was president, the Bridgeport plant was kept open. But there were layoffs. There were layoffs in 1978, 1979, right after the contract was signed.

Under the contract, the layoffs went according to seniority. We felt terrible, thinking of some of the workers who would be put out on the street. There was a Portuguese woman named Albertina who had little children. She was crying but she said, "It's OK. It's all right." The other women said, "That's unfair."

The workers took up a collection for her. I felt very guilty, and tried to talk to Albertina to make sure that she and the kids would be all right. We just didn't want to see her go.

When the next bunch of layoffs came along, somebody suggested, "We'll all work a few hours less each week. That way everybody can stay. Everybody will have health insurance." And they took advantage of the vacation and maternity leave, and that became the tradition in that factory.

The contract was never amended. Every time there was a layoff, we would sign a side agreement that everyone would agree to cut back. When the factory finally closed at the end of the 1980s, I think people were working four-and-a-half days a week.

VARIETIES OF ORGANIZING EXPERIENCE

There was a plastic factory down the street, which used chromium and nickel and mercury. About 175 men worked there. They had a horrible union. Someone got hurt in the factory once, and they called the union collect and the union wouldn't take the phone call. They never got to see their contract.

Someone who worked there heard about the UE, probably from someone at F-Dyne. We had a discussion, "Are we going to raid this place?" We concluded, "Maybe we can give them some tips about how to make the union work better for them." This was going on while we were trying to get the F-Dyne contract.

We arranged a meeting with the workers for a Sunday afternoon. It was a very cold day in February. People walked from all over the city to come. After they told their story it was decided then and there that we would work with the people for the UE to take over.

We started with a very militant committee. But as workers were lining up to vote, the National Labor Relations Board called off the election, because the company had said something in a leaflet the day before that they weren't supposed to say. The incumbent union filed charges.

People said to me, "Everybody knows that we are voting for the UE. Mia, we're going underground." There were a lot of people there from Latin America and they had experience in working underground. They said, "You won't know. We're not going to speak to you. You're just going to have to trust us." It was going to be nine months until the election.

I remember a day outside the factory, early in the morning. These guys in suits drove up in a huge Cadillac. The workers weren't even there yet. There was nothing except these guys, me, the garbage dump, Long Island Sound, and a public housing project. I said to myself, "This is it. I could disappear, and nobody would ever find me again." They walked up very menacingly and muttered obscenities. The wires in my car were pulled out.

When the election finally came, the UE won overwhelmingly. There was such celebration! We went to the union hall that night. People brought salsa records. We danced, and we danced, and we danced all night long. We stayed up making a flier saying, "WE WON!," as if people didn't know!

That factory, too, had to overcome differences. It was harder for me to work with because they were mostly men. There were Jamaicans in the shop who didn't get along with the Puerto Ricans. There were Dominicans who didn't get along with some other group. You show people their common needs, common interests. You work with them to believe that they can do it together, and not alone.

There was another factory outside New Haven, Bridgeport Plating, which we heard about from the son of a UE member in another plant. We set up what was supposed to be a small meeting. But instead of four or five workers coming to McDonald's for a cup of coffee, half the factory came. The McDonald's wasn't big enough for me to speak to the people and I didn't have any other place to go. I got up on a chair and the McDonald's manager started to get really nervous. So we went out in the parking lot, and continued our discussion. I asked people from different departments to get together in different parts of the parking lot and make a list of their problems, while I would rotate.

From that day, through the organizing drive, through the election, to the day we went out on an unfair labor practice strike, we had exactly the same amount of people. We called it "the grandmothers' strike." They were older women, who had never stood up for anything before in their lives. They made harnesses for jet aircraft. When you shook hands with them, you realized that their hands were deformed.

Our strike headquarters was a tent, like a tent you would use for a wedding. The women decorated the tent with artificial flowers. They cooked delicious meals. People were always meeting people: "Here, have a slice of cake, we'll tell you why we're on strike." There was a quiet woman, who at the beginning of the campaign wore her union button to work under her apron, in a skirt pocket. Her union button evolved. I had to work with her to get her confidence up, to say, "It's OK to be who you are, and believe in this. This is part of you. It is you. You can make it yours." She got up out of her chair—I'll never forget this—and she had her fists clenched up tight, and she said, "That's right." She was crying, and shouting at the top of her voice. "This company sucks! I've been waiting 28 years to say this! It sucks!"

BURNOUT

I burned out. I was in my mid-thirties. There were strikes in between organizing campaigns, national negotiations, immigration raids. There were campaigns that didn't take off, because for every one that did, there were at least three that didn't go anywhere, and people got fired. And at the time, there weren't many women organizers, either.

Hugh Harley, the director of organizing, wanted me to take a leave of absence. In retrospect, I probably should have taken a leave of absence and gone to work for a florist somewhere, and just taken it easy. But when you're in the midst of a burnout, you don't know your own abilities. I said, "No, no. I'm a terrible organizer. I can't do this anymore." So I left.

It was awfully hard! I didn't fit in anywhere. I worked at a shelter for battered women. I did an OK job, but there wasn't the same passion as in organizing. I worked very briefly for the hospital workers in New England. They had an organizing model with which I did not feel comfortable. From my point of view, it was too manipulative. It worked for them but it didn't work for me. And my age affected me, doing hospitals and nursing homes twenty-four hours a day, seven days a week.

There have been some things written about women's style of organizing versus that of men. Women tend to be nurturing, to look at the cycles: the cycles of the seasons, the cycles of life, the cycles that every organization goes through. Men tend to be, "Bam! Let's get it done!" Women are more patient. We look at things differently.

Workers' Memorial Day

Local 1199 sent me up to Waterbury to work on a long hospital strike. We did some creative things during that strike. We offered free health screenings to anybody in the community. The nurses did things for free to show that we weren't against community health care. We had a food bank. The maintenance people settled but the nurses were still out. So the maintenance people stayed out to support the nurses.

There was a luxury apartment building, L'Ambience, being built in Bridgeport. I came home from work at 7:30 one night in April, and got off the bus, and I was told, "The building that [my husband] Peter told the city council not to give a tax break to just collapsed. And there were men inside." A little later, an aide to the mayor called and asked me to come up to the school, just across from the building site. He said, "The Red Cross is here but we need help with the families."

I went. It was the end of the week, payday. People had been there to get their checks when the building collapsed. I immediately recognized a family that I knew from the Waterbury hospital strike. It was an Italian family, born in the same province as my grandfather on my mother's side. I remembered the family because I used to go to the picket line at

Waterbury hospital very early on Sunday morning. And I recalled a time when the whole family was sitting around a fire at the entrance to the hospital. A member of the family had just had a baby. They were celebrating with homemade wine and espresso in thermos bottles. One of the old men had gone into the woods to get mushrooms. My uncles who were miners also collected mushrooms. I felt very connected with them, and their celebration of their grandchild, or great-grandchild.

And there they were again, six months later, waiting for news of someone who didn't make it. I stayed with that family. It had been a warm spring but had turned very cold that day. The men who were digging for their coworkers in the rubble were chilled and wet to the bone. We went crazy looking for warm clothing, and long underwear, and wool socks. These guys did not stop digging. Their hands were bloody but they kept on digging. They were incredibly tough.

There were wonderful things that happened. Like anyone else, Italians can be very racist. By the end of those two weeks people had become long-lasting friends. Once they found the last body, the construction workers built an impromptu memorial for their coworkers. Poems and notes were written all over the walls. People took their tools, their hard hats, and laid them in a row.

I talked to the families, to the construction workers. They put it to me that they didn't want to talk to the shrinks but they had to talk to somebody.

You've heard of Workers' Memorial Day. This was how it began. The building collapsed because the wrong kind of bolts were used.

I never could figure out what to do with that experience. The best that I've been able to come up with is, looking at these people who have the same kind of look and build as my grandfather whom I never knew, and sitting with them by the firelight, and thinking, is this what I would have been doing if my grandfather had lived? Would we be talking, and drinking coffee and aniseth together?

I still plant bright, blood-red tulips every fall. I think of life and joy and the baby who was born that fall. When the tulips bloom in the spring, and as the petals drop, I think of the workers' blood in the ground that spring.

BILL DIPIETRO

BILL DIPIETRO WAS president of a small local of the International Association of Machinists at a Buick dealership in Youngstown, Ohio. He led a strike in 1992–1993 that lasted almost a year. Throughout the strike, Bill DiPietro insisted that no settlement would be acceptable unless it included a union shop. After the strike only a handful of the strikers chose to return to work, and DiPietro rebuilt Local 1519 with former strikebreakers. He hurt his back lifting a tire and is now disabled.

Bill DiPietro was interviewed at his home in Hubbard, Ohio, a suburb of Youngstown, in April 1998.

BILL DIPIETRO

They're Not Scabs Anymore

I WAS BORN IN 1950 and grew up on the north side of Youngstown. I was one of seven kids. My father worked in the mill, and my mother stayed home. She had her hands full.

I went to St. Anthony grade school and then to public school. My first job was working in a bowling alley. There was no union there. I worked for a Rambler dealer on Rayen Avenue. Then I worked for awhile in the steel mills, at the McDonald Mills of U.S. Steel. That was my first union job. I was nineteen then.

I filed my first grievance at the McDonald Mills. I burnt my hand at the mill, working hot wrap. We were working midnights, and the boss didn't want to give me a doctor's slip. So I went to the doctor myself. The boss got mad and wrote me up for not asking for gloves. But we did ask him. He never gave them to us. He gave those gloves out as if they were gold.

So they wrote me up, and I filed a grievance. Somehow the discipline got dropped. We went to the office, and I told them my side of it, and a union representative was with me, and the superintendent said to forget about it.

This was in the 1970s. I noticed that the mills weren't getting any better, and they weren't fixing them. I used to be real good friends with the electricians who would come out on the line when things broke down. They liked me. They told me, "Get out of here. They're just wrapping this place up to close it down."

So I quit and went back into the mechanical business. I went to a school through the Manpower program, and learned my trade there. I worked for Taylor Olds for awhile and got laid off. The mechanical business was up and down back then. Then I got a job working for a Ford dealer right here in Hubbard. I got married and we had a baby.

A friend of mine said, "Let's go to Buick Youngstown. They're hiring." I got hired, and then I really got into the union stuff.

A NEW BOSS

There was a union already there. To get sworn in, you had to go to a meeting. So I went to the meeting, and because it was an amalgamated local, there were forty or fifty people. There was the bus company, International Harvester, Schwebel's bread, a lot of little mechanical shops at the auto dealers on Wick Avenue. State Chevrolet was in our union. Valley Pontiac was in our union. The president, Carl Agnone, worked out of our shop.

I started to get interested. Our contracts were almost all the same, and it was a pretty good contract. It took care of any special tools you needed. It was a really strong union then.

When you used to go on strike, you would strike for maybe three weeks. Then the boss and the union rep would settle something. The weakness of the union was that contract expiration dates were not coordinated among the different shops. But if State Chevrolet went on strike, we would go and give them some relief. And if they got a three percent raise, every other dealership would get that, too.

Mr. Hopper, our boss at Buick Youngstown, was a nice guy. He was close to ninety, but he would walk through the shop and he knew everybody's name. He wanted workers who took care of the customers. He didn't care about speed. He didn't want flat rates.* He paid you a decent hourly wage. He didn't want to hear of a customer having any problems. And he handled his own contracts; he didn't have a lawyer.

Mr. Hopper died, and Bob Sweeney took over. Sweeney wanted to change things his way. He didn't like hourly rates. We tried to explain to him that hourly is the best way to go, because if you're trying to be a flat rater you're not trying to do a car right. He didn't want to hear that. He kept reading papers about flat rate shops, how they were producing. The men

---

*A flat rate is so much money for each kind of job, such as changing a muffler or installing a new fuel pump, regardless of the difficulty of the job on that particular vehicle. Thus doing a tune up correctly might take two hours but the flat rate might pay you for an hour and a half.

who were union officers in the 1980s kept explaining that numbers on a sheet of paper don't mean that the customer is going to be satisfied. That's where we locked horns.

Sweeney and his lawyer introduced the flat rates through a bonus system. They kept everybody working forty hours a week, at (let's say) ten dollars an hour. They said that most of the people weren't really making their money. What they meant by that was that a man might work forty hours, but only complete jobs worth twenty hours under a flat rate system. They checked every mechanic's work each week. The lawyer would say, "such and such a mechanic isn't pulling his weight." And the steward would say, "Well, what did he do in those forty hours? Maybe he had a broken bolt. Come on, you're not giving the guy a chance. You just throw it out there as if he's a bum." And Sweeney and his lawyer said, "He is a bum."

Then they said, "Here's what we're going to do. We're going to give you your forty hours. We'll give you your raises over three years. But we're going to introduce an incentive, a bonus." If a man completed jobs worth twenty-two hours, instead of twenty, they would give him a little extra money.

We all got together and the union officers said, "Look, they're trying to make you go faster." But I don't care how you explained it, there would be some guy who saw that money, that carrot, and go after it. They were killing themselves. We had half an hour for lunch and two fifteen-minute breaks. People started working through their breaks. The other guys would say, "You don't have to do that. You're making forty hours straight. Why get involved? You're playing right into their hands." We had debates at lunchtime!

Then at the next contract the boss would say, "Look what happened here. George used to do only twenty hours a week, now he's turning thirty-five." Next they wanted a guaranteed wage of only thirty, thirty-five hours. We went on strike for eight weeks to keep the forty-hour guarantee. That's when Bob Sweeney decided he didn't want the union.

The lawyer would call six of us upstairs at a time, and say, "I don't want to tell you how to do your jobs. I want to help you." One guy said, "You're a union buster." "No, no, no, I don't bust unions." This was maybe 1982, 1983. All the mills were going down, and they thought this was the time to make their move. It was like bringing a cannon in to shoot bugs.

When I first was hired there, you did all kinds of mechanical work. You did brake jobs, you did transmissions, you had to do everything. Our mechanics were very close-knit. We looked after each other. We were almost a family.

In the old days, you were really hired in as an apprentice. You followed the journeyman around for at least awhile. If you had problems, the journeyman was there to help you out. They used to hire a lot of kids from Choffin Vocational School who would come into the shop and learn. If you wanted to learn something at Choffin, you could go at nights and the company would pay for it. It was in the contract that we had to go, to keep up on things.

After Sweeney took over, he started cutting corners and said, "Let's specialize." Somebody did transmissions. Somebody did motors. I did alignments. Sweeney wanted everybody to take the ASE test to be licensed. I had no problem with it, but there were a lot of older mechanics who were very bright, but couldn't take the test. So we resisted putting the ASE test in the contract. We said, "It's great to be knowledgeable on a test, but it's also nice to have a guy with fifty years of experience on whom you can rely."

They wanted a fifty percent profit from everybody. Well, guys who did tune-ups made their own profit and other people's profits, too. They didn't want that. The shop steward would say, "It's impossible. The guy who does transmissions is not going to make a profit."

We had a wash department. After we got through working on someone's car, we'd send it to be washed. It was a nice thing. They started saying, "Why do we need a wash rack?" They got rid of the wash man. The guys got mad, and started leaving greasy fingerprints all over the cars. They called us in. We said, "You got rid of the wash rack. That was never a complaint until now." Then they wanted *us* to wash the cars: to pay ten dollars an hour for a job they used to pay five for.

They used to have a man who fixed interiors. He did beautiful work. They couldn't take away the job because it was in the contract, but they moved the man around until he had a heart attack.

Then they started working on the paint shop. The men there were older, but they were good painters. The lawyer called us in and said, "We're going to cut out the paint shop." The shop stewards, Joe Vasko and Bill Stevens, said, "Why on earth would you do that? That's your bread and butter, for collisions, everything." The lawyer pulled out a big chart and said, "You don't understand business." One time I said, "I'm just going to sign my paycheck back to you, I feel so sorry for you."

BECOMING A UNION SPOKESPERSON

We had three people on the negotiating team: one from the body shop, one from the parts department, and one from the mechanical. They were the elected shop stewards in the different areas.

Our union would send around a paper saying, "January 1st is the election for shop stewards. If anybody is interested, come at lunchtime and we'll nominate you." It was so small a shop that if you wanted to run for shop steward, you could do it. There were shop steward elections every year.

I never wanted to run for shop steward. But I saw that the men who were elected as shop stewards had a hard time with Sweeney in negotiations. And it seemed like everybody who became a shop steward got fired. I was getting madder. One day I just put my hand up and said, "I'll run." I won. This was in the late 1980s.

What I did, I went around and asked everybody what they wanted in the contract, and I would put it in the pot. The business agent didn't know mechanics. He didn't know what was going on in the shop.

The company wanted to close the body shop. I said there was no reason for that. They said, "Could you talk the men into taking a cut in pay?" I said, "Are you crazy? They'd cut me up into little pieces." I said I wasn't going to do it.

The lawyer looked at the faces of the other shop stewards, trying to find someone who would agree with him. We took a break. The body shop steward told me he wouldn't mind taking a cut, if the company was having a bad time. I liked the guy: we had worked together for fifteen or twenty years. But I said, "If you take a cut, that doesn't mean he'll stay. He'll stay for maybe a year or so. Then he'll cut you." He said, "Oh no, I've known Mr. Sweeney for a long time. Mr. Sweeney would never do that." So those guys took a 50 cents cut in pay.

When the company closed the body shop, I *wanted* to run again for shop steward. The men who worked there had forty years' seniority. They had done everything for this company. Sweeney called them in right before Christmas, and told them he was closing them down. He was going to subcontract the body work.

We wanted to call a wildcat, because the bargaining unit defined in the contract included the body shop. The union lawyer said, "You can't do that." We said, "Why can't we?" He said, "Because all these years they've been doing some subcontracting during busy times, and now it's past practice."

By this time Mr. Sweeney had given the business to his sons, Dave and Doug. The company brought in an accountant. I asked him, "What do you do? What are you here for?" The man said, "I'm here to explain something about insurance to you." I said, "Why do I have to hear this? That's the Sweeneys' problem, not mine." He said, "You don't understand. There are two people back there who have had heart attacks." I said, "You're nothing but a bean counter. So what?" He said, "You have a guy with Parkinson's disease." I said, "I don't care what they have. I don't want to get into that." He said, "Our insurance rates are going up and I can't find you good insurance."

I said to Dave Sweeney, "What about when your mother had a heart attack? Didn't that make your insurance rates go up? And you took her to a hospital in Texas. I'm not condemning you. I'd probably go for the best, too. But we paid for that ride." Sweeney said, "You guys are getting older. How about paying more for your insurance?" I said that wasn't going to fly but our new business agent started hemming and hawing. I suggested they just close the place down and open up an ice cream joint.

What triggered the strike in 1992 was that the company abolished the positions of the men who had had heart attacks. I told them they were looking for a strike, that they were bargaining for a strike. I asked, "What are those men supposed to do?" They answered, "Let them become mechanics at flat rates." I said, "One of those men is sixty-two years old. He has just come back from a heart attack. He's a good mechanic but you're not going to be able to give him engine jobs." They said, "That's *his* problem." I said, "No, that ain't right." All the stewards told them, you're just looking for a fight. I looked at Randy, and he looked at me, and we said, "We're not taking this contract back to the men."

The business agent said he would take it back for a vote. So we met at the union hall, and all three of us stewards said we wouldn't vote for this contract to save our souls. The men voted it down.

We went on strike. The company started hiring strike replacements right away.

THE STRIKE

This guy came by the picket line and blew his horn. He said, "Hey, my name is Jack Walsh. You want some help?" I said, "I'll take any help I can get." The guys didn't know who he was. I told them, "Well, we're out here on strike. The business agent is not coming around that much."

Jack said, "Why don't you come to a meeting?" I said, "What meeting do you want me to come to?" He told us about a retiree group that met in Hubbard, Solidarity USA. I went there, and started listening, and it sounded right.

Bob Moore, our lawyer, said we had to go to court. I asked the business agent, "Do you think the members should be there?" He said, "Nah, we'll take care of it." I said, "I think we should go." He said, "Nah, you don't need to." And here we got an injunction because we didn't go and explain our side of it. I asked the business agent, "How many strikes have you handled?" He said, "None. This is my first big one." I knew we were in trouble then. Here I am a mechanic, and I don't know too much about strikes, and I've got a greenhorn for a union rep that doesn't know anything.

Then we came up with the idea for a Beep-A-Thon. Under the injunction, we weren't allowed to march on the place. One Saturday Jack O'Connell was there from the Mahoning County central labor council, UAW people were there, Local 800 of the Food and Commercial Workers, Teamsters, and they all wanted to march. But I had a president and a vice president who didn't want to march. I had a lawyer calling me up at night telling me, "Don't march." So I think it was you, Staughton, that came up with the idea of driving by Buick Youngstown, blowing our horns.

We did say some things about the judge. The lawyer called me again that night and said, "You can't talk about the judge." I said, "Why?" He said, "Because you have to go in front of him. And don't put up a sign which says, 'Don't cross this line. The judge says you might be arrested'." I said, "Why not? It's the truth." He says, "I don't want to see a sign out there saying that." I said, "He's only going to arrest the president and the vice president. I'm just a shop steward."

The Beep-A-Thon was great! We started with the big one that Saturday. There were seventy-five cars, driving real slow. It went all the way from the school, up the back, and around. The cops were so tickled that we weren't marching that they held up traffic for us, remember? We went back and forth. People were in the cars, holding up signs, driving one after the other. The signs said "Scabs," "Sweeney's a union buster." We honked and honked. I burned out two of my horns. But it was well worth it.

After that, we did it two nights a week. It was good for morale. You didn't need very many cars. We tried to pick times when they did a lot of business.

Those Beep-A-Thons drove the company nuts. One time I was in Sweeney's office after the strike. He had a little reading light that was all busted up. I said, "Did you throw that at the lawyer during those Beep-A-Thons?" He said, "Those Beep-A-Thons!" He started going off about the people in the Beep-A- Thons. He said, "Where did you find those people?" I said, "Those are good people. They were better than anybody I ever had on the strike line." He knew all the names. "Where'd you get Bob Schindler? Where'd you get Staughton Lynd? Where'd you get Jack Walsh? Where'd you get Greg Yarwick?"*

We started in April and we were still at it in December. The vice president left the picket line and I became vice president. Carl Agnone, the local union president, was dying. I went to see him. Nobody had bought him anything. I got some cards and said, "These are from the men." Carl said, "You have to promise me one thing." I said, "Carl, I can't promise you anything. What do you want me to promise?" He said, "Make sure it's a closed shop." The men felt the same way.

I was fined $3,500 for violating the injunction. That very evening the president of the UAW Lordstown local called and said that they would cover any fines.

One day we were on the line, and Dave Sweeney pulls up in his truck. He said, "Let's go have some coffee." I said, "If it was the last cup of coffee in the world, I wouldn't drink it with you." He said, "Come on, Bill." All the guys were telling me to go. I said, "OK, I'll go, but only because these guys want me to." He said, "Where do you want to go?" I said,

---

*These are all names of members of the Youngstown Workers Solidarity Club.

"Someplace expensive. You're paying." So we went to Arby's.

He tried to get me to say who would come back. I said I wouldn't play that game. So I met with the men, and we met with the lawyer, and in the end we agreed that up to ten of the eighteen strikers could return. But a good half of the men had gotten other jobs, and Sweeney was offering money to buy people out. In the end, only three of the eighteen mechanics who had gone on strike went back to work in March, eleven months later.

REPRESENTING THE SCABS

I was the only mechanic who went back. The other two were parts men. Sweeney and I agreed that after thirty days, all the strike replacements who had not been discharged would be in the union.

Before the thirty days were up, Sweeney fired one man. As that man was walking out the door, I told him that if he wanted, the union would file a grievance and fight for him. He said he didn't want to be bothered.

There was a kid in parts who was really slow. The boss approached me and said, "I want to fire one more person." I said, "No, you can't do that." He said, "Why? You don't care about these scabs." I said, "They're not scabs any more. They're paying union dues. They're union brothers. I've got to help them out."

We went in the office. All the men were watching. The supervisor told the kid he was slow. The kid replied that he was still learning the computer, and I backed him up. Finally the supervisor said, "Well, I just want to warn you." After that the kid was our best union man. He came to all the meetings.

I started going to the lunch area and talking with the men who had been scabs. They said, "Why did you stick up for this guy?" I said, "Because he's in the union. That's what unions are about. It's not because I like you, or don't like you." I also said, "I don't want you to follow me. I want you to come up and tell me, 'Bill, you're wrong'." They liked that. They really liked that.

It's a terrible thing to say, but I wound up with a better group of men coming to the union meetings than I had before the strike.

TWO KINDS OF ORGANIZING

The international unions want to do good, but they don't know how to organize. You can't organize the way they want to do it.

The Machinists international had a class in Berkeley. They brought people in and said, "Here's how we figure we're going to organize." I gave them a good listen. I want to organize, too.

Then I went up to the man who made the presentation and said, "It's never going to happen." He says, "Why?" I says, "Because you're not going to bring maybe ten guys in, and zoom into this town, like maybe Youngstown, and say, 'OK, we're going to organize this. We're going to talk to people about why they should be in the union'." Those are great words. But if you aren't there every day, you can't do it. People will tell them, "I don't want to talk to you. I want to see what you can do."

I told those professors in Berkeley that if I were doing it, I'd have the staff man open up an office in Youngstown, where he could help people who were fired, and that sort of thing. That would do more than bringing guys into town and going door-to-door. It's nice to have people come and talk. But people remember more what you did for somebody.

ED MANN

E D MANN WAS a longtime activist at the Brier Hill mill of the Youngstown Sheet & Tube Company in Youngstown, Ohio. He was president and John Barbero was vice president of Local 1462, United Steelworkers of America, at Brier Hill from 1973 until the mill closed in 1979. They were strategically situated to respond to the closing of Youngstown's major steel mills and the resulting termination of ten thousand basic steel workers.

Resistance to the closings involved petitioning, picketing, filing grievances and NLRB charges, going to court, occupying company administration buildings, and searching for funds to reopen the mills under employee-community ownership. John Barbero argued that steel mills should be modernized in existing "brownfield" steelmaking communities, rather than in new "greenfield" sites. After the Brier Hill mill closed, Ed Mann led the occupation of U.S. Steel's Youngstown headquarters building.

Ed Mann and John Barbero speak often and vividly in *Shout Youngstown*, a documentary film by Youngstown natives Dorie Krauss and Carol Green-wald Brouder about the closings of Youngstown's steel mills. *Shout Youngstown* can be obtained from Cinema Guild, Inc., 115 W. 30th St., Suite 800, New York, NY 10001; 800-723-5522; www.cinemaguild.com.

After his retirement in 1980, Ed Mann was a vital member of the Workers Solidarity Club of Youngstown, Solidarity USA (a militant retiree organization), and the Industrial Workers of the World (IWW). He died in 1992.

What follows is excerpted from *We Are The Union: The Story of Ed Mann*, published by the Workers Solidarity Club. It is based on oral histories recorded by Pat Rosenthal, Bruce Nelson, and Staughton and Alice Lynd.

I'm Going Down That Hill

TREATING PEOPLE FAIRLY

I WAS BORN in 1928 in Toledo, Ohio. Treating people fairly was the undercurrent in our family. There were a lot of people we would call "homeless" today. In those days they were called "on the bum," and my mother always had something to share at mealtime if they came around.

My grandfather on my mother's side was a custom tailor. He came from what was Prussia at the time because he didn't want to fight for the Kaiser. He lived with us. He had been all over the world.

I remember how when I was a kid the old-timers in the neighborhood would come to our house on Sunday afternoons and discuss current events. The kids sat and listened and the old-timers talked. I can remember folks coming around recruiting for the Spanish Civil War. I think there was a Socialist tendency, which probably came out of the 1848 period in Germany. I got this just listening.

It was primarily a Jewish neighborhood and all the kids were raised Jewish. I went to a Reform temple, which is probably about as liberal as you can get in the Hebrew tradition. I saw some anti-Semitism as I was growing up. Toledo had a large Polish population. The kids would get in fights. During World War II we were very much aware of the Holocaust. I felt the attitude was, "Don't make waves. We don't want to create any more anti-Semitism than there is already."

I had an uncle who was somewhat of a hustler. He helped me to get an egg route. I could keep five cents a dozen. I had to fight to keep the boys in my neighborhood from breaking my eggs.

I never finished high school. When I was seventeen, I enlisted in the Marines and spent two years there, 1945–1947. After getting out of the Service I got a six-month membership in the YMCA. In Toledo, as in many other places, they had a Black YMCA and a white YMCA. I met this Black fellow. His name was Bell. He was going to box and he said to me, "Ed, I've got to take off four or five pounds" to get in a certain weight class. I said, "I've got this membership in the Y. Let's go down. They have a steam room."

So we go down there. Here I am, a returned veteran from the Second World War, Black fellow with me, and I went up to the desk and I said, "I want a guest pass." They looked at me like I was crazy! They said, "You better talk to the manager." So I said to the manager, "Hey, I want a pass for my buddy here. We want to work out." He said, "Look, don't cause any trouble. He's got his YMCA and this is yours."

I think it's things like that that politicize people. I was at an age where I was like a sponge, wanting to participate in society. Then I found out what society was like.

YOUNGSTOWN

When I was in the Service I met some folks from Youngstown. They said, if you want to earn good money and go to school, you can do both in Youngstown. The steel mills were paying well and the university would take anybody on the G.I. Bill.

It was so easy to get jobs in Youngstown at that time. I had eleven different jobs in one year and never got fired from any of them. They were decent paying jobs. The reason I quit was because the conditions were horrendous. They were all union jobs but unions were just starting to feel their oats. Unions had not yet settled into job descriptions and bonus systems and crew sizes.

I got a job in the cafeteria at the university. I was batching it and I wanted meals. That's where I met John Barbero.

John came from a family that had steel mills in their blood. His dad and mother were strongly involved in the 1937 Little Steel Strike. His dad was one of the folks that was blackballed at Republic Steel in 1937 and one of the I don't know how many who got their jobs back through the Supreme Court.

John was a very literate guy. He'd been in the Marine Corps during the Second World War. He was an interpreter. He learned to speak Japanese and married a Japanese woman. He felt strongly about what happened with the atomic bomb. He was sympathetic to many different ideas.

The Korean War started and in October 1950 I got a telegram: "Be in Philadelphia Navy Yard in ten days." I had a wife and a baby. I was going to college, had a job and no money. I had to quit school and quit my job. I got out in December 1951.

BRIER HILL

A friend of mine worked in the machine shop at Brier Hill. He said, "They're going to put on some more apprentices there." John Barbero was working in the Brier Hill Open Hearth. I went to the employment office. I said, "I want to be a machinist in the apprenticeship program." He said, "They're going to give the test this month. I'll put you in there as a rigger helper." This was in 1952.

You got a thirty-day probationary period. In that thirty days, I took the apprenticeship test. The fellow who gave the test said, "I can tell right now that you passed it." After they graded it, he said, "You got the highest score in the company."

In the meantime, the guys in the shop got me appointed as steward. Nobody else wanted the job. Going through the job descriptions, I found that a machinist working in the shop gets one rate, and when you're out in the mill you're supposed to get a nickel an hour more. I filed a grievance for all the machinists. I won the grievance! And I never heard a thing about the apprenticeship program after that.

A fellow with whom I'd gone to college said, "Look, if you want to make some money, come on up in the Open Hearth and get all the overtime you want." So I went up to the Open Hearth. A week later, they put on two new apprentices in the machine shop.

I really liked that Open Hearth. I think the first three months I was there, they must have had ten wildcat strikes. The guys wanted better working conditions. We'd say, "We want rubber-tired wheelbarrows," because the ones they had been using were steel-tired. They'd hit a rail, it would twist, and guys would get hurt. "We want a relief man!" "We want

cold water!" The refrigerator system would break down, and the superintendent was too cheap to buy ice. "We need safety masks today! Hey,
somebody got burned. We want safety jackets or we aren't going to
work on those furnaces!"

The grievance procedure wasn't working. That's why we had wildcat
strikes. We weren't going to get tied up in paperwork. The wildcats did-
n't last long: a day, two days at the most, maybe eight hours.

RANK AND FILE

When I started at Brier Hill it was a big plant. It was an integrated plant in
the sense that they started out with iron ore and made a finished product,
electric weld pipe. In that plant, there were three local unions. Local 1462
was the biggest, with about 3,300 members when I started there. It was
the first place I worked that had even the facade of a big union.

We had some strong young people with ideals. We believed in what
the union was supposed to be like.

Before the local was organized, a lot of Italians lived in the vicinity of
the plant. They were discriminated against as much as Blacks were discriminated against. They got the lousiest jobs. They did track labor. They
were helpers in the mason gang. They could not aspire to the jobs in the
shops that the Germans or the English had. Most of the Italians were of
limited formal education. They couldn't express themselves as well as
those that they called "Johnny Bulls," the English, Irish, and Scotch.

There was a young guy who was very literate named Danny Thomas.
He was tough. If a foreman was mistreating an old Italian guy, he'd grab
the foreman by the shirt and say, "Leave that old guy alone!" So he got a
lot of respect in the Italian community. Danny Thomas was president of
Local 1462 from the late 1940s until the early 1960s, when he became a
staff man for the international union. He was a real dictator as president.
He made all kinds of deals.

We had the most dishonest elections you can imagine. One time they
had a bottomless ballot box and they set it over a cold air return in the old
house that we used as a union hall. As you voted you put your ballot in
the box. It would drop down into the cellar. There were two people
down there. "This one's OK." They'd put it aside. "This one's no good."

They'd throw it in the furnace. (We heard this after these guys retired, years later.) We'd wonder, "There are three thousand people in the mill but we only got eight votes? Our caucus is bigger than that!" That was the game that was played. We learned early: if you don't have the power to count the votes, you don't have the power to win.

We knew we had two battles to fight, one with the company and one with the union. We weren't interested in breaking away or destroying the union. But we felt that the union had to be more responsive to what the members needed.

The union thought that what was good for the company was good for the union. I don't agree. I think the union should look out for its members. The company can look after itself. I got involved with the union because I thought it was the best way to be represented. You're on an equal footing with management. I always thought you had to demand your rights. You had to fight for them.

We spoke up in favor of union officers working at least one year in four in the mill; that no official should take more than the wages of the highest paid member he or she represents; that staff be elected, not appointed.

One of our main issues was, "We want to elect our stewards." Back then the local union president appointed all the stewards. In a 3,300-person plant, Danny Thomas had over one hundred paid people, like precinct committeemen. They had control over overtime and days off. We wanted stewards to be responsible to the people who elected them.

We won that issue many times on the floor. We'd bring a group of people to the union hall and we'd vote for electing them instead of appointing them. Next meeting, our people wouldn't show up, he had a majority, they'd vote it down. This went on for years until we took office in 1973.

RACE DISCRIMINATION

Blacks got the worst jobs. They worked in the coke plants, blast furnaces, track labor, plate mill, scarfing yard. There were very few Blacks in the skilled trades. The only Blacks I can recall in a skilled trade during my early years in the mill were bricklayers. There were none in the shops. No electricians. Maybe a few millwrights and motor inspectors but not many. Even in the Black departments, the top job was usually held by a white man.

Blacks did not get the jobs where there was a chance to promote. Maybe he became the truck driver, but he could never become the roller. Maybe he could become the craneman but he could never become the charging machine man.

Blacks had been brought in as scabs in 1919 and 1937. This gave any white racist an excuse to say, "The Blacks are going to take your jobs. They are scabs. They'll work for less." And it's an excuse because there were many Blacks who, when they found out they were being used as scabs, came out of those mills.

Blacks had their place and whites had their place. Nothing was done to discourage this by the managers or by the unions. It reflected the community, a very ethnic community.

It was maybe the first five years that I was in the mill that they started moving Blacks up on jobs. The people in the mill *knew* it was the right thing to do. They may have been racist but they knew it was the right thing to do.

In the Open Hearth where I worked most of the time there were Blacks in the pit (that's behind the furnace where they pour the steel). But on the floor where the first, second, and third helpers and the melters were, it was white until the early 1950s.

If you wanted to work on a furnace that meant you had to be able to take the heat. There were five doors on these furnaces. Let's say a Black guy was going to go up there and try to learn that job, shoveling into the furnace. The first helper would pull the door all the way up when the Black guy came near and the flame would shoot out twenty or thirty feet. We had some tough Black guys who stayed, who could do their own job and the jobs of the guys on either side of them.

You had to pick away, pick away at these various practices. Most of the people in the labor pool were Black because the coke plant, which was an almost wholly Black department, was shut down. Willie Aikens, a Black man who later became chairperson of the local's civil rights committee, was in the labor pool for a long time. So was I: the first twelve years I worked at Brier Hill I didn't have a full year's pay because of layoffs. He spent a lot of time on layoff and while he was on layoff white guys were hired off the street in some departments. That was a serious violation of seniority.

John Barbero and I supported the Blacks to press the issue in the Open Hearth. We got an agreement with the superintendent that he would open up all jobs to people in the labor pool. But we're talking about half a dozen jobs at the most.

By the time the mill shut down we had plant-wide seniority because of the [settlement of a lawsuit known as the] 1974 Consent Decree. There were people that complained, "We've been here all these years and now these Blacks are coming in! They don't know how to do this and they don't know how to do that." But it was the foreman's responsibility to train a new worker. The company said, "He's got to have the *ability* to do the job." Well, who determines the ability? The company. And who's supposed to train them? The company. The company wouldn't train the Black guys or wouldn't train them properly.

On the other hand, the company wanted production and didn't really care whether there was a Black or a white guy. I had a friend named Archie Nelson. He was a Black guy in the conditioning yard. The conditioning yard worked as a gang. They scarfed the steel, burned the impurities off slabs: a hard, hot job. In those kinds of jobs you develop leadership. Archie was the leader of the Blacks. He controlled that department. They knew how much they had to do. They did that much. They didn't work their heads off. All the supervisors were white. But if the Blacks folded their arms there would have been nothing done. So they let Archie run the crew.

Many Blacks had the feeling, "I've caught hell all these years. I've got a lot of seniority now. I'm going to go get Looey's job!" He could get Looey's job, but it had to be in a period when there was an increase in production and they opened up the bidding. Blacks would say, "Hey, how come I'm not getting that job?" There had to be an opening. If the Black was entitled to the job, we fought to see that he got it. If he wasn't, you had to tell him straight out, "Look, you're not going to get that job until it's posted or until there's a vacancy or until they put on more turns."

The Consent Decree was a good idea assuming everything was booming, but we were losing jobs. So you were fighting over the few jobs that were left. In a growth-type time it would have been much better. We were in a dying plant in a dying industry and that was the unfairness of it.

DIRECT ACTION

I believe in direct action. Grievances were backlogged sometimes two and three years. You got to settle these things right at the point of production, and RIGHT NOW! Sure, we could say, "You guys can't strike. You better get back on the job and file a grievance." But that won't get the problem resolved. If workers don't sympathize, they won't engage in direct action. That's their own way of saying whether or not it's a good grievance.

Once a problem is put on paper and gets into the grievance procedure, you might as well kiss that paper goodbye. The corporations saw this when they started recognizing unions. They co-opted the unions with the grievance procedure and the dues check-off. They quit dealing with the rank and file and started dealing with the people who wanted to be bosses like them, the union bosses.

We were the troublemakers. We'd have a wildcat strike. The international would say, "Either you get back to work or you're fired." It wasn't the company saying this. It was the union.

In a production department, say like the scarfing department where Archie Nelson was, if they slowed down it affected production. Sometimes the stuff is needed at the next point of operations on a certain timetable. The further a piece of metal gets through the operation, the more costly it becomes. So the further down the line you make your move or take your action, the more costly it is to the company.

In the Open Hearth, we worked on a big furnace that held two hundred tons of molten metal. If you slowed down the operation, the furnace would melt. The people who could slow down the procedure were the people who put in the scrap and molten iron, the charging machine men and cranemen. They had some control over how the operation went. If your first helper wanted two boxes of raw lime and a box of ore in the furnace to make the steel up to specifications, the charging machine man could give them a little extra or not enough and screw up everything.

Once they were going to change the bonus system. They were going to give the first helper and the second helper an increase in bonus and cut the third helpers. In other words, they were just moving the money around. Third helpers refused to go on the job. Second helpers stuck with them. Then there was nobody there to help the first helpers so they agreed to go out with us. It was a wildcat.

We were out that night. The midnight turn gets there and discovers this. We are all sitting in the washroom. The superintendent shows up with the president of the local, Danny Thomas. "What's the problem here?" I'm sitting there. As spokesman for the group, I said, "They're cutting our bonus. We don't want to hear it."

Danny Thomas says to the superintendent, "You get rid of that guy and your troubles are over." And the whole Open Hearth gang is sitting there. This doesn't hurt me at all politically. It got the guys hotter.

The superintendent was crying, "What am I going to do with this steel?" I said, "Tap it out on the ground. I don't care what you do with it." He said, "The blast furnace is ready to tap. We got to move that iron." "Dump it on the ground," I said. "We want our bonus." The company agreed not to cut our bonus.

We said, "Now who's going to get paid? Are we going to get paid for the time we've been docked here?" The superintendent said, "Oh, we can't do that. You guys didn't do any work." We said, "The furnace did the work. We want paid or we're going home right now." And it worked.

The wildcat over Tony's death was the first experience I had that showed that people really *can* be involved.* At the time I was recording secretary of the local, and John and I were both stewards in the Open Hearth. We filed a grievance with the superintendent about thirty-three different safety violations. One of the items was we wanted vehicles to have back-up signals. They used big heavy trucks in the pit. There was a lot of noise. It was hard to hear. We wanted a warning horn on the back so when a truck was going to back up the people working there could hear it. The company rejected the grievance out of hand.

I was working afternoon turn that day, three to eleven. I came out to work and somebody said, "Tony got killed." I asked, "How'd he get killed?" And I was told, "You remember that grievance you filed asking for back-up signals on the truck? The truck backed over him and crushed him."

---

*See "A Common Bond" by John Barbero, Ed Mann, and others discussing the wildcat strike and formulation of a committee that won safety demands after Tony was killed. Drawing both on Ed Mann's account and on family memories, Robert Bruno describes the death of Tony Pervetich in *Steelworker Alley: How Class Works in Youngstown* (Ithaca: Cornell University Press, 1999), pp. 77–78. Tony Pervetich was an uncle of Robert Bruno's mother.

So I got up on the bench in the washroom and I said to the guys coming to work, "What are we going to do about this? Are we going to work under these lousy conditions? Who's next? Who's going to get killed next? Don't we give a damn about Tony?"

Now some didn't want to go out. "That's not my problem. I don't work down there. I run a crane." We said, "Let's get out! Let's go!" We went up to the union hall. We tell them the situation. They agree, "Shut her down!" The guys called their buddies on the midnight turn: "Don't come out to work tonight."

They were looking to me for leadership. I said, "Here's what we'll do. Rather than get the stewards fired, let's appoint a committee for each area and let's start listing our demands on safety," bypassing the union structure. It worked.

We wanted this committee to meet with the company on a regular basis about safety conditions, bypassing the union safety committee because this was an immediate issue. (The union safety committee worked on things month by month: a meeting this month to say that this light-bulb had burned out, next month they come back and say, we didn't have any lightbulbs.)

Other departments didn't go out on strike in sympathy, but there was just no work for them, because we made the steel. That's a feeling of power. And it isn't something you're doing as an individual. You're doing it as a group.

If you're not going to *do* something, then you're not going to be a leader, are you? It wasn't prepared timing. It fell into place. You've got to recognize those situations. Be there when there are credible steps to take.

BEING A RADICAL

When we integrated the better jobs in the Open Hearth, it wasn't a popular position to take. It was a correct position but not a popular position. To be anti-Vietnam War, anti-Kent State,* wasn't a popular position.

---

*Ed Mann refers to the events of May 4, 1970, when National Guardsmen killed four students at Kent State University. The university is less than an hour's drive from Youngstown and one of the students killed was from a Youngstown suburb. To be "anti-Kent State" was to oppose what the National Guardsmen did.

I was Red-baited. But I found that the people didn't really care what my politics were as long as I won grievances, did my job as a union officer. Their question was, Does he produce as a union representative?

In the steel mill, the type of work we were involved in was gang-type work. You couldn't do the job yourself. You had to help the guy in the next furnace. He helped you. You didn't have to like him, but you knew that to get the job done and not die, you had to help each other.

So then you start talking. "How's the kids?" "What kind of car do you got?" Everyday stuff. And before you know it, "Come on over and have a beer. We're going to have a party. Why don't you bring your wife?" Before you know it you're friends.

You go to the union meetings and speak your piece. Somebody says, "Hey, I don't know him but that's the way I feel." So you go over and say, "Hey, I'm Ed and I work in the Open Hearth." If you're going to be a socialist, you got to be sociable.

We were communicative. We would talk to people. We could express ourselves. We weren't afraid of the boss. You got a job, you did it. You didn't do any extra. You helped your fellow worker. Over the years you develop a certain credibility.

For me to have gone out to the gate and pass out the Socialist Workers Party newspaper, and not know anybody there, and expect to recruit thirty people by the end of the month, would have been insane! You got to put down roots if you want to change anything.

PRESIDENT OF LOCAL 1462

It was always a part of our strategy to run people for local union office because we figured you had to have a base.

In 1970, I ran for president against Augie Naples and lost by about one hundred votes. It was an honest election. Steward elections were held a month later and I was elected steward in the department. In 1973, I ran for president and defeated Augie Naples. I ran two more times after that and won. The last time I ran unopposed.

You got ten percent of the folks in the union that are company and ten percent that are real union folks. The rest pay their dues and go home. People only come to union meetings when *they* have a problem. It's contract

time? OK. Are we going out on strike? Everybody's there and wants to
know. Or in one department, something may happen that brings everybody together. But no continuity. People aren't diehard dedicated. People
have other interests.

We knew we couldn't get them all to a union meeting, so we mailed a
newspaper to every member. If a guy didn't want to come to union meetings he was still entitled to information, and his wife could read about it,
too. We'd all contribute articles. We put articles in from anybody who
wanted to submit them. It was controversial as hell.

The international filed charges against us for what we printed. And
we'd print those charges, so the members could see. Then we'd have a
local union meeting and say, "What do you want to do about it?" They'd
say, "Just keep doing what you're doing. It's the members' paper." We
told the international that we'd give them equal time if they wanted it.

We gave them democracy in the local. Once we had elected stewards
for a couple of years, you couldn't appoint a steward, because the guys
would jump all over your ass. "We don't want that son of a bitch. Here's
the guy we want." That made it easier for me as president, too. I didn't
have to accept the heat for somebody I'd appointed. I could say, "You
guys elected him. If he's no good, get him the hell out of here."

Guys who didn't get elected could be appointed to committees. We
had committees on workers' comp, unemployment, pensions, hospital-
ization, that did their jobs. We had one guy who wasn't a good union
steward. We made him head of the Blood Bank. It was a non-controver-
sial job. He loved it. It gave him a role in the local.

WE ARE THE UNION

We had assumed the mill would always be there. In October 1978 we
learned otherwise. The Brier Hill Works were going to be shut down as
the result of a merger between the Lykes conglomerate, owner of the
Youngstown Sheet & Tube steel company, and the Ling Temco Vought
(LTV) conglomerate, owner of Jones & Laughlin (J&L) Steel. The first notice to the local union was in a prospectus concerning the proposed
merger that Lykes and LTV mailed to their stockholders. The prospectus
described phasing out Brier Hill as one of the "anticipated benefits" of
the merger.

We organized a picket line at the mill. About 200 steelworkers carried signs reading "Keep Brier Hill Open," "People First, Profits Second," "Impeach Griffin Bell" (a reference to Attorney General Bell's approval of the Lykes-LTV merger), "Youngstown Victim of Corporate Rape," and "Save Our Valley." This was the first direct action taken by steelworkers in response to the Youngstown shutdowns.

On January 22, 1979, Local 1462 held a meeting at the union hall. By coincidence, Gordon Allen, Sheet & Tube's superintendent, was speaking that same evening at the Mahoning Country Club not far away. At the meeting, I mentioned the fact that Allen was speaking nearby. I said that I still had the signs from the picket line in the back of my pickup truck. People began moving toward the door. We drove to the Country Club and set up a picket line outside the front door. Ken Doran moved up and down the line. He kept saying, "let's go inside." Finally, Doran opened the door and Barbero led the group through. In the lobby we set up a chant, "Where's Gordon Allen?" It was a way of saying, will we ever get to talk to somebody who can make a decision to save our plant?*

The management of the Country Club called the Girard police. The police arranged themselves inconspicuously and made no attempt to interfere.

Roger Slater, J&L's Youngstown district manager, and Gary Wuslich, superintendent of industrial relations, pleaded with me to keep the demonstrators outside. After a heated discussion, I agreed to hold people in the lobby until Allen came out.

We waited ten or fifteen minutes. When Allen finally approached he paused and said to me, "Now, Ed, you know we are handling this through the union." I and several others responded in one voice, "We *are* the union!"

We made the best fight we could. I think John Barbero and I had different attitudes. John thought we should fight to the end to keep the mill open. I felt that was unrealistic. You had to cut the best deal you could in the real situation that existed. We had people who were close to retire-

---

The Brier Hill Unionist, vol. 6, no. 4 (Feb. 1979), published a photo of members of Local 1462 with their picket signs inside the Mahoning Country Club confronting Gordon Allen. The documentary *Shout Youngstown* includes narration of the encounter by eyewitness Gerald Dickey, Local 1462 Recording Secretary.

ment, people who had very little seniority, and people in the middle group. I figured I was elected to represent everyone.

We bargained for Trade Readjustment Allowance. The company said, If you promise not to destroy the mill (they were paranoid as hell), we'll agree that we are shutting down because of foreign imports (which was a lie). I said, "I guarantee you the guys won't tear the mills down." It was a sure bet. The agreement included Campbell, Brier Hill, Rod and Wire, everybody from the plant manager down. It came to about $15,000 per employee.

"I'M GOING DOWN THAT HILL"

In November 1979, U. S. Steel announced that it was closing all its mills in the Youngstown area. Another 3,500 workers would lose their jobs. Later that month, about 300 Youngstown steelworkers together with Pittsburgh supporters occupied the first two floors of U. S. Steel's national headquarters in Pittsburgh. The occupation lasted several hours.

Then on January 28, 1980, there was a rally at the hall of Local 1330, USWA, in Youngstown. The hall was just up a hill from U. S. Steel's Youngstown administration building. The politicians came and made their speeches. They didn't say anything. I think the crowd thought they were there to get votes.

I began my speech by saying, "You know, we've heard a lot about benefits this morning, but I thought we were here to save jobs." I went on:

I think we've got a job to do today. And that job is to let U. S. Steel know that this is the end of the line. No more jobs are going to be shut down in Youngstown. You've got men here, you've got women here, you've got children here, and we're here for one purpose. Not to be talked to about what's going to happen in Congress two years from now. What's going to happen in Youngstown today?

There's a building two blocks from here. That's the U. S. Steel headquarters. You know the whole country is looking at the voters, the citizens. What are you going to do? Are you going to make an action, or are you going to sit and be talked to?

The action is today. We're going down that hill, and we're going to let the politicians know, we're going to let U. S. Steel know, we're going to let the whole country know that steelworkers in Youngstown got guts and we want to fight for our jobs. We're not going to fight for welfare! [Cheers.]

In 1919, the fight was on for the 8-hour day and they lost that struggle and they burned down East Youngstown, which is Campbell. Now I'm not saying burn anything down but you got the 8-hour day.

In 1937, you wanted a union and people got shot in Youngstown because they wanted a union. And everything hasn't been that great since you got a union. Every day you put your life on the line when you went into that iron house. Every day you sucked up the dirt and took a chance on breaking your legs or breaking your back. And anyone who's worked in there knows what I'm talking about.

Now, I don't like to read to people, but in 1857 Frederick Douglass said something that I think you ought to listen to:

"Those who profess to favor freedom and yet discourage agitation are men who want crops without plowing up the ground. They want rain without thunder and lightning. They want the ocean without the awful roar of its waters. This struggle may be a moral one [and you've heard a lot about that] or it may be a physical one [and you're going to hear about that] but it must be a struggle. Power concedes nothing without a demand. It never did and it never will. Find out what people will submit to and you will find out the exact measure of injustice and wrong which will be imposed upon them. And these will be continued until they are resisted in either words or blows or with both. The limits of tyrants are prescribed by the endurance of those they oppress."

This was said in 1857 and things haven't changed. U. S. Steel is going to see how much they can put on you. And when I say you I mean Youngstown, you know. We've got lists. We've got an obituary of plants that were shut down in the last twenty years. When are we going to make a stand?

Now, I'm going down that hill and I'm going into that building. And anyone that doesn't want to come along doesn't have to, but I'm sure there are those who'll want to.

People liked the idea! At least 700 people were involved. When we got to the U. S. Steel building we told the property protection people to step aside, and they did. We took over the building.

On the top floor we found an executive game room no one ever knew about. My daughter Beth changed her baby's diaper on the executives' pool table. At the end of the afternoon Bob Vasquez, president of Local 1330, decided to end the occupation. But if we had it to do again, I know that he, and I, and everyone I know who was there, would have stayed in that building for as long as it took.

"I THINK THERE'S A BETTER WAY"

I retired in 1980. In 1981, the Workers Solidarity Club of Youngstown was organized. It's a pretty free-wheeling organization. We don't have membership lists. We don't have dues. I think the makeup of the Club is exciting: people from different unions, unemployed folks, retirees, people from all walks of life. We do a lot of support work for people on strike. We make an effort to organize the unorganized.

I joined the Industrial Workers of the World (IWW) about 1984. And in 1986, after LTV filed for bankruptcy, I became active in an organization of LTV retirees called Solidarity USA.

The IWW is a lot like the Solidarity Club. Whoever wants to do their thing at the moment, does it. If you want to participate, you participate, and if you don't, you don't.

I like the Wobblies'* history: the Bill Haywood stuff, the Ludlow mine, the Sacco-Vanzetti thing. I like their music. I like the things they were active in.

These folks believed that workers should exercise power, instead of handing it over to bureaucrats they elect, and letting the bureaucrats make the decisions. The people have to live with the decisions. If you make a decision that's bad, and you have to live with it, you can't blame somebody else. But what happens when a bureaucrat makes a decision and you have to live with it?

A lot of our folks belong to established unions and they don't want to attack the AFL-CIO because they feel that by doing that you're attacking the union movement. I don't sense that there's any movement there at all. We have people who are sensitive about attacking the AFL-CIO for not doing its job. But it's not going to do its job. It's not structured to do its job.

I don't regard the AFL-CIO as "the union." I think the union's in the people. Don't forget, there are only 13 million workers organized in the AFL-CIO, but there are probably 100 million workers. As long as people work they are going to have grievances. Now, who is going to handle those grievances? Some kind of organization, that is, people together. Bureaucrats aren't going to solve our problems.

---

*IWW members were pejoratively called "Wobblies."

It's very unpredictable. If we read our history, we know that back in Debs' time the railroads were one of the biggest industries in the country. They had a lot of shops: people worked as blacksmiths, machinists, whatever. The company cut their pay so much a day. They didn't do anything about it. Six months later the company cut their pay again, quite a bit. Then the company came up with a pay cut that was infinitesimal. That was enough! The whole country went down. It was like a general strike. They burned the railroad yards in Pittsburgh and in many other places. Who knows what is going to make the workers say, This is enough! But the point is, somebody has to be there when they say, This is enough!

Maybe the cio has run its course. Maybe there will be unions but they won't be structured as we see them today.

The companies say they want workers to participate in the work process, in management. But they're not giving away any decision-making. The company's rights are very clear-cut and defined. You may able to discuss how many parking places there will be in the parking lot, or what kind of pop will be in the pop machine. But when it comes to hiring, firing, disciplining, the rules of production and so on, you're not involved. They talk about "work teams." This is garbage. A work team tends to say, Hey, this guy isn't keeping up, let's get rid of him.

The Wobblies say, Do away with the wage system. For a lot of people that's pretty hard to take. What the Wobblies mean is, you'll have what you need. The wage system has destroyed us. If I work hard I'll get ahead, but if I'm stronger than Jim over here, maybe I'll get the better job and Jim will be sweeping floors. But maybe Jim has four kids. The wage system is a very divisive thing. It's the only thing we have now, but it's very divisive.

Maybe I'm just dreaming, but I think there's a better way.

JAMES TREVATHAN

J AMES TREVATHAN is an African-American from Youngstown, Ohio. Like his father, he sought employment in the basic steel industry. In 1974, a suit filed by two black steelworkers in Alabama against both the steel companies and the union resulted in a Consent Decree that made it possible for Trevathan to move from the Mason Department to the Machine Shop. A few years later the mills in Youngstown shut down.

Trevathan developed second and third careers, as a painter and as a counselor on employment problems for the local NAACP and Urban League. Trevathan has not found unions very helpful in addressing the problems of minority workers.

This conversation took place at the Lynds' kitchen table in November 1998.

JAMES TREVATHAN

War on Black Males

I WAS BORN in Youngstown, Ohio, in July 1925 in a wooden apartment house they called a "flat." I don't remember the exact year, but I was about eight, nine, ten years old when my father used to get up every morning about 4:30, 5 o'clock, and go down to Republic Steel on Poland Avenue. They had this system. There would be fifty, sixty men. One of the foremen or supervisors would come out, and he would pick who he wanted, and how many he wanted. The others had to go back home.

My father did that five, six days a week. Some weeks he was fortunate. He might get picked three days that week. Sometimes it was four days, and a whole lot of times, none.

So my father developed a little side skill to support his family. He was a painter and a paper hanger. That went on until we moved from a street right up the hill from Poland Avenue to the South Side. Then he went full-time as a painter and an interior decorator with my grandfather.

He used to do a lot of work on the north side of Youngstown, for people who could afford it. He used to do, say, a $900 interior painting job and get paid maybe $350–400. At one time, when he didn't have transportation, I remember seeing my father carrying a paper-hanging board, a table that folded up, and a stepladder, and walk eight, ten, twelve blocks to get to the job.

As we started getting a little older—I must have been, oh, twelve, thirteen—he began to take us with him, and teach us. We would start off painting garages, cellar windows. As we got older he taught us how to hang paper. That's how, later on, I got involved in it myself.

SEGREGATION IN 1945

I've had a good life, wife and children, and things. For a black man, it's been OK. But I've had nasty experiences with people that caused me to be the way I am. And it hurts; it hurts.

I went in the Service in 1942. In 1945 my mother was living on West Federal Street and she had a massive heart attack. The Red Cross interceded for me to get a leave to come home. They gave me fourteen days.

So I came home on the trains. When I got here, she was in South Side hospital. After I had been here six or seven days, they released her from the hospital. She came home. And when my fourteen days were up, she was home, and my oldest brother was there. I said, "I'm going to go to the train station by myself, Momma."

The B & O railway station was on the near West Side. Now, I had on my uniform. I was in the 82nd Airborne. I was a paratrooper. I had my jump ribbons on. I had a couple of little combat ribbons. So I went to the train station and they said I had about an hour and a half to wait.

Right across the street was a little bar. I had never been in a bar in my life before. But I did drink a little bit. So I went across the street and sat there at the counter. I was going to have me maybe a shot of whiskey and a couple of beers, waiting on the train.

There was a white lady behind the bar. After I sat there for about five minutes she came up and said, "May I help you?" I said, "Yes. I'd like to have a double shot of Calverts and a bottle of beer." She said, "I'm sorry, we don't serve colored."

Now this was in 1945. I'd been over there. I'd been shot at. I had gone through the training at Fort Bragg, North Carolina, I had jumped out of airplanes and was scared to death. I had done all of this and I hadn't bothered anybody. I did it because the white man said, "Do it: sign here, go here, and do this." Why did I have to go through all this mess?

I got up to leave. And this shows you that there are some good white people in the world. There were two white guys (I didn't know they were truck drivers) sitting at a table. One of them got up and came over. He said, "What did you say to this soldier? Did I hear you say you don't serve colored?" "Well yes, that's our policy." He started cussing her. His buddy came up to try to stop him. They started talking about how they were going to turn the place completely out. I said, "No, no. Come on. This might get back on me because I'm in uniform. Please, don't, come on."

We went outside. The one truck driver almost had tears in his eyes. He said, "Come here, soldier." They took me over to the tractor parked over on the side. It didn't have a trailer, just a cab. He reached up under the seat and he had a brand new quart of Johnny Walker Red Label Scotch. He said, "Here. Take it with you. Keep it." Gave me the whole bottle, sure did.

I don't understand it. All because of this [tapping the skin on his forearm].

TAKE YOUR HAND OFF MY WIFE

When I first came out of the Service, I went to Youngstown State University for a semester and a half on the GI bill. Then I fell in love and got married. My uncle got me a job at Valley Mould and Iron. I was working out there in 1949, 1950.

One payday I had asked my wife to meet me downtown. There was a bar called The Rainbow Bar, which used to cash paychecks. This particular morning I was working 11 to 7, and I was going to give my wife my money and go fishing with my buddy.

When we pulled up in front of the bar, I looked up the street at the new furniture store, Haber's. My wife was standing there and a police officer was holding her by the arm. So I got out of the car, and I walked up there, and I said, "Hello. Hey, what's going on?"

He said, "Who are you?"

I said, "Well, that's my wife."

He said, "We've been getting reports about women hanging out down here on paydays. We watched her standing here fifteen or twenty minutes."

I said, "I told her to meet me here. I'm going to give her some of my paycheck." I showed him my paycheck.

He said, "How do we know that this is your wife? You got any papers?"

I said, "No, I don't carry no wedding papers with me. That's my wife, and you take your hand off her."

My first wife was a small, short lady. The cop was about six feet. He must have tightened up on her arm, hurting her, so she started to cry.

Then I used some profanity and told him to take his hand off my wife. When I said that, he turned her loose and took a step back. Now, I don't know for sure, and I doubt I'll ever know, but something inside of me said he was going to pull his gun, and shoot me. I didn't have anything. I just ran and grabbed him, and picked him up, and threw him through the plate glass window of the furniture store.

They told me later in court that it wouldn't have been so bad, but I picked up a big piece of the glass. I intended to kill him. But his buddy got out of the car, and ran over and started beating me across my shoulders with his stick. I dropped the glass, and they were able to subdue me, and arrest me.

That was in the morning. About ten or eleven o'clock that night, they came and got me out of the cell, and took me downstairs in the basement. They bent me over the back of a chair, and used wet towels, and beat me in the kidneys. The towels don't leave a mark, that's why they do that. But you can't control your water for a couple of weeks.

After my father got to see me, they were able to get me some pills, and it was all right. There was no permanent damage. I guess I had to be taught a lesson for assaulting a police officer.

My father was a Mason, and Mr. Oates, who was a barber, was a Mason, and an attorney we knew was a Mason. They decided that if I was indicted by a grand jury, I would go on trial in the county. They would surely send me away, because the jury would all be white.

So they used their Masonic connections and got me out of jail. But I had to leave Youngstown. They knew that the police would be picking me up every weekend, harassing me, and they told me to get out. I left Youngstown and went to Chicago.

I got a job as a bus driver up there. But the cost of living was so high, with a wife and two kids, I had to come back to Youngstown.

BUS DRIVER

Then I got to be the second black man to drive a city bus in Youngstown. The company was called the Youngstown Municipal Railway Company. It was privately owned, and there was no union.

I could understand that the city had never seen Black bus drivers.

People got on the bus, and some were all right, and some would roll their eyes at you.

One day I was working the Elm Street bus line. At that time there were a lot of Black women who went up and down that part of town, doing housework. A white lady got on the bus. She threw her fare on the floor. There were fifteen or twenty people on the bus, mostly Black women.

I told her, "Missus, you have to put your money in the fare box." She looked at me and said, "If you want it in there, you Black son of a bitch, put it in there yourself," and went back and sat down.

I didn't move. I just sat there. In our training we were taught not to curse anybody out, not to argue, but to get to a telephone and call a supervisor. So I sat there for about five minutes. The bus was not moving. The women got mad, and started to call this lady all kinds of names, because they had to go to work. They talked about throwing her through the window. Finally she got up, and ran off the bus, leaving the money laying there on the floor.

The pay was so low! One day a friend of mine was riding the bus. I was taking him to work down in Struthers, and telling him that I needed a better-paying job, so he told me to put in an application at the steel mill.

YOUNGSTOWN SHEET AND TUBE

I went into the Rod and Wire Mill in Struthers in 1952. You had to join the union at the company employment office. When you signed your W-2 forms, you signed a card to be in the union. Union dues were deducted from payroll.

In the Wire Mill, it was about fifty-fifty Black and white. You started as what they called a wire drawer helper. They had great big machines called bull frames. They took a wire coil about three inches in diameter and ran it through the machine and brought it down to a smaller size, stretched it out. You started off with a big spool of rod on the floor. You pulled the rod up to what they called a pointer machine, stuck it in, and put a point on it. Then you took it out and took it over to the die box on the bull frame, and stuck it in there. Then the wire drawer operator ran the machine.

They had one department there called "the die room," where they made all the dies. They worked in nice warm conditions, shirt sleeves

in the wintertime, clean, and good money. There were never any
Blacks in there.

MACHINE SHOP

After the Rod and Wire Mill shut down, I was transferred to the Mason
Department at the Campbell Works. I was a bricklayer helper for a while.

Then I got to be a labor foreman, what they called a "pusher." It
wasn't really a foreman because the foremen were on salary. It was a
crew leader.

I used to see the way the big bosses would talk to the foremen, the
guys on salary. They weren't in the union. They couldn't say anything. I
knew I couldn't handle that. As a crew leader, if they cussed me out, I
could cuss them back and just go back to the gang and start loading
bricks again.

After the Consent Decree came in, I went up to the employment office
and took an aptitude test. I passed it. Then they gave you a list to select
which trade you wanted to go into. They had bricklayer, welder, carpenter, millwright, pipe fitter, machinist.

Well, when I had first gone to work in the Mason Department, we
used to go over to the Machine Shop where they had a pop machine.
When you went in there, the Machine Shop was a great big, nice, warm
building, the machines just a running, the guys in the wintertime, in January, with little short sleeved shirts on, clean. We used to go there and
stand by the machines while we drank our pop. We couldn't hang out
too long, or the foreman would come get us.

I thought it was a nice place to work. So when I passed the aptitude
test, I marked "Machine Shop." The gentleman at the employment office said, "Oh, no. You don't want to go there." I said, "Why not?" He
said, "Oh, it's hard." I said, "No, it ain't hard." He said, "Did you graduate?" I said, "Yes, I graduated from East High School." He said, "Well, you
know, it's math, and it's been awhile." He did everything he could to dissuade me from going into that Machine Shop. All that did was to make
me more determined.

So I went in there. I had been out of high school for a lot of years. The
math was hard. But I got my oldest daughter and my oldest son, and they

would sit up with me at night, and we would go over Algebra 1, Algebra 2, trigonometry. They'd teach me.

And there was a Black machinist in the mill, the first one in there, named Hubert Clardy. We would go to his house. And he would teach us. There were only six of us out of some 120-some machinists. Then in the shop he would teach us. You had to put so many hours in the shop, and so many hours at the Buckeye School.

You'd go in the shop in the morning, and the foreman would say, "Trevathan, you go over there and work with Blackie Naples." Blackie was a white machinist. I would go over there. He'd look at me and tell me, "OK. Have a seat over there." So I'd sit down. Twelve o'clock would come, and I'd be sitting there. The whistle would blow at three o'clock, I'd still be sitting there.

They weren't all like that, but a majority were. And the supervisors didn't seem to care. There were a couple who were different. There was one white fellow who was married to a blind lady. He was real nice. He would teach you.

One time a foreman was sick and the company made Hubert Clardy an acting foreman on afternoon turn. A lot of the machinists went home. The next day they came back to ring in for afternoon turn, because you worked the same turn the whole week. The superintendent, a big German fellow, was standing at the clock. As they were coming in the door, he was standing there with their time cards. He had taken them out of the racks. They asked him where their cards were, and he said, "You're not working today. Go back home." He did it for three days. Work was starting to pile up, and it was going to cause a lot of confusion. Finally, from what I understand, the big bosses across the river, plus the union, stopped him. But thirty-five or forty men, almost the whole afternoon turn, lost three days' work. That superintendent was a fair man, and he didn't have any more problems out of them about working with us Blacks.

After the company made Hubert Clardy a foreman, the men knew that they had to be more cooperative. After they saw that we were going to be there, most of them would help us.

The apprenticeship was four years. Then you took your final test and got your journeyman's card. If you worked a lot of overtime, you could do it in less than four years. We didn't get a lot of overtime.

In the test, you had to run the machines by yourself. There was a lathe machine, a planer, and a boring mill. Those were the three basic ones. They would give you a job. The foreman would come by at the clock and give you an order. It would have drawings on it. It could be a gear, or a rod, or a shaft. You would take that and go to whatever machine you needed. If it was a big shaft, you'd probably go to the lathe machines. If it was a big gear, you'd go to the boring mills. Then you would call a crane and go down in the back where they had all the material, metals, stocked up. You would measure what you needed, bring it up to the machine with the crane, and put it on the machine. Then you would get your tools and mark it and measure it, what you needed, which way you had to go. Diameter, length, circumference. Then you started up your machine.

We carried our plant-wide seniority into the Machine Shop. That was another contention in that shop. A couple of us who went in there, a couple of Blacks, had more seniority than some of the white machinists. So when it came time for vacations, we would be able to pick the June, July, and August months, because we had more seniority. Then sometimes if things got slow, and there was a layoff, they had to go out before we did.

The Machine Shop was shut down in 1982. I had been there seven or eight years, making decent money. By that time I had thirty years' seniority and the age to qualify for the magic "rule of 80." So I took my retirement.

Looking back, the union helped only when it was backed into a corner. The union president at the Campbell Works was a piece of work. Some of the Blacks in the mill had some very serious thoughts about doing some violent things to that president. The union did just what it had to do for us Blacks. No more. That's all. The least possible. Sometimes they would reach out and make a couple of Blacks shop stewards, or grievance people, but these Blacks were well-chosen. They did what they were told. No, the union wasn't nothing to rave about.

I was a member of the union, but I never wanted to be involved in it. I had no time for activism.

PAINTING

All the time I was in the mill I worked at two jobs, taking care of five children. I never stopped painting. When I was in the Wire Mill, the

Mason Department, the Machine Shop, I would always try to trade shifts. You would be scheduled day turn for one week, 3 to 11 for one week, 11 to 7 next week. For eighteen years I almost always worked 11 to 7, so I could do my painting in the daytime. It wasn't hard to get.

You got children running around, you've got to get shoes, and pants, you don't worry too much about sleep. You do what you have to do. I would take small jobs, living room, kitchen. Sometimes in the summer I would take outside jobs. I had a couple of guys that used to help me. We would paint together.

There were two brothers who founded the Haber's furniture store. (Yeah, the same place where I threw the cop through the window.) They had come here from New Castle, Pennsylvania. They gave me a contract to paint the whole downtown store. I rented some scaffolds and things. The union came down and stopped the job.

I had my cousin, Oscar Hill, and another friend, Harry Venable. There were going to be four of us. We were going to work evenings, after the store closed.

On the second or third night, the union started picketing in front of the store. Mr. Haber called me in the office the next morning. Mr. Haber told me, "Jim, I'm going to have to stop your job." I said, "Why?" He said, "You see those pickets out there. That's no good for my business. I don't know what to tell you."

So I went out and talked to one of the union guys who was picketing. He told me to go to the union hall on Rayen Avenue. I went up there, and asked if I could get in the union. I said I would be willing to pay my initiation fees, dues, whatever it took for the four of us to get into the union.

They told me that they weren't accepting new memberships at the time but I could form my own local. I didn't know how to form a union local! I said, "You need lawyers to do that, don't you? There are a lot of legal issues there. I don't know anything about it."

So I went back to Haber's, got my stuff, and we left. That's all we could do.

MY WIFE'S FAMILY

I married again in 1960. When I met my second wife, she was from

Clinton, South Carolina, down near Spartanburg. You drove down the main highway, then you turned off to go to where her parents lived. I must have driven ten miles down this dark road to get to where they lived, back in a big clearing. There were a number of houses up on wooden poles.

She had a couple of elderly uncles. Her grandfather on her father's side was still living. One of her uncles had his own whiskey still, way back in the woods. They came up to the house one morning, about four of them, with their shotguns and hound dogs. You drove way down there to a beautiful creek. It was so clear you could count the bricks at the bottom. That's where they made the whiskey.

They would be drinking, and I would be right there with them, too, because that was some good whiskey. They told me some of the experiences that they had in the South. Things that people up here could never, never, never dream would happen.

They told me how one man, my wife's father, lived on the white man's land. He had four daughters and a son. They all worked. The girls and their mother worked in the big houses, the men worked in the fields.

A white man named Copeland had three sons. His sons used to come down to where my wife and her family lived, in the evenings, and ask for the two daughters. The father would be sitting on the porch. He'd say, "They're back there in the house doing dishes or baking pies." "Tell them we want to see them." He had to call his two daughters out, and they'd get in the car with these white boys, and they'd take them down into the woods, bring them back maybe an hour, two hours later, their hair all over their heads. And they'd go back in the house.

Now, the father had to sit there and see this happen. If he had raised his voice, they would have kicked his family off the land, they wouldn't have had anywhere to stay. Or he would have been a dead man.

I know that God teaches, "Don't hate. Don't hate. It's a sin to hate." He wants you to love this man just like he was your brother. But then when you see things with your own eyes, and hear things with your own ears, how can you do that? How?

It started to get to me. It may have had something to do with me getting involved with the NAACP or the Urban League.

TROUBLESHOOTING

In 1988 or 1989 I met Willie Oliver, the head of the NAACP. We used to sing in male choruses in churches. He sang with Friendship Baptist Church and I sang with Mount Zion.

He was always telling me that he needed somebody to be chairman of the Labor and Industry Committee. He kept bugging me, and bugging me, and I was starting to wind down my painting work, so I had some spare time. I said I would give it a shot.

The office was downtown, right across the street from the police station. I was there until about three years ago, when I left and came to the Urban League.

The NAACP didn't pay. It was all volunteer. After I was there for about a year, they voted to give me $50 a month for gas. But out of all the years I was there, I never got but about $300 or $400. They never had any money.

I learned how to get people to talk to me. I learned how to get the confidence of workers. I would listen. I would go to a meeting, and just sit there and listen, take notes. Basically, you just need to have common sense, "mother wit."

I learned that if a person came to me with a complaint, the first thing you have to do is to use your own judgment. You have to look at this person while they are talking, look into their eyes. You have to make sure that they are being 100 percent straight with you, because you don't ever want to go to a meeting where you start saying something, and people start pulling out papers, documents, showing you that you are way off base. That can be totally embarrassing. So you try to investigate anyway you can: check it out.

I've had individual cases from Big John's car wash to a good job downtown working at the TV stations, how they discriminate against them, how they mistreat their Black employees. Big John's car wash, on Belmont Avenue, makes all the tips go into one box, and claims to keep it to divide it up at Christmastime. Who's going to still be there at Christmas the way turnover is at a car wash? Then he would take the Black employees and in winter time, put them out in front, drying off the cars with towels, where it's cold, while the whites are in the back, where they vacuum out the cars, with great big heaters; then in the summertime they reverse it.

You know about Denny's Restaurant, McDonald's Restaurant, Burger King. It doesn't matter where Blacks go. Look at how they do with good-paying jobs at a plant like Packard Electric. We were trying to get blacks into the apprenticeship program. Blacks would pass the written test and then they would go to the interview. Interviewing a person is perception. They were flunking us out at the interviews.

BLACK AND WHITE

This society has declared war on Black males. I'm the father of three boys, the grandfather of four grandsons, and the great grandfather of four more boys. They have declared war on Black males. They are building prisons today for my great grandsons.

This is my belief: they are out to genocide the Black race in this country. If you don't have seeds to plant grass, no grass is going to grow. If you incarcerate all the young Black males between the ages of 17 and 25 or 30, and all that you don't incarcerate, you make sure that they have plenty of drugs to sell, and plenty of guns to kill each other with, slowly but surely, you're going to kill off Blacks in the United States.

The white man plans, fifty, sixty, a hundred years ahead. We don't do this. We are more reactive than proactive. Just as sure as God is in heaven, if nothing changes the way it is now, forty-five or fifty or sixty years from now, the Black race will be almost gone in this country.

As I said before, there are some beautiful white people in this world. Yes, I've met some. That one truck driver was ready to do something very upsetting. That big German supervisor at the Number One Machine Shop. He wasn't friendly or buddy-buddy, but he made sure everything was straight. He kept everything on an even keel. There was no mistreating. When he did find out about it, he stopped it the best he could. His hands were tied by the other workers and the union and the big shots across the river, so he had his limitations, too. Otherwise he wouldn't have had a job.

I keep going for two reasons. Number one, I can't sit still. I've been working all my blessed life and I'm too dumb to sit down and relax. Number two, maybe, just maybe, I may go out here tomorrow morning and I may help two little young Black people keep their jobs. I can't do anything for these forty or fifty other ones. But I may help these two. And maybe, some of that will rub off on one out of the two, and maybe he'll go and help two more.

ANDREA CARNEY

A NDREA CARNEY HAS for many years been a steward at Kaiser Permanente in Los Angeles for Local 399, Service Employees International Union (SEIU). Local 399 carried on the celebrated "Justice for Janitors" organizing campaign in the late 1980s.

Andrea tells how the newly organized janitors, many of them recent immigrants from Central America, joined with Anglo health care workers like herself to form a Multiracial Alliance. In June 1995, the Alliance elected a new Local 399 executive board. Just before he became head of the AFL-CIO, SEIU president John Sweeney imposed a trusteeship. The trustee appointed by Sweeney removed Andrea and others from the offices to which they had been elected. Andrea concludes her account with a letter in which she refused a full-time staff job offered by the appointed trustee.

This account is drawn from two narratives of events at Local 399 that appeared in the rank-and-file newsletter *Impact*, and from an interview with Andrea Carney on June 5 and 7, 1998. Andrea's husband David Hughes was also present, and is the "David" referred to in what follows.

ANDREA CARNEY

I Declined to Join the Staff

I WAS BORN RIGHT before World War II broke out, in 1941. The war had an impact on me as a small child. My dad was drafted. From all the talk I heard, I knew something was very wrong.

My father was a landscape gardener. My mother was a housewife until the time I was fifteen, when she went to work on the assembly line in a toy factory. She stayed in that job for a number of years until she went to work for an answering service. I have two sisters.

My parents were pretty apolitical. But my grandfather on my mother's side was not. He lived with us for a period of time in the early 1940s, when he became chemically imbalanced and psychotic from a drug. Eventually he went to a state hospital where we would see him periodically. But he wasn't sick at all. He just didn't fit in, like a lot of people in the 1940s who kind of went against the grain. He finally escaped, and from time to time came back to stay with us.

It was my grandfather who interested me in the injustice that was going on in our country and in the world. He would bring things up, such as what was happening in the South. I paid attention to him. The other family members unfortunately did not.

I never had a teacher who motivated me except in fifth grade. He was a substitute teacher. I'm surprised he lasted as long as he did because it was the McCarthy period. He gave us ideas. He told us there was a fuel for cars that was made from animal waste, and there was a conspiracy by the auto and oil industries to buy up patents for technologies by which they felt threatened.

I was impressed with this guy. He would sit on top of a little desk and tell us all kinds of things. That's how I learned about "buyer beware" and "laissez-faire." One time he talked to us about who the Russian people really were. At school we were told that now the Russians had the atom bomb they were going to come and bomb us any day. We went through air raid drills. They would ring the fire bell, and we got under our desks. It went on through the 1950s.

But he told us that the people in the Soviet Union were working moms and dads, with kids, people just like you and me and everybody else. There was no difference between them and us. They had the same desires, they went about their business just as we did. He wasn't there the next year.

I got very interested in the Rosenberg case. When they were executed I was the same age as their oldest son. I was convinced by all the propaganda that they had probably given some secret away, but I felt that that is not something for which you should be killed. These were somebody's parents. Even though I had grown to be very patriotic following the war, I never again had any faith in our government.

I don't remember any adult who felt the way I did. I don't remember discussing the Rosenberg case even with my grandfather, as he was probably out of my life in that period. It was just what I was reading in the newspapers and seeing on TV. There were thousands of people demonstrating to save the Rosenbergs, not only in this country but everywhere else.

I was rather shy as a child. When I got to junior high I became a little more outspoken. I became a radical, although I didn't know I was. My mother was upset that I was so outspoken and had opinions. She wanted to know why I couldn't be more like my sisters. I felt alone but I was not a loner. I ran with a lot of friends at school, and when I went to work it was the same. It's always been that way.

After I got most of the way through high school I sought out older women to talk to. I wanted to hear their experiences, I wanted to know what they'd been through. I wanted to know right away. And I didn't want to go to school. I wanted to get out and work. So I quit school in my senior year of high school and went to work as a riveter in San Fernando.

WORKING

At that time, in the late 1950s, it was easy to get a job. A lot of industry was booming, especially in electronics.

I stayed at my first job only a few months. The guy wouldn't give me a dime raise, so I said, "Forget you. I'm out of here." I walked off the job, went across the street and got a job as a floor girl in a sewing factory.

There I observed women, most of whom were Latina, being abused by piecework. A floor person made less money than the women on the machines but it was her job to distribute the bundles of material. I realized what was going on, and had to run around and make sure everybody got her fair share. Some of the workers tried to pay me to give them the big bundles of material. I said, "No. *Everybody* gets a big bundle and everybody gets a small bundle."

I stayed there for a year. Unfortunately, I didn't speak Spanish. I grew up in Pacoima and I should have learned Spanish, but I didn't. However, the women came to respect me.

Then I went into electronics. I met some wonderful people who taught me a lot. I learned how to wind transformers, to put them together from scratch. I learned how to follow a diagram. It was sporadic. We were in and out of work.

I left that job and found work in another big plant. There I stayed for two years, testing diodes. Diodes end up in little circuit boards that are used in aircraft and electronics. It was a mixed group of white and Asian workers. That was a new experience for me.

One day I was sitting out in the yard, eating my lunch by myself. A group of African-American women came by and said, "Is this place hiring?" I said, "Yes, they are. They have been running ads." They wanted to know where the personnel office was. I told them. They were back in less than five minutes. They said, "They're not hiring."

During the next few days I heard my supervisor ask one of the Korean workers if she had any friends who wanted to work there. I went to another Korean worker, and I asked her to go back to her community, and get the Korean newspaper, and see if the company was running an ad. She came back and said, "Yes."

I wrote to the NAACP and told them exactly what had happened. As a result, the company hired one very light-skinned African-American woman. It was hard to tell that she was African-American. And they slapped up posters all over the place saying, "We are an equal opportunity employer."

About the same time, I heard that two women in another part of the plant were trying to organize a union. One of my coworkers was an older woman with a couple of children. I went to her and said, "Why don't we check this out?" She said, "Yeah, we should." So we went to a union meeting. We sat and listened to the concerns of other workers, and talked about what we felt. The next week the two women were fired. And everybody got quiet again.

HOSPITAL WORK

I decided that I should try another field. I went to work in St. Joseph hospital in Burbank as a nurse's aide. That was a real eye-opener. In a hospital you have to work as a team. If you don't, the work doesn't get done and patients will suffer. The camaraderie with the other nurses was like a community.

I met a woman who became a very close friend. She helped me and I helped her. Ardath had taken the job in her fifties after not working most of her adult life. She had only been working there a few months when I was hired. She talked to her patients, she fussed over them, and the patients really loved her. Management had the attitude, "Ardath can't finish her work. She spends too much time with certain patients."

I said to myself, "She's going to make it, and I'm going to help her." I would say to her near the end of the shift, "I'll help you." I would finish my patients, and then make sure that her patients were completed by the time we were supposed to fill out reports.

I burnt out after a year and a half at St. Joseph hospital. I worked on the medical floor. People came in to die, so I saw a lot of death. I got very close to some patients who died. Many of them were young. Finally I felt, "I can't do this anymore."

Several years later, I found work at Kaiser Permanente. I was on the verge of taking it when I was offered a job by AFSCME. I was in a radical women's therapy group at the time, and one of the women who came to the group had a high-ranking position in AFSCME. She told me that I would be a great organizer. I turned down the AFSCME job. I told her that I didn't think I had the experience to be an organizer.

Of course, in another way I had been organizing all my life. From junior high on, I noticed that I could motivate people to do things with me if they were good things. And there have been times over the years when I have thought, I could be a lot further along in the labor movement if I had taken that job with AFSCME. Then I realize that I am so glad I didn't do it, because I learned so much more in twenty years at Kaiser by doing it on my own, by being rank and file.

I went to work at Kaiser in 1978. By 1981 or 1982, I was saying, something really is wrong with this union, and maybe I ought to step in and figure out what we can do. I'd call a business agent and he wouldn't call me back, or, rather than help, he'd tell me, "I'll make you a steward." I'd say, "I don't want to be a steward." But things kept getting worse, so I finally called him and said I would be a steward.

WHAT I LEARNED AS A STEWARD

In one department where I worked, there was a lot of racial discrimination.* The Latinas were harassed by supervision. I went to the Latinas and said, "Do you realize that the only people being written up are Latina, that the only people who are fired are Latina?" I said, "We need to do something about this. That's why I became a steward. We need to stop it." Three of us filed a class action grievance on racial discrimination: one African-American, one Latina, and myself.

Then I began to be severely harassed. I was written up regularly for lateness when other people who came in as much as forty-five minutes late were not being written up. I tried to get the officials down at the union hall to deal with this. We met with the senior business agent and the vice president. They told me, "You just have to be on time."

I concluded that my friends and I were going to be terminated if we stayed in that department. We looked for any position that was open. We took positions in a brand new department called the "float pool."

We floated to every department in the medical center, and I filed grievances in them all! I uncovered all kinds of issues that would never have been brought to light had the people only grumbled to each other. They would say to each other, "This isn't fair!" And I talked with them and said, "This isn't fair! You need to be paid more for what you're doing." I filed requests for reclassification, and we won a lot of them.

---

*Local 399 was made up of approximately 27,000 members, broken down, roughly, as follows: 14,000 health care workers, 8,000 janitors, and 5,000 workers in allied industries. As of the summer of 1995, 48 percent of Local 399 members were Latino, followed by African-Americans (20 percent), Caucasians (20 percent), and Asians and Asian Pacific-Americans (10 percent).

Clinic assistants had been doing ear washes, they had been removing sutures, they had been doing catheterization. Finally we were told that, under state law, clinic assistants could not perform many of the duties they had been doing. Kaiser gave us memos saying that the assistants would be paid retroactively for two years' work but henceforth they could not do it. Well, guess what? Right now I have filed a grievance and Labor Board charges against Kaiser for asking clinic assistants to do the very things that, during the 1980s, they told us we could not do.

In the early 1990s we formed a Solidarity Committee. Thirty or forty of us met at a restaurant. The issue was Kaiser's practice of hiring hundreds of on-calls. They had to be on call 24 hours, seven days a week, and received no medical benefits.

We started a campaign. We picketed the hospital. We made signs and walked up and down before work, after work, and during lunch. The hospital took pictures of us. The union leadership said that the union was not supposed to do informational picketing without giving the hospital ten days' notice. So we said, "We'll do it on our own."

I called the Labor Board to find out if we could be fired for picketing. I said, "We are exercising our right to free speech during our off hours. Doesn't that supersede anything in the contract?" They couldn't give me a clear answer. We did it anyway. And we weren't fired.

Local 399 removed two stewards without explanation. There was a stormy union meeting. A third steward said, "Give me an explanation as to why these two were fired or I will consider resigning." President Jim Zellers said, "There was Communist rhetoric in their leaflets." The NLRB held that the stewards could be legally removed because they were appointed, not elected.

One time in 1993 six parking lot attendants at Los Angeles Medical Center were fired for allegedly stealing money from parking lot receipts. The supervisor's cousin had a non-union parking company, and had the supervisor been able to get rid of the unionized attendants, Kaiser would have been free to subcontract with his cousin's company.

We went down to the union hall and said, "We want to do a demonstration for these men and women at their Step II hearing." The business agent agreed. (I think he thought that I would be the only one who showed up.) The night before the hearing, about ten of us got together and made picket signs. In the morning we showed up at the hospital. The regional personnel director came down and told us it was against the law, because the union officials hadn't given a ten-day notice. I said, "We're all staying." Then the senior business agent was sent down. I said, "I have taken the day off, and I'm not leaving here till that grievance is done." He said, "Well, at least take '399' off the picket signs." So we agreed to cross off 399, and we stayed.

One third of the workers at the Los Angeles Medical Center were undocumented. There was a woman from the Philippines whom I will call Lupita (not her real name). Her husband was a resident alien, and she had a baby.

One day Lupita was called to the personnel office and did not come back. I resolved not to go home until I found her. When I went to her house, her husband had to bring her out of hiding and I had to drag out of her what was wrong. She was suspended for undocumentation.

The union business agent referred her to a management attorney! The attorney told her to resign. I appealed to President Zellers who referred me to a second business agent, who recommended another attorney. That lawyer said the company had acted unlawfully and Lupita should file a grievance. The attorney also told me that I could not fight the employee's battle for her. I told the attorney I wanted to quit Kaiser. She said to me, "If you do, someone will take your place who doesn't give a damn."

I left the attorney's office and drove toward Lupita's apartment. On the way I was rear-ended. When I got to her place I was physically shaken. I told Lupita what the second attorney had said. I lay down on the floor, saying, "I'll support you whatever you decide." Lupita said, "I'll file."

THE MULTIRACIAL ALLIANCE

It was very difficult for health care workers in Local 399 to meet with janitors. Janitors worked the night shift. If they came to general membership meetings it was at two in the afternoon. Most of the health care workers worked the day shift.

We repeatedly asked the union leadership to inform us of any activities they were conducting with the janitors, and to give us a chance to be involved. The union was waging the "Justice for Janitors" campaign. We wanted to be at any demonstrations if we could get time off from work. If we knew in advance we could take the day off to go and help.

The leadership would not let us know. They would not give us the janitors' fliers. They would not let us participate. It was very difficult to get to know any of the people who worked in the union's other division.

Executive board members had been appointed throughout the union's existence. They were always staff members. They were insiders beholden to the local union president. In 1991, there were some open seats on the executive board and I said to my friends, "Let's go down there and ask Zellers to appoint us." At that meeting, he denied that there were any openings, but over the next six months he appointed three janitors and three health care workers, one of them from Kaiser.

In 1992 we decided that we should run a group of people for the local union executive board. I talked to a friend from another union who looked at our bylaws and said, "Andrea, these are the most undemocratic bylaws I've ever seen, but your power is on the executive board. Get on the executive board."

We went to a general membership meeting. I asked President Zellers to give us nomination petitions. He said there weren't any. So David helped me design a nomination petition, and six people ran, myself among them. All of us ran for seats held by staff members.

We weren't prepared for what came next, and that was disqualification. People were disqualified if they couldn't find in the computer the name of every person who signed their petitions. One person was disqualified because she'd given her petitions to someone else, and the other member didn't know what they were, and kept them in his pocket. One after another the five persons other than myself were eliminated. I never felt so alone in my life.

I ran, and I lost. The janitors later told me the union led them to believe that I was a Communist, and that I hated Mexicans. I also learned later that the man who beat me won illegally, because the union stuffed the ballot box. On election day, there were only two of us at the polling place. One of us would campaign near the parking lot and the other watch the ballot box. Then we would trade roles. Because of this some persons were able to vote two or three times without my friend and me knowing it.

THE 1995 CAMPAIGN

The successful 1995 campaign began in 1994. A group of health care workers met and called themselves "Change 95."

A group of janitors had already been meeting for two years. They were upset because they had tried to break into the union, and participate, and direct it the way they wanted to direct it, and they weren't allowed to do that. So they formed their own group called "Grupo Reformista."

I came into Change 95 in September 1994. I could see that they were talking too much to a particular staff member, a director of research and chief negotiator for the contract. A woman at my first meeting, a Chilean health care worker in a wheelchair named Lizbeth, suggested that it would be a good idea to meet the janitors. She said they were going to have a conference and after that, a march. I missed the conference because I had to work that day. But I made the march. And Lizbeth made a speech that we all had to unite, and come together, and figure out how to do this as a group. The janitors came up to her afterwards and wanted to know how we could connect.

We told the janitors we were meeting on Sunday, and five of them showed up. Change 95 and the janitors worked together for a while but eventually they broke apart. I left with the janitors. I felt, "These are the people that are going to move this thing."

By January 1995, I was working with the janitors. There was one other health care worker with us. She was bilingual but I am not. Sometimes the meetings were in Spanish, and there was no interpreter.

I was one of those who argued that we should run a candidate against Jim Zellers as well as running candidates against the whole executive board. The staff who were sympathetic to us had inside information from a reliable source higher up in the union that if we ran someone against Zellers, SEIU president Sweeney would put the local in trusteeship a week before the election. We weighed that, and finally decided that it was too risky to run someone for president. We wanted to get through the election. We wanted to prove that we could win. We named our slate the Multiracial Alliance.

According to Alliance literature, before 1995, the union was governed as an "old (white) boys' network." The only difference was that in this case the old boys were "liberals," "progressives," even self-described "radicals," who had fallen into practices associated with more traditional union bureaucracies. These practices included grievances that were never pursued, inadequate training for members and stewards, and an executive board that functioned only as a rubber stamp for the autocratic decisions of top officials.

The Alliance faced tremendous odds in the election. The campaign was funded by contributions from the members themselves, depended entirely on volunteer labor, and had to unite workers who spoke different languages. The Alliance organized vans to transport workers to the polls, stationed observers at every voting site to prevent electoral fraud, formed reception and education committees to provide information to the voters, conducted phone banking, and set up organizing committees at the worksites to get out the vote. There were even coordinators at each polling place equipped with cellular phones.

On June 8, 1995, the entire local union executive board was voted out of office. The twenty-one successful candidates of the Multiracial Alliance included eleven Latinos, four African-Americans, and six Caucasians. A particular target of the Alliance was David Stillwell, executive vice president and director of the Allied Services Division. The division's membership is ninety percent Latino. Stillwell was defeated by Cesar Oliva Sanchez, a janitor from Guatemala.

On July 13, 1995, the new executive board was installed and immediately convened a meeting that passed a number of resolutions. Article XV of the Local 399 Constitution states: "The Executive Board shall meet . . . at any time at the call of a majority of the Board." Article XV also states: "The Executive Board is hereby authorized and empowered to take any and all lawful action not inconsistent with this Constitution to safeguard and protect this Local Union."

Nevertheless, four days after the executive board's initial meeting, Local 399 president Jim Zellers asked national SEIU president Sweeney to rule that the meeting of the new executive board on July 13 had been held in violation of Local 399's Constitution and Bylaws, and that its resolutions were improper.

We tried to negotiate a peaceful resolution with the international. According to the *Los Angeles Times*, a member of President Zellers' staff stated that the newly elected executive vice president, Cesar Oliva Sanchez, "cannot speak English to conduct negotiations with cleaning company executives and lacks the experience to do the job." I heard the same sentiment expressed *several* times. A Vision Statement from the Alliance, dated July 25, 1995, stated: "as people of color, we are very sensitive to rhetoric about 'competence' and we wonder if the same rhetoric would be used if the majority of us were not Latino and African-Americans."

On August 3, 1995, a dozen Alliance supporters including Sanchez began a hunger strike in front of Local 399 headquarters. A banner said: "Respect the will of the workers! Let us govern!" I was one of the hunger strikers at the union hall. I lasted eleven days. Some of the men stuck it out until the 23rd of August. Some of them had been on hunger strike in their own countries, El Salvador, Guatemala, and Honduras.

On September 14, 1995, Sweeney announced that a trusteeship would be imposed. That same day, Trustee Mike Garcia wrote a letter to the members-elect of the new executive board, stating: "Pursuant to my authority, I am hereby removing you from your elected position in Local 399, effective immediately."

In the summer of 1996, I was offered a job as a full-time business agent for Local 399. For years I had thought that I could help fix what was wrong with the union by being on staff. But I gradually came to realize that it didn't matter who got the staff positions. And the aftermath of the 1995 campaign showed me that it didn't matter who was elected. I'd seen good people tossed out by the trustees. I'd also seen the way good people changed for the worse when they ran for office.

I was afraid of changing, too. When the offer came, I felt torn and depressed. Then I got a letter that named the Ed Mann Labor School and other organizations back east. It made me realize there were other people struggling, too. And I felt, "I'm not alone. I don't have to work on staff to change things."

I declined to join the staff. My letter stated in part that "were I to join the staff, I figure I'd be expected to support an International team for election."* I also mentioned male leadership in what was largely a women's union, and that activism of any stripe was looked upon as sedition by Local 399 leadership. I recalled a recent meeting of the SEIU Western Conference Latino Caucus. Although approximately 48 percent of Local 399 members were Latino and the meeting was to be held in our own union hall, the meeting was not publicized in our local. I ended the letter by saying that when I got home that day, "I broke down and wept: tears for myself and what I could look forward to on staff, and tears for my dear union." I signed it: "Your sister, Andrea Carney, Shop Steward, East L.A. Clinic, Kaiser Permanente."

*The full text of the letter appeared in *Impact*, Dec. 1996.

CHINESE STAFF
AND WORKERS'
ASSOCIATION

THE CHINESE STAFF and Workers' Association (CSWA) grew out of struggles by restaurant and garment workers on New York City's Lower East Side at the end of the 1970s. The concept is that where an employer offers a product or service to the ultimate consumer (as does a restaurant) the employer may be more vulnerable to a neighborhood picket line than to the grievance and arbitration procedure.

Unlike many labor organizations, CSWA fights sweatshop conditions in the United States. Some of its members work in unionized garment factories where workers are paid less than the minimum wage and where an eight-hour day is considered part-time work. CSWA's aim is not simply to fight for economic gain—although it has won improvements for many workers—but to mobilize workers to fight for control over their time and their lives, as a human right.

In addition to workplace struggles, CSWA has led the fight against the displacement of Chinatown residents by luxury condominiums and resisted the spread of casino gambling in Chinatown.

The following group interview was arranged by Jeannette Gabriel, and conducted at the CSWA office in September 1998. Trinh Duong translated for some of the participants, as well as contributing her own story.

CHINESE STAFF
AND WORKERS' ASSOCIATION

Sweatshops, Restaurants, and Community

J IM ONG: I worked as a restaurant waiter for 30 years, retiring in 1992. I still care about the labor movement in New York City, so I still come to the Association. I feel deeply about the sweatshop conditions in New York. In my judgment, these conditions are more serious than on the Chinese mainland.

Many Chinese immigrant workers are not in the economic mainstream. Most Chinese workers are in the restaurant and garment industries, or in the low-income service industry. In our experience, whatever we complain about they have excuses, and we don't have the power, or the money, to make them change. If we push very hard they give us something. People come from Washington, but they don't have the will, the determination to resolve the sweatshop problem in the United States. It's a joke!

We have discovered that labor law cannot change sweatshop conditions. If we want to do something effective, it must be by our own action, our own efforts, like a demonstration. That can make something happen.

In 1978, I tried to organize my friends who were working in the same restaurant. When I reached the age of fifty, the boss began to complain. The boss said, "You're too old." I was the head waiter and all my friends respected me very much. They said, "That's not fair. Your work is so good. We have to do something!"

I tried to join a trade union. But I discovered right after I joined, the union did not offer real protection. So six of us set up a picket line. The boss was really frightened. After three hours, the restaurant was closed down.

We found that we could form an association, and talk to the boss ourselves. We could protect our own rights as workers. On the opening day for our association, about two hundred people came.

WING LAM: In 1978, I was working in the garment industry. I worked in a union shop in Long Island City. It had been organized by the International Ladies' Garment Workers' Union (ILGWU). It was one of the ILGWU's biggest shops. There were four hundred people, most of them Dominican. A couple were Puerto Rican. I was the only Chinese.

I worked as a shipping clerk. My partner was a Puerto Rican. He spoke English, and I spoke a little broken Spanish. I also read some English. I found out that for the past ten years the workers had been paid fifty cents less than the wage in the contract. We were being paid $2.75 an hour. We should have gotten about $3.25.*

One hundred of us marched down to the union from the shop. We went to the Garment Center and raised hell with the union. At the time our local union had about 3,000 members. Whoever controlled our shop was going to run the local.

In that union they didn't have "union representatives." They called them "business agents." The highest position in the local, the president, was called the "manager." These people were paid by the union.

The manager of our local was the union representative from our shop. He was no stranger. That's why everybody was being underpaid.

So when we marched down there, the union manager said, "Oh, really? We've got to do something about it. Tomorrow, you know what? I'll go there first thing in the morning." People reacted that the union sounded OK.

Next day, the union manager came and talked to the boss. After he talked to the boss, the union manager said as he was leaving, "Everything is taken care of. You guys keep working. Everything is going to be fine." At the end of the day, all the leaders of the protest got pink slips. There

---

*A leaflet entitled "Welcome to the U.S.A. The United Sweatshops of America" by the National Mobilization Against Sweatshops (NMASS), states: "80–90 percent of the garment sweatshops in New York's Chinatown are unionized and conditions are deteriorating . . . . Union workers are making $1–3 an hour, working 10–16 hours a day." See also Peter Kwong, *Forbidden Workers: Illegal Chinese Immigrants and American Labor* (New York: The New Press, 1997), Chapter 8, which states that union members in sweatshops in the United States often work long hours without overtime pay.

were about eight of us. We were the most outspoken. Both my partner and I got laid off.

So of course we went to the union. "What the hell are you doing? You went there, we got laid off." "Really? That's bad! We've got to do something about it. We've got to go to arbitration."

I said, "Why arbitration? Why don't we picket or strike?"

"Well, we can't strike, you know. Trust us. We're really able to help you."

They had been able to identify all the leaders. We weren't experienced. We didn't designate a leader to stay underground. All the leaders were spotted right away. Obviously the workers got scared.

We tried to talk to civil rights organizations in the Chinese and Latino communities. They didn't see workers' issues as that important. They were looking at race, nationality, that kind of thing.

All we could do was to wait for the arbitration. A few days before the hearing, I asked to talk to the union lawyer. The union president finally gave me the phone number. So I called the lawyer. I said, "I want to sit down and talk to you about what happened." He said, "No, there's no need to do that. Your union leader already told me what happened." I said, "You've got to hear from me. I have more detail. I know what's going on." He said, "I'm the lawyer for the union, not the lawyer for you." I said, "But look. I got fired, not the union leader. You've got to talk to me." He refused. I knew then that something really funny was going on.

During the arbitration, all this lawyer knew to do was pound the table. He looked mean. He looked as if he was fighting for us. But he hadn't prepared anything. He didn't even bring witnesses. We brought all the witnesses. He said, "We don't need them. It's a very clear-cut case." This was my first experience of the grievance-arbitration procedure. I saw how the union worked.

We lost the arbitration. The boss said I instigated a slowdown. Some foreman testified that I told people to take it easy. What I told them was, "Don't worry. Take it easy." He said that "take it easy" meant to slow down.

However, the boss admitted that one of the reasons he fired me was because we demanded a union wage. Some people suggested that I should go to the National Labor Relations Board. Later on we did this, and we were able to turn the arbitration decision around.

After I won before the NLRB, the lawyer for the boss said, "We don't want this guy to go back. We'll pay him. If you defy us, we'll never stop fighting you. We can drag this out for six or seven years. You had better settle or you'll never get anything." My lawyer told me, "Yeah. They could do that." People were having hard times. There were not that many jobs. During the whole process, many of our coworkers had left. If we had gone back it would have been a different workforce, anyway. So we said, OK.

When we charged the boss we also charged the union. The union told us that if we would drop our charge against the union, they would give us valuable information. My lawyer was pretty pro-union. So she convinced me to drop the union from the suit.

WORKING FOR THE UNION

At that time I was just working for money. The union was curious how I had been able to organize all the Spanish workforce, although I did not speak Spanish. They asked me to work for them. They offered much more than I received in the shop. In the shop I had made about $125 a week. I was offered $200 a week by the union. To me, it was a pretty good job.

I was a paid picketer for the union. Wherever there was trouble, I went. If you needed a picketer, I was there. I worked around the clock. Sometimes I worked at night, watching the gate, to make sure that the boss didn't ship something out. I wasn't paid to organize, I was paid to picket. The union told me to make sure I didn't talk to the workers. They were afraid I might say something wrong.

Sometimes we used our muscle. We followed people to the train station. We said, "Hey folks, don't do that." Maybe that worker never came back to work for that boss. I learned that's how the union worked. The union used fear, rather than trying to win over the worker. I found out that many unions were like that.

Later on I worked as a "colonizer." You went to the shop and looked for a job, just like any other worker. One shop I went to made perfume. I think the union sent me there to put me in Siberia. They didn't mean to unionize that shop. They sent me there to make sure I was there, away from the Garment Center.

JIM ONG: It was exile.

WING LAM: I kept asking the union when we were going to do something. They said, "Get information. Get information." Finally they told me, "Forget it." The union paid me the difference between my wage in the shop and the union salary.

Another time I worked in a Korean shop. I was a very good worker. In two or three months that I worked there, I got five increases. The boss paid me more than the union.

The workers were either Korean or Latino. I don't speak Korean. I don't speak Spanish. But somehow, I unionized that place. First I got the Latinos. They are the easiest people to unionize. After they were all signed up, we pulled a strike. We found out where the work came from and put pressure on the manufacturer.

The boss didn't know who had done this. It was the only Korean-owned garment shop that had been unionized. I wanted to stay there because I was learning to become a presser. The boss told the union he would sign a contract if the union told him who had organized the place. One day the manager of the local came to the shop. After he left, the boss called me in. He said, "Wing! I treat you very well. I treat you like a son. I pay you good. Why did you do that?"

I said, "What are you talking about?" He said, "You're the guy." He was confused: he didn't know if the union had told the truth, or I was telling the truth. I *was* a good worker. Probably he wanted me to become a foreman. He didn't fire me.

I went back to my local and asked, "What the hell are you guys doing? You want to get me killed?" They told me, "Why don't you get out of there? We need you."

I want you to know how unions work. I colonized in a shop where the boss was Italian. I worked as a grader. They had been in the industry thirty or forty years. The shop had never been unionized.

When I went there, I was supposed to unionize the whole shop, and then pull a strike. After I had been there about five months, we had privately signed up most of the workers. We were ready to strike. But before we could do it, we had to tell the union, "We're ready. Do it."

My boss in the union said, "Wait. I've got to make a phone call. Call me back tomorrow." I called him and he said, "Get out immediately. We're not going to strike." I said, "What?" I went to a friend in the union who said, "We did not get permission to do it." That particular shop was protected by the Mafia. No one could touch it. My boss in the union had somehow sent me into the wrong shop.

So this was how at least the Garment Workers' union worked. It had a very militant history. But this was 1978. One time we asked the Amalgamated to help us form a union of organizers. Before long most of the Black organizers were gone, and only the white guys stayed.

In my heart I decided that what we needed was a workers' organization, not just a union to sell our labor.

STARTING THE ASSOCIATION

The association was to be not just for garment workers, or restaurant workers, but for all workers. The original idea was for the association to be a bridge between the unions and the community. Many workers were frustrated when the union sold them out. At that time we wanted to be a bridge, to make the unions look better. But we wished also to be a watchdog against the unions. That meant that if a union didn't do its thing, we'd kick their butts.

We helped several shops to unionize. Every one got sold out by the restaurant workers' union. The bosses learned faster than the workers. They learned how to buy the union off. For some unions the whole idea is money. So we began to think, everyone that we send into the union gets trapped. It's as if we were sending people to suicide.

In Chinatown at that time, most garment shops were unionized but very few restaurants. Silver Palace was the first. At the Silver Palace Restaurant, the boss fired all the workers. We were able to rally the community behind them. Everybody went back. After they went back, we tried to decide whether to join the AFL-CIO, or what? We decided that up to then we had sent several shops to suicide. We had better do something else.

We utilized the energy of the Silver Palace campaign to form a union that was independent from the AFL-CIO. We knew nothing about independent unions. But also, we didn't want the Chinese Staff and Workers' Association to be a union. We wanted to be separate. We had seen the limits of the unions. Each time we sent a worker to the union, and they got a contract, the worker would sit back and wait for the contract to expire. The workers thought they had the American Dream now, they had protection.

Many workers, both in union and non-union shops, joined the CSWA. We decided we needed to deal with community issues as well as workplace issues. We wanted the worker to have more say in the community. In the

Silver Palace case, CSWA got not only worker support but also small business support against the wrongdoing of Silver Palace. We were able to get community support from the beginning because we asked people to fight against the practice of management taking workers' tips. This practice hurts all workers in the industry.

The Association was the first grassroots movement of the Chinese worker in this country. Even in San Francisco, everything was from outside. This was a labor movement from inside.

YEE TOM: I worked in a restaurant all my life. When I began, we worked ten to twelve hours a day, six days a week. We never had a vacation.

We tried to form a union. The union lost the election, and I got fired. The boss used the excuse that the subways were shut down because of a subway strike, and I couldn't get to work. The union's attitude was, "Why spend money on this guy?"

JIM ONG: Tom came to the Association about this. It was very unfair. We sent a delegation of five persons. One of them was me. The name of the restaurant was Ho Ho. It was a little fancy place, about ten blocks from Radio City. We went there and told the boss, "We are from the Association." I said, "If you don't take Tommy back by tomorrow, I will be picketing in front of your restaurant."

YEE TOM: They took me back. They paid me back pay!

JIM ONG: We did everything by ourselves. It was much, much stronger than a union. None of this, "We're going to have arbitration, next week I'll call you." It was very clear. "If you don't rehire him, I will come back tomorrow."

YEE TOM: That's very true.

WAH LEE:* As an immigrant to this country, my first job was at the Silver Palace restaurant. A union had been in place there for a long time. The problem was that some of the workers' representatives agreed more with the boss than with the workers. They didn't really want to be concerned with the workers' issues. Sometimes they got favors from the boss.

In 1993, when our contract ended, the employer tried to force us to sign an illegal contract. It provided that the boss could take our tips, and cut all our benefits. During negotiations we saw that some of the representatives were not strong.

*Wah Lee is an older Chinese-speaking woman. She spoke in Chinese.

The boss locked us out in the middle of negotiations. We were very angry. We felt we had to take back a little bit of justice. We demanded reinstatement and a good contract.

We began to picket but it was difficult. In 1993, if you can remember, it was very hot and later very cold. That year there were twelve big snow storms. The snow piled up as high as a human being.

We didn't just picket once a day. We picketed two hours during lunch and at nighttime, during dinner, every single day. We picketed for seven months. We involved many different kinds of workers: Jewish, Latino, Japanese, Korean. We went to high schools and colleges and told people why we were picketing at the Silver Palace. Every weekend we had a large demonstration. The boycott was not only in Chinatown.

There was no way out for the boss. He had to come back to the negotiating table and sit down with the workers. All the workers returned to work and we got a good contract. We went back to work March 18, 1994. A new group of organizers and leaders had emerged.

I worked there for six years and I don't think the boss ever learned my name. After we came out and fought for our rights the boss had to say, "This person knows that she has some rights, and she fought for them."

VIRGINIA YU: I became active during the summer of 1995. There was a struggle at Jing Fong, at the time the largest Chinese restaurant in the Northeast. A worker was fired after he started asking questions, and a campaign began in February 1995. I was in school, in the first year of my master's program in social work. When I came back from school in the summer, I was informed of the campaign. The campaign had come to a standstill because of collusion between the police, Chinese newspapers, the tongs* and the Chinese Restaurant Association.

I feel I should tell you about my background. My parents came here twenty-six years ago and they have been working in the factory ever since. My father worked as a button machine operator. My mother worked as a seamstress. My grandmother worked in the factory until she retired.

When I was a young child my mother worked at home. I remember when I was five or six years old, my mom sewing and my older sister helping out. My mother would bring work home from the factory. She

---

*A tong is an association of businessmen with connections to street gangs that enforce their policies.

had to go to the factory to get the garments. She would have to bring the garments back to the factory after they were sewn. My mother still tells me today how she would drag the three of us, on the train, going up and down the staircases, with this huge cart full of sewn garments.

I myself didn't start working in the factory until I was in junior high school. It was illegal for me to be working but I had to help my father. In addition, my two sisters worked there.

I remember how I, after Chinese school, would go to the factory where my father worked. This might be on a Sunday evening. I hated going there, but I had to help out as best I could. I didn't like to do the actual machine work because at the time I was so young. Sometimes my grandmother or my sisters would work with us, if the garments had to get out the next day. When my mother finished her own work, she would come help my father. We were always there. We would not leave until nine or ten in the evening.

I remember my mom coming home late, and complaining of aches and pains in her shoulders, her back, her hands. Almost every night, after we ate, I would give her a massage to ease her pain. After twenty years of work she developed an occupational disease and could not work for nine months. Even today, she can only work seven or eight hours a day. The sad part is that seven or eight hours is considered part-time!

My father is still working in the factory even though my sisters and I now have jobs. I had always thought that I would go to school and make enough money so that my parents didn't need to work in the factory. But my parents are still working to make sure they earn at least the $7,000 a year necessary to maintain their health insurance.

Until I found Chinese Staff, I didn't know that I could do something, that there was an organization with which I could try to change the situation of my family. Now, I realize that the only way *really* to make change is by organizing workers of all trades in the community. When I found this opportunity, I jumped in with both feet.

The worker who was fired at Jing Fong said that he was made to work over seventy hours a week, making seventy cents per hour. This was very similar to what my parents and my family had to go through, and are still going through now.

We formed a student organization. We called it Students for Workers'

Rights. We wanted to organize a big rally to show that students and youth supported this campaign to enforce labor laws in our community. Then we thought, "What's a rally going to do? This has gone on for three months. We want to do more."

After many discussions, a group of us decided that on June 4—the anniversary of the Tienanmen Square massacre—we would begin a hunger strike for seven days.

THE HUNGER STRIKE

VIRGINIA YU: Five students did it. It was pretty tough out there. We were right in the street, in front of the Jing Fong restaurant. I remember the first night.

The police gave us a really hard time, especially the captain. At first they said, "Oh, you can put up something for when it rains or gets too sunny." Then they turned around and said, "No." When we tried to put something up to cover ourselves, the police drew a picture of a structure that they thought could not be built. To the police captain's surprise, construction workers actually built what the police had drawn. After all that, the police demolished it.

That was a pivotal moment for me. I saw firsthand what was going on. It was everything the Chinese Staff was talking about: the collusion between the police, the tong, and the Restaurant Association was very clear. I remember seeing gang members across the street. I knew about all this, but being there and seeing it really strengthened me.

The police station was across the street from our picket, but they wouldn't let us use the bathroom. The smell of garbage from the restaurant reeked that summer. In the late evening, garbage trucks would drag the garbage right across the area where we had set up tables to sleep. They were trying to intimidate us but we were even more determined to continue the struggle.

Since we were outdoors, right in the heart of Chinatown, every day, we were able to make an impact on the community. We were able to publicize to the community and to the city that things needed to be changed. Most people stopped to see what was going on. Some students even went into the factories to get people to sign our petitions.

Nelson, my boyfriend, wrote a letter about our campaign to an anchor for Channel 9 news. She was touched by the letter and came out to do an exposé on conditions in Chinatown. Nelson was able to discuss our campaign on TV.

We didn't get much rest. I felt I was on display in a museum. I remember waking up with cameras in my face. Every day was a new adventure since the enemy was on either side of us: to the left was the police and to the right, the restaurant. The sun finally took its toll. In the middle of the week, three of the five students had to go to the hospital because of dehydration.

My whole family didn't want me to do the hunger strike. I didn't tell my mom until the night before, because I knew that if I told her earlier, she wouldn't let me do it. In time, I was able to get my mother and my younger sister involved. My mother wanted to see why I was willing to go without eating for seven days, and if I was part of a cult.

After my mother came around, and saw what the issues were, she began to see what this organization is about. She even began to talk about workers' power and workers' rights. She is now a board member of Chinese Staff.

My mother has been involved with cswa for three years. I am constantly amazed by the resilience with which she continues to fight for workers' rights, even though she could be blacklisted. My mother believes in justice and dignity for working people. I have gained so much strength from her determination.

NATIONAL MOBILIZATION AGAINST SWEATSHOPS (NMASS)

WING LAM: I think Chinese people and other sweatshop workers tend to marginalize themselves and have been marginalized by others. We unite based on color, race, sex. In a way we unite based on our differences to fight our common oppression. But such a movement does not find common ground between the people who have been exploited. If we just ask for people's support or sympathy, that won't last. Movements like that, such as consumer boycotts, have failed many times. We must find common ground.

In America, the labor movement concentrates on wages. That separates the garment worker who makes $1 an hour and the college graduate who makes $20. The college graduates believe that raising the minimum wage is no concern of theirs.

We advocate that people should have more control of their lives, their time. The labor movement should not narrow itself to the purely economic that concerns only a particular trade. We have to cut across all trades and sexes and become a class movement. Even the person that makes $20 an hour is still a slave, who has to change that. NMASS advances the right to a 40-hour work week at a living wage as a human right.

In America, people are subject to a culture of compromising in which they choose the lesser of two evils. We say, "Oh, we aren't doing as well as before, but at least we're not as badly off as people in a Third World country." We think that in order to have a different kind of movement you need to have a different culture, a different perspective. We should not have to earn money just to survive. People should have a life, people should have control of their time.

The labor movement often looks at people and says, "You are higher-skilled and get paid more, while you are lower-skilled and get paid less." In our community we see that that's not true. To be able to make an entire garment takes more skill than putting a screw in a hole on an auto-assembly line. You can't say that the female garment worker, who makes a whole garment, is less skilled than a man on the assembly line.

TRINH DUONG: I was born in Vietnam. I stayed in a refugee camp about two years, from four to six years old. That refugee camp taught me, you don't want to be poor, and, you don't want to be at other people's mercy. And so, for all the years that I was in the United States after I got here when I was six, what I really learned is that you just take care of yourself. You go out and try to make a lot of money. Forget anything else.

I learned to look down on a lot of people. In 1992 or 1993 I read about the Silver Palace in *The New York Times* and *The Village Voice*. I said to myself, "These people seem to have a lot of time on their hands. Why are they picketing all the time? They should just go to work." I was going to school to learn how to be a stockbroker.

In 1995, when we were eating at Jing Fong, I met some people on the picket line. It was a curiosity to me. I didn't feel that I was part of any community. I thought that the picketers would look like activists: have nose rings and so forth. Instead, they looked pretty ordinary. Some were forty years old, with little kids.

I took the flier, and went home, and about a month later I tried to find the picket line, just to see what it was like. It took me about two hours before I found the office. When I came up here, it seemed like a different world. Why were people still here at nine at night, talking, when they could go home and take care of themselves?

There was something that drew me. It was as if you got a glimpse of something that you're not allowed to see. I didn't know how to describe it, but I came back.

I was a pretty racist person. At first I said to myself, "The only reason I'm coming down to this picket line is to help these people chant in English." I really thought that. But as I was there, time after time, I changed.

One night before a picket I was here in the office. Again, I was going to give diction to the picket line. But what people were talking about was that the police said they were going to arrest everybody who went out and picketed, in the same way that we had picketed all along, for the past couple of months. The discussion was, "Is it worth it for me to be arrested?" Some people had green cards. Many of them were working in restaurants or garment factories.

At the beginning I thought, "There is no way I am going to do this, no way I am going to get in trouble." But then I saw all these people who had more reason than I to say, "No." And everybody said, "We have to go out there. This is our voice. The picket line is our voice. We have nothing else if we lose it. So we have to take it back, even if they arrest us."

That made me rethink a lot of things. It made me feel proud. These were not people you should think of as unskilled, because they work in garment factories or they are poor. For me, it taught me something about human strength and determination, and that change is possible. For a long time I had believed that you can't change anything, so you might as well join it, and be the best.

I still didn't want to be arrested. I went to the picket line. People put bags over their faces in case they got arrested. But they still walked in the picket line, and were prepared for arrest. Seeing that, I felt that I couldn't stand on the sidelines anymore.

List of Abbreviations

AFGE	American Federation of Government Employees
AFL	(AF of L) American Federation of Labor
AFSCME	American Federation of State, County, and Municipal Employees Union
AWOC	Agricultural Workers' Organizing Committee
CIO	Committee for Industrial Organization; later, Congress of Industrial Organizations
CP	Communist Party
CSWA	Chinese Staff and Workers' Association
FASH	Fraternal Association of Steel Haulers
GM	General Motors
ICWU	International Chemical Workers Union
ILD	International Labor Defense
ILGWU	International Ladies' Garment Workers' Union
IWO	International Workers Order
IWW	Industrial Workers of the World
J&L	Jones & Laughlin
KKK	Ku Klux Klan
LTV	Ling Temco Vought
MAPA	Mexican American Political Association
NAACP	National Association for the Advancement of Colored People
NLRB	National Labor Relations Board
NMASS	National Mobilization Against Sweatshops
NMU	National Maritime Union
OEO	Office of Economic Opportunity
RAFT	Rank And File Team
SEIU	Service Employees International Union
SIU	Seafarers International Union

SNCC	Student Nonviolent Coordinating Committee
SP	Socialist Party
SUP	Sailors Union of the Pacific
SWOC	Steel Workers Organizing Committee
UAW	United Automobile Workers
UE	United Electrical, Radio and Machine Workers
UFWOC	United Farm Workers Organizing Committee
ULP	United Labor Party
UMW	United Mine Workers
UOPWA	United Office and Professional Workers of America
UPWA	United Packinghouse Workers of America
USA	(USWA) United Steelworkers of America
YCL	Young Communist League
YPSL	Young Peoples' Socialist League

Index

during Briggs strike, 61–62
attitude toward contracts, 283
Ed Mann on, 364–365
Stan Weir encounters, 182–183
informal work groups
Stan Weir on, 196–199

job classifications
at University of Chicago, 303
Justice for Janitors, 379, 386. *See
also* Multiracial Alliance

Ku Klux Klan
in Iowa after World War I, 16–17
in Northeast Ohio, 153

layoffs, 23, 47, 262, 354
and organizing, 77
work-sharing as alternative, xii,
25, 161–162, 262, 322, 330
lumberjacks, 41–42
lunchtime meetings
debates among auto dealership
mechanics, 338
in packinghouse organizing, 87
of University of Chicago clerical
workers, 301, 302
in UE organizing in 1970s, 329

Mann, Ed, xiv, 267–268, 281–284,
346–365
meat packers. *See* packinghouse
workers
Memorial Day Massacre, 94–96, 103

Multiracial Alliance, xiii, 379,
386–390

nationality. *See* immigrants
nonviolence
demanded by Chavez, 307–308
no-strike clause, 3–4
and dues check-off, 256–258
in steel contracts, 105, 170, 173
in miners' contract, 165
during World War II, 88, 184
Nowicki, Stella (Vicky Starr) xiv,
xv, 297, 300

organizing. *See also* autoworkers,
chemical workers, clerical
workers, coal miners, Farm
Workers, garment workers,
health care workers, packinghouse workers, public em-
ployees, railroad workers,
restaurants, rubber workers,
seamen, steelhaulers, steelworkers, sweatshops, unemployed, women
blitz, x
by international unions, 3–4,
345, 364
through servicing the
community, xiii, 306–307,
329, 333, 397–398
women's style of, xii, 77, 84,
327–328, 332, 333
overtime
during layoffs, 262

Also from Haymarket Books

The Civil Wars in U.S. Labor:
Birth of a New Workers' Movement or Death Throes of the Old?
Steve Early · From forced trusteeships to hostile inter-union raids, the labor movement has been gripped by civil war. Steve Early argues that these policies are an extension of the strategy of labor management collaboration that must be replaced with rank-and-file initiative. ISBN 9781608460991

Fields of Resistance: The Struggle of Florida's Farmworkers for Justice
Silvia Giagnoni · In Immokalee, Florida, the tomato capital of the world, farmworkers organized themselves into the Coalition of Immokalee Workers, and launched nationwide boycott campaigns that forced McDonald's, Burger King, and Taco Bell to recognize their demands for workers' rights. ISBN 9781608460939

The Lean Years: A History of the American Worker, 1920–1933 and
The Turbulent Years: A History of the American Worker, 1933–1941
Irving Bernstein, Frances Fox Piven (Introduction) · The complex fate of individual American workers, both organized and unorganized, definitively shaped the era of the 1920s and early 1930s. Irving Bernstein's classic texts narrate an era of wrenching hardships but also great victories for American labor. ISBN 9781608460632

Live Working or Die Fighting: How the Working Class Went Global
Paul Mason · *Live Working or Die Fighting* celebrates a common history of defiance, idealism, and self-sacrifice, one as alive and active today as it was two hundred years ago. ISBN 9781608460700

Revolution in Seattle: A Memoir
Harvey O'Connor · In this moving, political memoir, labor journalist and activist Harvey O'Connor captures the courage and defiance of workers on the march against the carnage of the first World War, and dramatic inequality, along with his remembrances of the Seattle General Strike of 1919. ISBN 9781931859745

Subterranean Fire:
A History of Working-Class Radicalism in the United States
Sharon Smith · This accessible, critical history of the U.S. labor movement examines the hidden history of workers' resistance from the nineteenth century to the present. ISBN 9781931859233

About Haymarket Books

Haymarket Books is a nonprofit, progressive book distributor and publisher, a project of the Center for Economic Research and Social Change. We believe that activists need to take ideas, history, and politics into the many struggles for social justice today. Learning the lessons of past victories, as well as defeats, can arm a new generation of fighters for a better world. As Karl Marx said, "The philosophers have merely interpreted the world; the point, however, is to change it."

We take inspiration and courage from our namesakes, the Haymarket Martyrs, who gave their lives fighting for a better world. Their 1886 struggle for the eight-hour day, which gave us May Day, the international workers' holiday, reminds workers around the world that ordinary people can organize and struggle for their own liberation. These struggles continue today across the globe—struggles against oppression, exploitation, hunger, and poverty.

It was August Spies, one of the Martyrs targeted for being an immigrant and an anarchist, who predicted the battles being fought to this day. "If you think that by hanging us you can stamp out the labor movement," Spies told the judge, "then hang us. Here you will tread upon a spark, but here, and there, and behind you, and in front of you, and everywhere, the flames will blaze up. It is a subterranean fire. You cannot put it out. The ground is on fire upon which you stand."

We could not succeed in our publishing efforts without the generous financial support of our readers. Many people contribute to our project through the Haymarket Sustainers program, where donors receive free books in return for their monetary support. If you would like to be a part of this program, please contact us at info@haymarketbooks.org.

Order these titles and more online at www.haymarketbooks.org or call 773-583-7884.

About the Editors

Staughton Lynd was born in 1929 and grew up in New York City. His parents, Robert and Helen Lynd, co-authored the well-known Middletown books. Staughton went through the schools of the Ethical Culture Society. Above the auditorium of the main school were written the words: "The place where men meet to seek the highest is holy ground."

Staughton received a BA from Harvard, an MA and PhD from Columbia, and a JD from the University of Chicago. He taught American history at Spelman College in Atlanta, where one of his students was the future Pulitzer Prize–winning novelist Alice Walker, and at Yale University.

Staughton served as director of Freedom Schools in the Mississippi Summer Project of 1964. In April 1965, he chaired the first march against the Vietnam War in Washington, DC. In August 1965, he was arrested, together with Bob Moses and David Dellinger, at the Assembly of Unrepresented People in Washington, DC, where demonstrators sought to declare peace with the people of Vietnam on the steps of the Capitol. In December 1965, Staughton, along with Tom Hayden and Herbert Aptheker, made a controversial trip to Hanoi, hoping to clarify the peace terms of the Vietnamese government and the National Liberation Front of South Vietnam.

Because of his advocacy and practice of civil disobedience, Lynd was unable to continue as a full-time history teacher. The history departments at five Chicago-area universities offered him positions, only to have the offers negatived by university or state administrators. In 1976, Staughton became a lawyer and until his retirement at the end of 1996 worked for Legal Services in Youngstown, Ohio. He specialized in employment law. When the steel mills in Youngstown were closed in 1977–1980 he served as lead counsel to the Ecumenical Coalition of the Mahoning Valley, which sought to reopen the mills under worker-community ownership, and brought the action Local 1330 v. U.S. Steel. After retiring, Staughton was for a time Local Education Coordinator for Teamsters Local 377 in Youngstown.

Staughton met Alice Lee Niles at Harvard Summer School. Alice's parents had recently become members of the Society of Friends, and Staughton had become aware of Quakerism through a cousin who served as an ambulance driver during World War II. Staughton and Alice were married at the Stony Run Meeting House in Baltimore in 1951. They have three children and seven grandchildren. In the early 1960s, the Lynds became convinced Friends, and joined the Atlanta Friends Meeting. They are presently sojourning members of the 57th Street Meeting in Chicago.

Alice was a member of a union of clerical workers in the 1950s, and a member of the Amalgamated Clothing Workers' Union in the 1970s. As a labor lawyer she helped visiting nurses to organize an independent union; assisted laid-off workers when they lost pension, health care, and other benefits; filed occupational health and safety claims; and litigated employment discrimination cases.

The Lynds have been deeply involved in opposing the death penalty, and in probing the cases of men sentenced to death or very long sentences for their alleged roles in a major prison riot in 1993. They were co-counsel in a major class action suit challenging conditions at Ohio's supermaximum security prison that went up to the United States Supreme Court, *Wilkinson v. Austin*. This case, now being applied in other states, established procedural standards for placement and retention of prisoners in supermax prisons.

Staughton has written or edited numerous books, including:

Class Conflict, Slavery, and the United States Constitution (1967) and *Intellectual Origins of American Radicalism* (1968), re-issued by Cambridge University Press in 2009; with Michael Ferber, *The Resistance* (Beacon Press, 1971); *Solidarity Unionism: Rebuilding the Labor Movement from Below* (Charles H. Kerr, 1992); *"We Are All Leaders": The Alternative Unionism of the Early 1930s* (University of Illinois Press, 1996); *Living Inside Our Hope: A Steadfast Radical's Thoughts on Rebuilding the Movement* (Cornell University Press, 1997). Chapter Four of *Living Inside Our Hope* is an essay co-authored by Alice and Staughton called "Liberation Theology for Quakers," which first appeared as a Pendle Hill pamphlet; *Lucasville: The Untold Story of a Prison Uprising* (Temple University Press, 2004); with Andrej Grubacic, *Wobblies and Zapatistas: Conversations on Anarchism, Marxism and Radical History* (PM Press, 2008); with Daniel Gross, *Labor Law for the Rank & Filer: Building Solidarity While Staying Clear of the Law* (PM Press, 2008); and *From Here to There: The Lynd Reader* (PM Press, 2010).

The Lynds have co-edited four books together: *Homeland: Oral Histories of Palestine and Palestinians* (Olive Branch Press, 1994); *Nonviolence in America: A Documentary History* (Orbis Books, 1995); *Rank and File: Personal Histories by Working-Class Organizers* (Monthly Review Press, 1988); and *The New Rank and File* (Cornell University Press, 2000), which includes oral histories of labor activists in the past quarter century.

Most recently, the Lynds have written Stepping Stones: Memoir of a Life Together, published in hardcover and paperback by Lexington Books in 2009.